Stanislas Chaillou

The Architect's Sourcebook

Dimensions and Files for Space Design

Birkhäuser
Basel

Author: Stanislas Chaillou

Acquisitions Editor: David Marold, Birkhäuser Verlag, A-Vienna
Content and Production Editor: Angelika Gaal, Birkhäuser Verlag, A-Vienna
Proofreading: Alun Brown
Layout and Design: Stanislas Chaillou
Cover Design: Floyd Schulze
Image editing: Stanislas Chaillou
Printing and binding: FINIDR, s.r.o.
Printed in the Czech Republic
Paper: Magno Natural
Typeface: Neue Haas Grotesk

The CAD Blocks can be downloaded from the Rayon SAS website. The download and copyright free use of the data will be free of charge for anyone who has access to the QR codes. The use of the CAD Blocks is governed by Rayon's Terms of Use, presented on this webpage: https://www.rayon.design/terms-of-service. Essentially, users are not allowed to resell the blocks or start a competing content database with them. The publisher accepts no responsibility for the provision and/or consequences of the use of the data and the associated implications. Rayon guarantees the provision of the CAD Blocks until the end of 2027. It is therefore recommended to download all CAD Blocks before expiration.

The dimensions provided in this book offer generic guidelines, and are not tied to any specific regulation; both Rayon and the author cannot take responsibility for the validity of these guidelines for any specific context or location.

Library of Congress Control Number: 2024931446

Bibliographic information published by the German National Library; The German National Library lists this publication in the Deutsche Nationalbibliografie; detailed bibliographic data are available on the Internet at http://dnb.dnb.de.

ISBN 978-3-0356-2845-6
e-ISBN (PDF) 978-3-0356-2847-0

Im Westfeld 8, 4055 Basel, Switzerland
Part of Walter de Gruyter GmbH, Berlin/Boston

9 8 7 6 5 4 3 2 1 www.birkhauser.com

Acknowledgment

This book goes out to the Rayon team, without whom none of this would have been possible!

About the Author

Stanislas Chaillou is a Paris-based architect and data scientist. He is the co-founder of Rayon, a company building a new generation of design software for the AEC industry. Stanislas received his Bachelor of Science in Architecture from the Swiss Federal Institute of Technology of Lausanne and his Master's degree in Architecture from Harvard University. Since 2018, his work has been focusing on the theoretical and experimental aspects of Artificial Intelligence in Architecture.

Stanislas was the curator of the exhibition "Artificial Intelligence & Architecture," organized at the Arsenal Pavilion. He is also the author of "Artificial Intelligence & Architecture, From Research to Practice" (2022) edited by Birkhäuser (Basel).

About this Book

The Architect's Sourcebook provides readers with an accessible and playful space planning manual for the digital age. The Sourcebook conveniently brings together general dimensions, layout tips, and the CAD data designers actually need to draw spaces in their software.

A 1000+ readily downloadable CAD blocks, provided by the software company Rayon, are offered throughout the Sourcebook, to help architects address generic typologies (housing, office and outdoor spaces). The quality and diversity of this digital repository will become the architect's best friend to create most kinds of space layout.

At a time when Architecture's tool set and knowledge leaves increasingly online, this book represents both a much-needed update to traditional architectural handbooks, and a timely complement to well-known design manuals.

Table of Contents

You don't have time?
See you p.14 ;)

You have time? Read this!

Taken at face value, this Sourcebook will first and foremost help designers, and aspiring architects to represent space layouts in any kind of CAD environment. 1000+ CAD blocks provided by the software company Rayon, and a comprehensive space planning guide wrapped in a comic book-like look-and-feel, is what the next 440+ pages is all about. Useful and uncomplicated: before anything else, readers will find here a lighthearted manual for space planning.

As well as finding a playful manual, readers will also see in this Sourcebook an expression of how a certain side of design knowledge has become an increasingly online, crowdsourced, and digitally crafted corpus.

This reality is one we would like to touch upon before this book begins.

Technicity: an age of manuals & catalogs

Architecture's rise in technicity throughout the XXth century forced the discipline to document much more the various facets of the act of building. This reality gave birth to countless manuals and catalogs that structured for a long time both the discipline and the very practice of Architecture. From the jobsites to the accreditation exams, handbooks and catalogs have been omnipresent for a long while.

The Early Standards: The **Architects' Data**, conceived by Ernst Neufert in 1936 as part of his teaching at the Bauhaus in Weimar, is a testimony to the growing importance of manuals throughout the past century. This handbook initially found a growing readership in German-speaking countries in the first half of the XXth century, under its initial name "**Bauentwurfslehre**." Translated into English in 1970, and now titled the Architects' Data, the manual quickly spread throughout the English-speaking world. Today, adapted and translated in 17 languages and with over 500,000+ copies sold worldwide, Neufert's handbook is recognized as a must-have reference by practitioners around the world. The success of this book, besides the obvious quality of its content, lies in Neufert's acute, early-on understanding of the upcom-

1 p. 447

2 p. 447

ing evolution of Architecture: with the industrialization of building products and systems, architects would soon have to rely on a corpus of formulated technical knowledge. Having identified this trend, the Architect's Data found itself ideally matched with the discipline's concern of losing its ability to build in the face of the growing complexity of buildings themselves.

Neufert's Architect's Data will prove to be the tip of a much larger iceberg: the past century saw many similar manuals go to print. As Architecture is first and foremost a local industry, handbooks published would be curated to address specific language regions, with shared building standards. Among the many, we can point to a few well-known publications:
3 p. 447 the **Architectural Graphic Standards** by Charles George Ramsey (first print run in
4 p. 447 1932, 1+ million copies sold); the **Architectural Graphics** by Frank Ching (first edition 1975, 500,000+ copies sold); and the more recent
5 p. 447 **Constructing Architecture** by Andrea Deplazes. This corpus, meant to help architects plan and control the construction process, soon became deeply intertwined within the discipline's academic culture. If countless manuals today populate architects' shelves, it is first and foremost because this corpus of books underpins the very accreditation exams that safeguard entry to the profession. By embracing these publications, practitioners found an ideal way to document the "hard skills" that any aspiring architect should exhibit before entering the practice.

The Catalog Tradition: Far from these disciplinarian concerns, and during roughly the same period, the industrialization of building products and systems gave rise to yet another type of publication: catalogs. Chairs, desks, booths, brick systems, appliances, etc.: objects produced at scale would be marketed by means of catalogs, blending together their technical specifications ("how to use") and their marketed qualities ("why to purchase"). Printed catalogs played a central role in the fast-paced commercial expansion of furniture brands of the past century such Knoll, Kartell, Vitra, etc. And as standardized objects soon started flooding interiors, from

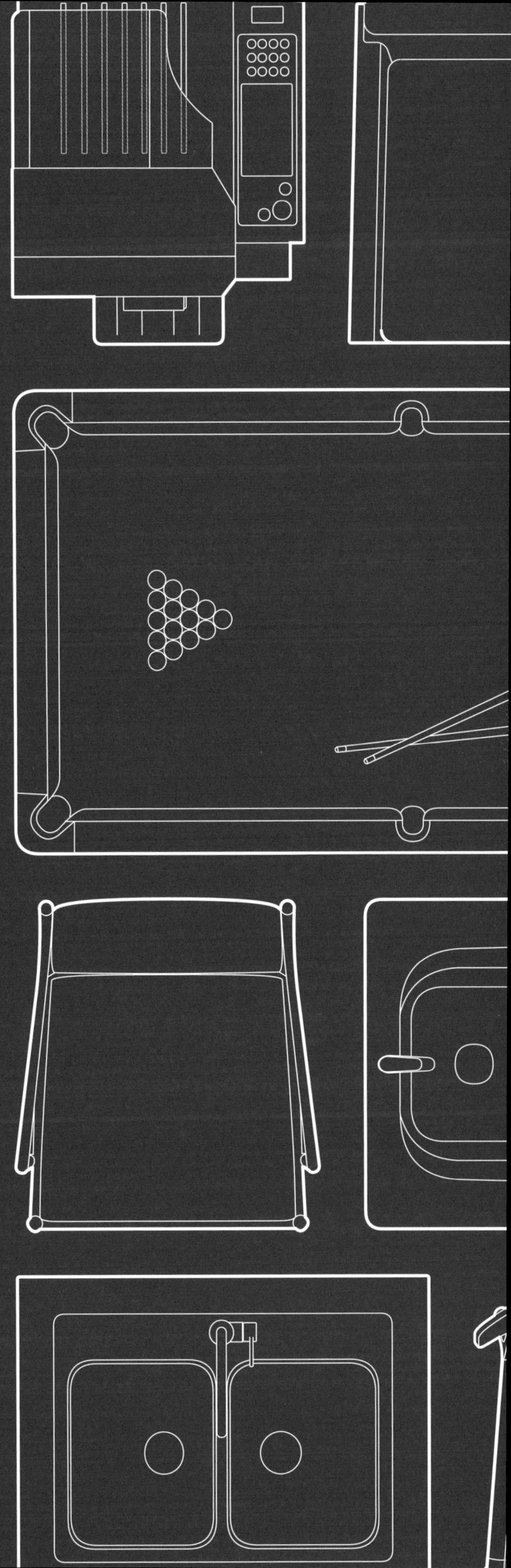

residential projects to commercial spaces, their dimensions began bleeding into the discipline's knowledge. For an architect, being able to plan most types of spaces would mean mastering the generic sizes offered by manufacturers; at times, a competence of equal importance to more scholarly knowledge. Simultaneously, as technology became ever more ingrained in the majority of building products, architects had to become familiar with products' technical specifications; to the point where these constrains 6 p. 447 would force designers to **specialize in the use of certain offerings or systems**: such practitioners would be expert in the use of terracotta thermal bricks, when this other one would be in the use of mechanical air ducts of a given manufacturer, etc.

Although fairly different both in scope and intent, printed handbooks and catalogs shaped the last century's architectural practice; sometimes more so than the scholarly literature wishes to admit. Today, however, these formats seem to belong to a distant past as the Internet profoundly transformed the landscape of printed publications at the turn of the XXIst century.

Offline > Online

7 p. 447 In 2020, Ikea decided to **suppress its paper catalog**, thereby confirming a much deeper trend that had already been looming for decades. Let's remember that in 2016, at its 8 p. 447 peak, Ikea's catalog had a distribution of **200 million copies in 69 different versions, in 32 languages, and to more than 50 markets**. For a publication that started in 1951, such a pragmatic pivot represents a turning point for manufacturers' catalogs in general; away from the paper format and towards a more dominant web presence. Of course, Ikea had not waited to build its online presence before shutting down its catalog. For two decades already, Ikea had been enriching its website to host and market its entire offering. The very technical specifications of its furniture had even been disseminated on each product page. But Ikea's website is just the front of a much deeper overhaul of the manufacturer's strategy. Inventory management, logistics, fulfillment, and supply chain: at every step of its value chain, the company digitized its processes to become a category leader. From the real-world showrooms of the 1950s to the web giant of the 2020s, Ikea's turnover is a case study today for many.

Its radical transformation offers an ideal vantage point from which to consider a much broader reality: most manufacturers these past decades have undergone a similar evolution; the paper catalogs of yesterday have migrated online, while distribution strategies now revolve around web traffic KPIs. To acknowledge the growing importance of designers' mainstream software, all manufacturers even provide the dimensions of their furniture by releasing the actual **CAD and** 9 p. 447 **BIM data**. After all, building products and systems naturally followed a trend, common to most industries, rebalancing their acquisition channels and offerings from offline to online. And if Architecture's reliance on manufacturers' catalogs has been ongoing for a long time, this sudden online relocation certainly has swayed the profession towards the web as an essential repository of information for builders.

In fact, Architecture itself experienced a similar motion over roughly the same period of time. This drastic "offline>online" relocation today permeates all facets of the discipline; a motion in four steps that is, although apparently obvious, worth understanding; especially in its latest developments.

The Web 2.0: Things began early on, as the Web 2.0 propelled the world of knowledge. In the image of the very page dedicated to "**Architecture**" on Wikipedia, first created in 10 p. 447 October 2001, the 2000s saw architectural information blossom online. If architectural knowledge's online presence today is a given, it is worth remembering its inception: the first efforts were actually placed around organizing online some of the discipline's written knowledge, beginning with building codes, news and educational content. Spearheaded by institutional players, building codes started being present online in the early days of the Internet. As for most regulatory content, governments and administrations around the world saw an opportunity to release and keep the construction codes of their respective jurisdictions up to date. At the same time, and although faithful to its tradition of printed reviews, Architecture saw the rise of its online news outlets. Media like 11 p. 447 **ArchDaily** (launched in 2008), **Dezeen** (launched in 2006), **AD**, **The Architect's Newspaper**, and countless others have seen their traffic skyrocketing over the past decades; in fact, their influence and viewership has largely exceeded the sole realm of the discipline. Most notably, educational content has benefited from the web in order to gather resources and structure knowledge in a myriad of different ways, from the early database system of academic libraries to the written content of classes leveraging the simplicity of blog publishing.

CAD & BIM: With the increasing bandwidth of web connections, the Internet started offering the ability to host large databases. Communities of architects harnessed this option and started building shared or gated repositories of assets such as PDFs of well-known books, CAD blocks, entire drawing sets, textures, images, etc. Websites such as BiblioCAD, Toffu, ArchiTextures, Dimensions.com, Studio Alternativi and many others started addressing practitioners by means of curated marketplaces. With the uptick of BIM software placing an emphasis on drawing buildings using actual building elements carrying detailed metadata, new repositories of BIM items followed in the footsteps of the marketplace trend: websites like BimObjects, BIMcomponents, bimStore, etc. today gather vast amounts of manufacturers' references for designers to download. On the side of knowledge production, publishers started understanding the importance of their web presence. Publications began leveraging the web to expand their content to other mediums, while publishing houses found an upside in aggregating the knowledge found across publications into content portals. To name only two iconic expressions of this
12 p. 447 trend: Wiley's all-too-famous **Architectural Graphics Standards** first started its web-
13 p. 447 site in 2016, whereas Birkhauser's **Building Types Online** got released in 2013, to offer a wide library of architectural floor plans to practitioners. With the increasing possibility of uploading and streaming heavy videos, educational content turned to this new medium and leveraged online portals to offer free or affordable access to rudimentary architectural design curricula. Heralded by universities and more generalist content platforms, this effort saw architectural education get democratized and reach wider, newer audiences worldwide.

Social Media: Soon enough, the Internet turned "social" when social media started acting as a catalyst of this early online infrastructure of architectural content, and propelling its reach to a much (much) wider audience. The importance of self-promotion in a creative profession like Architecture had social networks deeply resonating with the need of designers to find an audience. As a by-product of this period, we see portfolios today being published on Behance or Issuu rather than being plotted at the local print shop, or projects being shared (and reshared) on Instagram, TikTok or Twitter to maximize design studios' reach. This phenomenon has become so deeply ingrained in the habits of the profession that it is almost impossible to discern its extent, let alone its ongoing growth. However, one thing is certain: social media has been a spectacular springboard for architects, offering them a pedestal that no other outlet had been able to provide before.

The Legacy Players: The turn of the 2020s recently confirmed a new inflection point in this offline>online motion. A new step in the chronology is happening as we speak: this decade will see software migrating to the cloud in a final attempt to bring online the entire value chain of Architecture. Among the many reasons explaining this shift, a few key elements can help clarify this development. Above all, this situation stems from recently attained technological maturity: new frameworks are finally ready to support the transition online of architectural software. In fact, for a long time, mainstream browser technologies could not afford to host and operate heavy architectural models. Until very recently, a CAD file, often composed of hundreds of thousands if not millions of entities, could simply not be opened in a browser without crashing. That reality has changed, and new, powerful frameworks are today finally available for companies to build robust online applications that can hope to compete with the power of native software. Concomitantly, designers are starting to question legacy desktop-based software; especially at a time when other tools they use daily are already online and often allow for a multiplayer edition experience, while the majority of design tools architects use every day is still single player and desktop-based: AutoCAD, ArchiCAD, VectorWorks, Illustrator, etc. Perhaps most importantly, architects are witnessing other design disciplines operating the same transformation, ahead of them. Most notably, the online web design software Figma has caught the attention of all other design domains in its ability to ramp up its presence and challenge the incumbent in **just a few years**. 14 p. 447 The San Francisco-based startup managed to build an online, multiplayer web design software platform and dislodge the incumbent, once said to be "impossible to remove." Figma appears today as a perfect case study, showing how much design tools can today embrace the web for the better.

(Online) Tools: As a window of opportunity opens for Architecture, we are discerning the early signs of a blossoming ecosystem of online software. Most telling is maybe seeing legacy players beginning to rethink their offering. The example of Autodesk is certainly interesting in this respect: considering the recently acquired Forma, formerly called Spacemaker, as the cornerstone of its strategy, the software provider is beginning its transition to a cloud-based ecosystem. In the meantime, an entirely new ecosystem of web-apps is consolidating. This young generation of tools is being built from scratch using browser technologies; 2D or 3D, CAD, BIM or somewhere in between, these tools aspire to meet the hope of practitioners to see a better online ecosystem of design tools one day. Rayon, Snaptrude, Arcol, Modumate, etc.: **this new generation is racing to find acceptance** in the vast, global market of the AEC. 15 p. 447

By the end of this chronology, this new ecosystem we have described powers a different culture altogether. The design communities that this offline>online motion serves are ones that display in certain respects new types of dynamics, common among online communities. Designs and projects are shared with a certain spontaneity, pragmatism and simplicity of use take precedence over disciplinary concerns, while design teams function as distributed bodies. All in all, behind the evolution of Architecture's technological infrastructure, a new type of work culture seems to be appearing across the discipline.

Data, content, software, work culture: the Internet is gradually rebalancing our discipline. And in this wind of change, knowledge and tools are gradually converging online; it is, in essence, in this landscape that this publication lands.

On bits & paper

All is online; and yet here we are, publishing a book!

At first glance, one could wonder how books, even more so ones describing generic knowledge, could survive? How could they keep their rank in this evermore digital landscape? To this interrogation, we see the Architect's Sourcebook, along with similar works, having an essential role to play. These publications seemingly "stitch together" some of the virtues of the legacy forms of knowledge consumption with the obvious advantages online content offers. By leveraging the intersection between "bits and paper," they represent a timely answer to the transitory state our discipline finds itself in.

The Status Quo: The divide between digital and print still appears today as an airtight frontier, despite what each format could bring to the other. On one hand, architectural knowledge is still on the fence with web-based content. While the digital age has undoubtedly democratized access to information, its overwhelming profusion has often obscured the path to relevant and reliable content. The sheer quantity of information may sometimes render the search for valuable insights quite tedious, if not impossible. More importantly maybe, unlike the curated and carefully vetted nature of printed publications, online architectural resources frequently suffer from inconsistencies and a general lack of dependability.

On the other side, existing handbooks in Architecture, although information-rich, might today lack certain qualities professionals would hope for. This type of book frequently comes across as dry or overly technical, making it much less accessible and relatable to a broad audience. Moreover, a notable gap still exists today between traditional manuals and the catalogs of items essential for effectively designing spaces. To get the full picture, architects often find themselves juggling between various handbooks and catalogs. The advice offered in existing handbooks also often fluctuates between being overly specific or excessively generic, leaving little room for practical applications. These publications are notably challenged by timing itself: while it takes a considerable amount of time to compile and publish them, their content quickly becomes outdated in this fast-paced architectural world, especially at scales where trends and regulations move fast.

An Age of Hybrids: At first sight, the current status quo fails to reconcile both formats: terabytes of online, poorly-curated information are sitting next to mountain-like piles of increasingly obsolete technical manuals. Ernst Neufert himself, in his **preface to the Architect's Data**, rightfully pointed out how Architecture should embrace change and look towards solutions the future might hold! To us, the hybridization of digital and print not only helps fill each medium's shortcomings, but also represents a direction that has the potential to help Architecture keep pace with the evolution of knowledge consumption.

16 p. 447

Above anything else, the book format still sets a high bar for quality and curation. The editorial process that publications usually go through reasserts the importance of curation and reliability of information. The vetting that precedes the publication of most work, be it through peer review or the editor-author collaboration, ensures a minimum level of information integrity that confers to the printed format a certain authority.

Then the structure of the book format, the general clarity of the organization of its information, starkly contrasts with the swarm of data that one can find online. That is why books can in fact offer an ideal entry point, a gateway to the information present online. Publications like this one are the very demonstration of this possibility: if anything, this book will help readers browse and make sense of a rather flat **database of CAD items**. It is the user manual to entire "stacks of data," a map to a vast, foggy wasteland of bits. Through the sequence of chapters, catalogs, kits, etc., this publication simply queries Rayon's repositories to provide a legible, understandable, pedagogical reading of its content. It only demonstrates how, in digital time, the printed medium can give meaning, structure and trustworthiness to the "knowledge in bulk" that increasingly exists online. On the flip side, online content can afford to be continuously updated; in this sense, web-based content can be sustained longer than printed material. That is why, as books touch upon topics prone to evolve over time, offloading time sensitive information to online portals can be an apt strategy. This way, information can remain current much longer, as online content can afford to go through revisions and updates. More importantly, online content's extent can grow over time, as hosted databases can be complemented and expanded at any point.

17 p. 447

All in all, stitching together the advantages of the book format, and that of the Web, has a promising future for disciplines where knowledge access and integrity matter. That's why we think that there is a future for architectural handbooks at the frontiers between bits and paper.

The Sourcebook

Both a book and a website, a manuscript and a database, a stack of pages and collections of QR codes: the Sourcebook belongs to this category of strange hybrid publications we see these days; halfway between physical and digital. As such, it hopes to express in print the wealth of space planning information that is today bubbling online!

Space Planning in Architecture: As a manual, this book focuses on a specific scale of Architecture: space planning. That dimension of Architecture might be better understood when contrasted with other levels of building design. American theorist Frank Duffy's famous assertion might come in handy here: "There isn't any such thing as a building. A building properly conceived is several layers of longevity of built components." For him and disciples of his like architect Stewart Brand, buildings are not integral entities, but rather assemblages constituted of multiple "layers." Brand will go as far
18 p. 447
as to coin five distinct layers: **Structure, Skin, Services, Space Plan, and Stuff**. Each system would be nested within the next one and would correspond to a very different lifespan, set of constraints and level of care. To this day, this classification still resonates with the architectural profession, especially at a time when durability is a rising concern for the built world. Most notable in this taxonomy is the idea that space planning and the items it comprises (the "Stuff") stand as the innermost layers of the classification, and display the shortest life cycle. Looking at Brand's layers, it is fair to say that architects absolutely excel at handling the three outermost ones (Structure, Skin, Services). As these are the most long-lasting systems of buildings, they naturally carry the most risk and therefore naturally deserve the profession's full attention. However, the innermost layers of Brand's classification sometimes appear to be neglected in Architecture. Unlike other aspects of building design, they are often treated as an afterthought; a by-product of other (more external) architectural considerations. Yet Space Plan and Stuff are critical components that deserve attention in their own right. These layers together carry their own language, dimensions, and know-how. Not only do they represent a distinct part of building design, they are more "free" than other dimensions: as space planning is less bound by strict regulations and building codes, it is a rather global and relatable dimension of Architecture. Less technical than other scales, yet equally crucial, this side of space design matters today to an ever-increasing crowd of online designers.

The Internet has, in fact, proven to be especially welcoming to the hosting of information, discussions, and all forms of media documenting this scale of Architecture. And as with most forms of online knowledge, it displays all the cruxes and benefits we would expect: messy and imprecise, fragmented between gated websites or community forums, the information remains scattered around in all forms. The data itself either lacks reliability or is too specific to given locations. On the plus side, however, it is possible to find there all one needs to plan space: curating and digesting this sea of information might be a tedious exercise, but one cannot deny that at the heart of this haystack lies a wealth of good sense and useful tips. Better than that even: this space-planning-online-knowledge is a living, breathing form of knowledge, where discussions and contributions continuously bring to the surface the latest information about space dimensions or catalog updates. Browsing forums, or reading threads, is at times simply fascinating.

This handbook hopes to do justice to this online culture, and distill in the print some of its richness. As it tackles space planning, the Sourcebook wants to both address this underappreciated scale of building design, and pay tribute to the ever-increasing contributions to this topic of online design communities.

Content: So what do readers "get" out of this manual?

First and foremost, the Sourcebook offers generic dimensions and space layout ideas. The publication covers three essential typologies — **housing, office, and outdoor spaces** — and 19 p. 447
touches upon most rooms that constitute these types of spaces. To that end, we blend

together the rules of thumb of the handbook format and the wide palette of choices of the catalog format; in other words, guidelines and items!

Three types of chapters allow us to cover most bases: "Dimensions" chapters tackle the size of generic items and general rules for placing them in space. Then, "Kits" chapters offer entire collections of furniture to plan a specific type of space. For each type of room, a pack between 20 and 40 items is offered, ready for use, while illustrations give to readers layout ideas, or just goofy scenarios. Finally, "Catalogs" considers each family of items, and provides the full spectrum of possibilities within that category.

This book most importantly gives readers access to the CAD data needed to actually draw spaces: the Sourcebook takes advantage of Rayon's high-fidelity repository of CAD blocks, and offers, by means of QR codes disseminat-
20 p. 447 ed throughout the book, **1000+ CAD assets** readily available for download (see page 13 for instructions). Together, these items represent more than a simple collection of vector illustrations: they document Brand's innermost layers. They offer a generic, extensive toolbox for practitioners to work with, while bringing the notion of an architectural manual one step closer to architects' modern workflows.

Last but not least, the Sourcebook gives this seemingly technical topic a slightly more light-hearted touch than usual manuals; it blends together a bit of Ernst Neufert's rigor
21 p. 447 with a dash of **Gary Larson**'s wit. After all, rules and guidelines are already quite a dry topic to begin with; can't we give this all a twist? At least it is what we have tried to do here by keeping things on the fun side, rather than mimic the stern aesthetic common to specification manuals. We hope in this way to broaden the appeal and reach of planning knowledge to a much larger audience.

In the next few pages, we lay down the basic principle of this handbook: the table of contents can then be found on p. 20, while the book chapters begin as of p. 22 (the Basics), p. 32 (the Office), p. 172 (the House) and p. 304 (the Outdoor). A DIY segment will conclude the publication on p. 430.

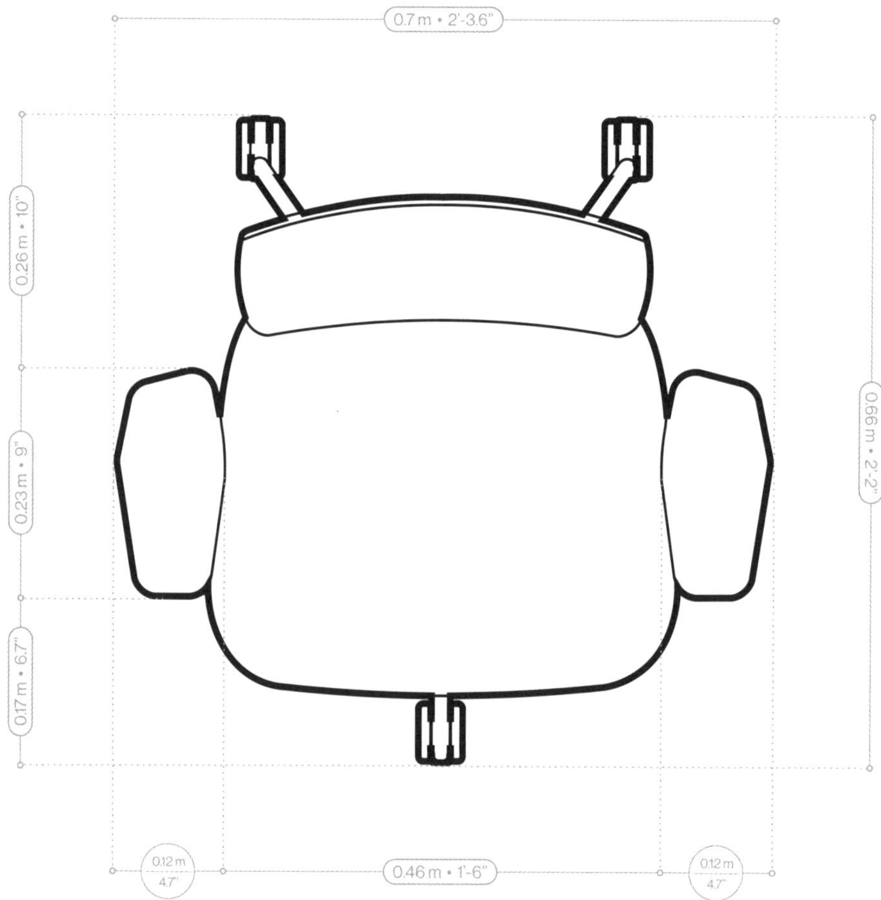

Objects we use everyday come in (oddly) specific dimensions, and when it comes to remembering them all, designers understandably struggle. For one thing, this book will provide readers with the **generic sizes of the things** that they most likely use in 99% of their projects.

Most **items in this book carry a tag!** Each tag details the object's properties (name, size, etc.). In addition the tag's **QR code** will redirect you to a downloadable CAD block, hosted online. Instructions for downloading all items can be found by scanning **the QR code above!**

This book contains in fact
more than 1000 CAD blocks,
available online and sorted by category.
So take out your phone,
and start scanning!

Kit for a
Bedroom
Catalog of
Appliances
Catalog of
Urban Furniture
Kit for a
Open Space
Kit for a
Private Office
Kit for a
Meeting Room
Kit for a
Kitchen
Catalog of
Office Fixtures
Kit for a
Skatepark
Lounge
Kit for a
Bathroom
Kit for a
Conference Room
Catalog of
Sport Fields
Catalog of
Office Desks
Kit for a
Playground

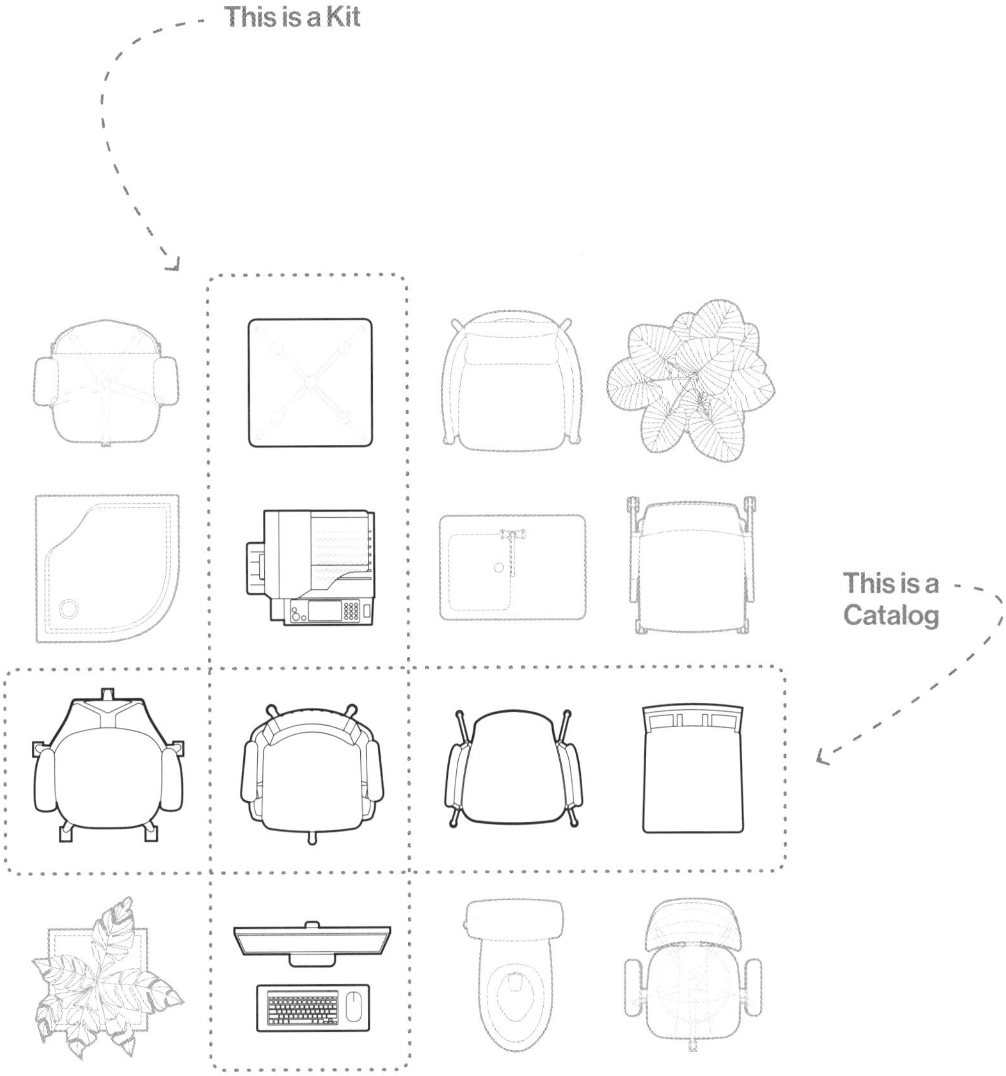

Finally, blocks are organized in
kits and catalogs.

On one hand, **kits** will provide readers with different types of items, **grouped together to furnish a specific room**: a bedroom, an open space, a garage, etc. On the other hand, **catalogs** cover the different **possible versions of a single item**: for instance, the chair catalog ranges from light kitchen chairs to comfy office chairs.

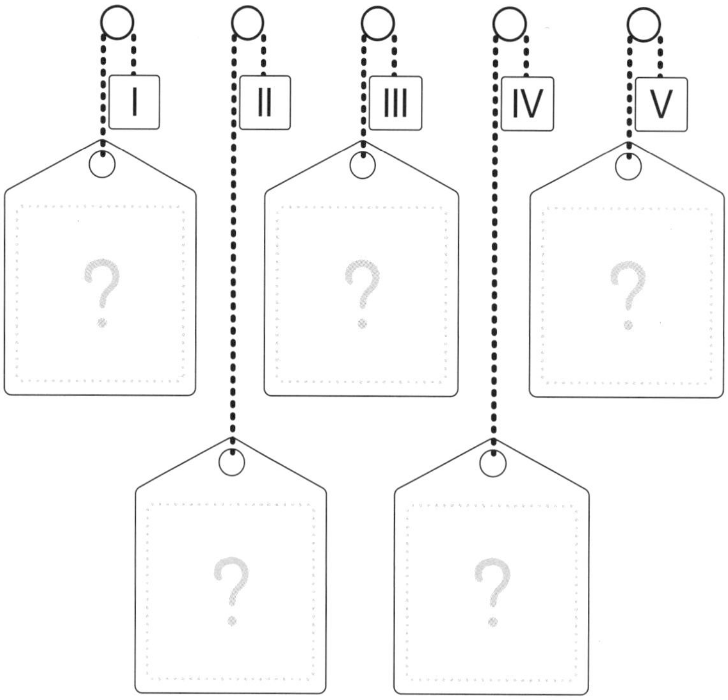
I
II
III
IV
V
?
?
?
?
?

Bonus

? ? ? ? ?

I II III IV V

One last thing!

Many more blocks are waiting for you! As you browse through the pages, keep an eye out for **the 5 clues** (see opposite page). Each one is carrying a number. Once you have spotted them, **head over to the website above (see QR code)**, and enter your **5 letter code.**

Good luck!

The Basics

People, Openings, Stairs, Elevators, etc.

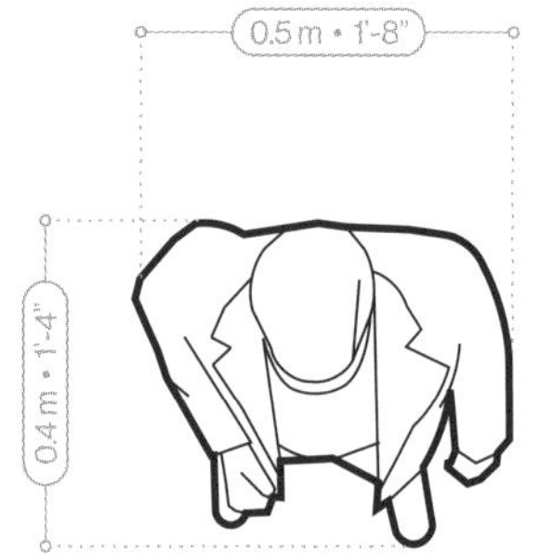

Standing

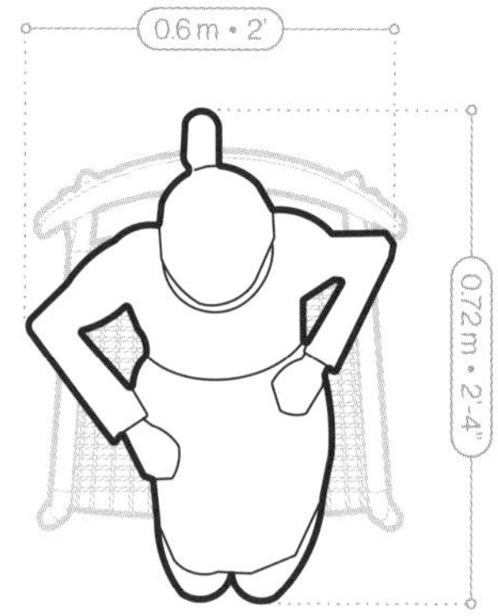

Sitting

Walking

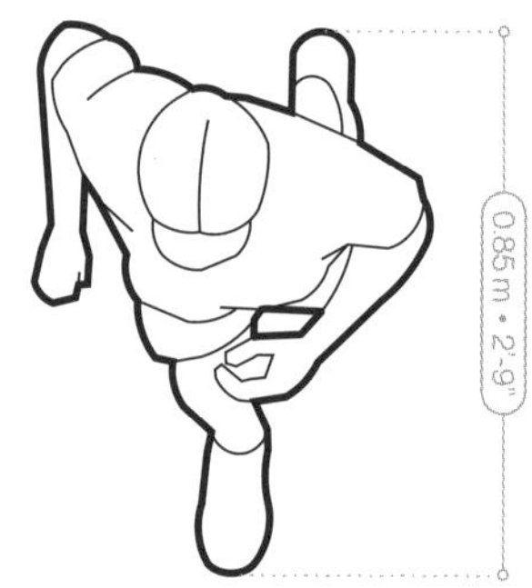

Running

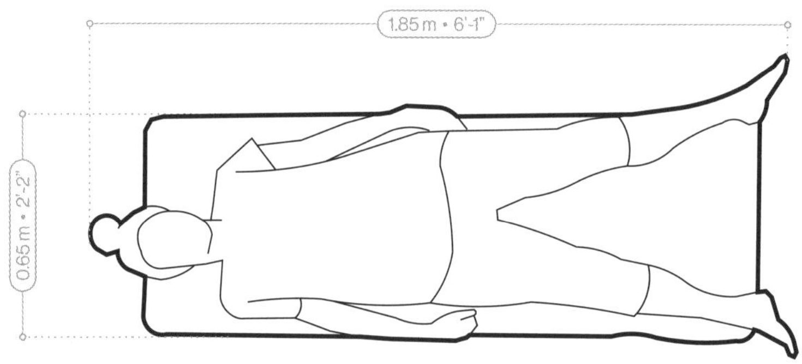

Lying

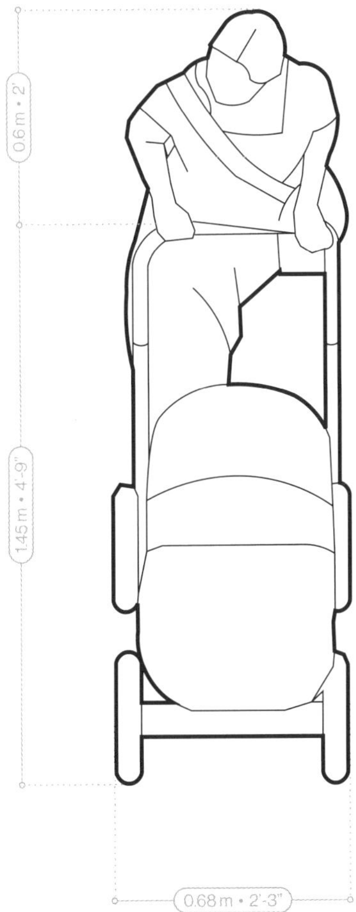

Stroller

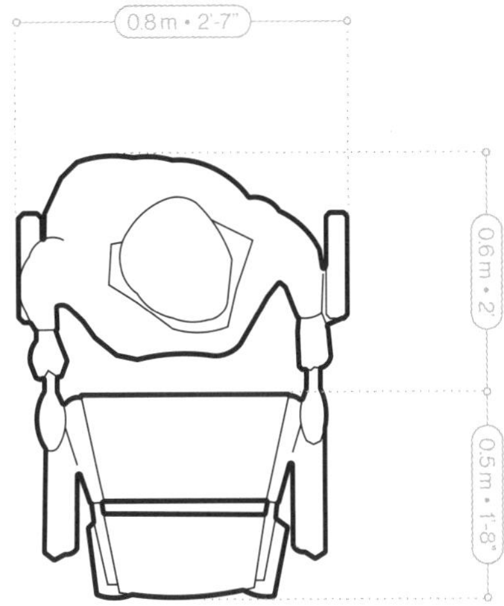

Walker

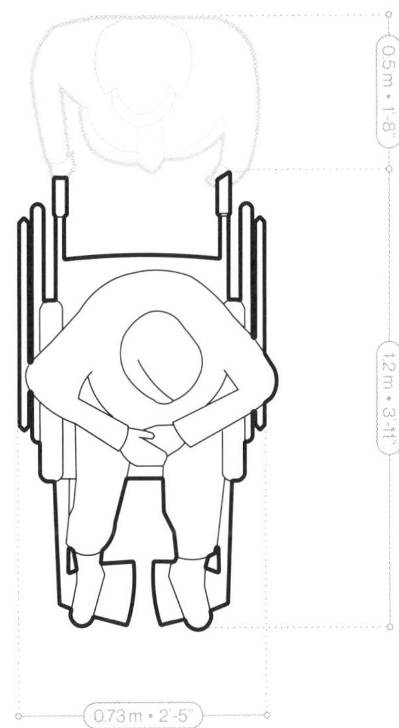

Wheelchair

Groups

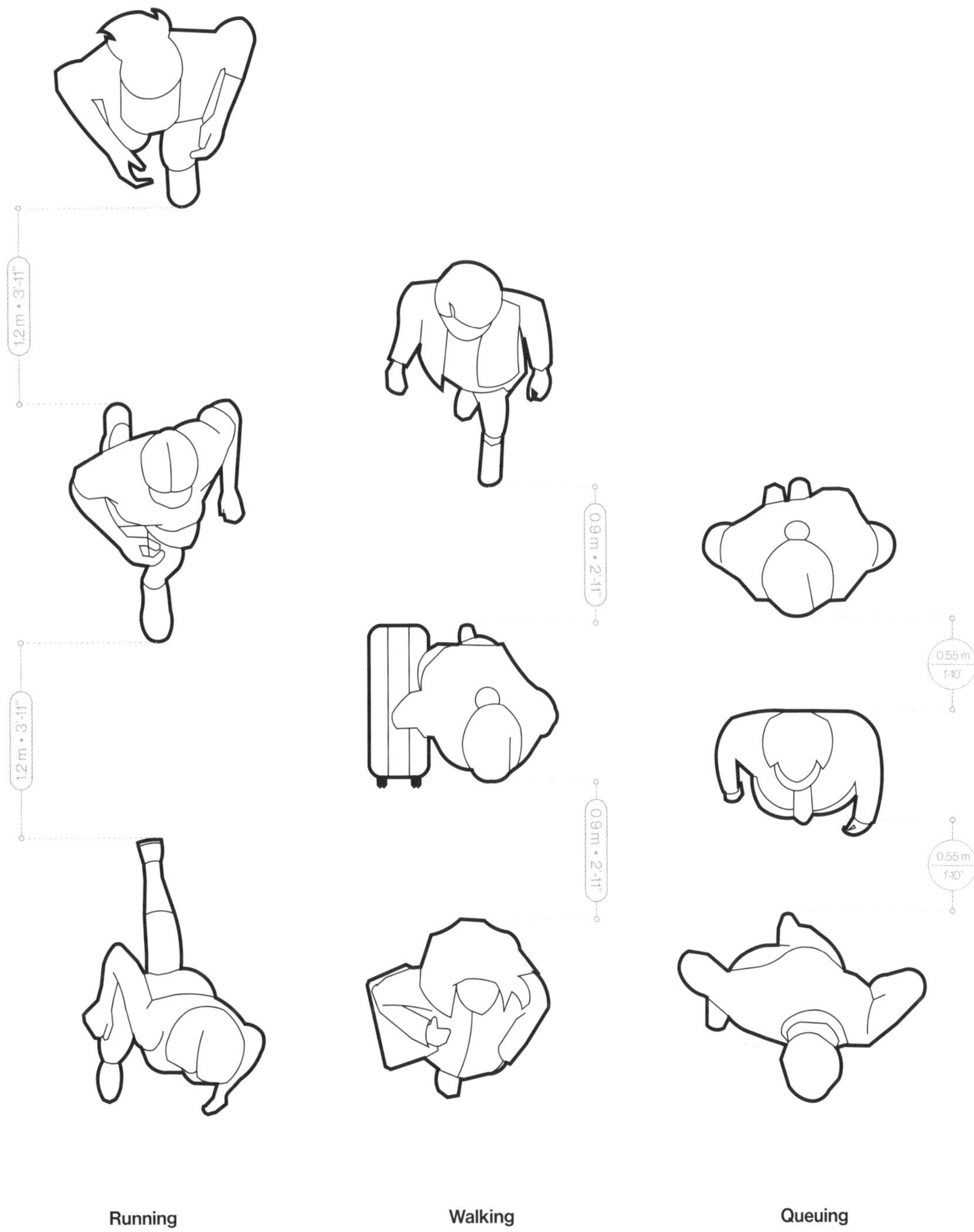
1.2 m • 3'-11"
1.2 m • 3'-11"
0.9 m • 2'-11"
0.9 m • 2'-11"
0.55 m
1'-10"
0.55 m
1'-10"
Running
Walking
Queuing

Gaps

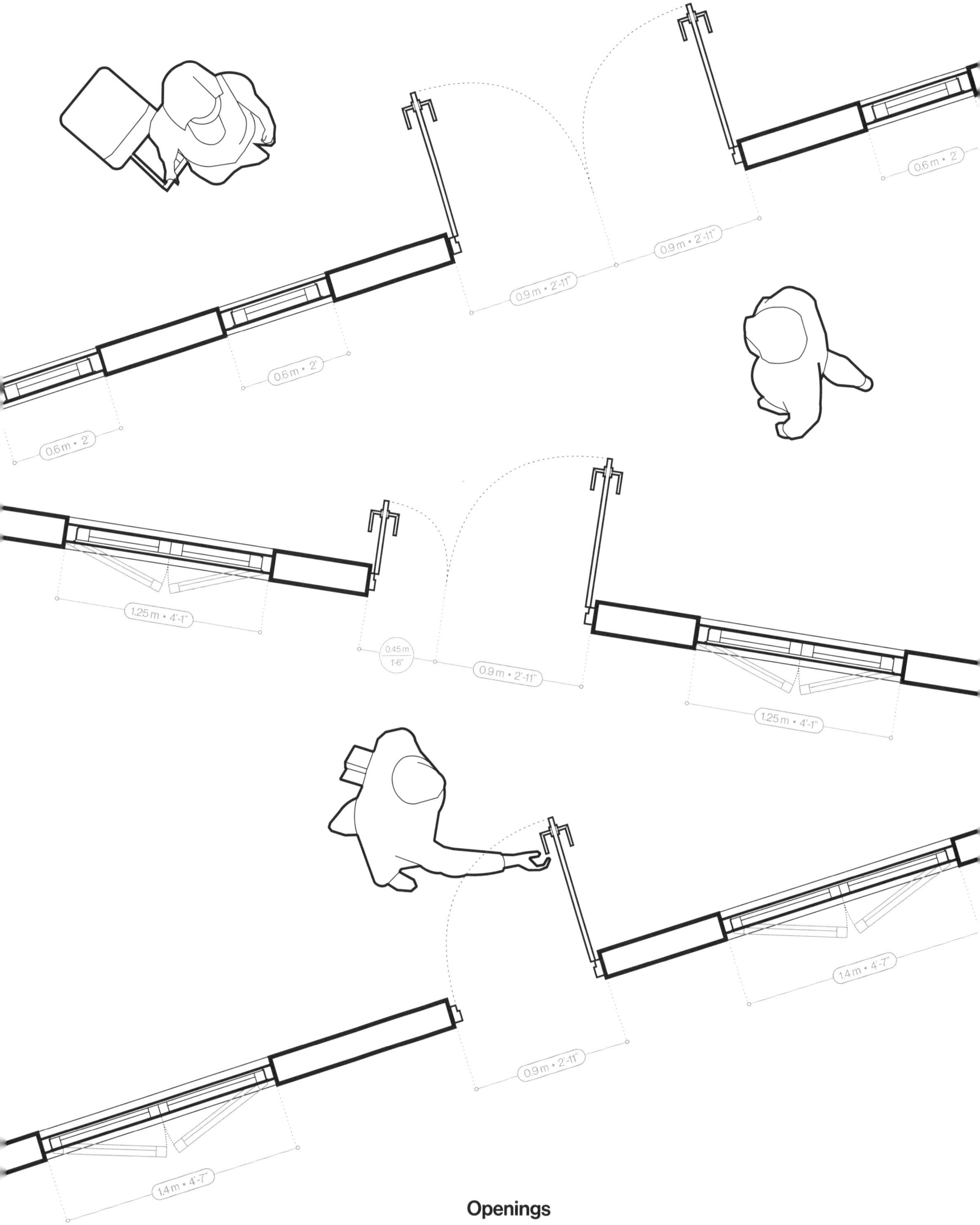
0.6 m • 2'
0.9 m • 2'-11"
0.9 m • 2'-11"
0.6 m • 2'
0.6 m • 2'
1.25 m • 4'-1"
0.45 m
1'-6"
0.9 m • 2'-11"
1.25 m • 4'-1"
1.4 m • 4'-7"
0.9 m • 2'-11"
1.4 m • 4'-7"

Openings

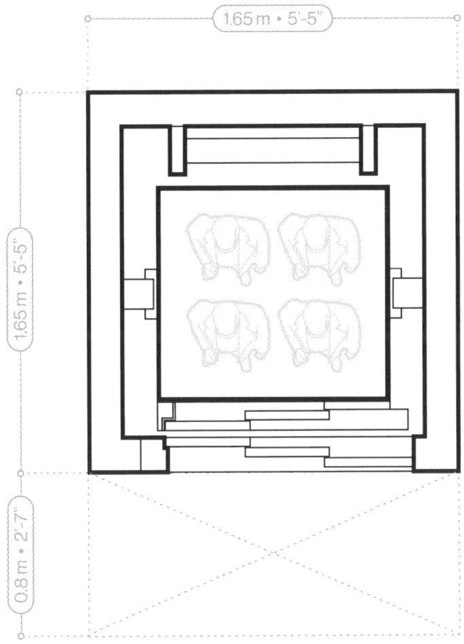

4 people

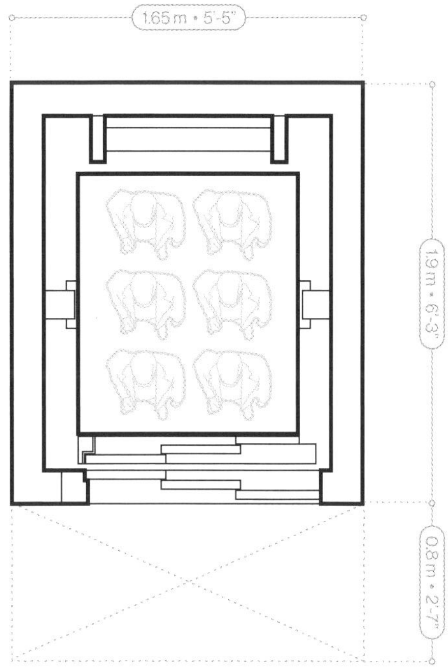

6 people

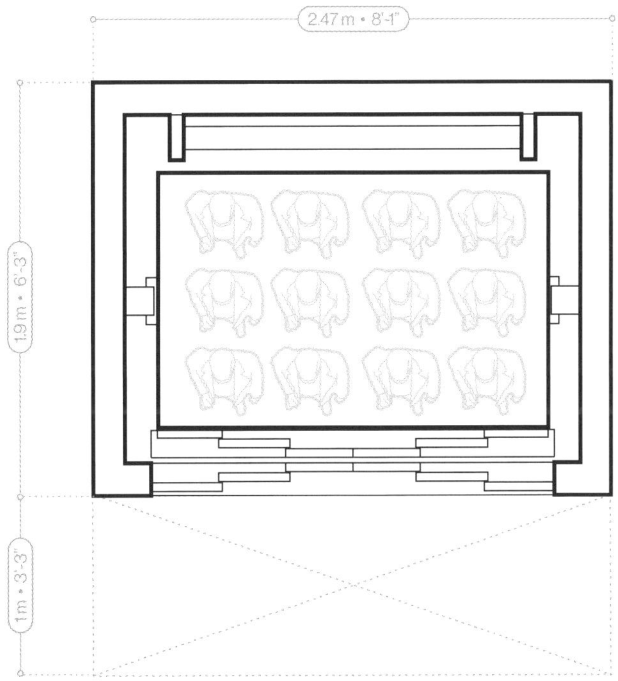

12 people

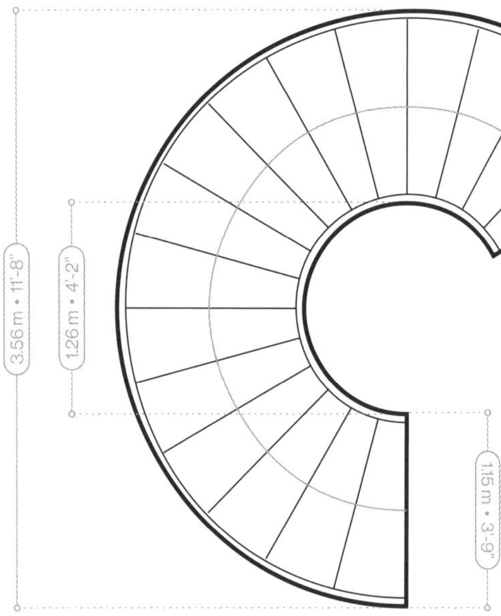

Round stair

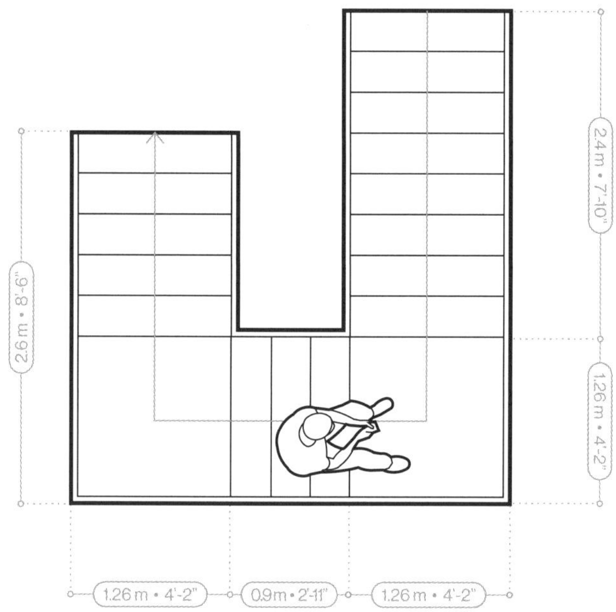

U stair

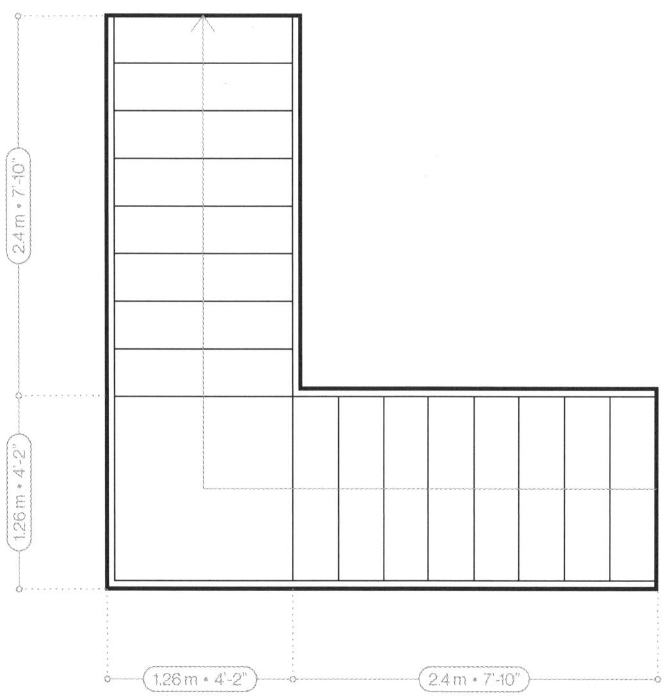

L stair

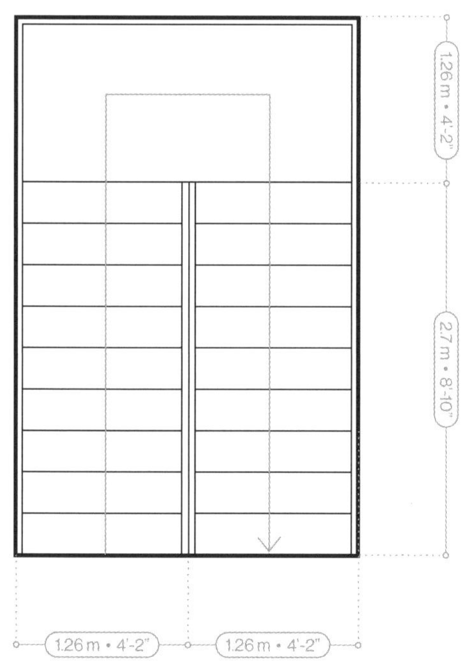

Compact U stair

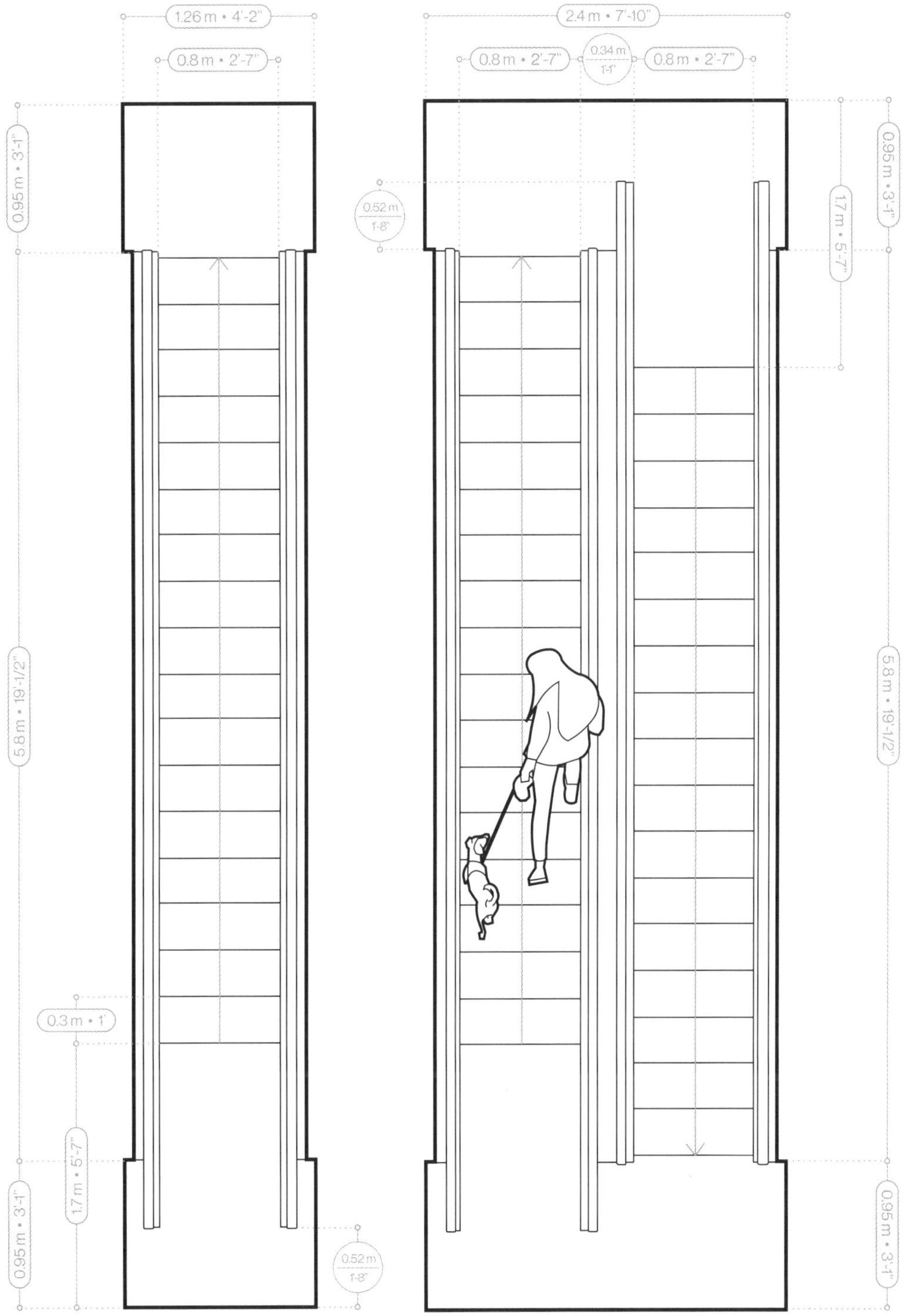

One-way escalator **Two-way escalator**

For the Office

Desks, Chairs, Booths, Armchairs, etc.

We open this book's first chapter on the topic of the workplace, an environment that has undergone significant transformations over the past decades. The rise of wireless technology has been an essential vector of change, liberating workers and office infrastructure from the limitations of fixed internet connections. This technological advancement has prompted a critical reassessment of traditional office layouts, particularly the open-plan design, which has faced criticism for its lack of personalization and potential impact on employee interaction and productivity.

The shift towards hybrid work models, integrating both remote and on-site working methods, has also posed new challenges for conventional office design. These evolving work patterns have emphasized the importance of wellness and care in the workplace, leading to the development of strategies focused on creating more human-centric and supportive work environments.

As a result of these evolving work dynamics, the past decade has seen a shift in the composition and design of office spaces. Modern workplaces
1 p. 87 now frequently feature a **variety of booths** tailored for individual focus or collaborative activities, reflecting the changing needs of the workforce. The traditional **meeting room** has evolved, 2 p. 61 giving way to more dynamic brainstorming areas and enclosed meeting spaces, designed to foster creativity and collaboration while providing privacy when needed.

The first twenty years of the millennium were marked by the emergence of new types of spaces that offer many "shades of gray" between the traditional open-plan layout and the seclusion of the private office. This includes **hot-desking areas** for transient use and quieter 3 p. 89 zones within open spaces, providing employees with a range of options in terms of privacy and interaction. The principles guiding office layout have also evolved dramatically. The once prevalent free-form layout of **open spaces** has 4 p. 79 been reimagined, introducing innovative, more fluid circulation patterns and redefining the boundaries between dedicated work zones and communal areas.

Flexibility has emerged as a cornerstone in contemporary office design, focusing on fluid and adaptable spaces that respond to the varying needs of employees. This approach is evident in the strategic placement of furniture and office elements, encouraging natural movement and interaction. Modern office furniture has adapted to this trend, becoming more versatile and reconfigurable to support the dynamic nature of modern workspaces. This shift is facilitated by a 5 p. 143 broad spectrum of **modular furniture collections**, which allow for a flexible and responsive office environment.

The focus on wellness has become increasingly pronounced in recent office design choices. 6 p. 155 Amenities like **gyms** have been reintroduced, aiming to enhance the overall workplace experience by promoting physical health and well-being. 7 p. 115 The **cafeteria**, a staple of office life, has also evolved. Many are now designed as open-kitchen spaces adjacent to work areas, blurring the lines between professional and leisure spaces. In some extreme cases, the cafeteria even merges with the lobby, creating a barista-style reception area that fosters a sense of community.

8 p. 121 The resurgence of **plant** life in office settings is a reflection of the growing trend towards biophilic design, which emphasizes the integration of natural elements into the built environment. This approach is rooted in the understanding that a connection to nature is essential for mental and physical health, leading to a more balanced and productive workspace.

In addition to these design trends, the integration of technology in office spaces has become increasingly sophisticated. Smart office solutions, including automated lighting and climate control systems, have become more prevalent, enhancing both the environmental sustainability and the comfort of the workplace. The adoption of ergonomic furniture and adjustable 9 p. 55 **workstations** highlights a growing recognition of the importance of physical well-being in the workplace, acknowledging the diverse needs of a modern workforce.

Mindful of these different trends, this upcoming chapter covers the main typology of spaces necessary to plan an office space. Diversity of meeting areas, modular furniture, different types of workstations and booths, rich plant catalogs, etc.: we have tried to reflect the different changes that these past decades have witnessed within the various kits and catalogs available in the chapter.

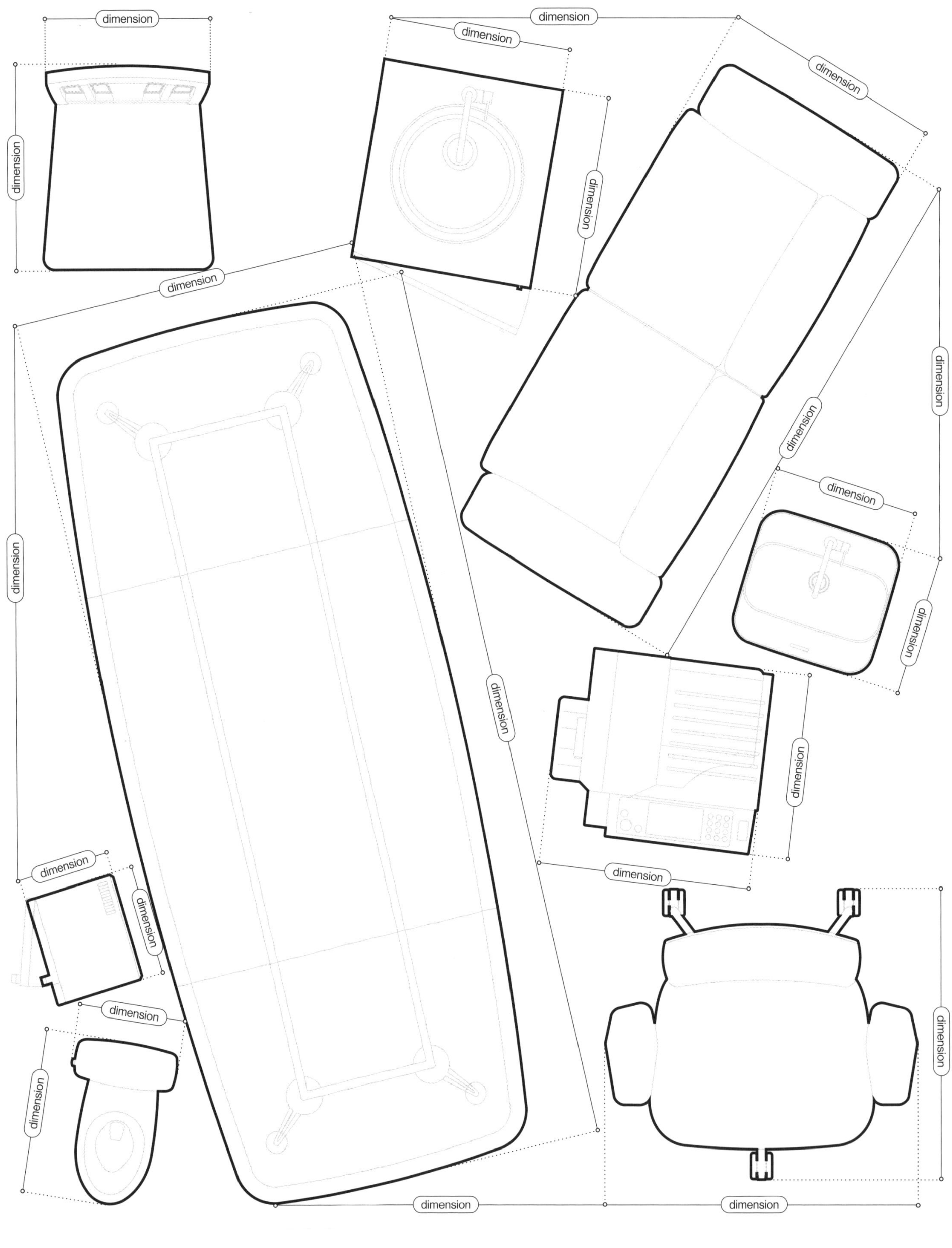
dimension
dimension
dimension
dimension
dimension
dimension
dimension
dimension
dimension
dimension
dimension
dimension
dimension
dimension
dimension
dimension
dimension
dimension
dimension
dimension
dimension
dimension

Dimensions

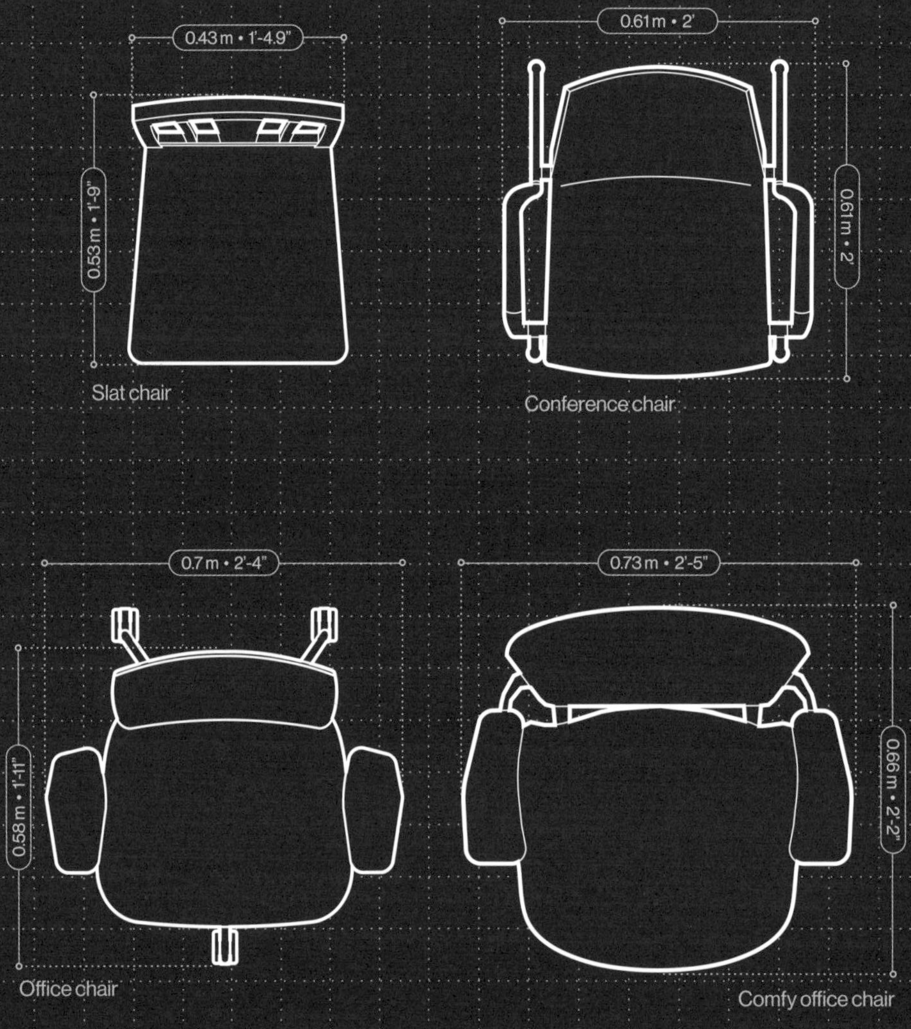
0.43 m • 1'-4.9"
0.53 m • 1'-9"
Slat chair
0.61 m • 2'
0.61 m • 2'
Conference chair
0.7 m • 2'-4"
0.58 m • 1'-11"
Office chair
0.73 m • 2'-5"
0.66 m • 2'-2"
Comfy office chair

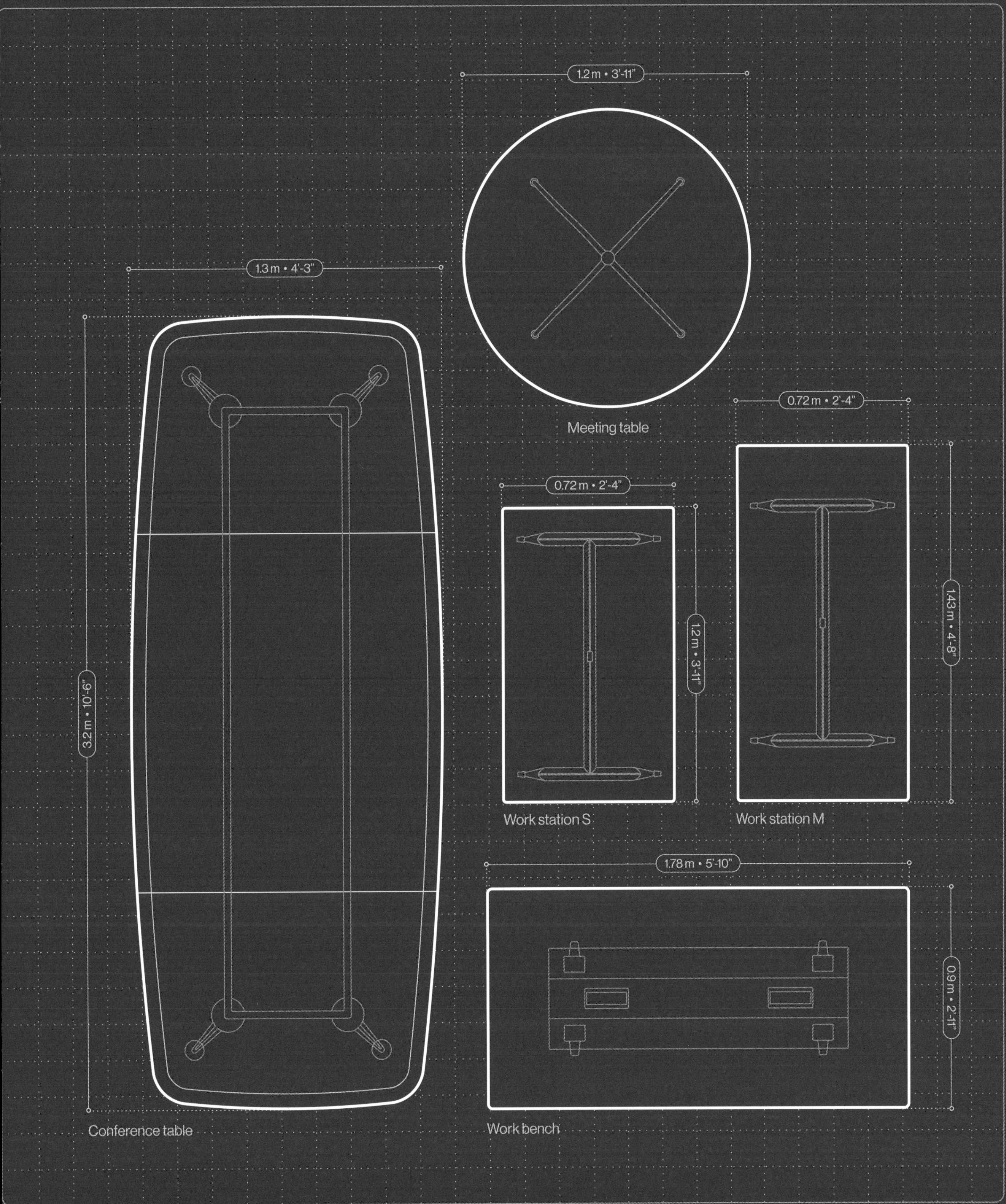
1.2 m • 3'-11"
Meeting table
1.3 m • 4'-3"
0.72 m • 2'-4"
0.72 m • 2'-4"
1.2 m • 3'-11"
1.43 m • 4'-8"
3.2 m • 10'-6"
Work station S
Work station M
1.78 m • 5'-10"
0.9m • 2'-11"
Conference table
Work bench

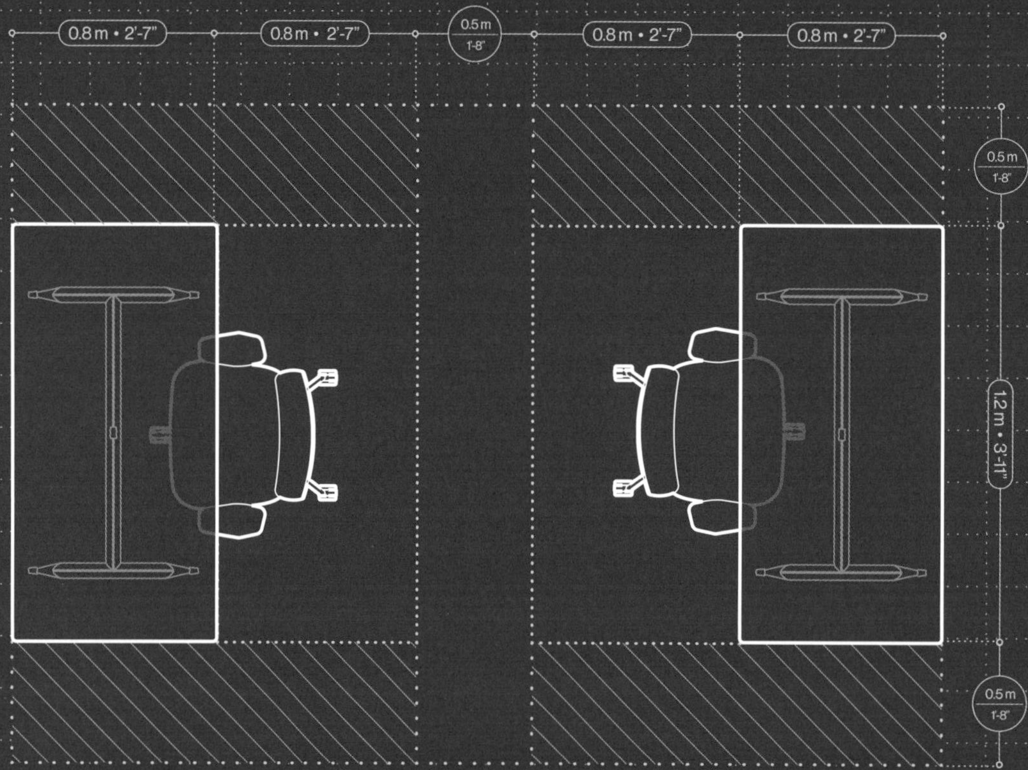

Office desks

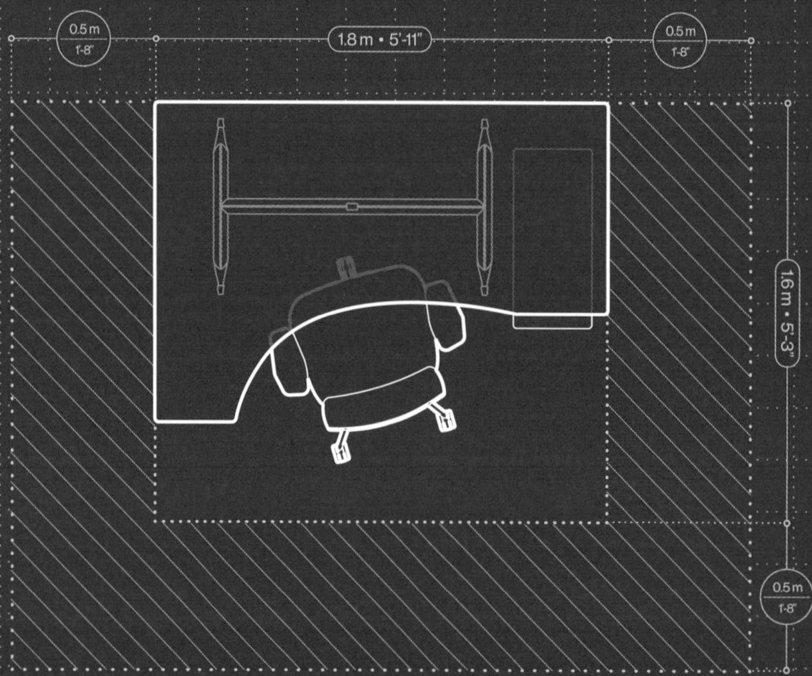

L-shaped office desk

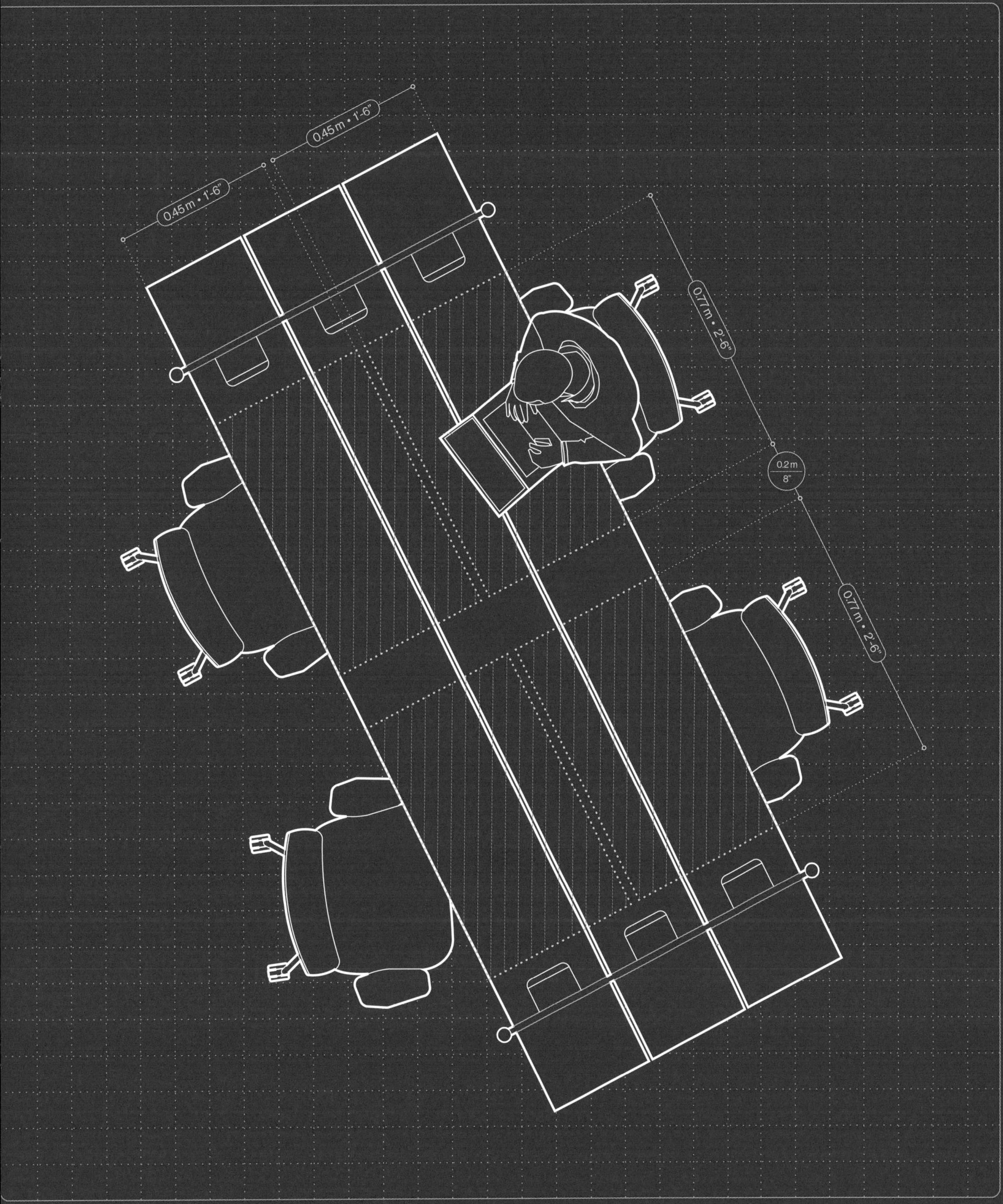
0.45 m • 1'-6"
0.45 m • 1'-6"
0.77 m • 2'-6"
0.2 m
8"
0.77 m • 2'-6"

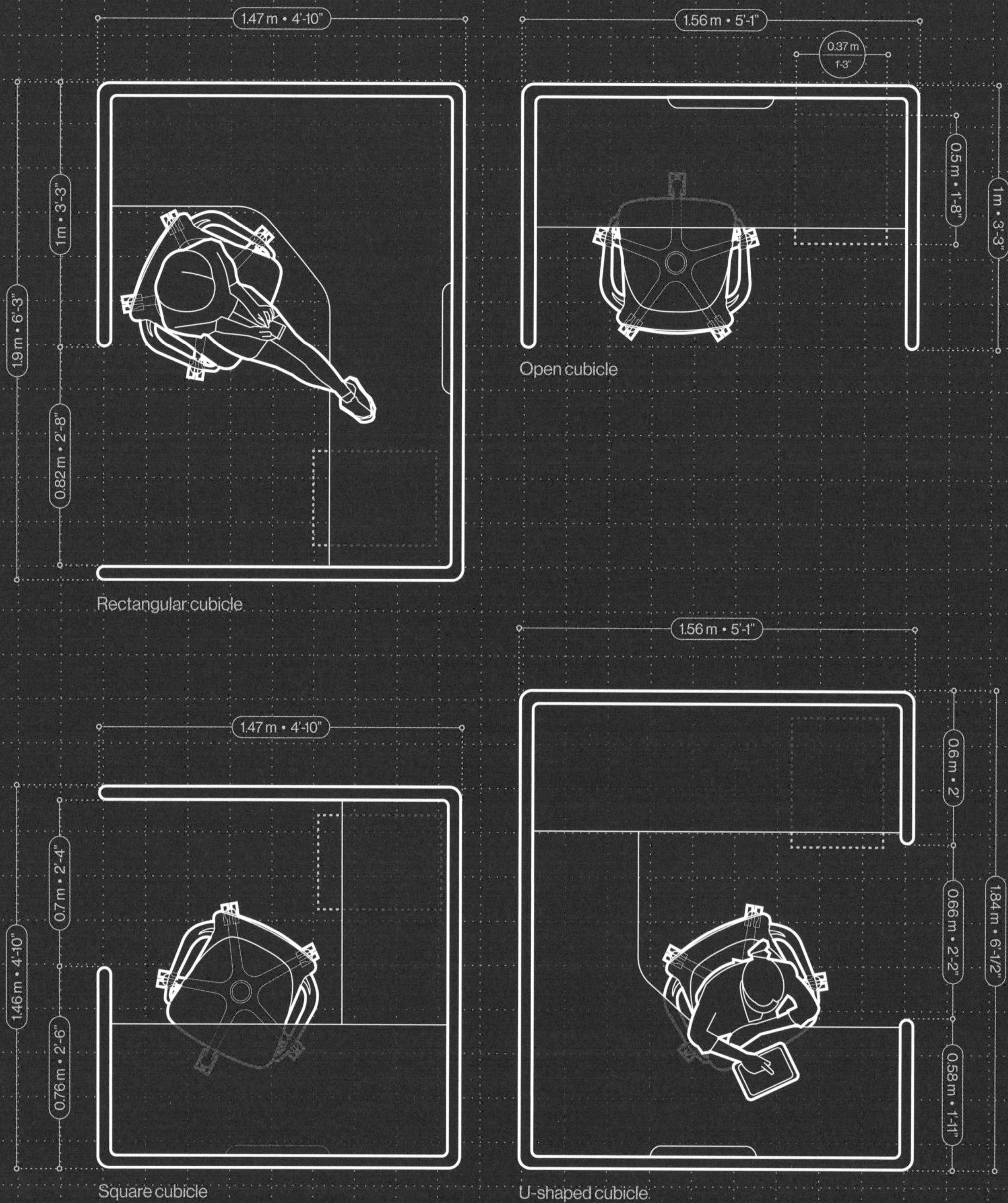
1.47 m • 4'-10"
1.9 m • 6'-3"
1 m • 3'-3"
0.82 m • 2'-8"
Rectangular cubicle
1.56 m • 5'-1"
0.37 m
1'-3"
0.5 m • 1'-8"
1 m • 3'-3"
Open cubicle
1.47 m • 4'-10"
1.46 m • 4'-10"
0.7 m • 2'-4"
0.76 m • 2'-6"
Square cubicle
1.56 m • 5'-1"
0.6 m • 2'
0.66 m • 2'-2"
0.58 m • 1'-11"
1.84 m • 6'-1/2"
U-shaped cubicle

Cubicles

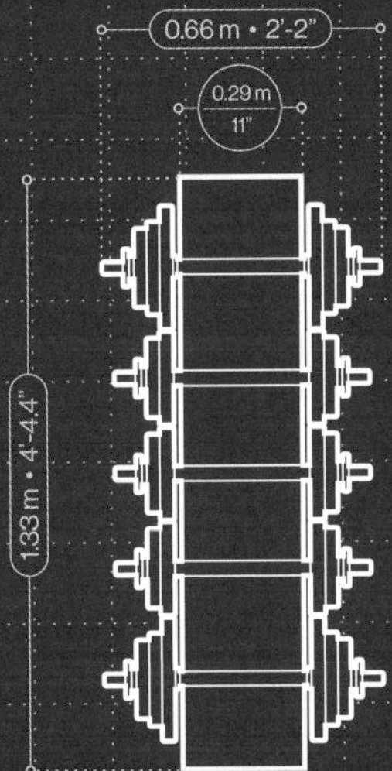

Weights

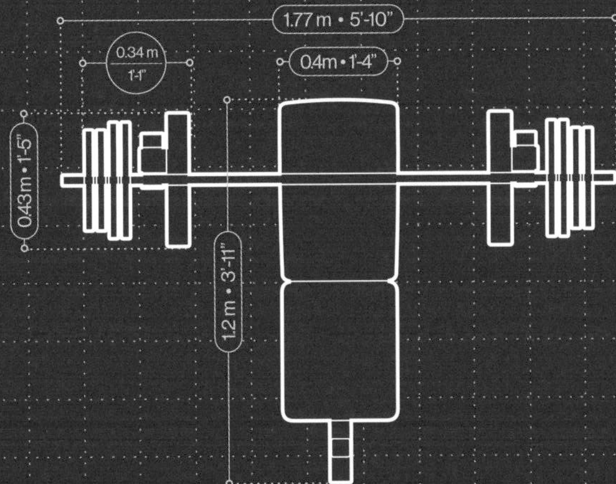

Bench press - L

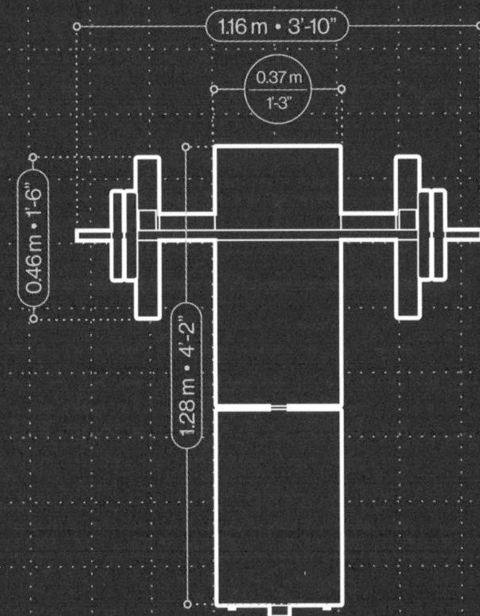

Bench press - S

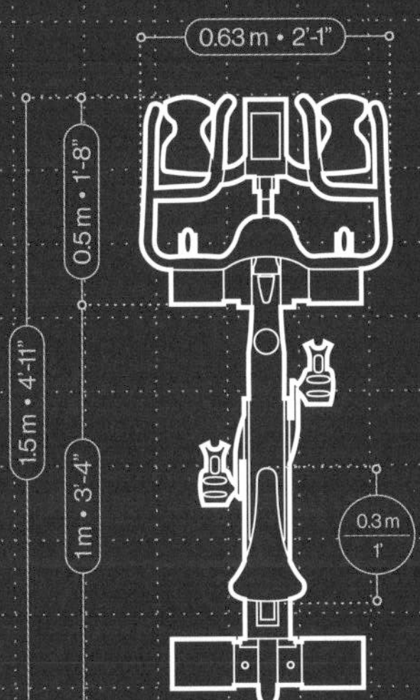

Indoor cycle

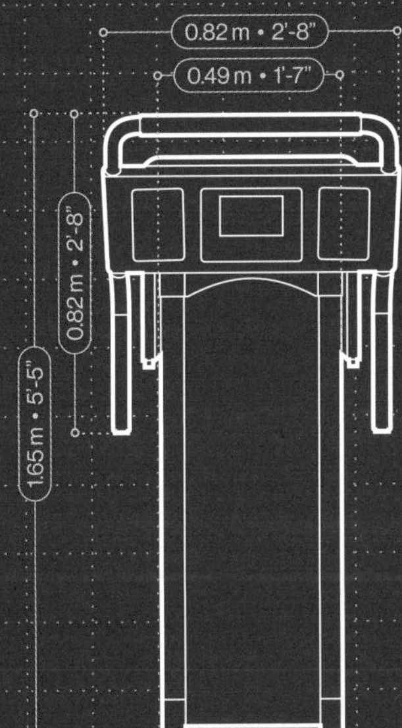

Treadmill

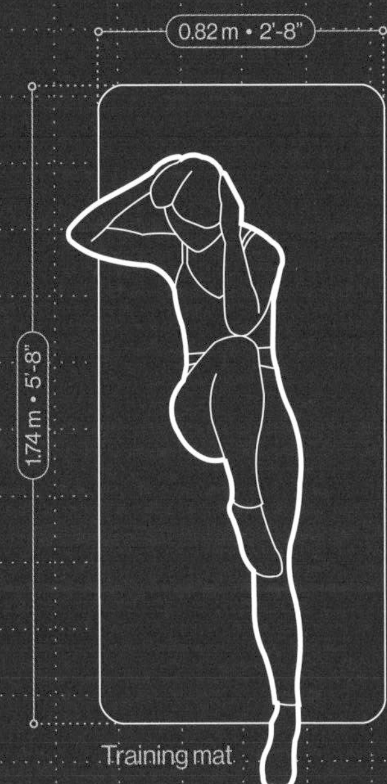

Training mat

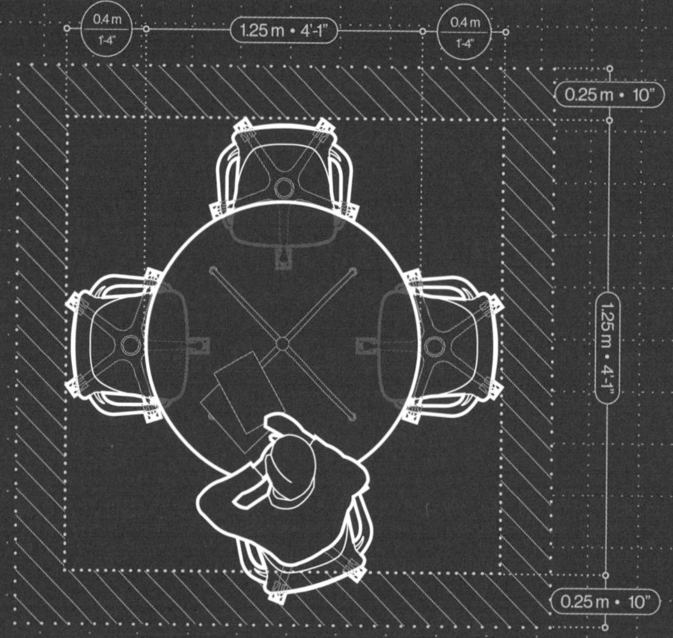

Meeting room - S

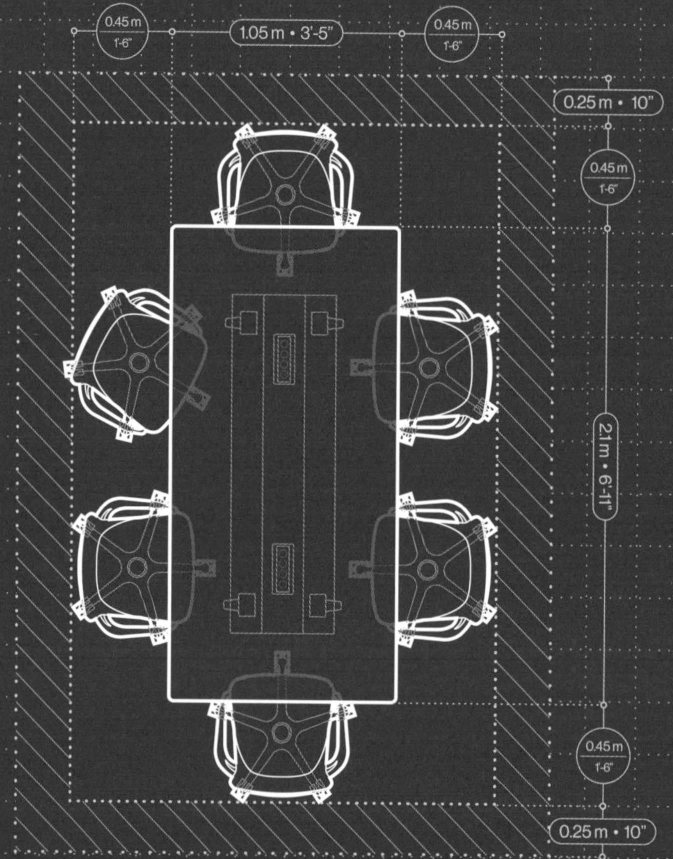

Meeting room - M

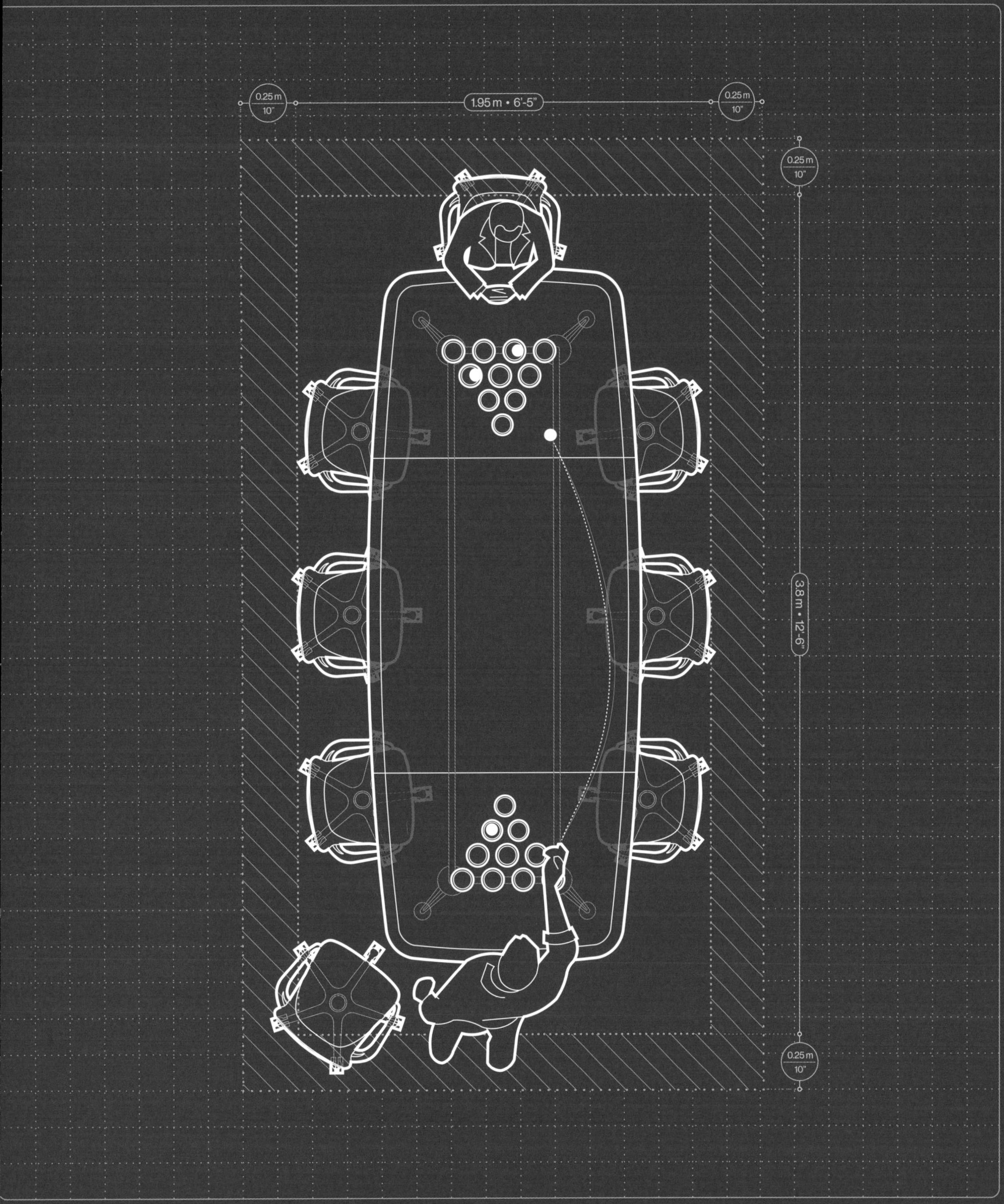

Conference room

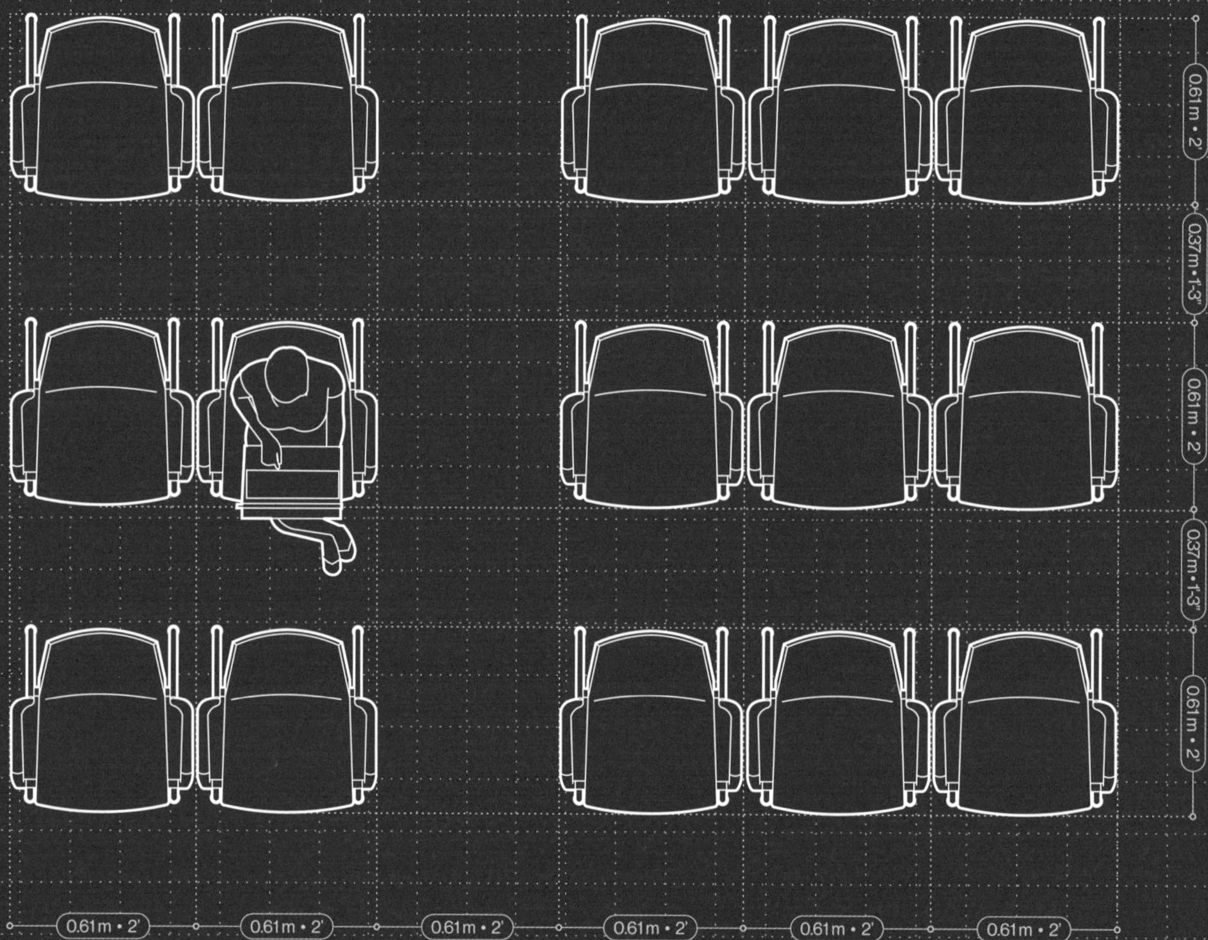

Lecture room

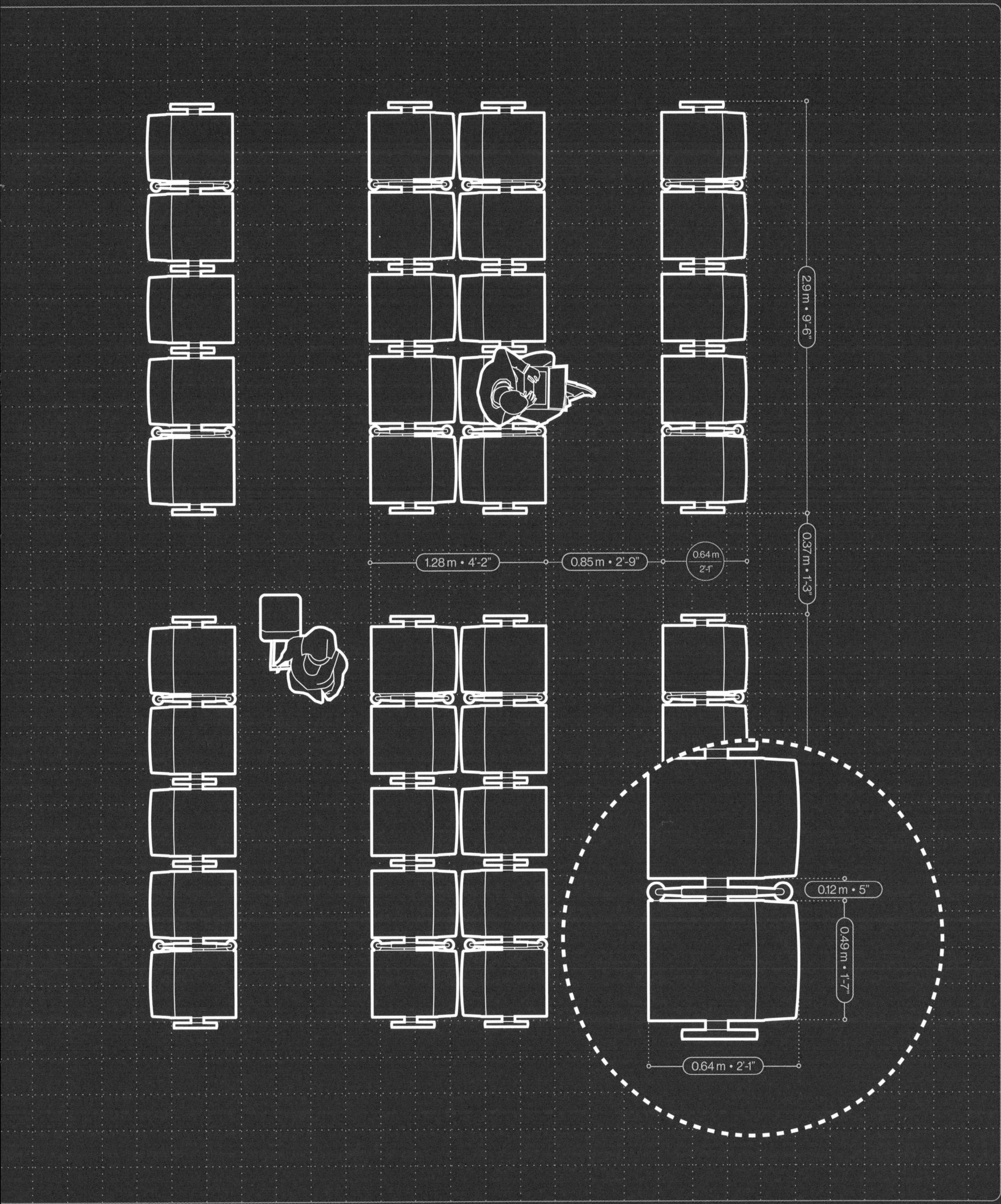
2.9 m • 9'-6"
0.37 m • 1'-3"
1.28 m • 4'-2"
0.85 m • 2'-9"
0.64 m
2'-1"
0.12 m • 5"
0.49 m • 1'-7"
0.64 m • 2'-1"

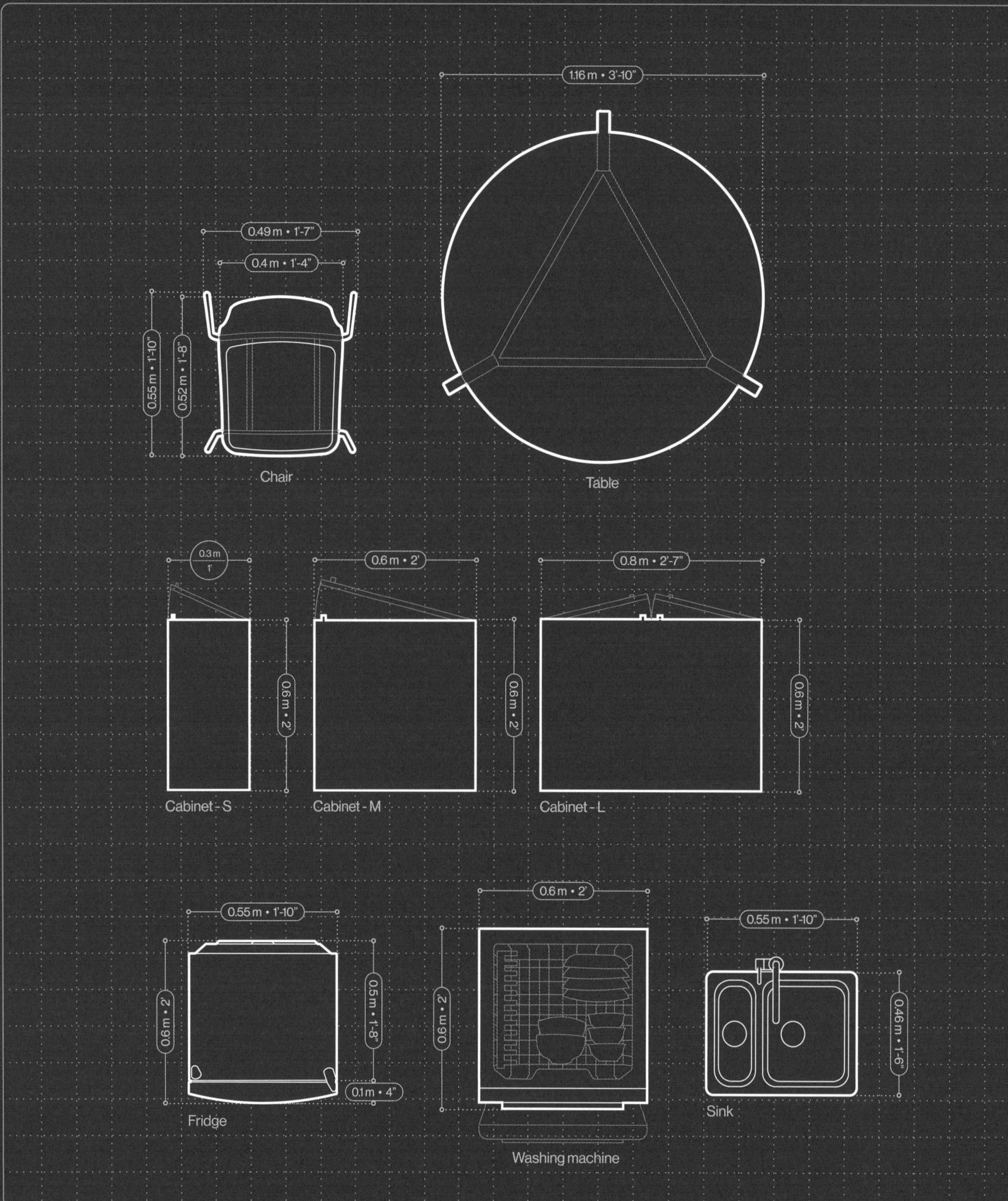

1.16 m • 3'-10"
Table
0.49 m • 1'-7"
0.4 m • 1'-4"
0.55 m • 1'-10"
0.52 m • 1'-8"
Chair
0.3 m
1'
0.6 m • 2'
Cabinet - S
0.6 m • 2'
0.6 m • 2'
Cabinet - M
0.8 m • 2'-7"
0.6 m • 2'
Cabinet - L
0.55 m • 1'-10"
0.6 m • 2'
0.5 m • 1'-8"
0.1 m • 4"
Fridge
0.6 m • 2'
0.6 m • 2'
Washing machine
0.55 m • 1'-10"
0.46 m • 1'-6"
Sink

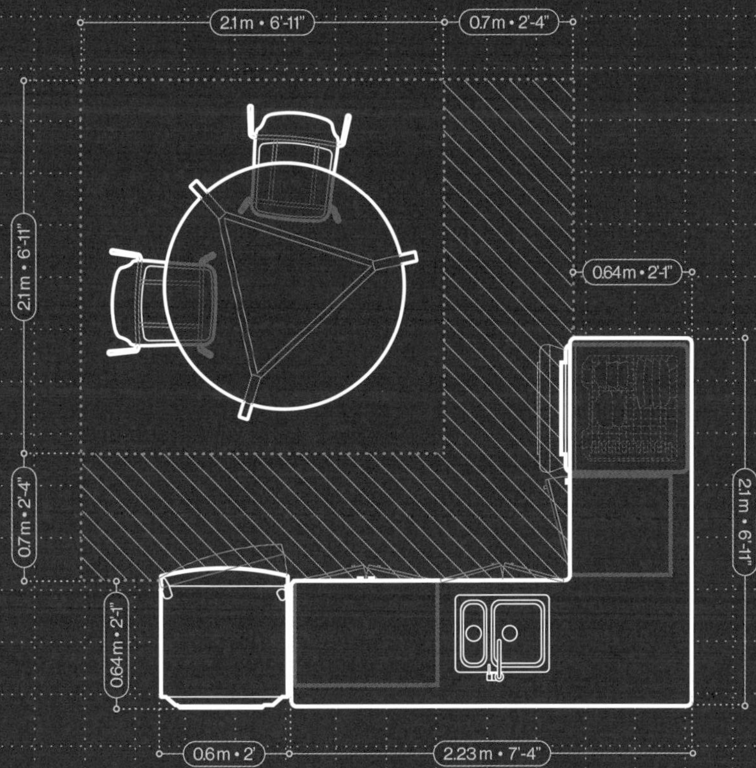

Corner kitchenette

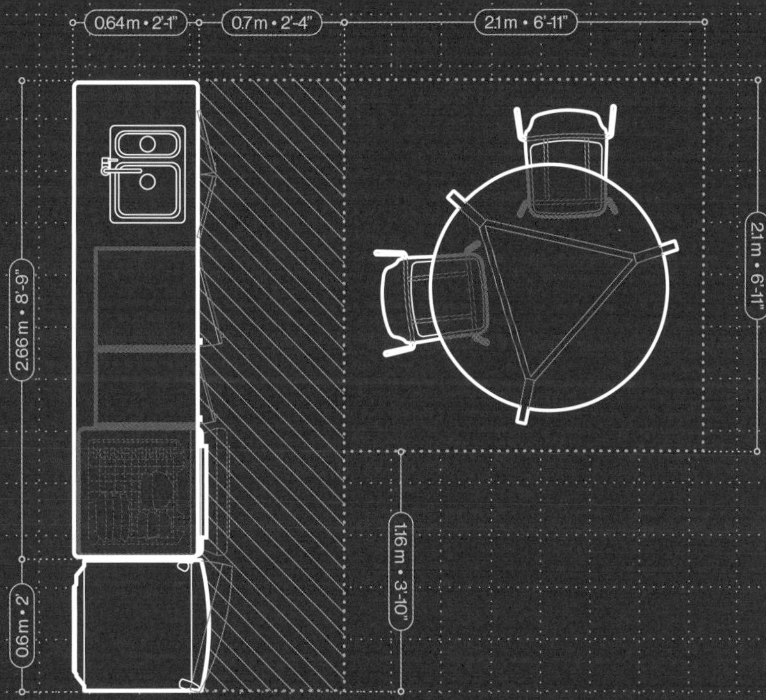

Open kitchenette

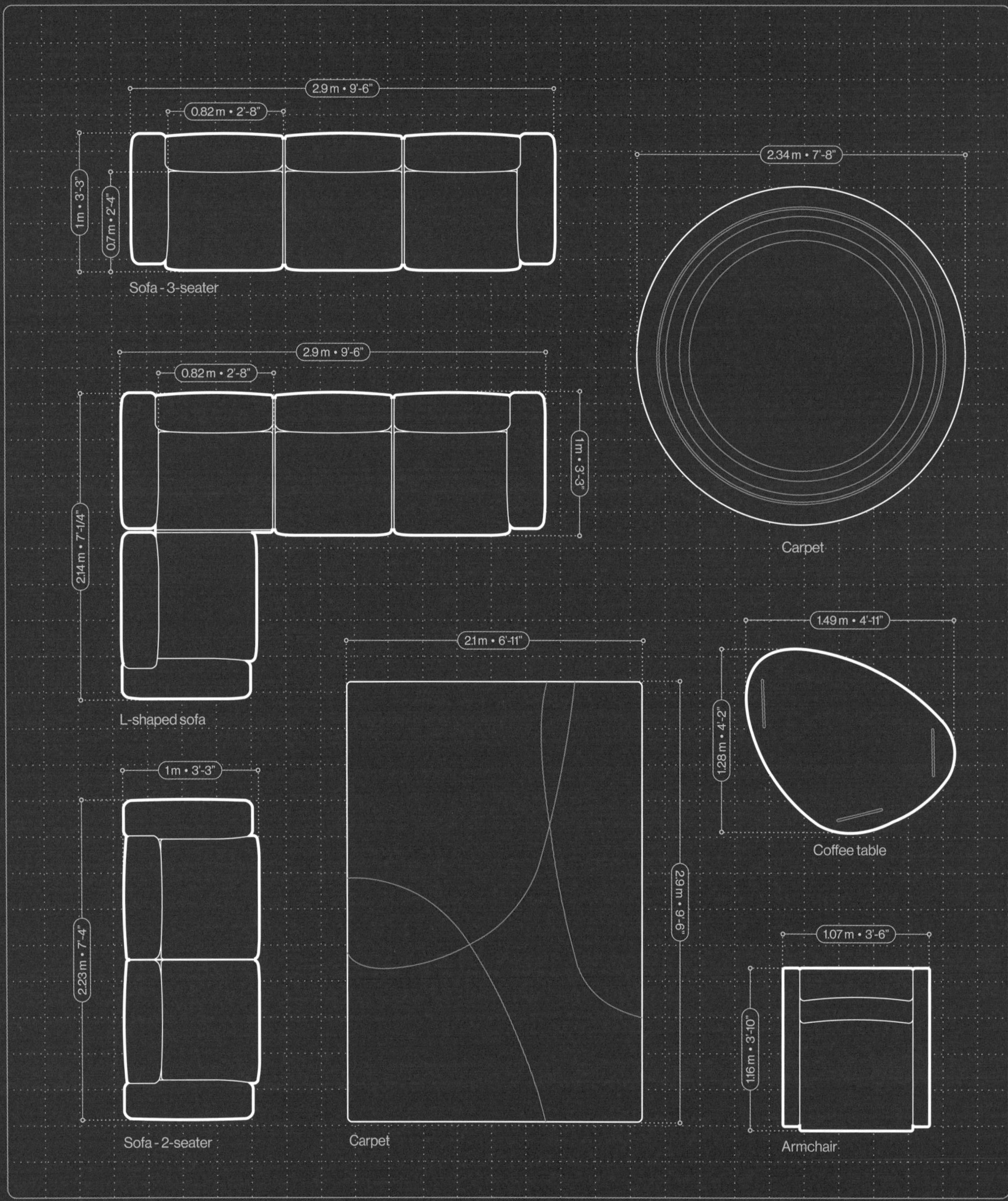

2.9 m • 9'-6"
0.82 m • 2'-8"
1 m • 3'-3"
0.7 m • 2'-4"
Sofa - 3-seater
2.34 m • 7'-8"
Carpet
2.9 m • 9'-6"
0.82 m • 2'-8"
1 m • 3'-3"
2.14 m • 7'-1/4"
L-shaped sofa
1.49 m • 4'-11"
1.28 m • 4'-2"
Coffee table
2.1 m • 6'-11"
2.9 m • 9'-6"
Carpet
1 m • 3'-3"
2.23 m • 7'-4"
Sofa - 2-seater
1.07 m • 3'-6"
1.16 m • 3'-10"
Armchair

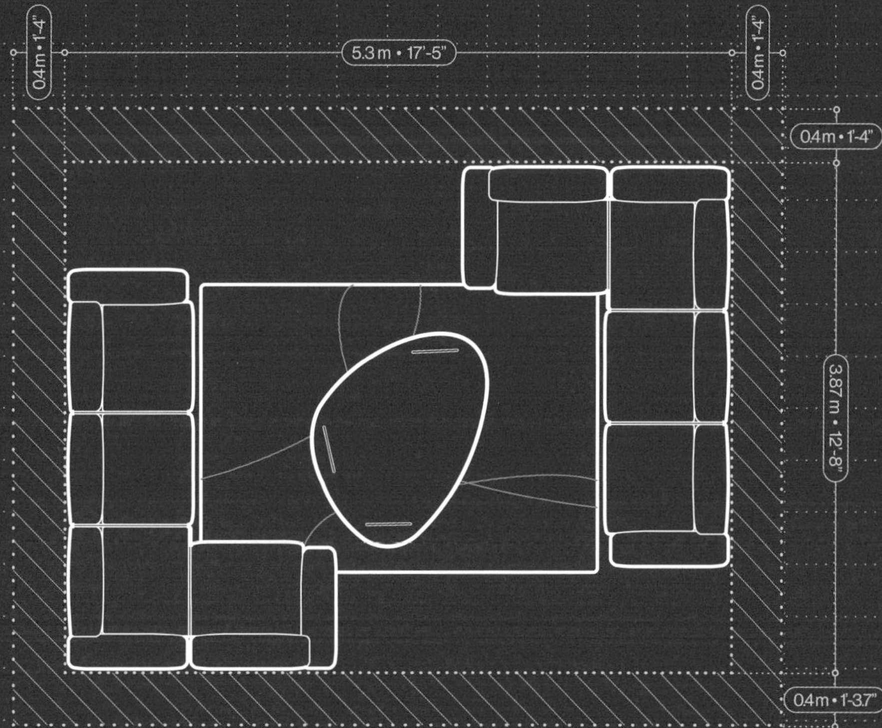

Lounge - L

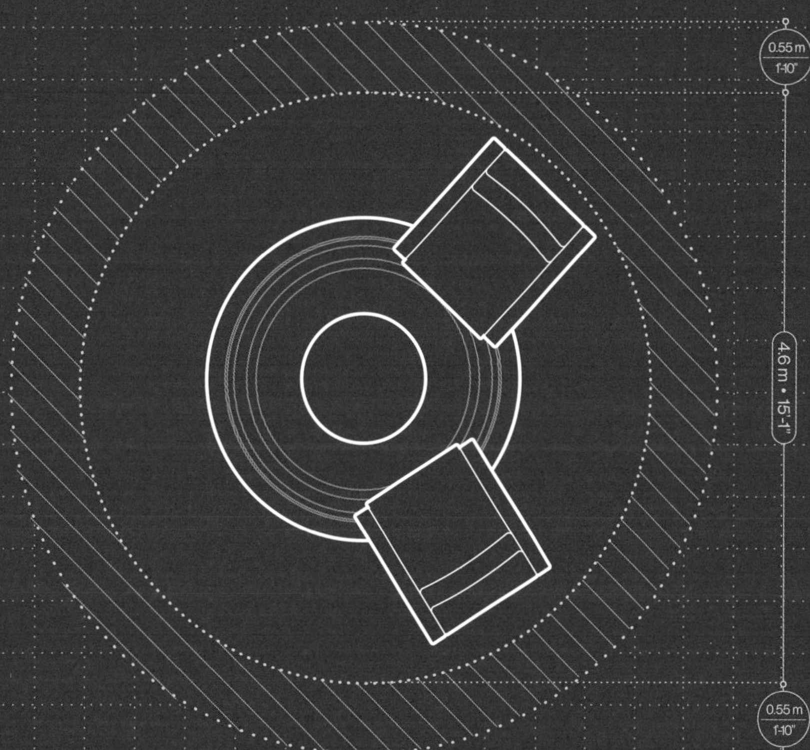

Lounge - S

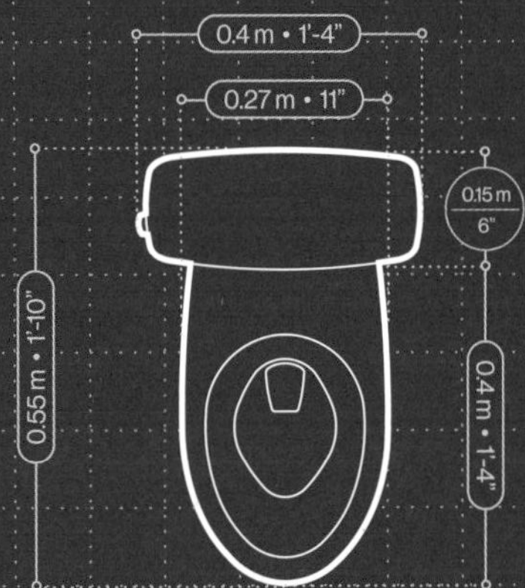

Toilet

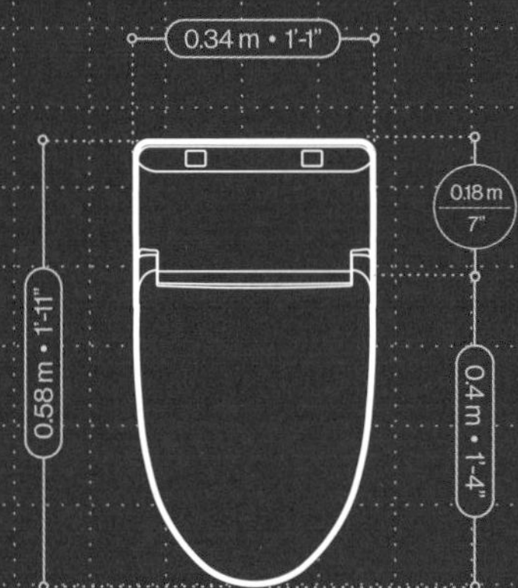

Toilet

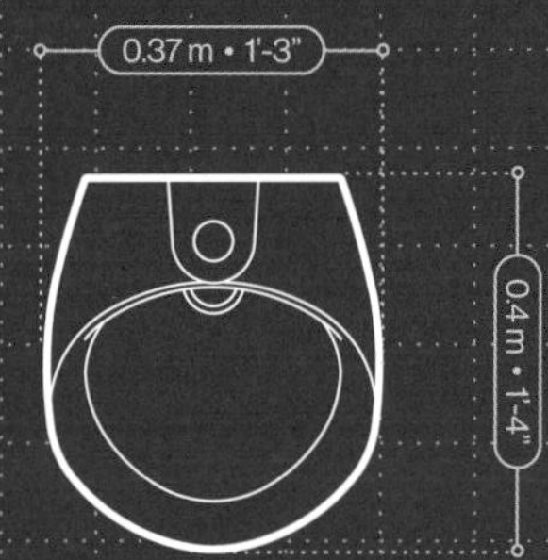

Urinal

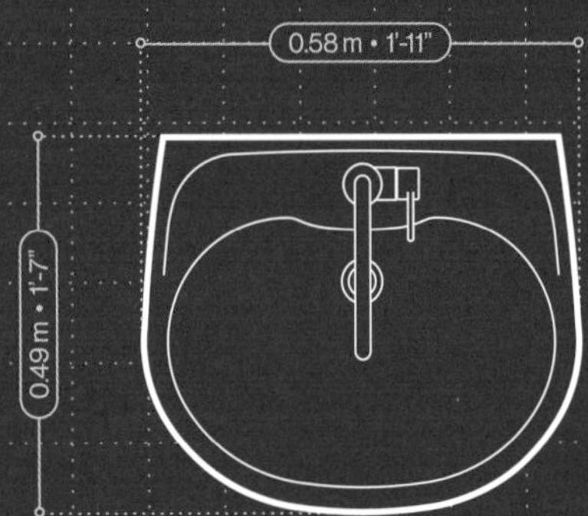

Sink

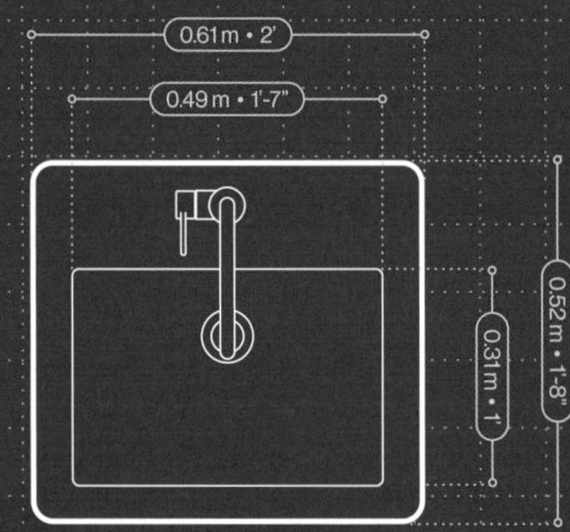

Sink

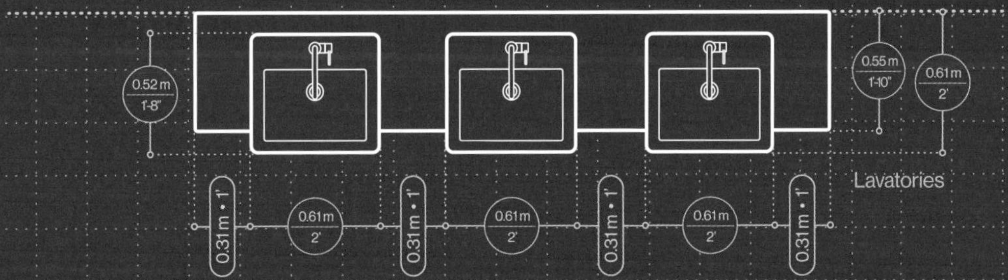

Lavatories

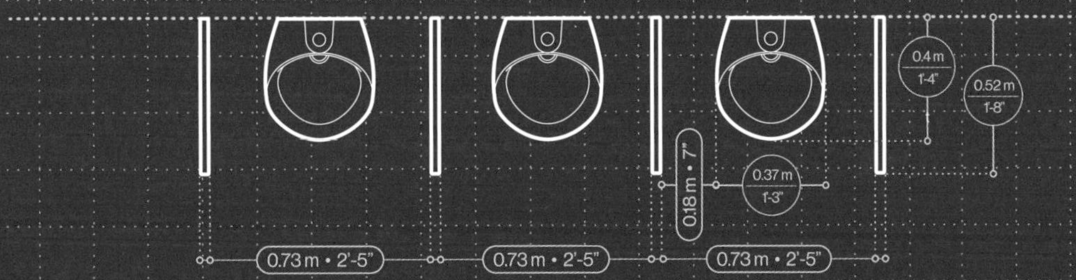

Urinal partitions

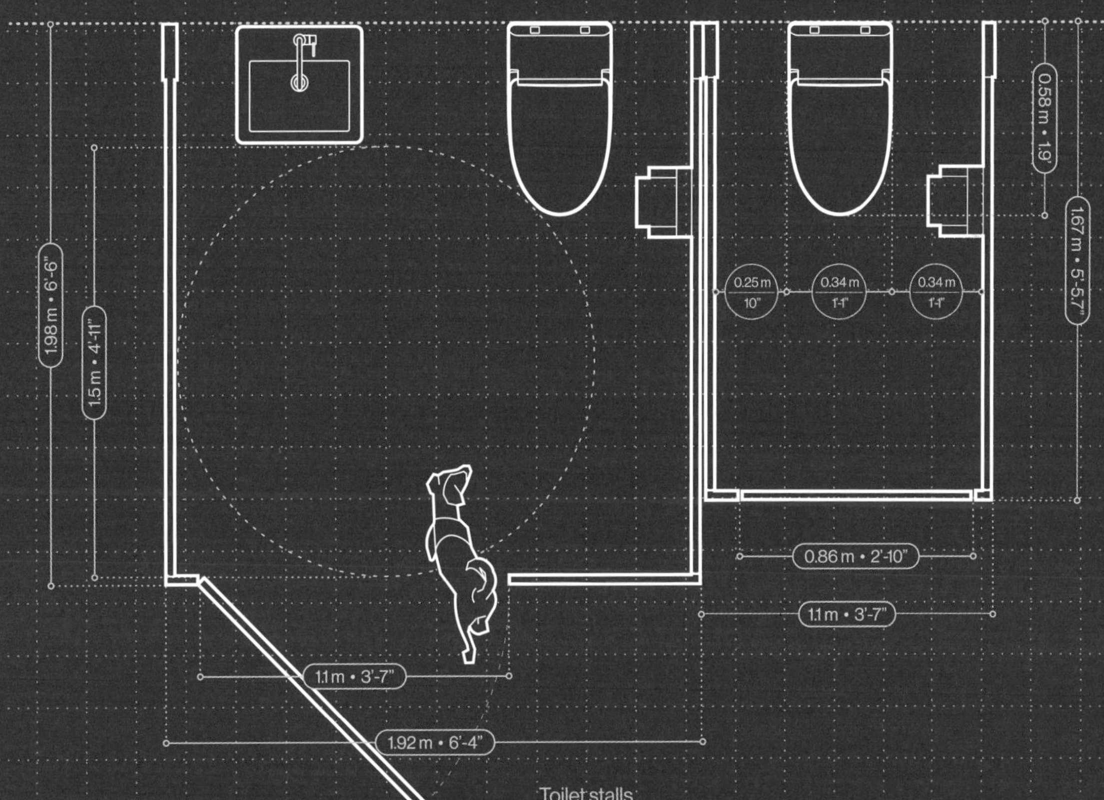

Toilet stalls

Kit for a
Private Office

Workstation desk
Private office kit
0.8×1.72m • 2'-7.5"×5'-7.7"
Calathea
Private office kit
0.85×0.83m • 2'-9.5"×2'-9"

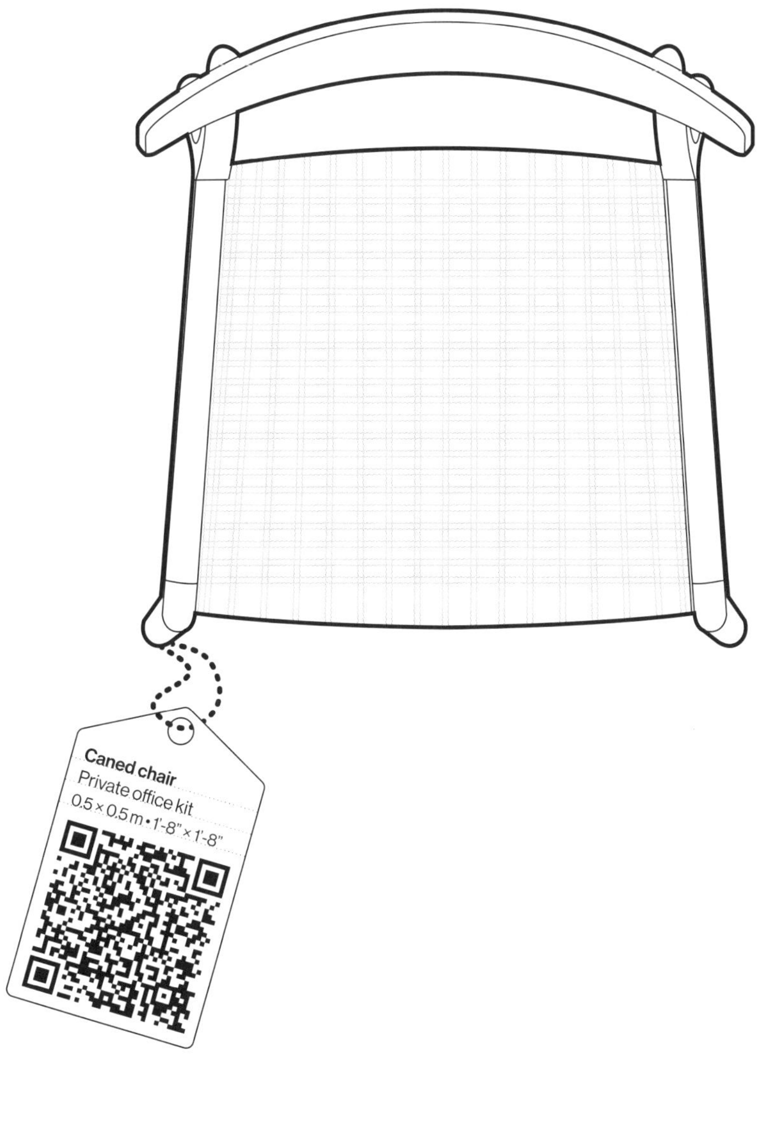
Caned chair
Private office kit
0.5 × 0.5 m • 1'-8" × 1'-8"

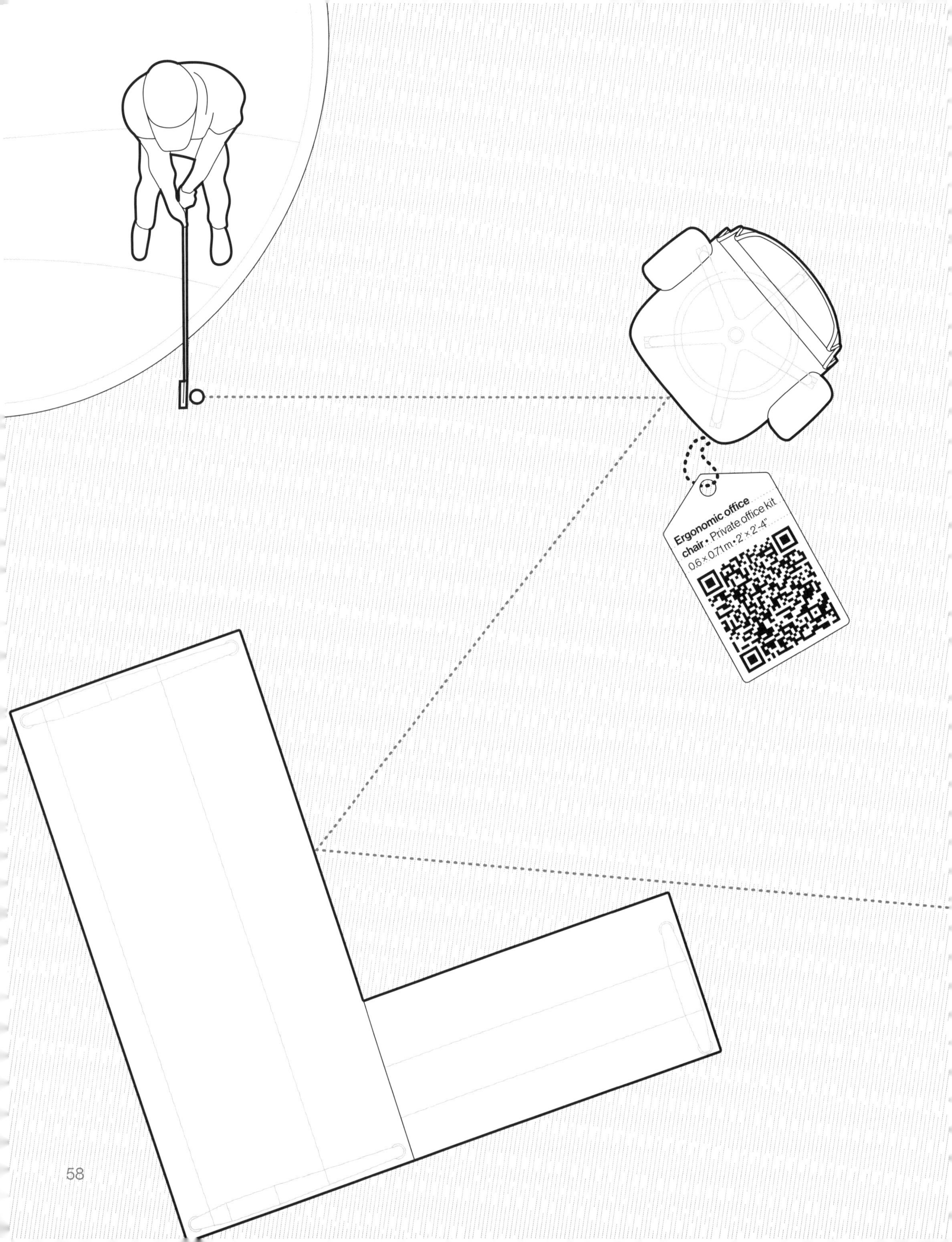
Ergonomic office chair • Private office kit
0.6 × 0.71 m • 2′ × 2′-4″

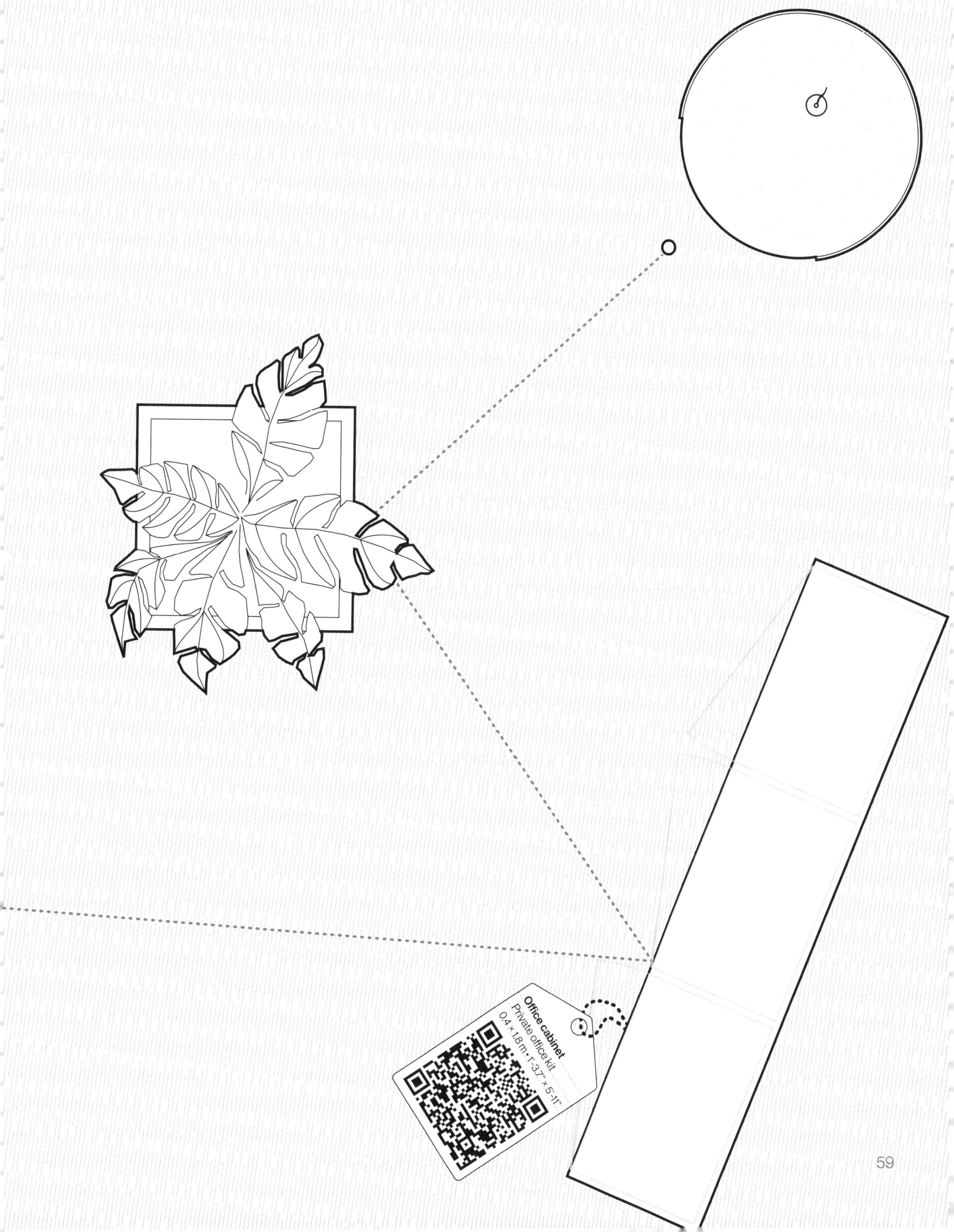
Office cabinet
Private office kit
0.4 × 1.8 m • 1'-3.7" × 5'-11"

Kit for a
Meeting Room

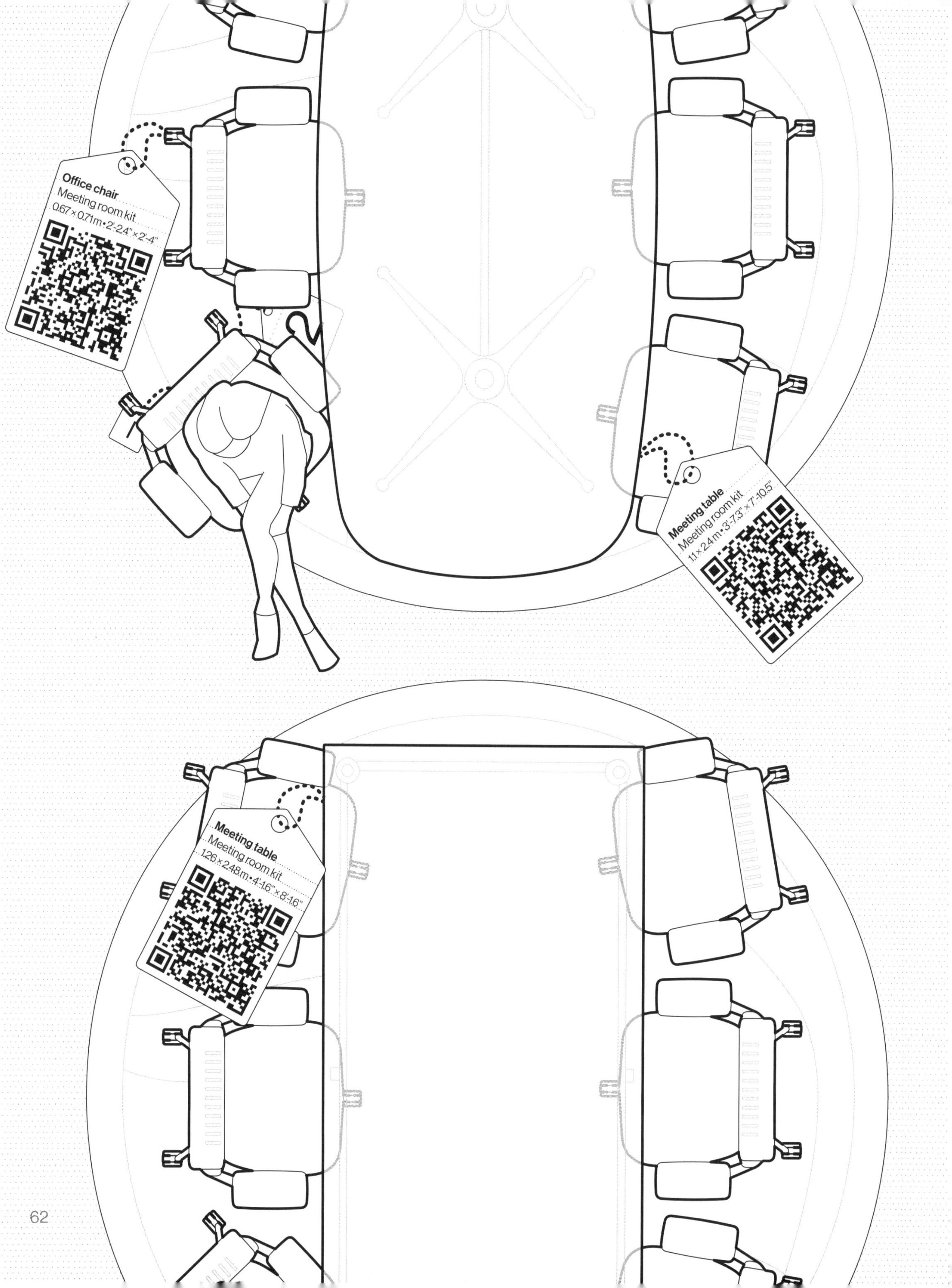
Office chair
Meeting room kit
0.67 × 0.71 m • 2'-2.4" × 2'-4"
Meeting table
Meeting room kit
1.1 × 2.4 m • 3'-7.3" × 7'-10.5"
Meeting table
Meeting room kit
1.26 × 2.48 m • 4'-1.6" × 8'-1.6"

Palm tree
Meeting room kit
1.57 × 1.85 m • 5'-2" × 6'-1"

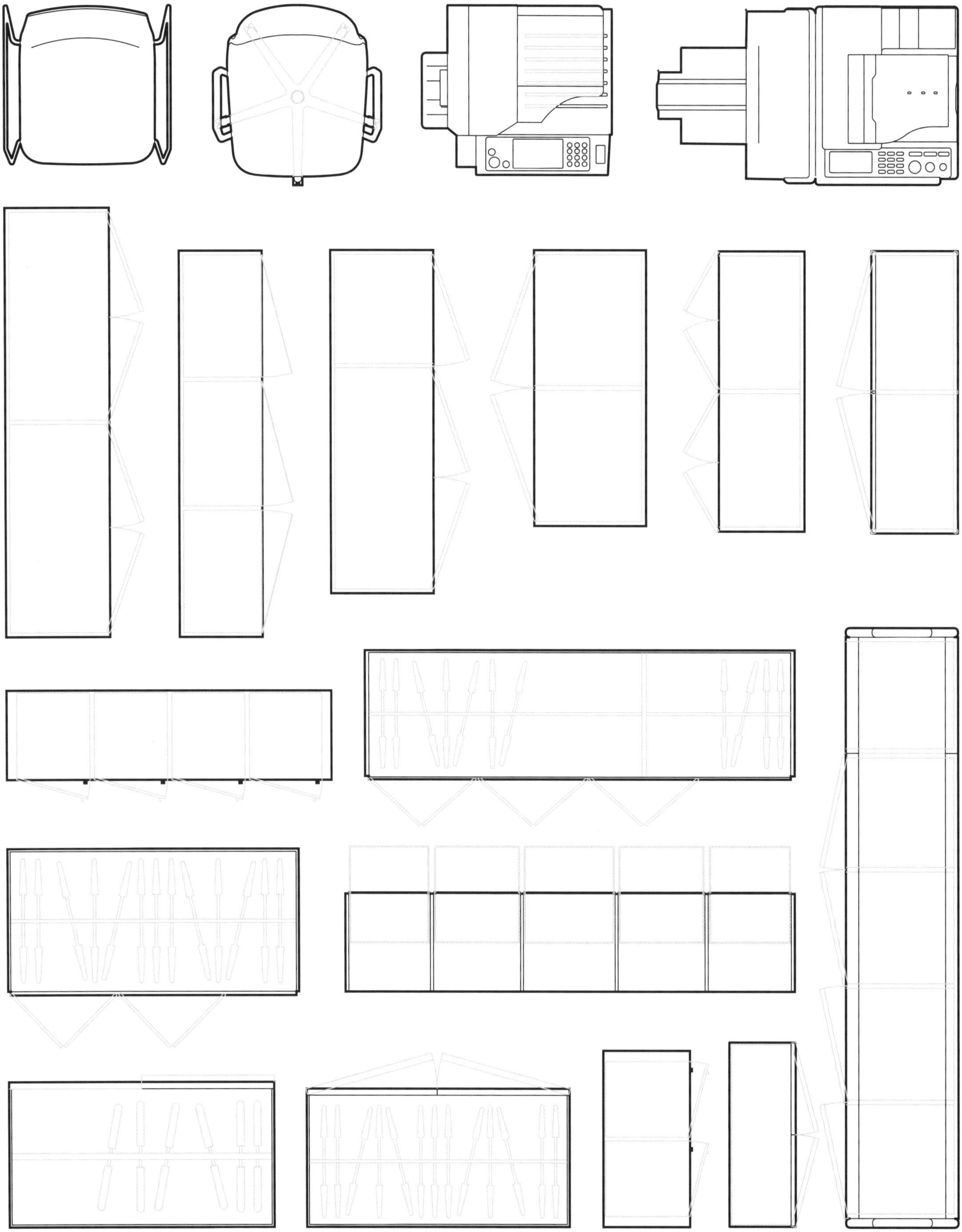

Kit for a
Archive Room

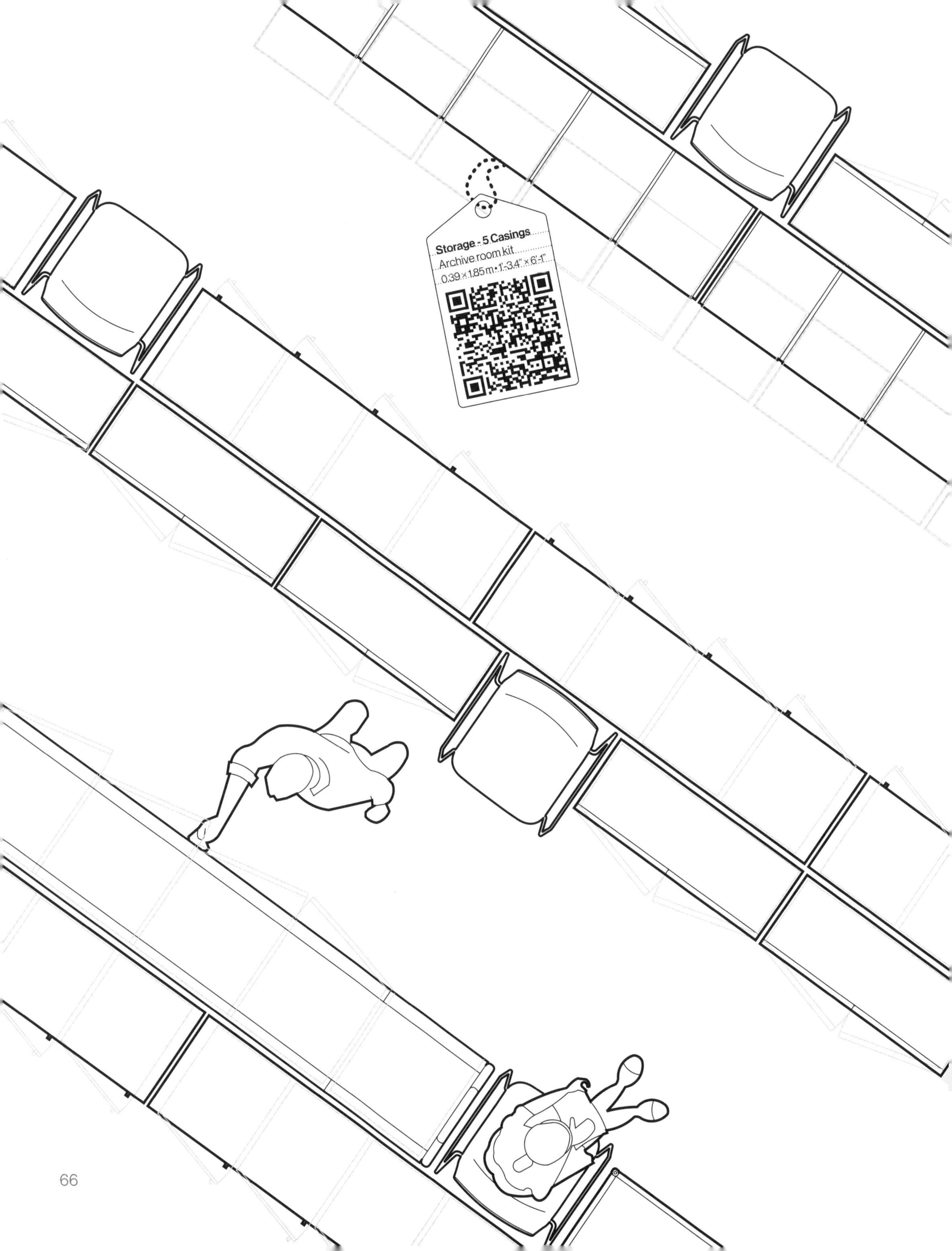
Storage - 5 Casings
Archive room kit
0.39 × 1.85 m • 1'-3.4" × 6'-1"

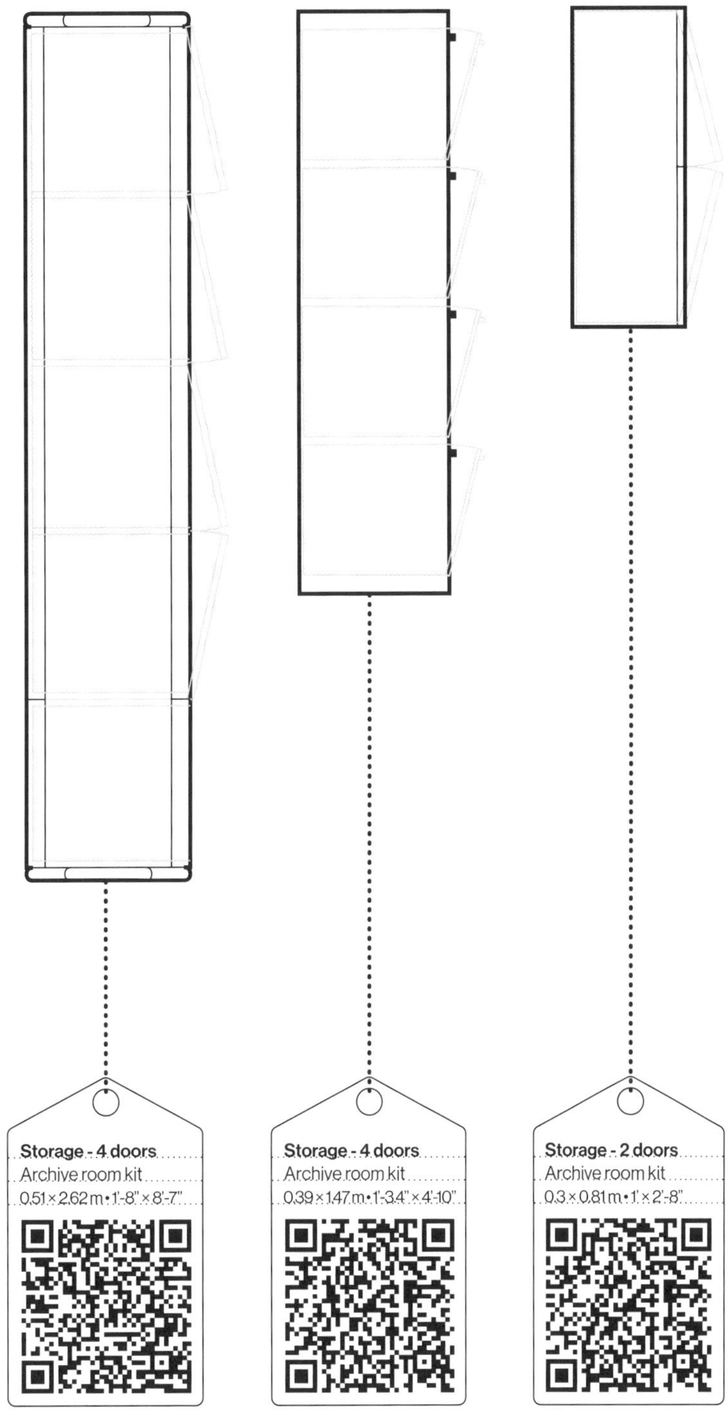
Storage - 4 doors
Archive room kit
0.51 × 2.62 m • 1'-8" × 8'-7"
Storage - 4 doors
Archive room kit
0.39 × 1.47 m • 1'-3.4" × 4'-10"
Storage - 2 doors
Archive room kit
0.3 × 0.81 m • 1' × 2'-8"

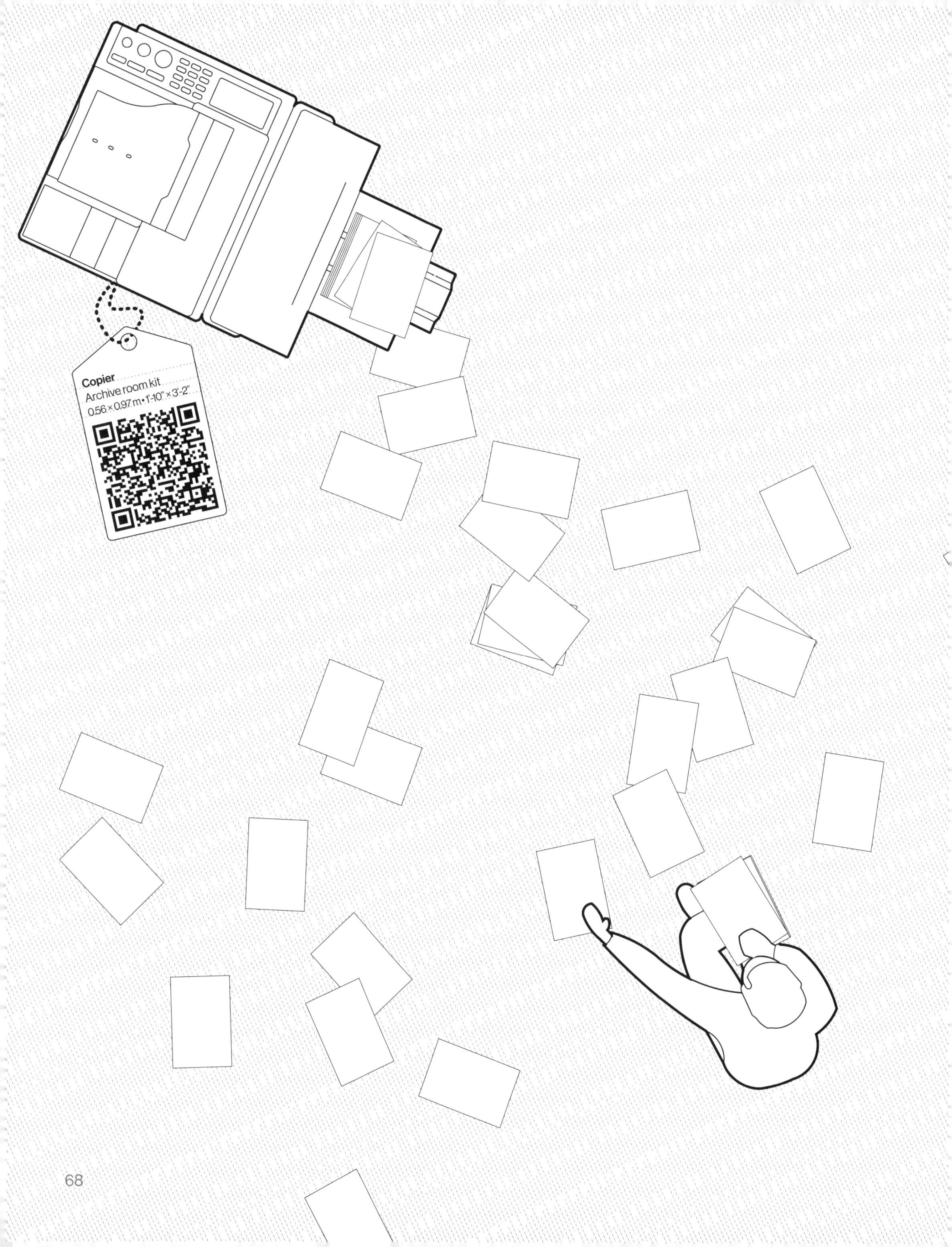
Copier
Archive room kit
0.56 × 0.97 m • 1'-10" × 3'-2"

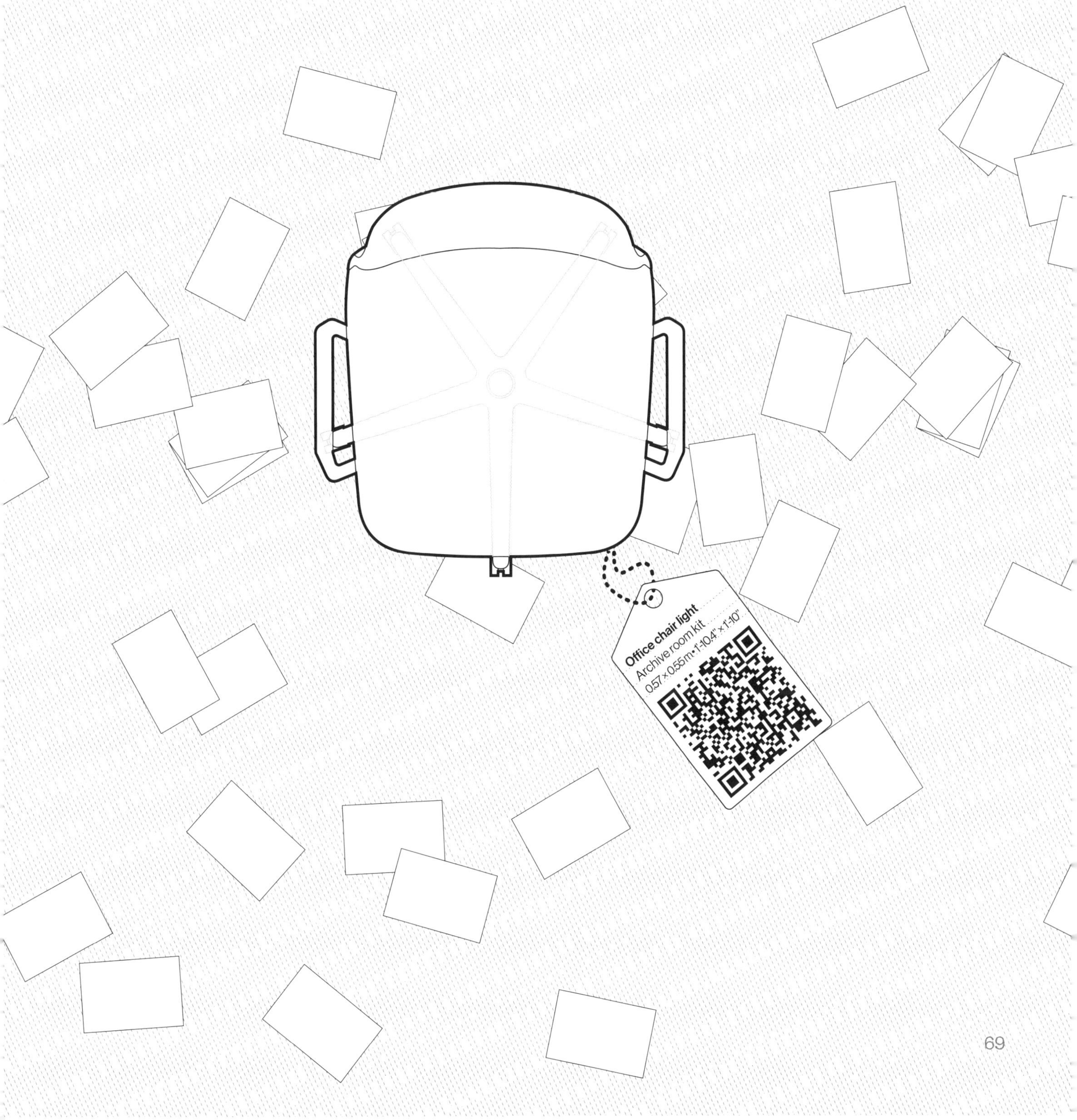
Office chair light
Archive room kit
0.57 × 0.55 m • 1'-10.4" × 1'-10"

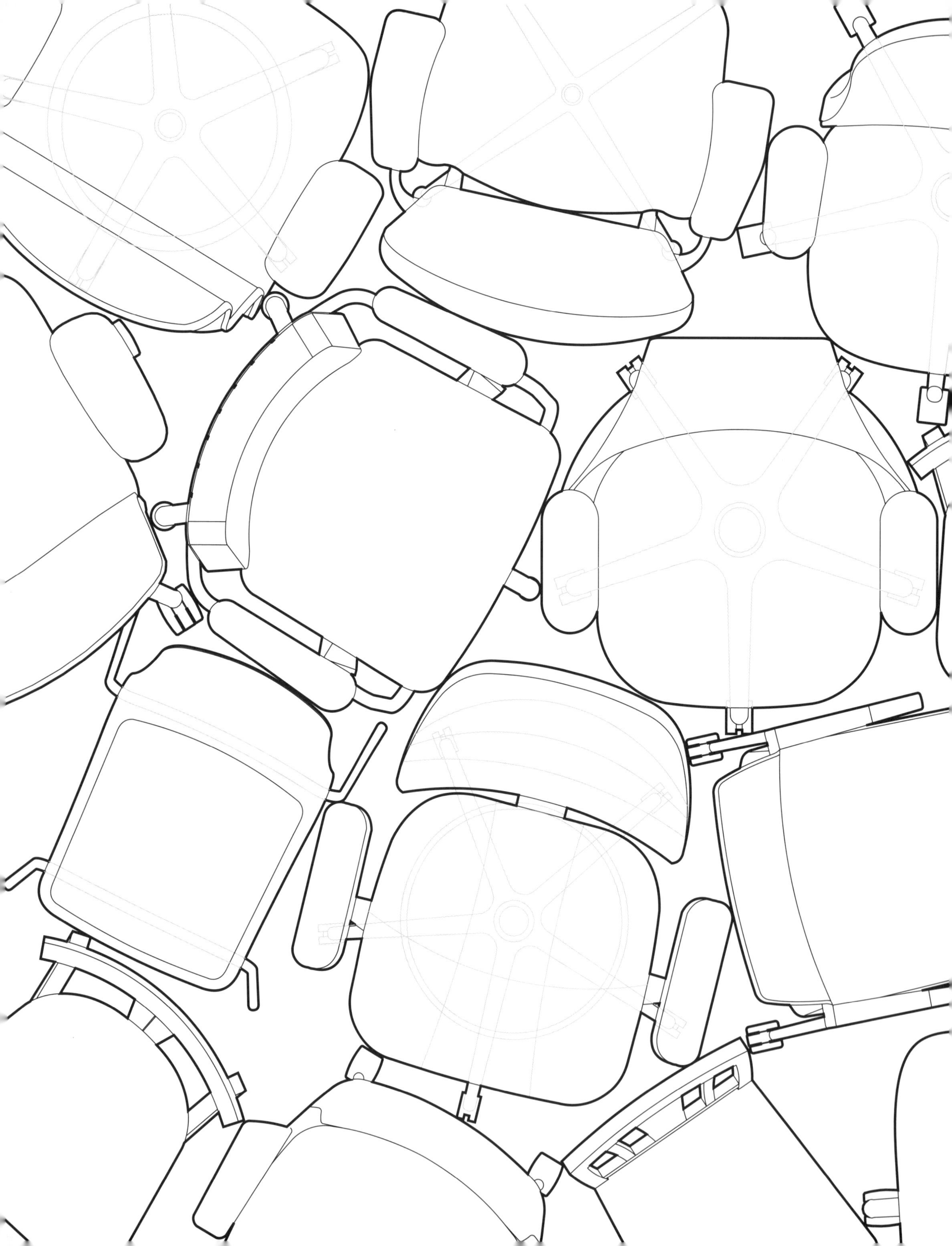

A Catalog of Office Chairs

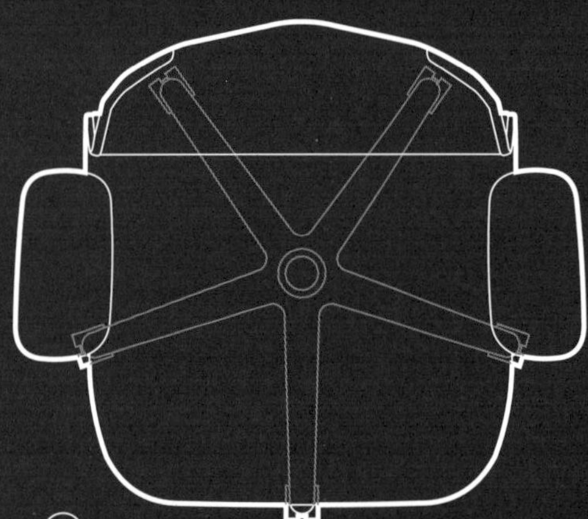

1

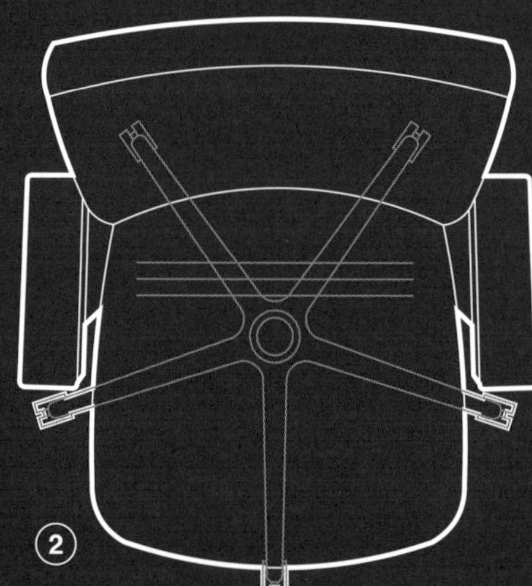

2

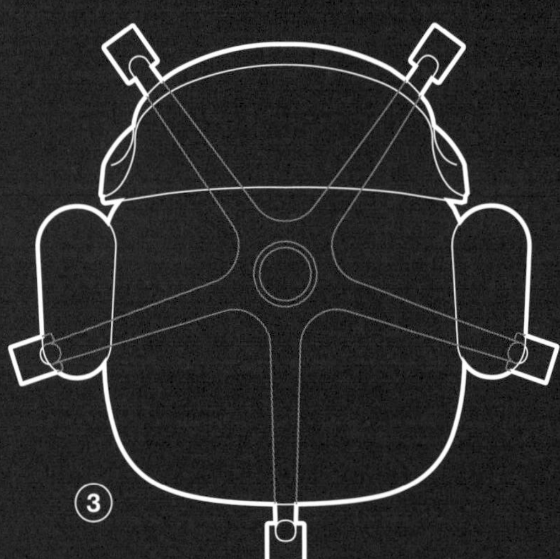

3

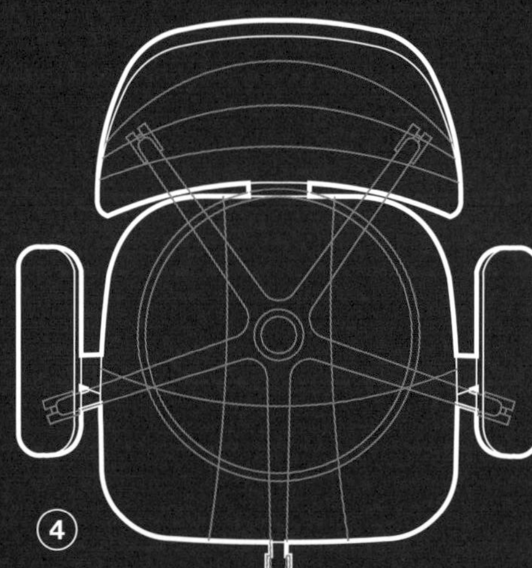

4

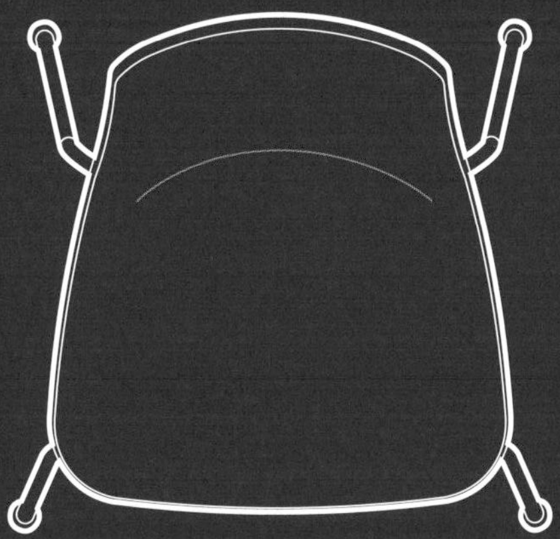

5

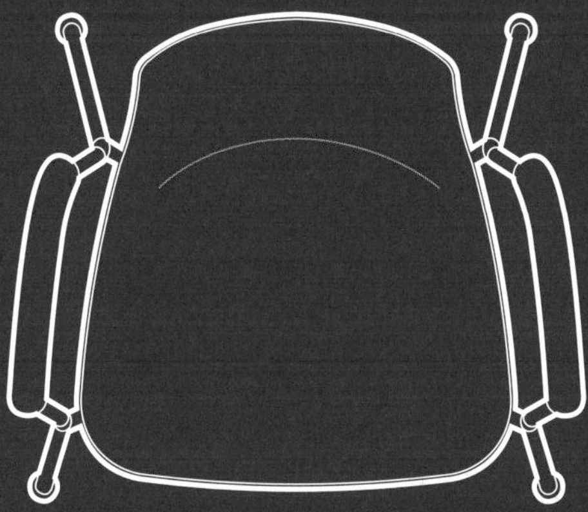

6

7

8

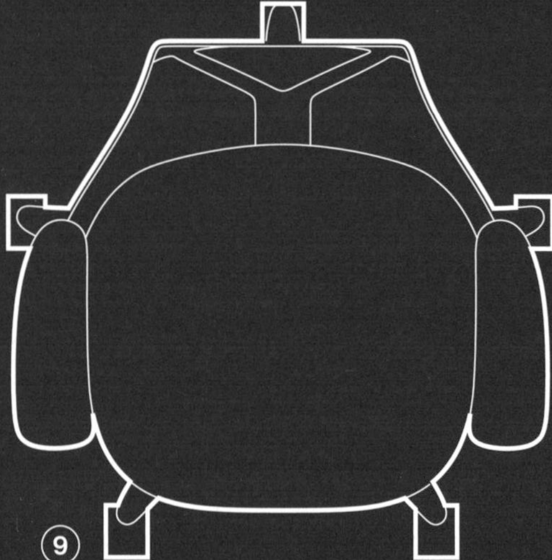

9

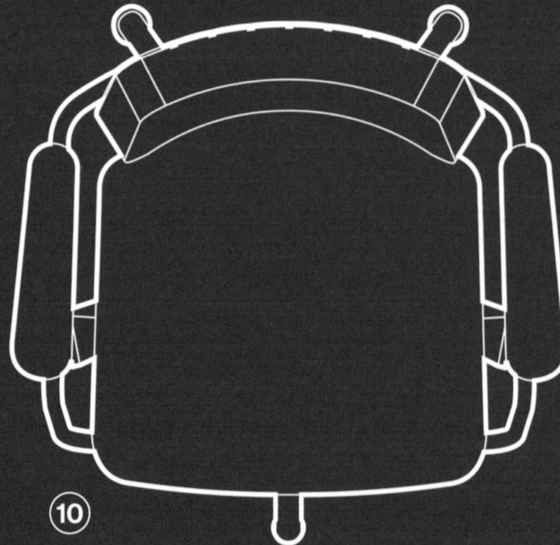

10

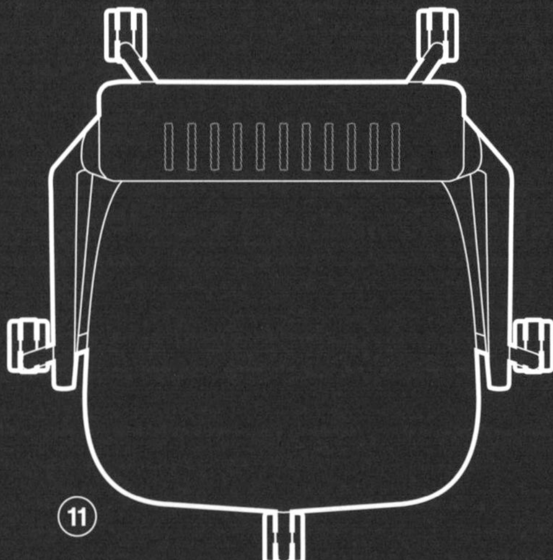

11

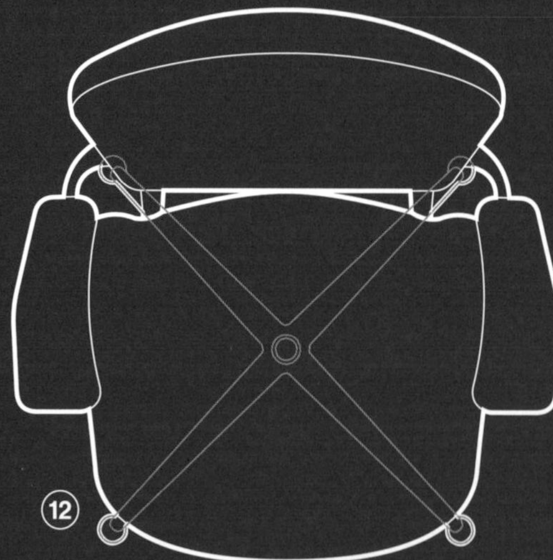

12

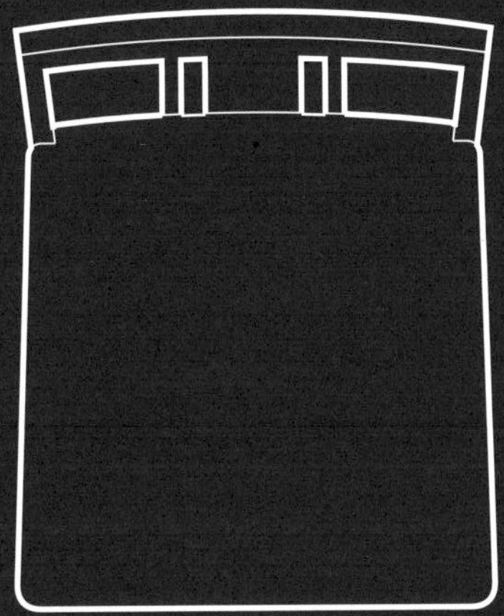

13

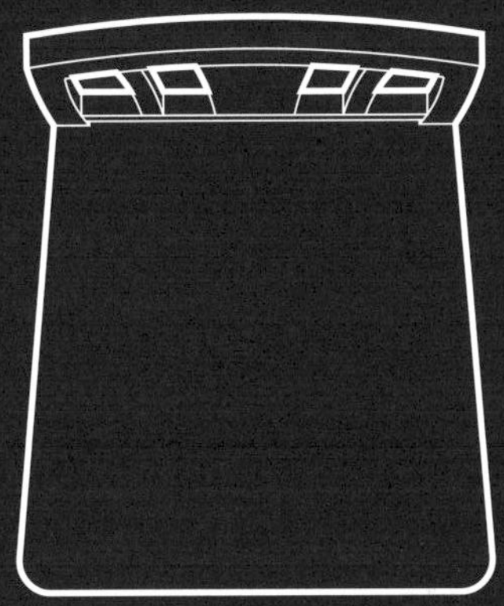

14

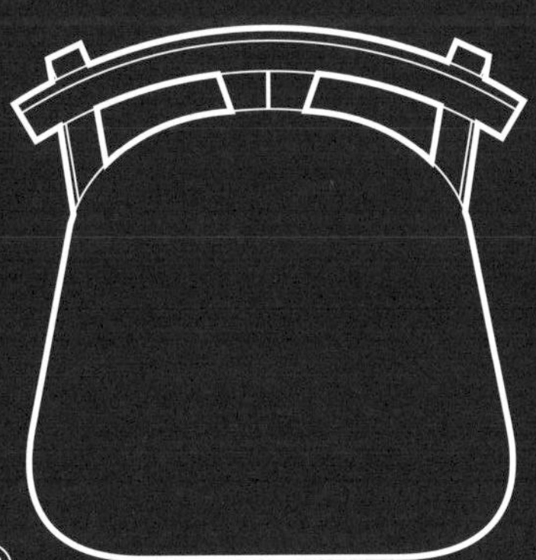

15

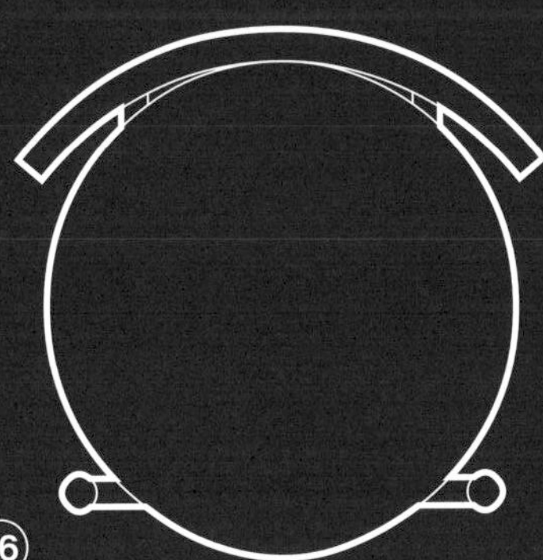

16

1
Comfy office chair
Office chairs
0.6 × 0.71 m • 2' × 2'-4"

2
Office chair prestige
Office chairs
0.7 × 0.66 m • 2'-3.6" × 2'-2"

3
Office chair swivel
Office chairs
0.72 × 0.76 m • 2'-4" × 2'-6"

4
Comfy swivel chair
Office chairs
0.71 × 0.67 m • 2'-4" × 2'-2.4"

5
Conference chair
Office chairs
0.51 × 0.55 m • 1'-8" × 1'-10"

6
Conference chair w. armrest • Office chairs
0.5 × 0.61 m • 1'-7.7" × 2'

7
Chair light
Office chairs
0.53 × 0.51 m • 1'-9" × 1'-8"

8
Conference chair with wheels • Office chairs
0.58 × 0.58 m • 1'-11" × 1'-11"

9

Mesh chair
Office chairs
0.68 × 0.69 m • 2'-3" × 2'-3"

10

Fauteuil pivot
Office chairs
0.62 × 0.66 m • 2'-1/2" × 2'-2"

11

Office Chair
Office chairs
0.67 × 0.69 m • 2'-2.4" × 2'-3"

12

Chair upholstered
Office chairs
0.68 × 0.7 m • 2'-3" × 2'-3.6"

13

Side dining chair L
Office chairs
0.6 × 0.5 m • 2' × 1'-7.7"

14

Side dining chair S
Office chairs
0.53 × 0.46 m • 1'-9" × 1'-6"

15

Low back chair
Office chairs
0.5 × 0.5 m • 1'-7.7" × 1'-7.7"

16

Chair round
Office chairs
0.48 × 0.5 m • 1'-7" × 1'-7.7"

Kit for an
Open Space

L desk module
Open space kit
1.1 × 2.1 m • 3'-7.3" × 6'-10.7"
Standard office desk
Open space kit
0.6 × 1.2 m • 2' × 3'-11.2"

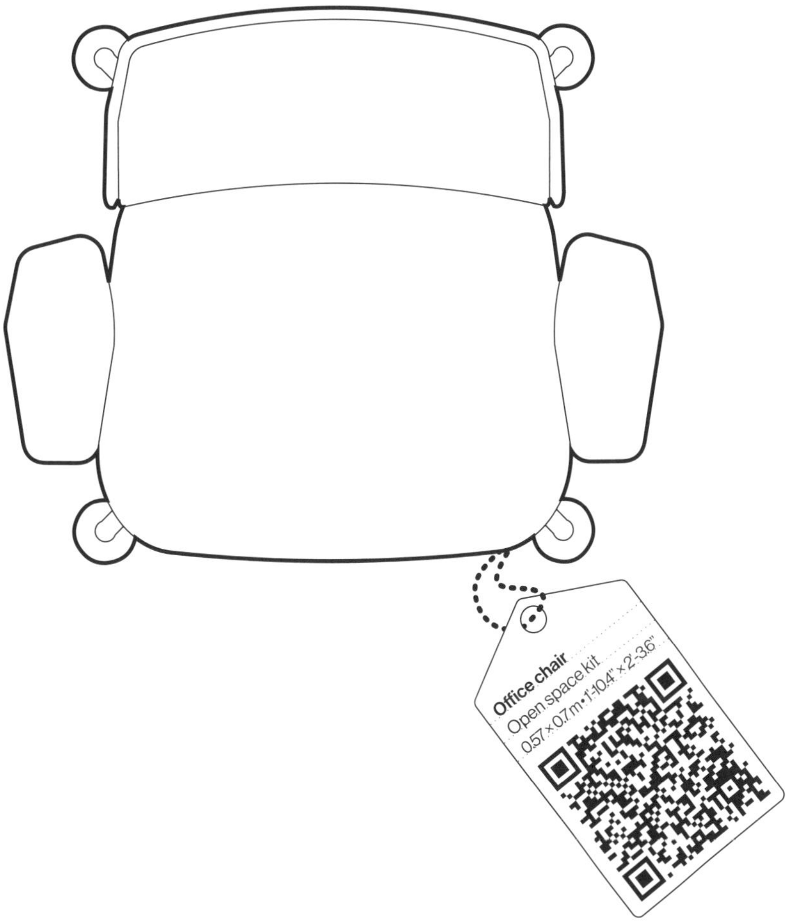
Office chair
Open space kit
0.57 × 0.7 m • 1'-10.4" × 2'-3.6"

Kit for a
Quiet Open Space

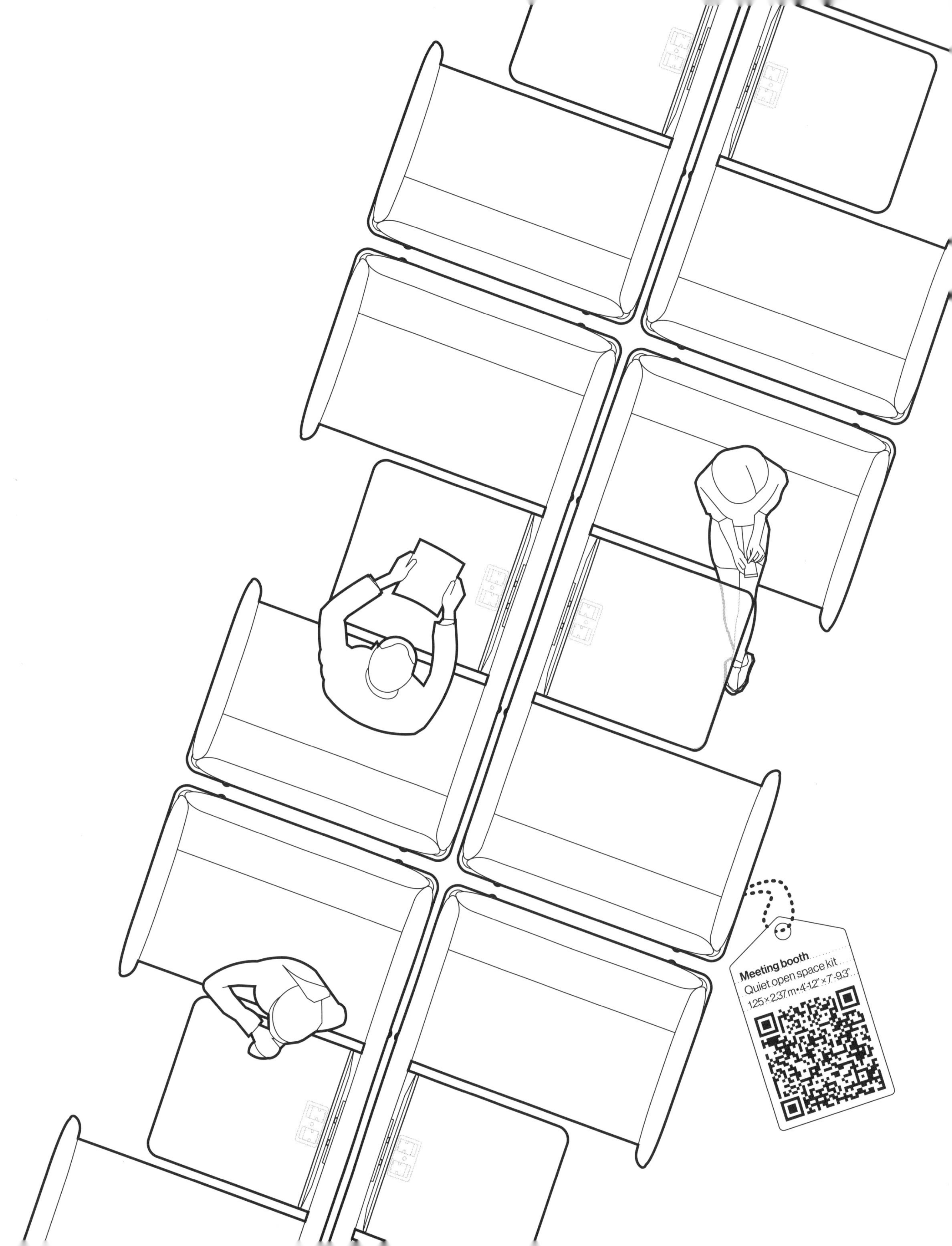
Meeting booth
Quiet open space kit
1.25 × 2.37 m • 4'-1.2" × 7'-9.3"

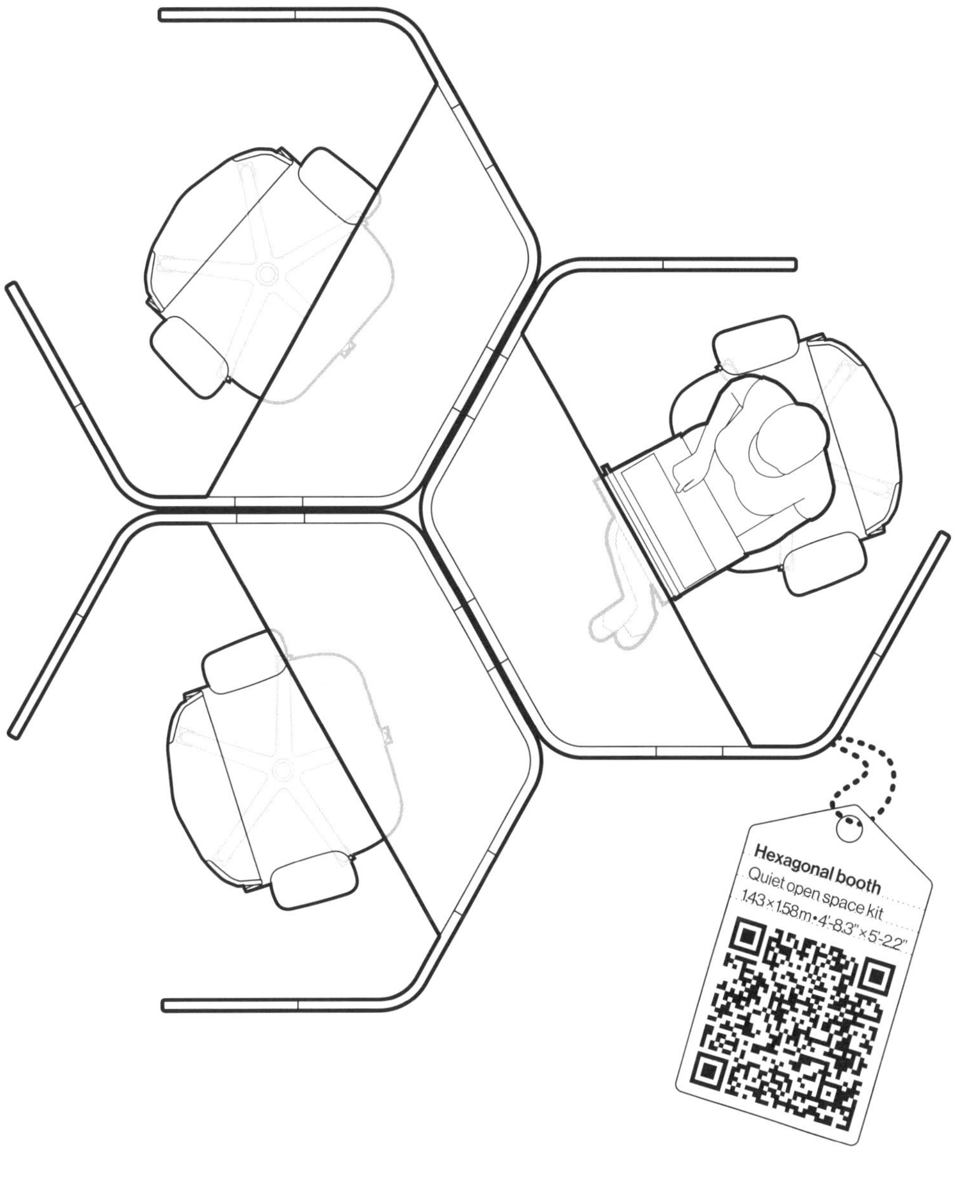
Hexagonal booth
Quiet open space kit
1.43×1.58m • 4'-8.3"×5'-2.2"

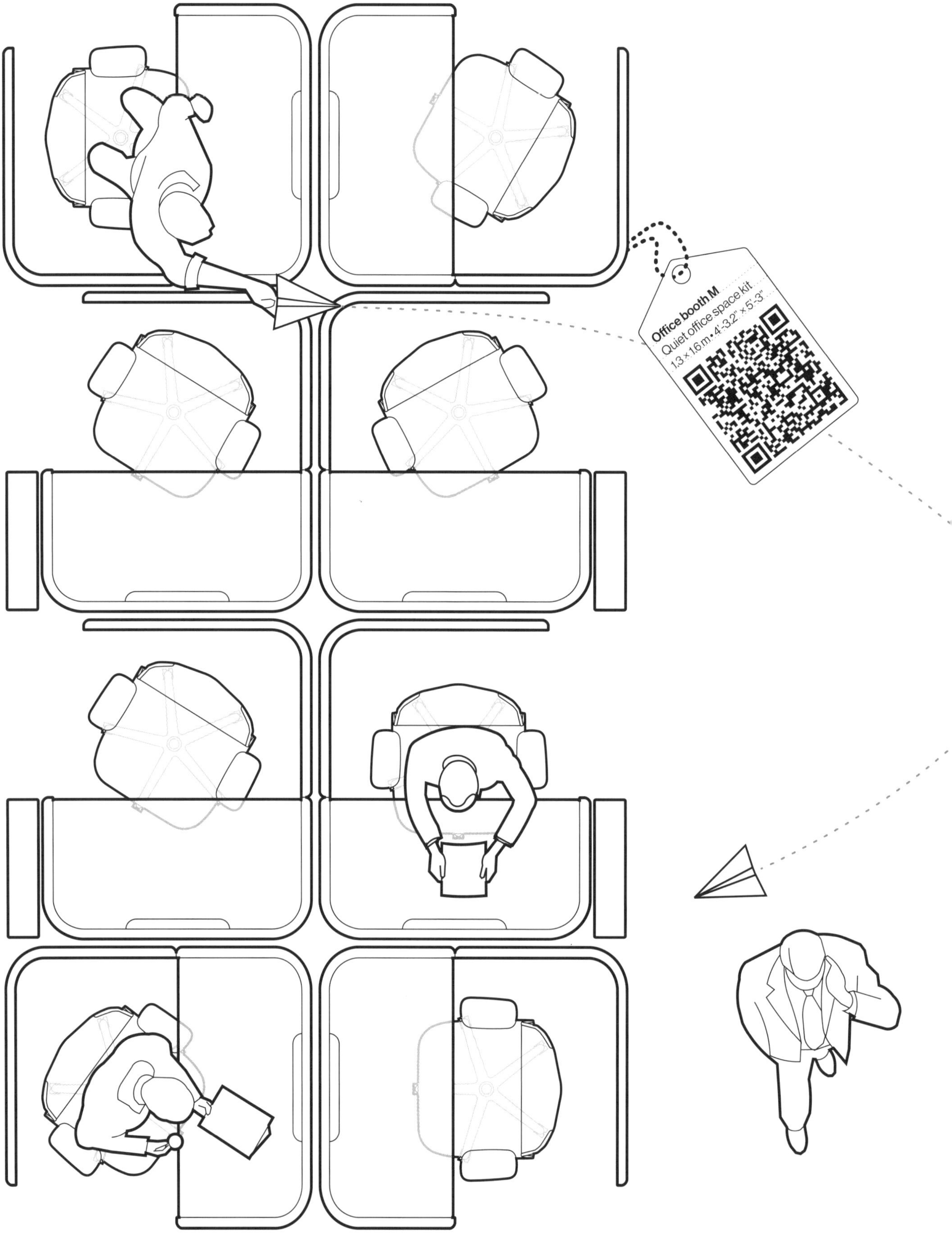
Office booth M
Quiet office space kit
1.3 × 1.6 m • 4'-3.2" × 5'-3"

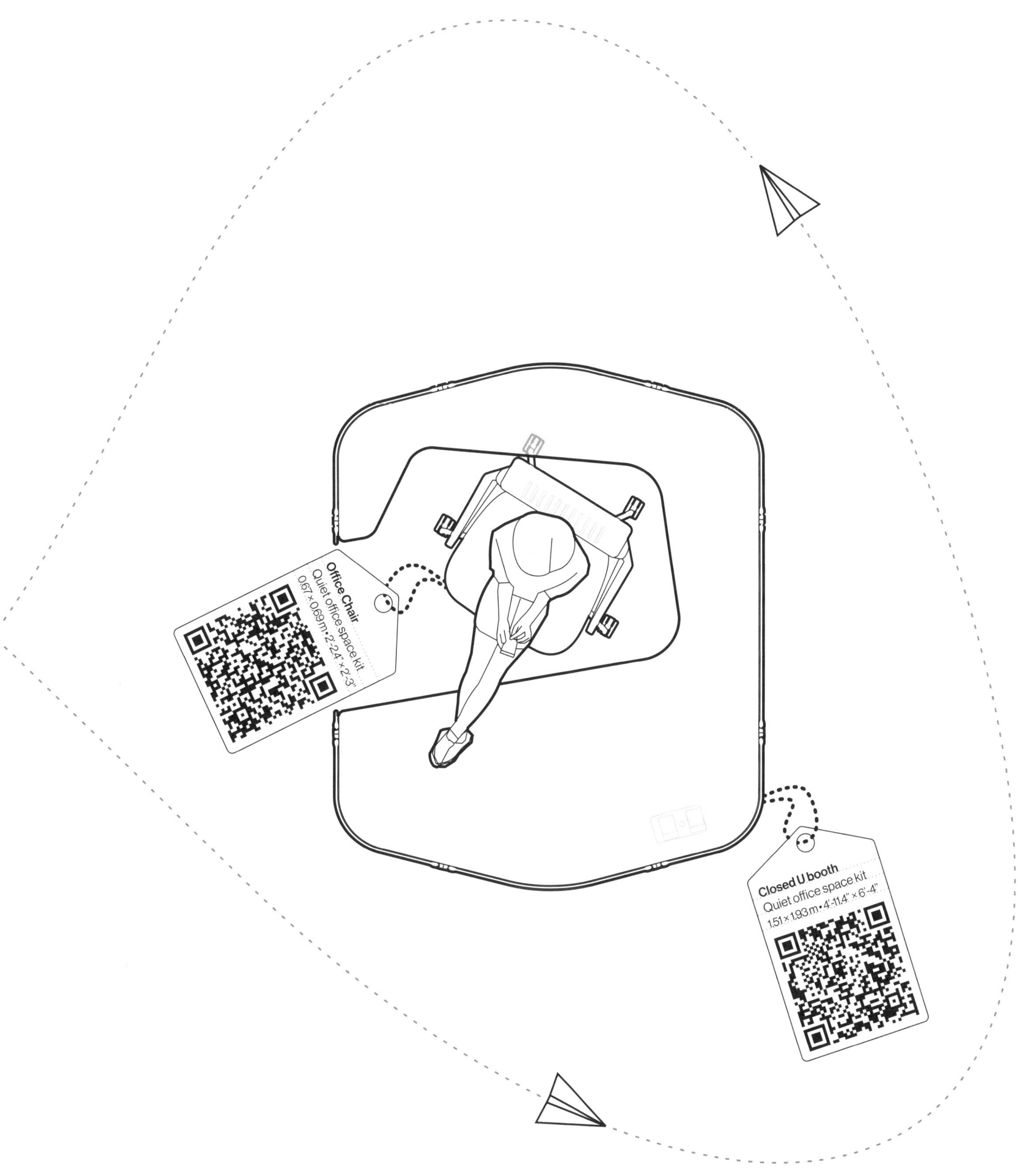
Office Chair
Quiet office space kit
0.67 × 0.69 m • 2'-2.4" × 2'-3"
Closed U booth
Quiet office space kit
1.51 × 1.93 m • 4'-11.4" × 6'-4"

Kit for a
Hot Desking Space

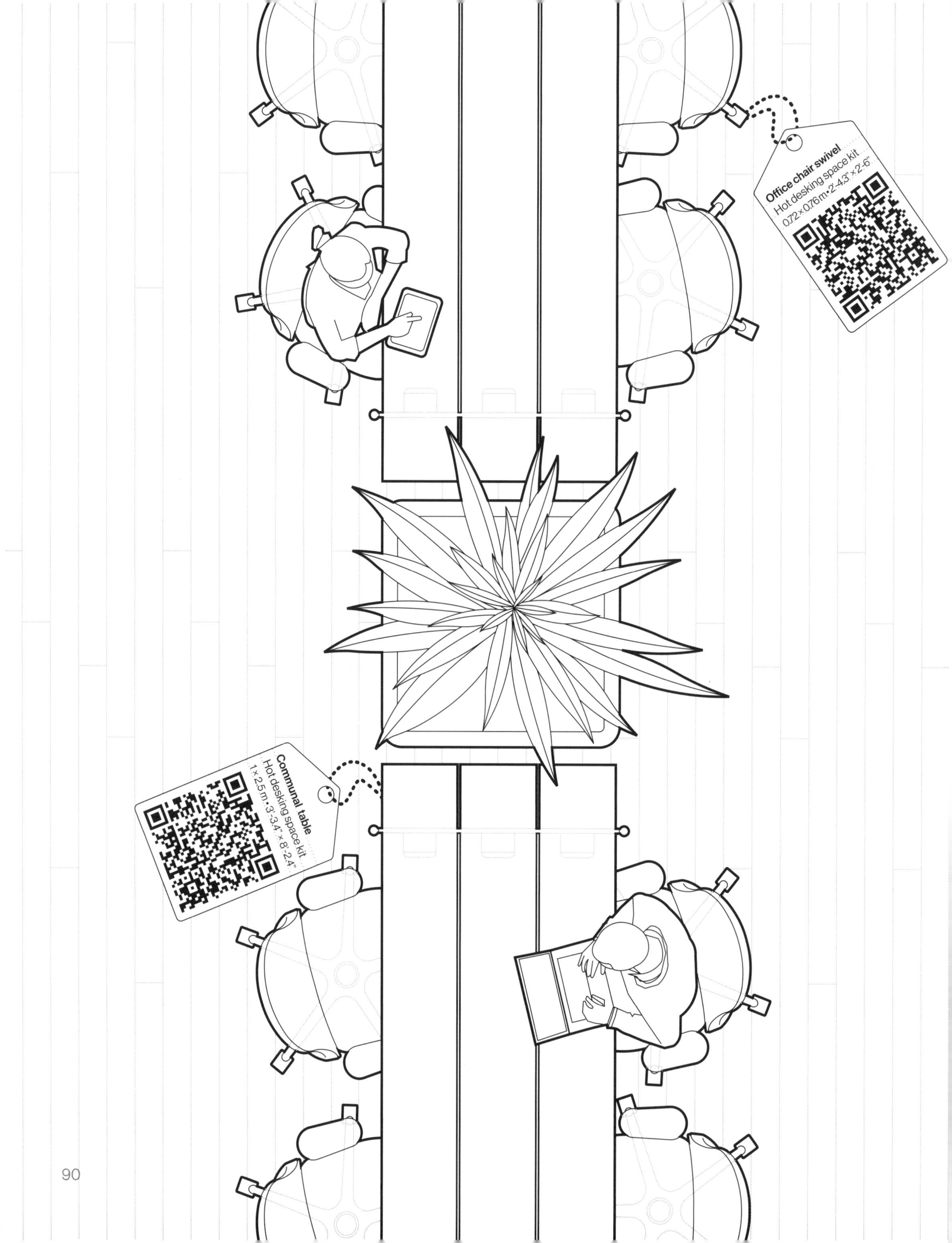
Office chair swivel
Hot desking space kit
0.72×0.76m • 2'-4,3" × 2'-6"
Communal table
Hot desking space kit
1×2.5m • 3'-3.4" × 8'-2.4"

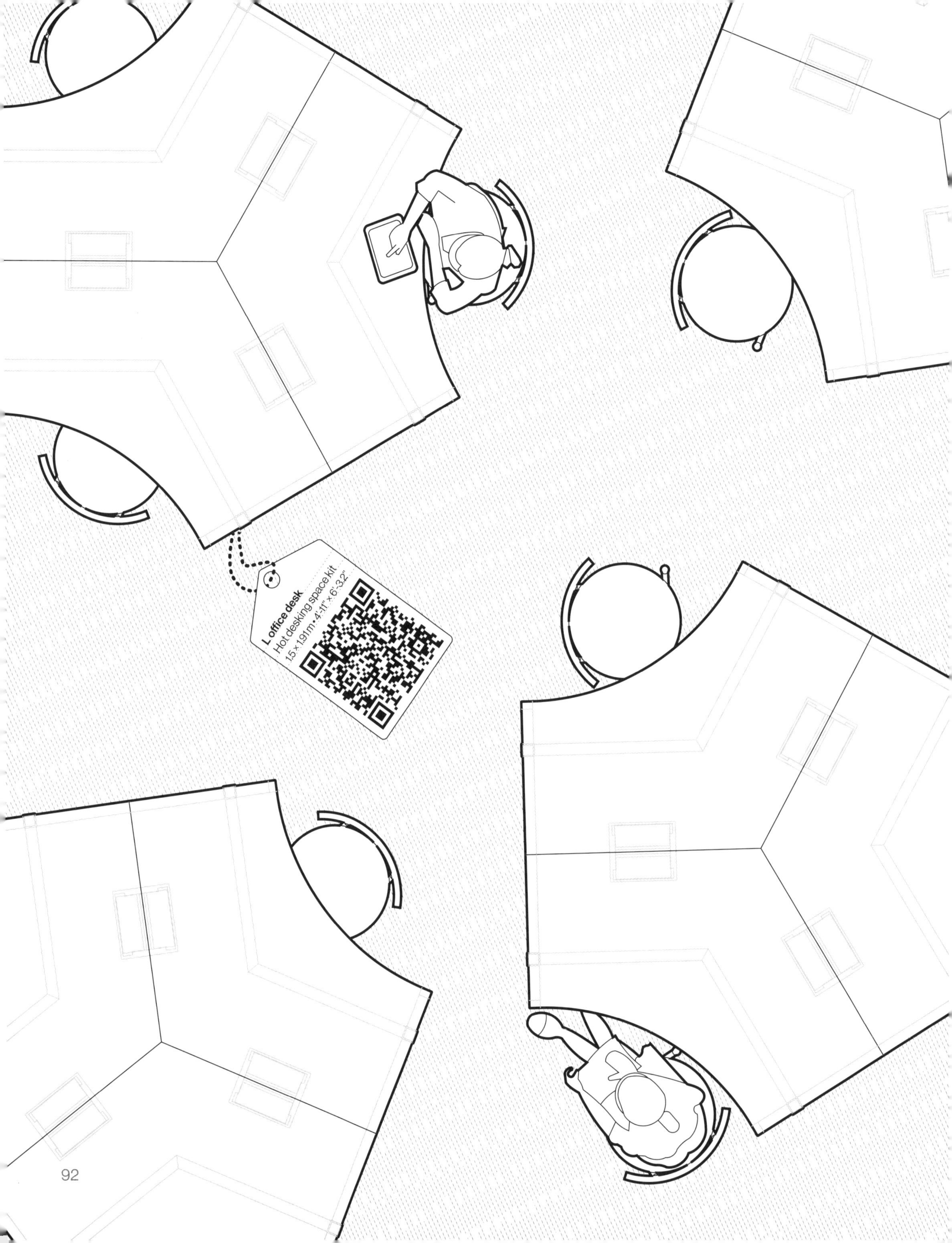
L office desk
Hot desking space kit
1.5 × 1.91 m • 4'-11" × 6'-3.2"

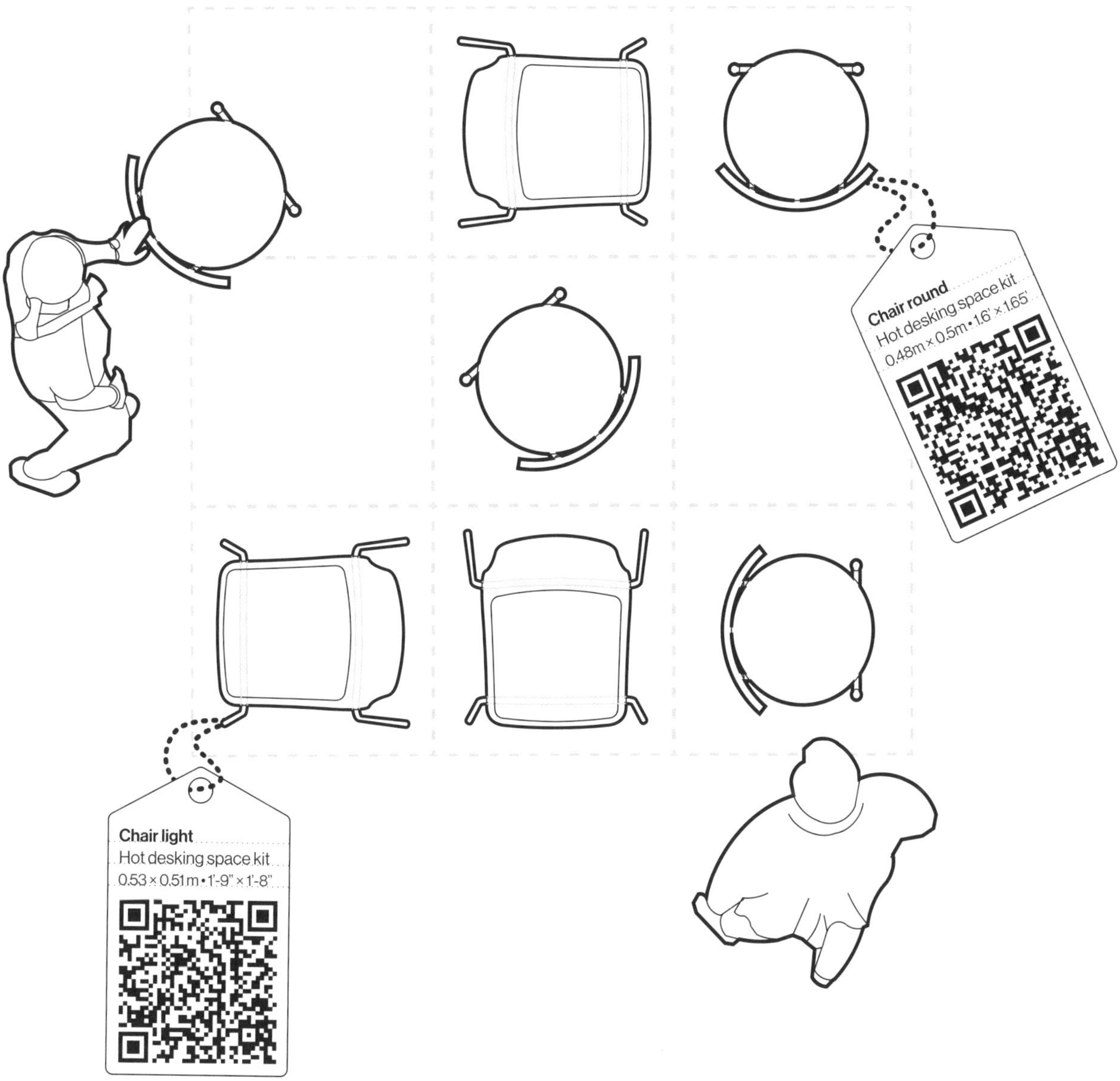
Chair round
Hot desking space kit
0.48m × 0.5m • 1.6' × 1.65'
Chair light
Hot desking space kit
0.53 × 0.51m • 1'-9" × 1'-8"

A Catalog of

Office Desks

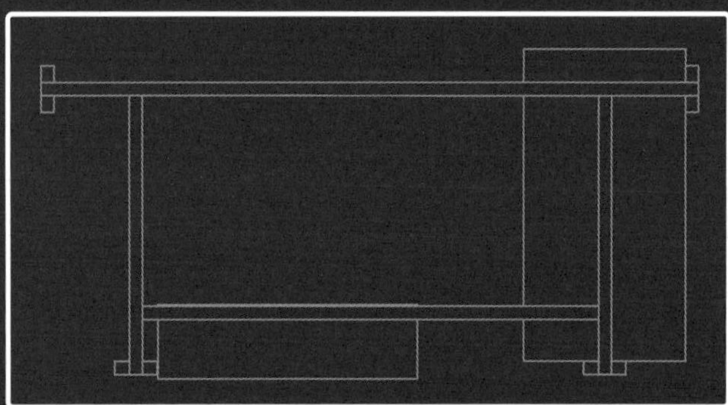

1

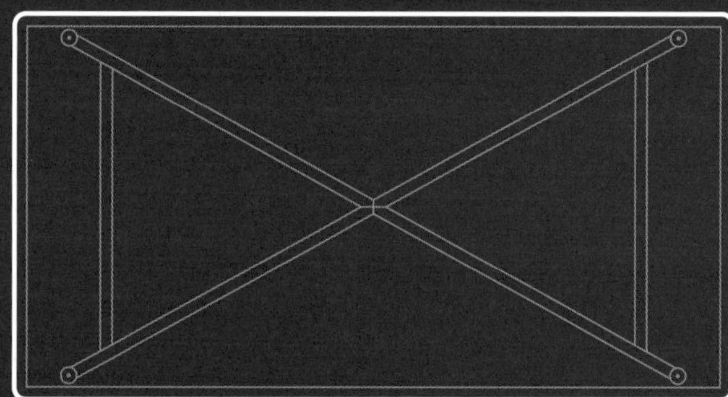

2

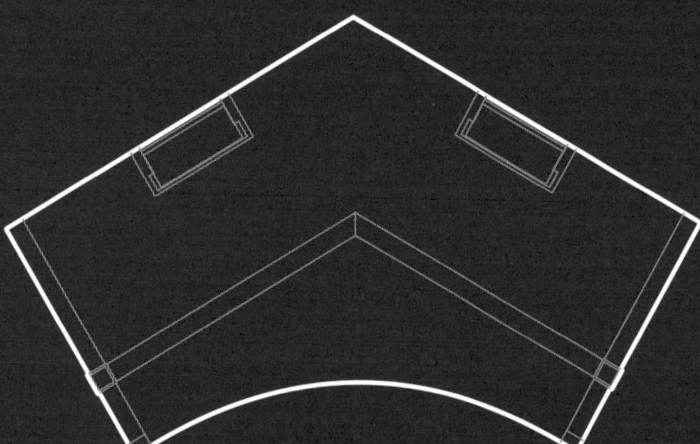

3

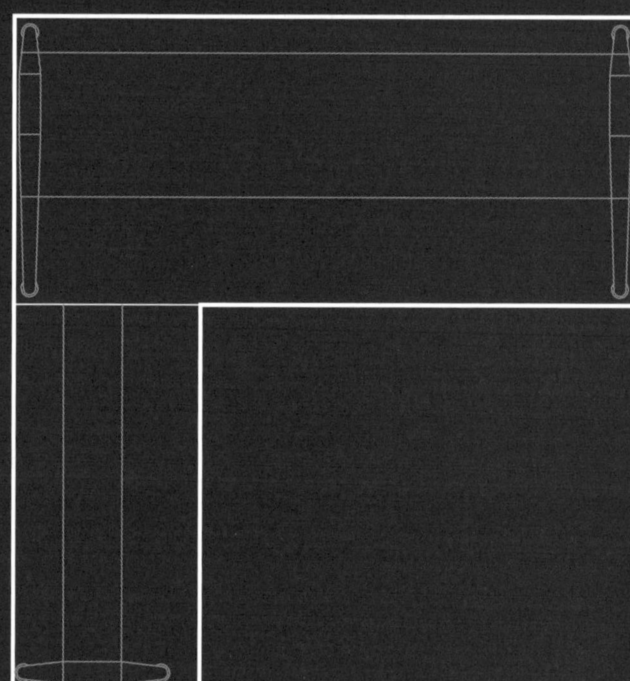

4

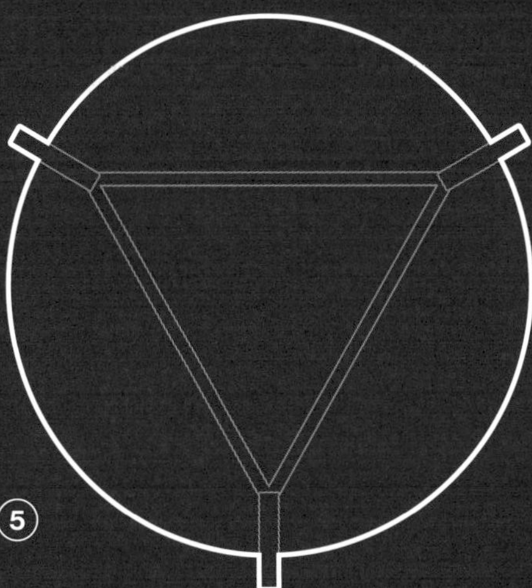

5

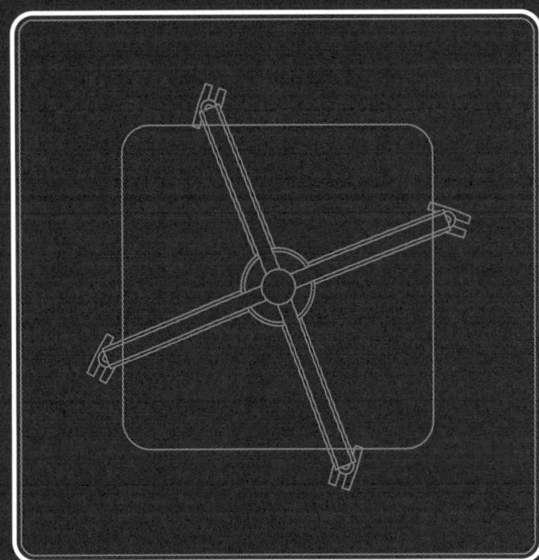

6

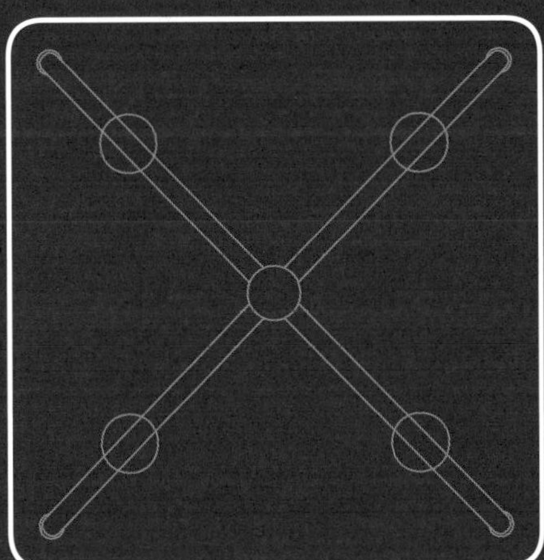

7

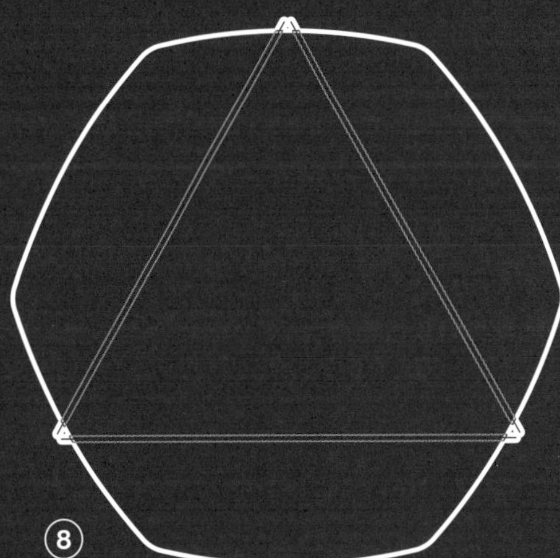

8

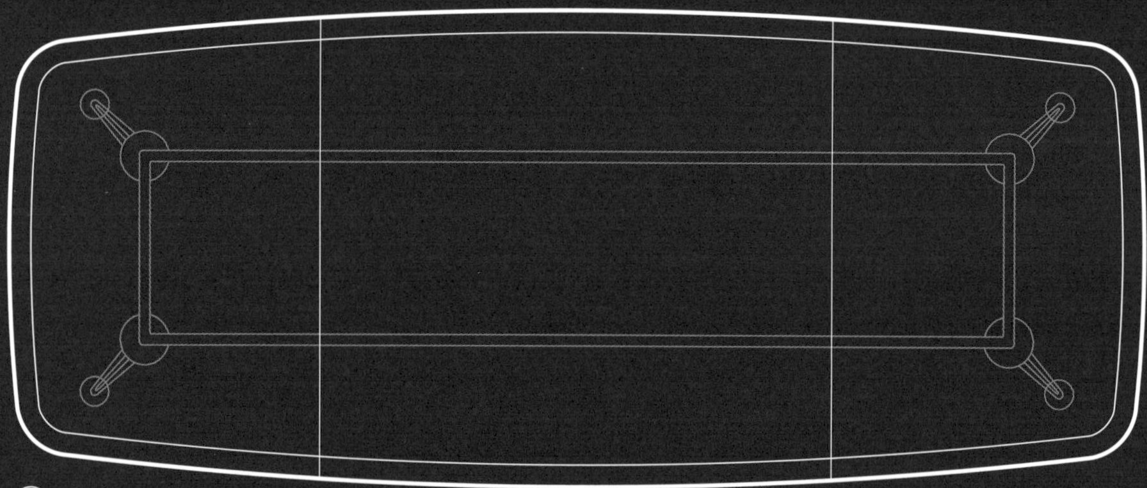

9

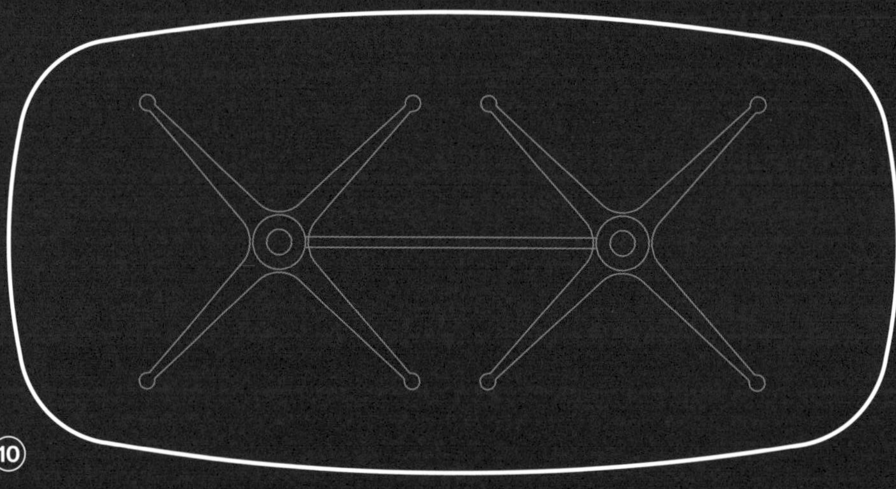

10

⑪

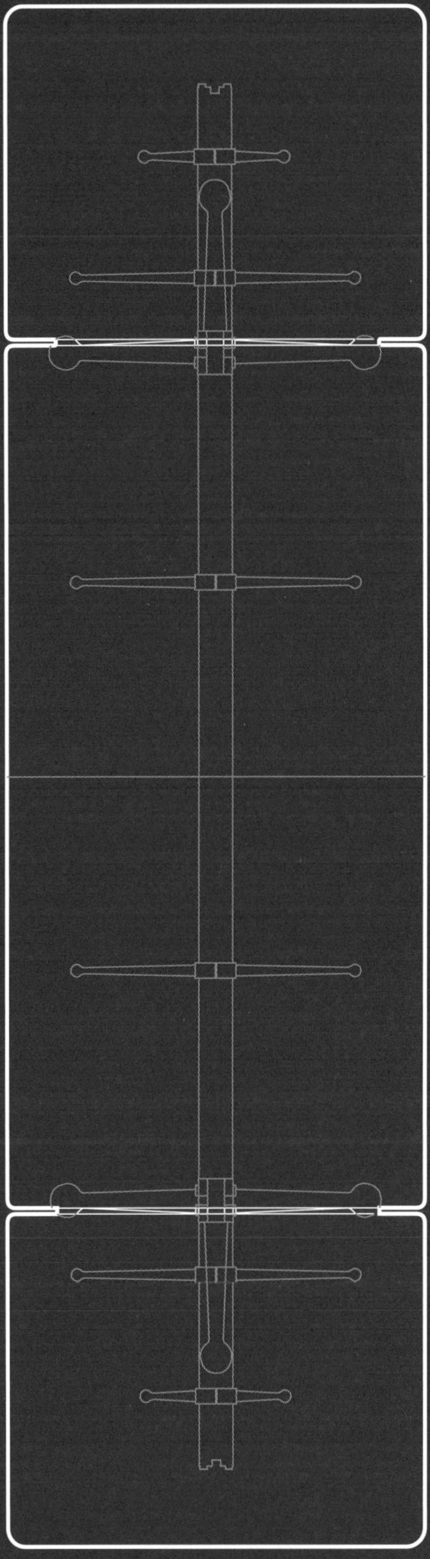

⑫

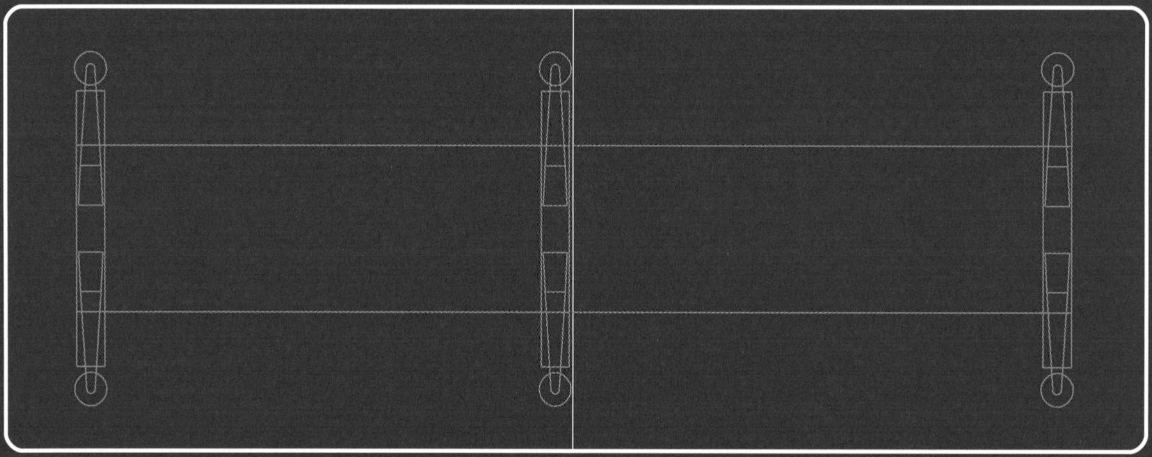

⑬

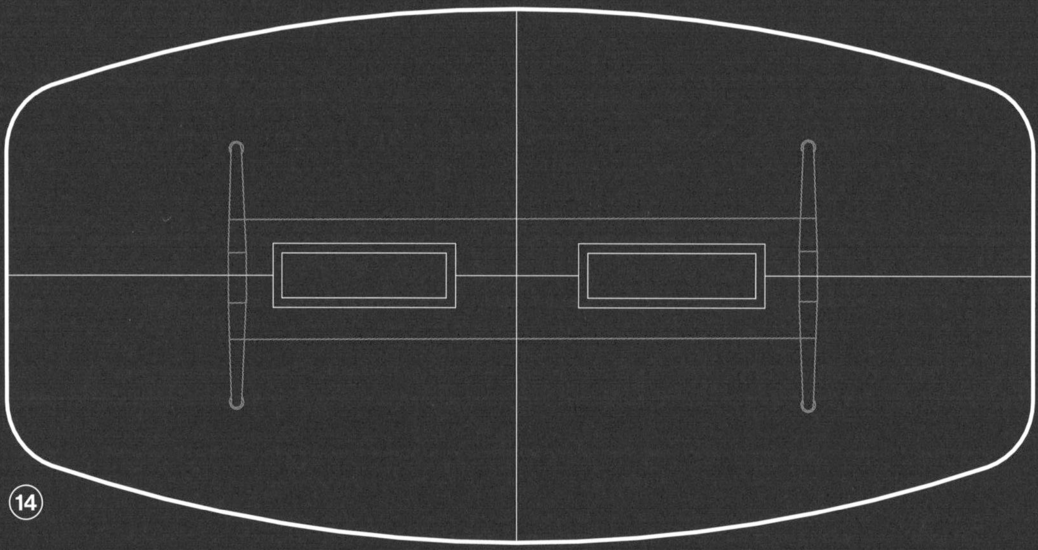

⑭

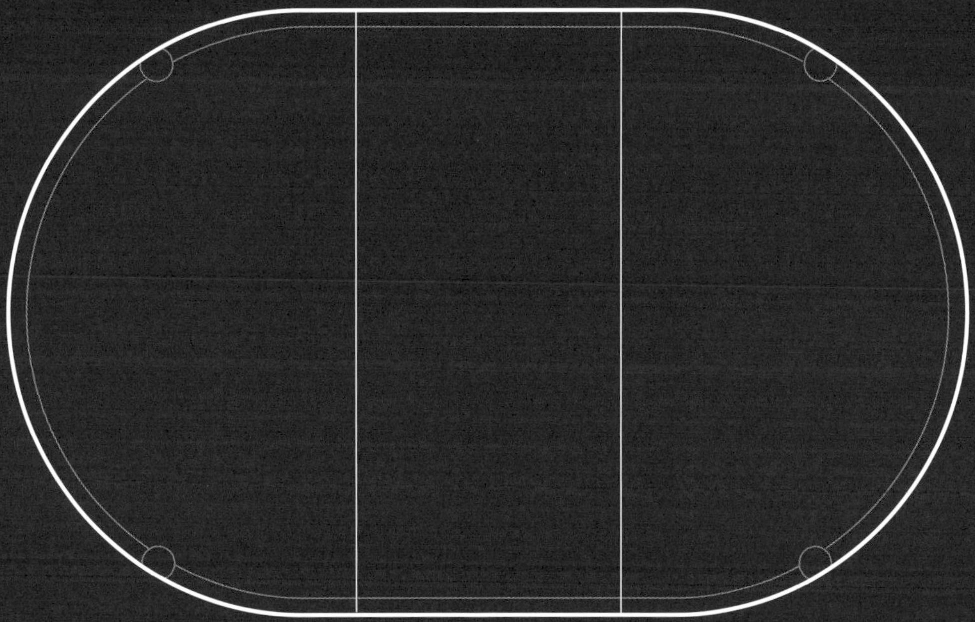

15

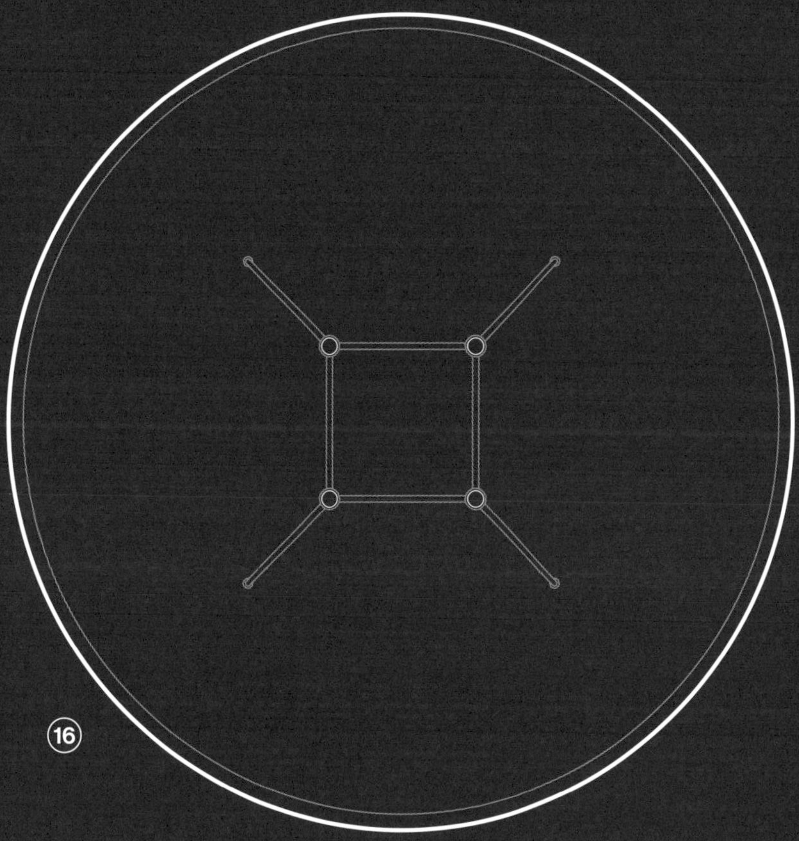

16

1

Private office desk
Office desks
0.56 × 1.07 m • 1'-10" × 3'-6"

2

Office desk light
Office desks
0.6 × 1.17 m • 1'-11.6" × 3'-10"

3

L office desk
Office desks
1.5 × 1.9 m • 4'-11" × 6'-2.8"

4

L desk corner
Office desks
2.1 × 2 m • 6'-10.7" × 6'-6.7"

5

Gueridon
Office desks
1.7 × 1.61 m • 5'-6.9" × 5'-3.4"

6

Dining table on wheels • Office desks
0.78 × 0.78 m • 2'-6.7" × 2'-6.7"

7

Square table
Office desks
0.75 × 0.75 m • 2'-5.5" × 2'-5.5"

8

Coffee table
Office desks
0.84 × 0.89 m • 2'-9" × 2'-11"

(9)

Meeting table 6 pers.
Office desks
1.1 × 2.2 m • 3'-7.3" × 7'-2.6"

(10)

Meeting table 8 pers.
Office desks
1.3 × 3.2 m • 4'-3.2" × 10'-6"

(11)

Kitchen table
Office desks
1 × 2.5 m • 3'-3.4" × 8'-2.4"

(12)

Conference room
Office desks
0.91 × 3.22 m • 3' × 10'-6.8"

(13)

Meeting desk rect-angular • Office desks
1.2 × 3.2 m • 3'-11.2" × 10'-6"

(14)

Meeting desk oval L
Office desks
2 × 4 m • 6'-6.7" × 13'-1.5"

(15)

Meeting desk oval S
Office desks
1.7 × 2.8 m • 5'-6.9" × 9'-1.8"

(16)

Meeting room table circular • Office desks
3.1 × 3.1 m • 10'-2.4" × 10'-2.4"

Kit for a
Conference Room

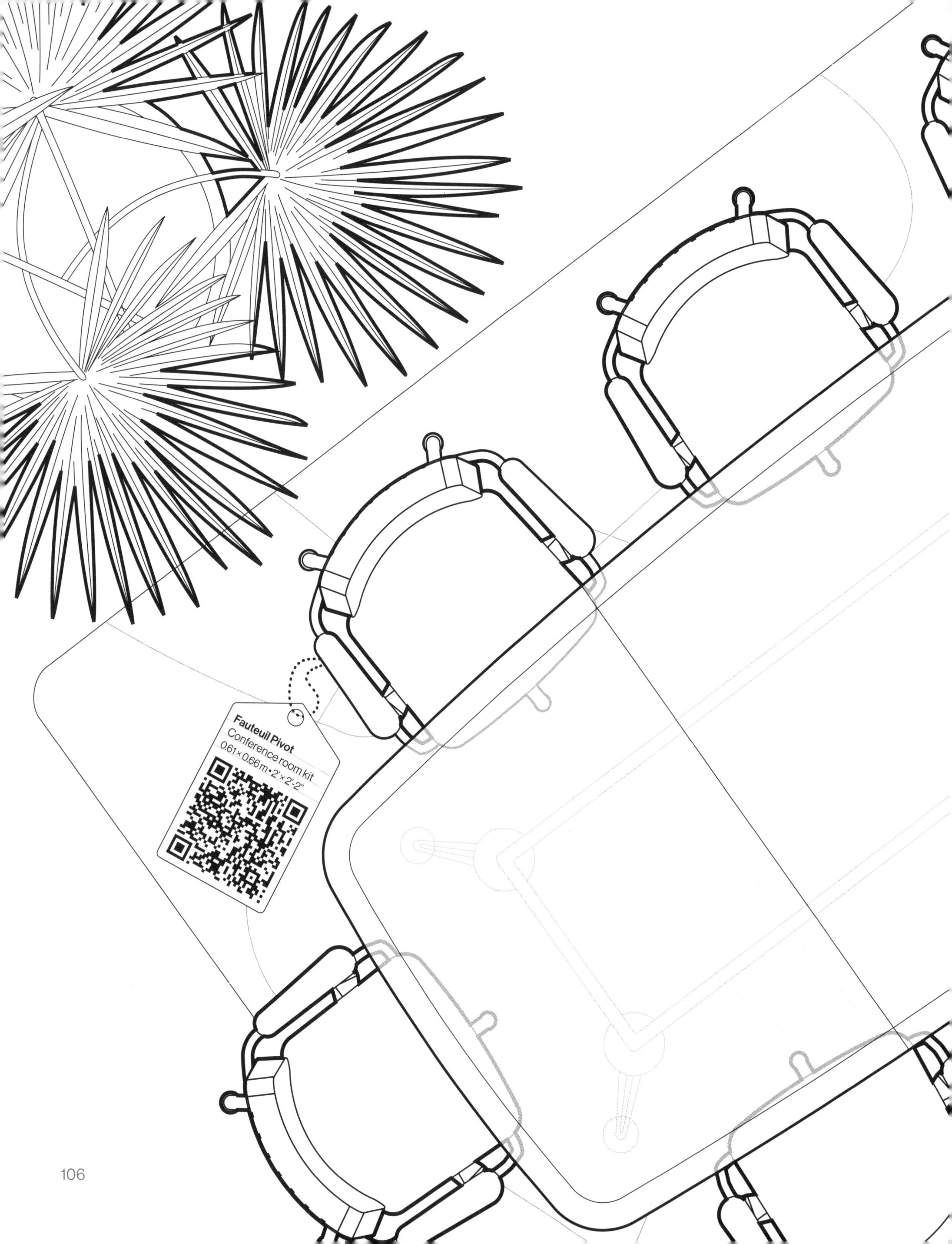
Fauteuil Pivot
Conference room kit
0.61 × 0.66 m • 2' × 2'-2"

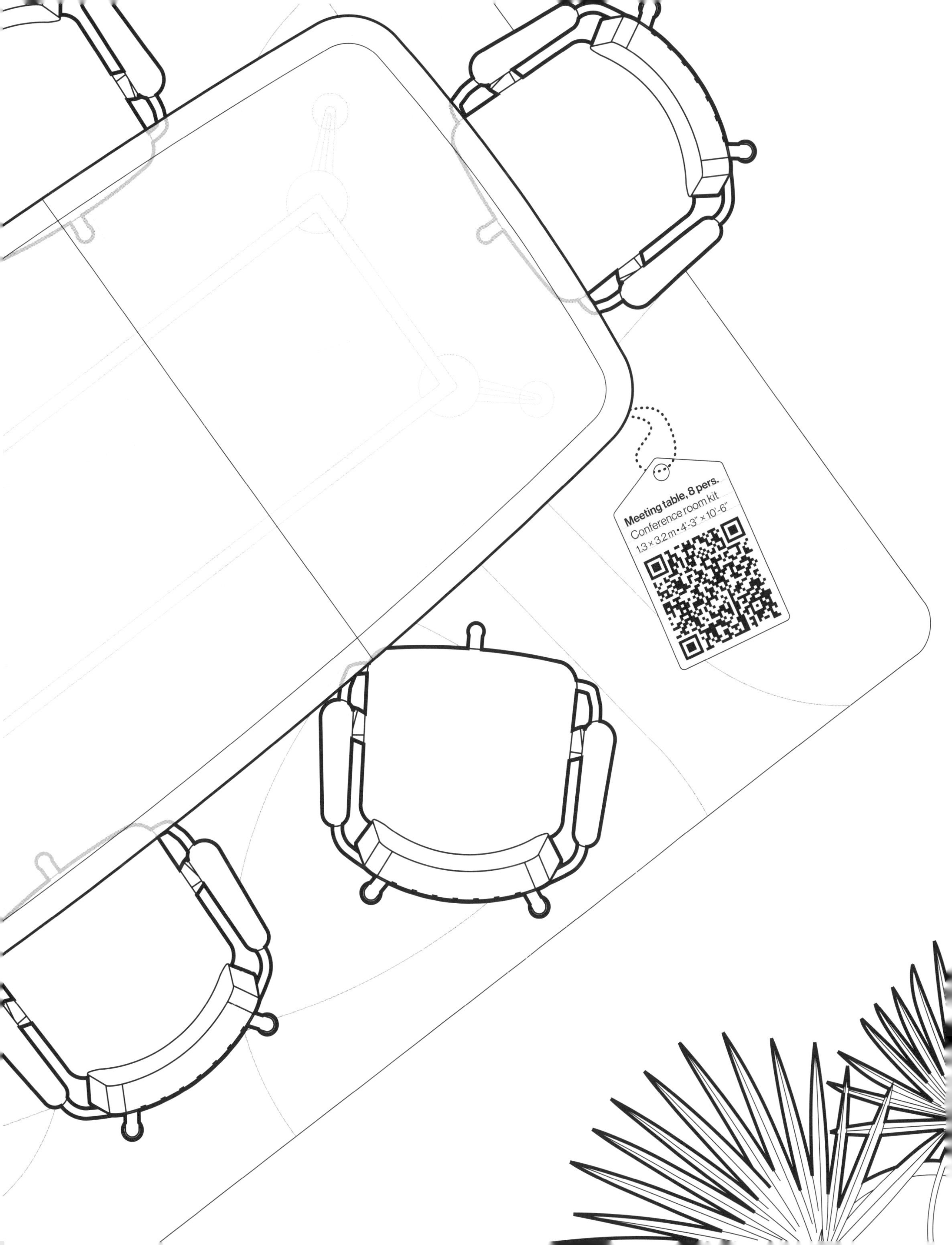
Meeting table, 8 pers.
Conference room kit
1.3 × 3.2 m • 4'-3" × 10'-6"

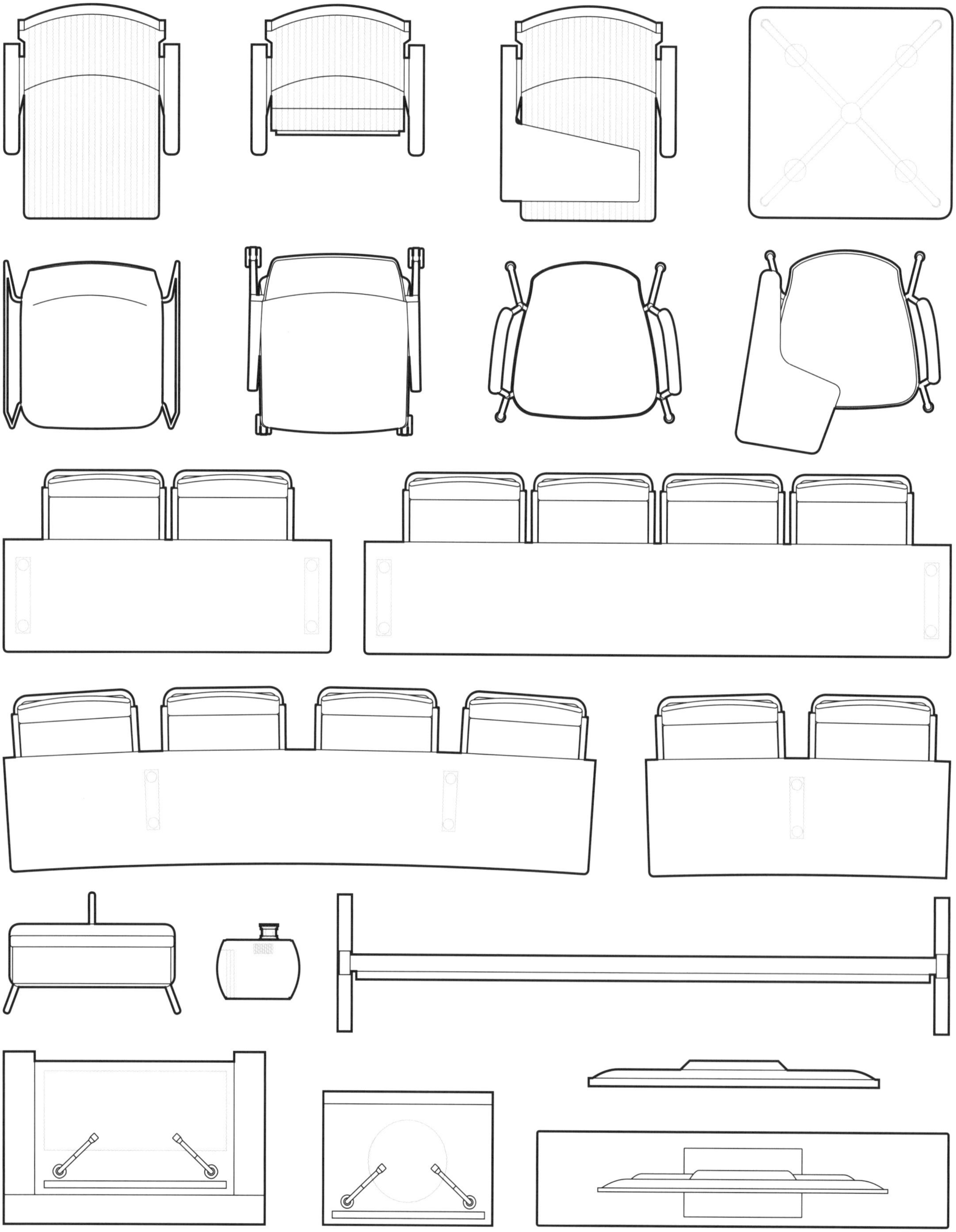

Kit for a
Lecture Room

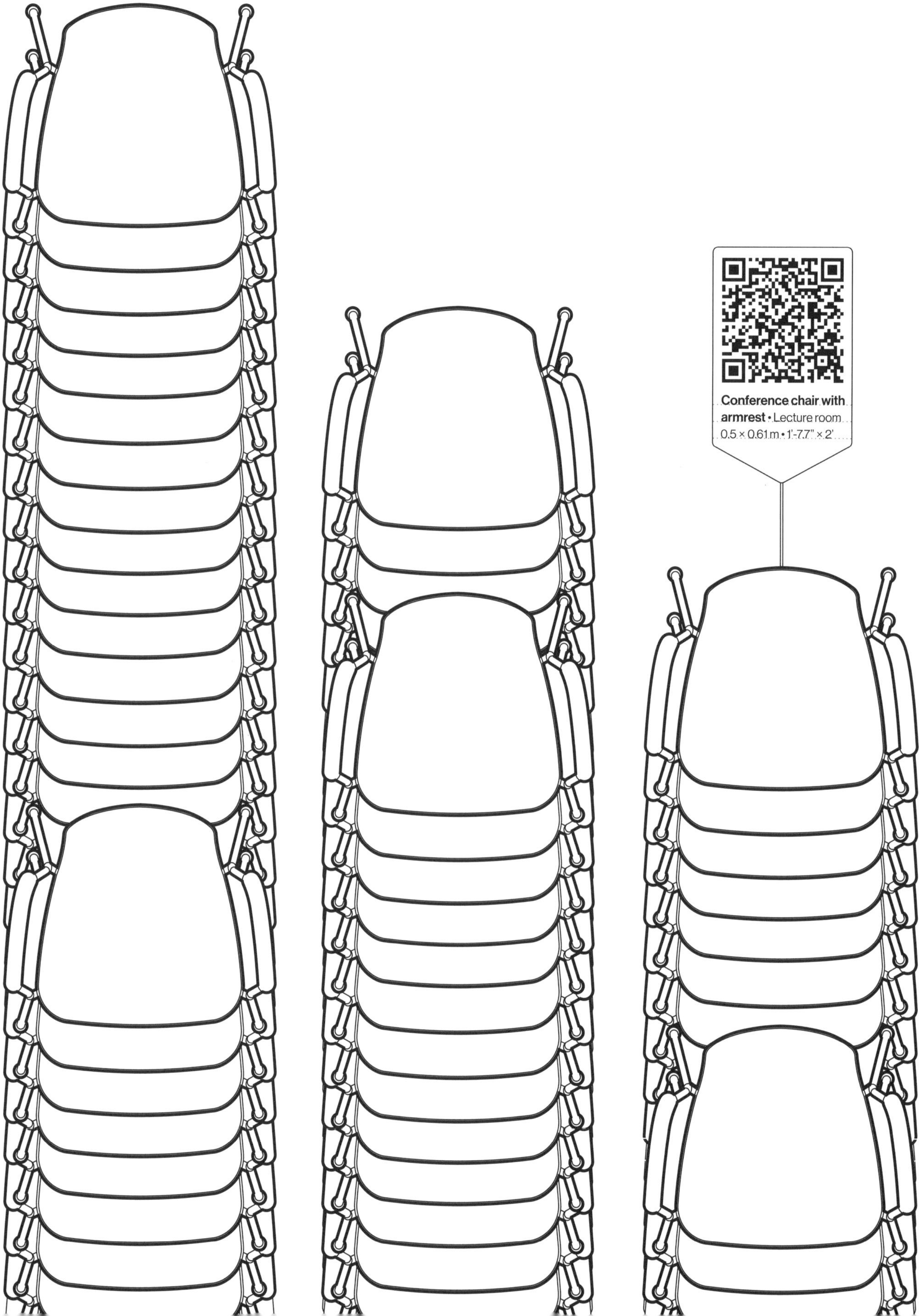
Conference chair with armrest • Lecture room
0.5 × 0.61 m • 1'-7.7" × 2'

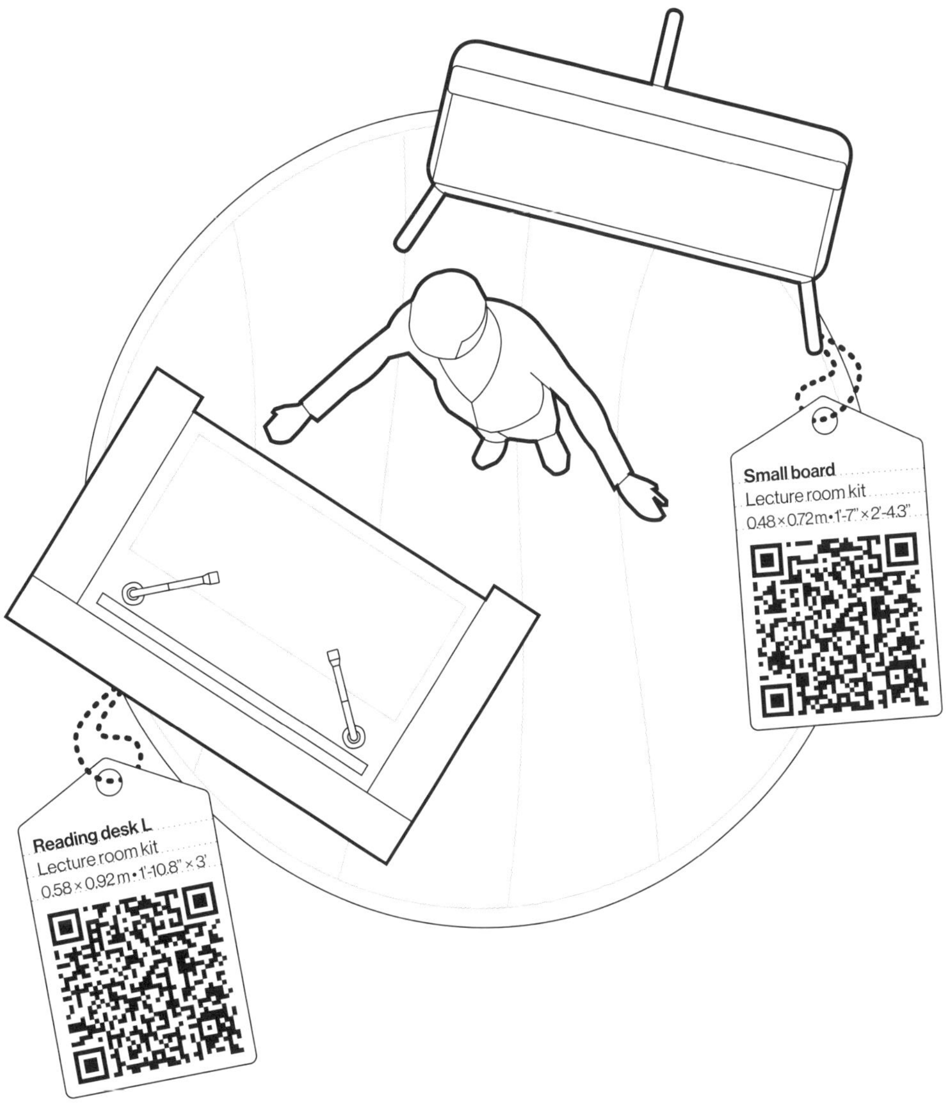
Small board
Lecture room kit
0.48 × 0.72 m • 1'-7" × 2'-4.3"
Reading desk L
Lecture room kit
0.58 × 0.92 m • 1'-10.8" × 3'

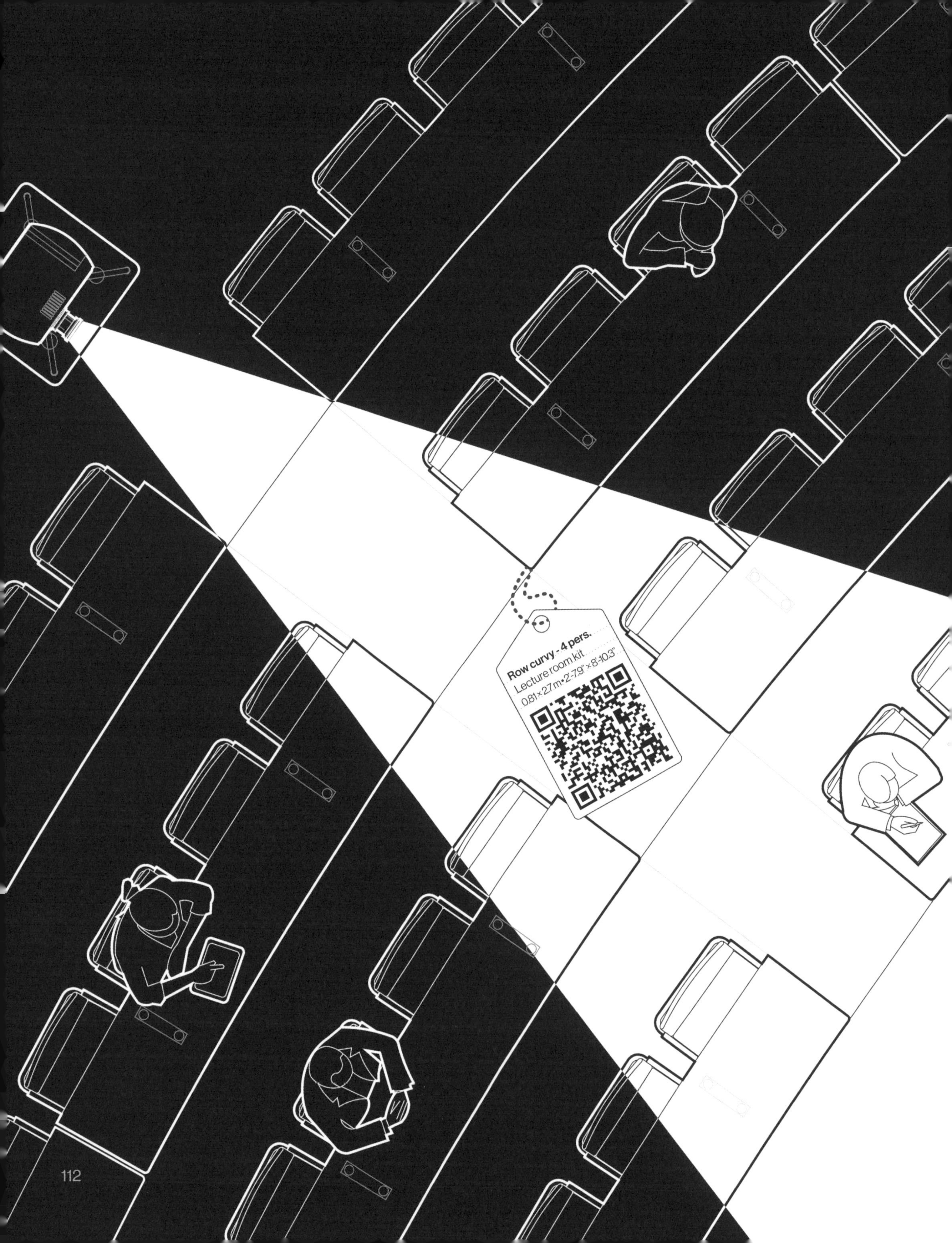

Row curvy - 4 pers.
Lecture room kit
0.81×2.7m•2'-7.9"×8'-10.3"

Conference chair folded • Lecture room kit
0.48×0.58m•1'-6.9"×1'-10.8"
Conference chair
Lecture room kit
0.7×0.58m•2'-3.2"×1'-10.8"
Conference chair with desk • Lecture room kit
0.7×0.58m•2'-3.2"×1'-10.8"

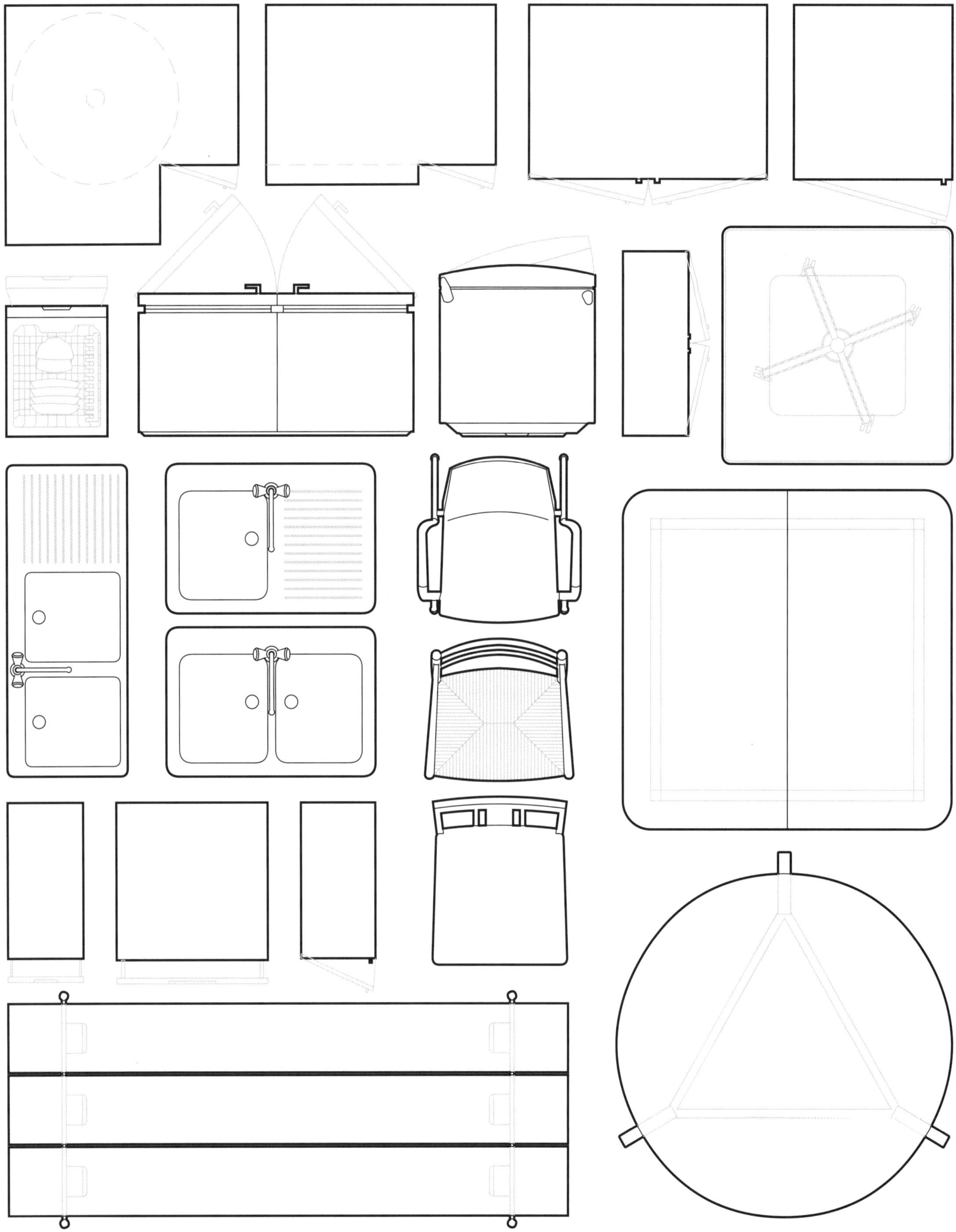

Kit for a
Communal Kitchen

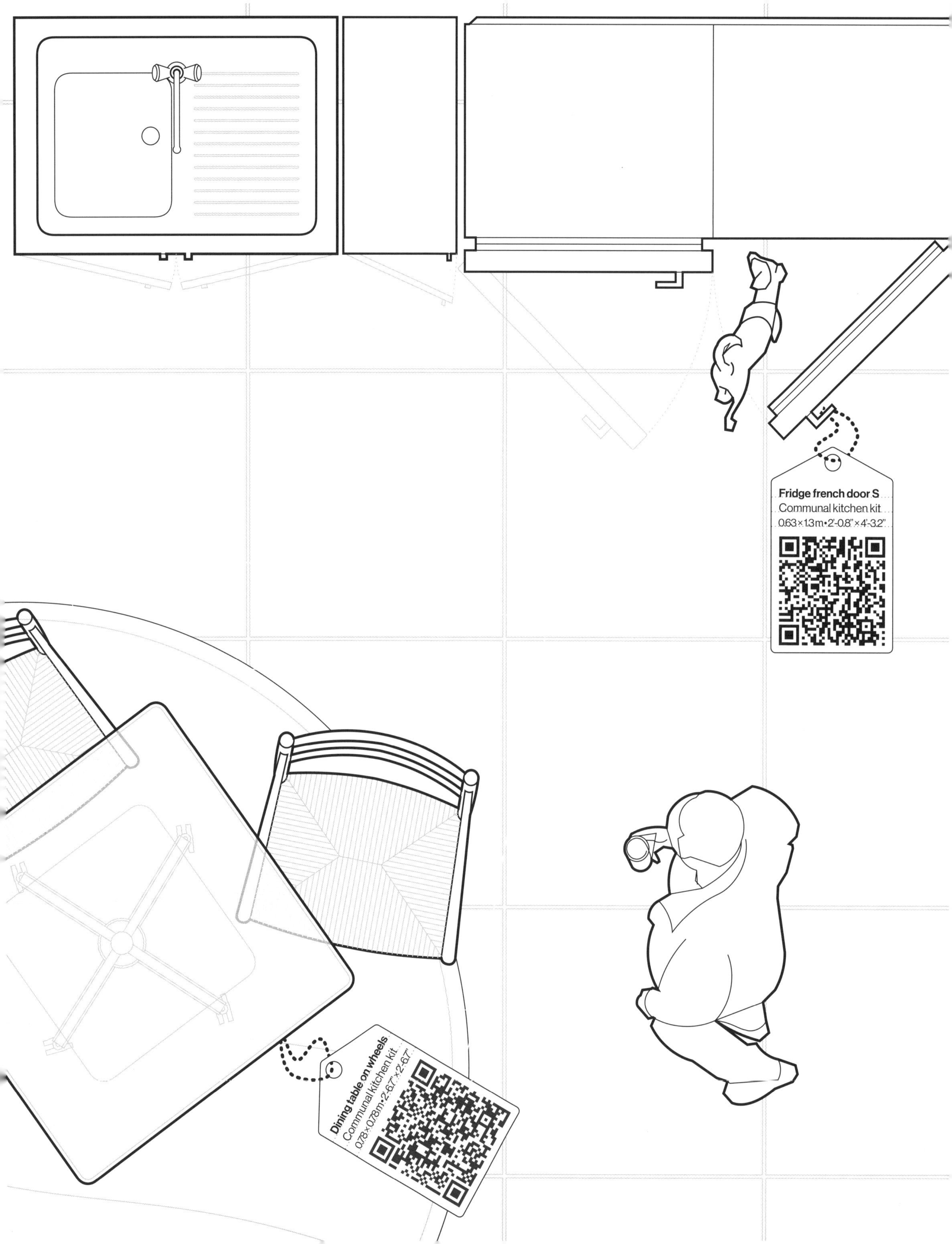

Fridge french door S
Communal kitchen kit
0.63×1.3m•2'-0.8"×4'-3.2"
Dining table on wheels
Communal kitchen kit
0.78×0.78m•2'-6.7"×2'-6.7"

Chair
Communal kitchen kit
0.5 × 0.55 m • 1'-8" × 1'-9.7"

Gueridon
Communal Kitchen kit
1.7 × 1.6 m • 5'-6.9" × 5'-3.4"

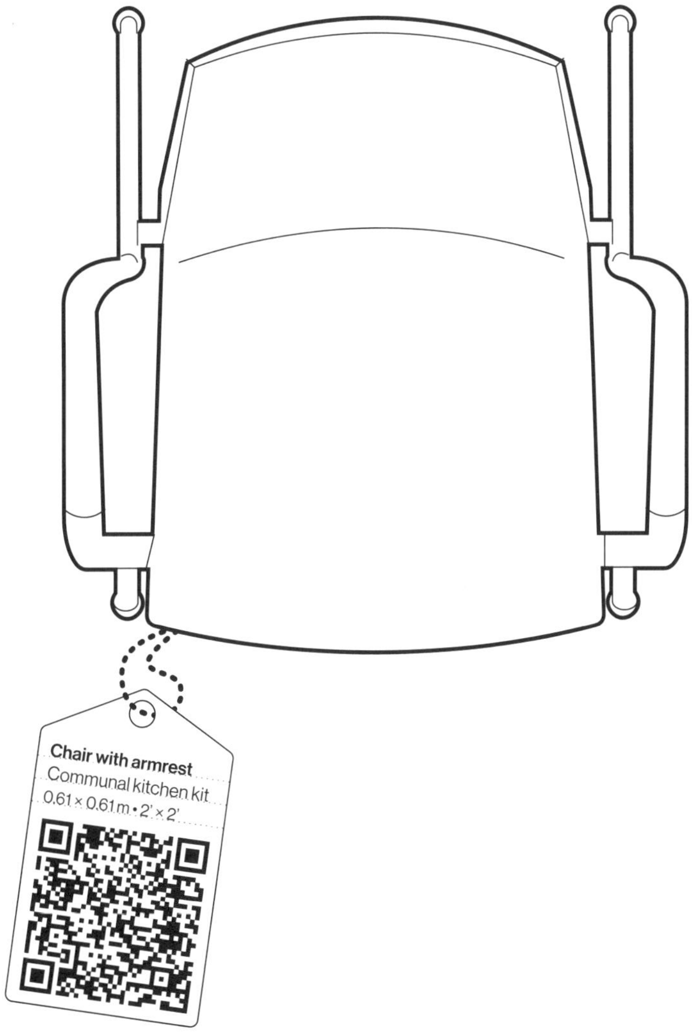
Chair with armrest
Communal kitchen kit
0.61 × 0.61 m • 2' × 2'

A Catalog of Plants

1
2
3
4

5

6

7

8

9

10

11

12

13

14

15

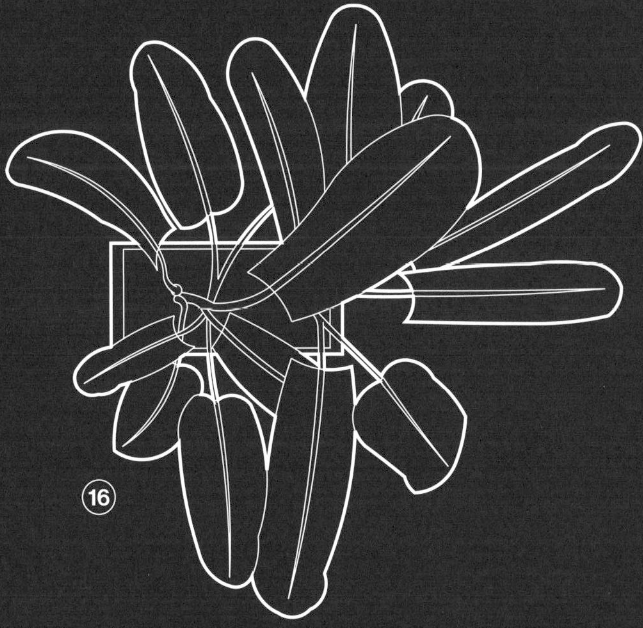
16

1
Fan palm S
Plants
1.3 × 1.16 m • 4'-3.2" × 3'-9.7"
2
Calathea
Plants
0.87 × 0.83 m • 2'-10" × 2'-8.7"
3
Philodendron
Plants
0.84 × 0.84 m • 2'-9" × 2'-9"
4
Geranium L
Plants
0.63 × 0.77 m • 2'-1" × 2'-6.3"
5
Asplenium
Plants
1 × 0.95 m • 3'-3.4" × 3'-1.4"
6
Ficus elastica
Plants
1.57 × 1.71 m • 5'-1.8" × 5'-7.3"
7
Calathea ornata
Plants
1.28 × 1.16 m • 4'-2.4" × 3'-9.7"
8
Monstera
Plants
1.29 × 1.4 m • 4'-2.8" × 4'-7"

9

Ficus
Plants
0.69 × 0.79 m • 2'-3.2" × 2'-7"

10

Howea forsteriana
Plants
1.57 × 1.85 m • 5'-1.8" × 6'-1"

11

Geranium S
Plants
0.6 × 0.63 m • 1'-11.6" × 2'-1"

12

Scindapsus
Plants
0.7 × 0.78 m • 2'-3.6" × 2'-6.7"

13

Dracaena
Plants
1 × 1.16 m • 3'-3.4" × 3'-9.7"

14

Scindapsus pictus
Plants
0.8 × 1.1 m • 2'-7.5" × 3'-6.9"

15

Tradescantia L
Plants
0.82 × 0.9 m • 2'-8.3" × 2'-11.4"

16

Peperomia
Plants
0.8 × 0.93 m • 2'-7.5" × 3'-0.6"

Kit for a
Lounge Area

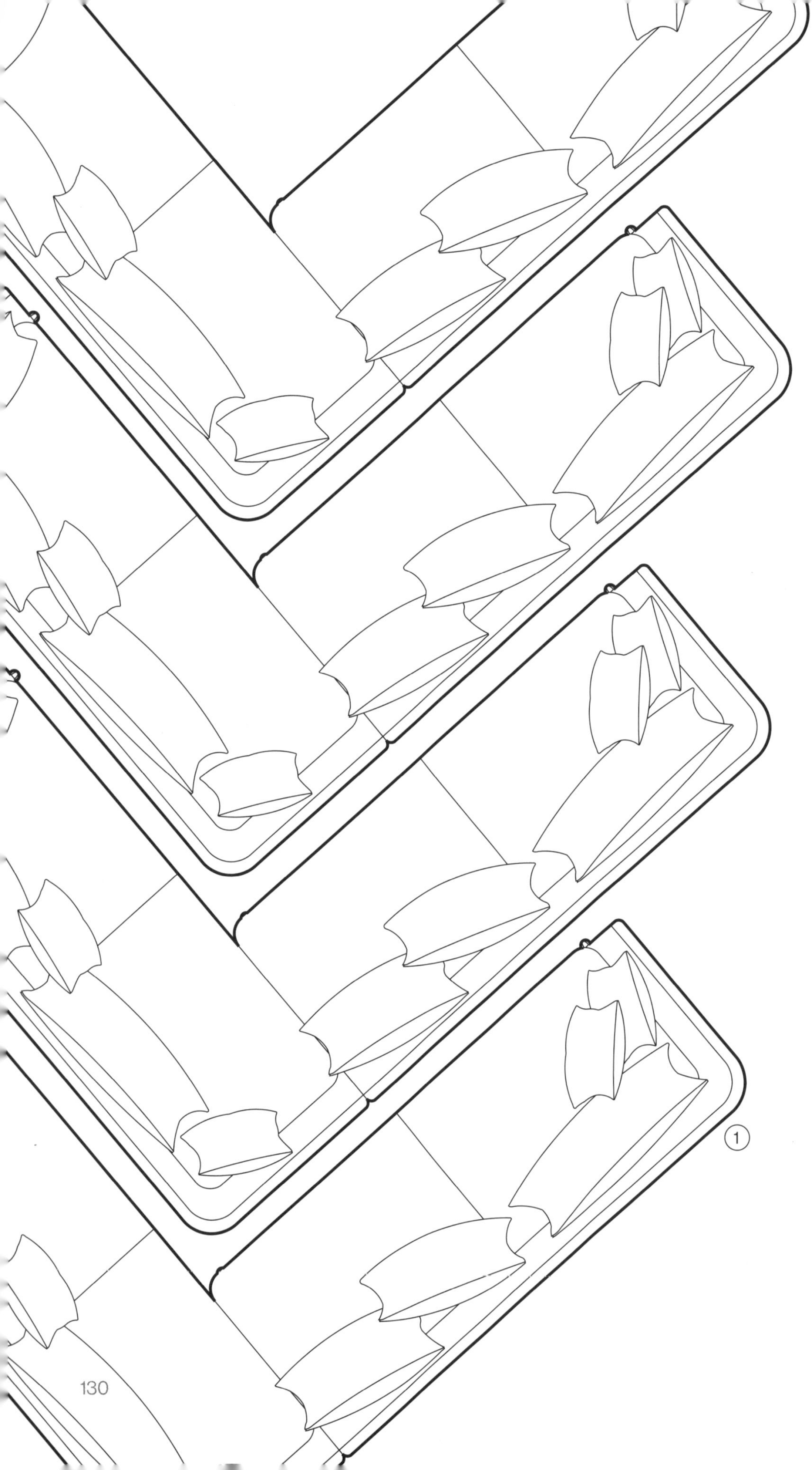

1
L-shaped sofa
Lounge area kit
2.33 × 3 m • 7'-7.7" × 9'-10"

2
Square table
Lounge area kit
0.75 × 0.75 m • 2'-5.5" × 2'-5.5"

3
Flow carpet
Lounge area kit
2.3 × 1.6 m • 7'-6.6" × 5'-3"

4
Alcove sofa M
Lounge area kit
0.95 × 2.2 m • 3'-1.4" × 7'-2.6"

3
2
4

Kit for a
Lobby Area

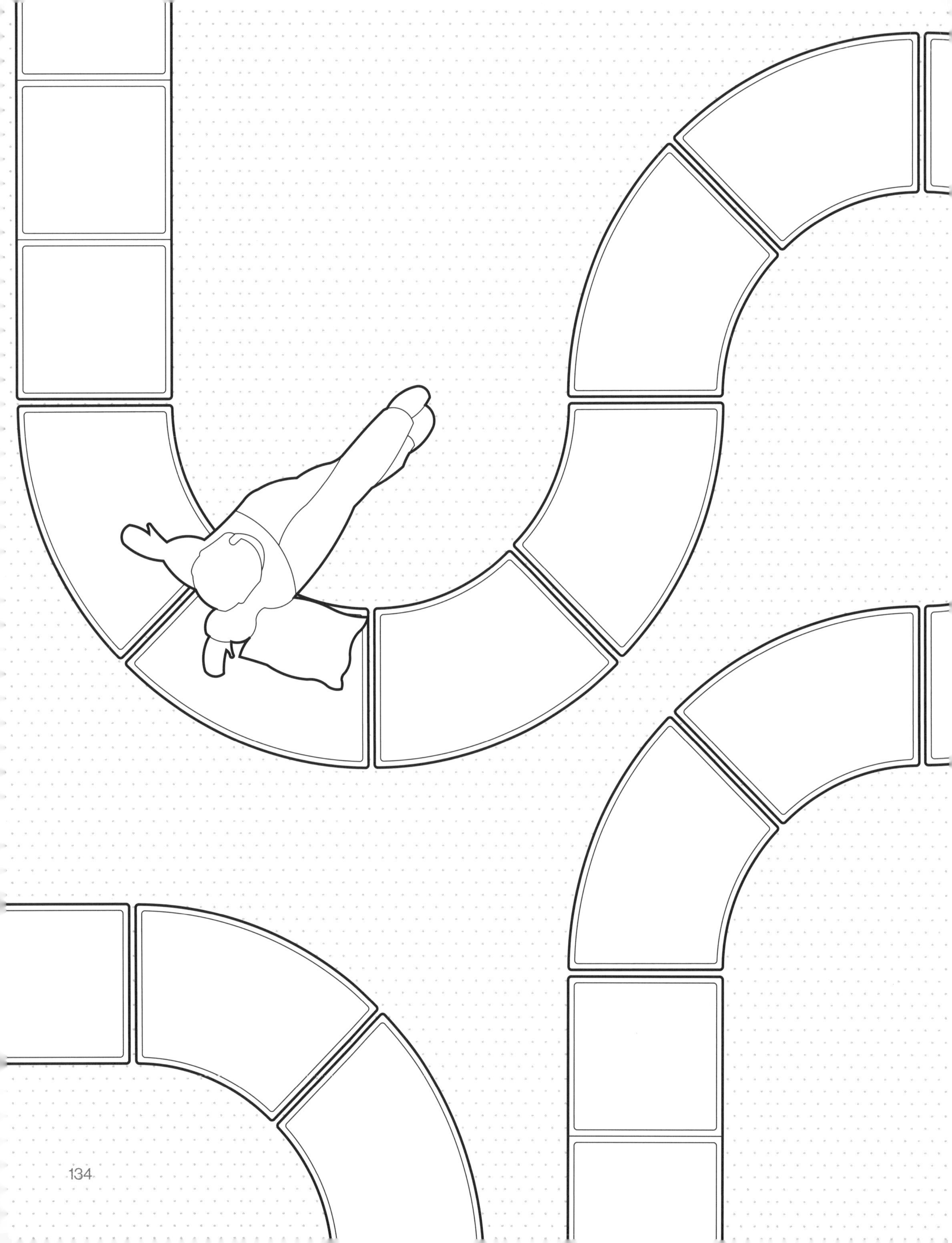

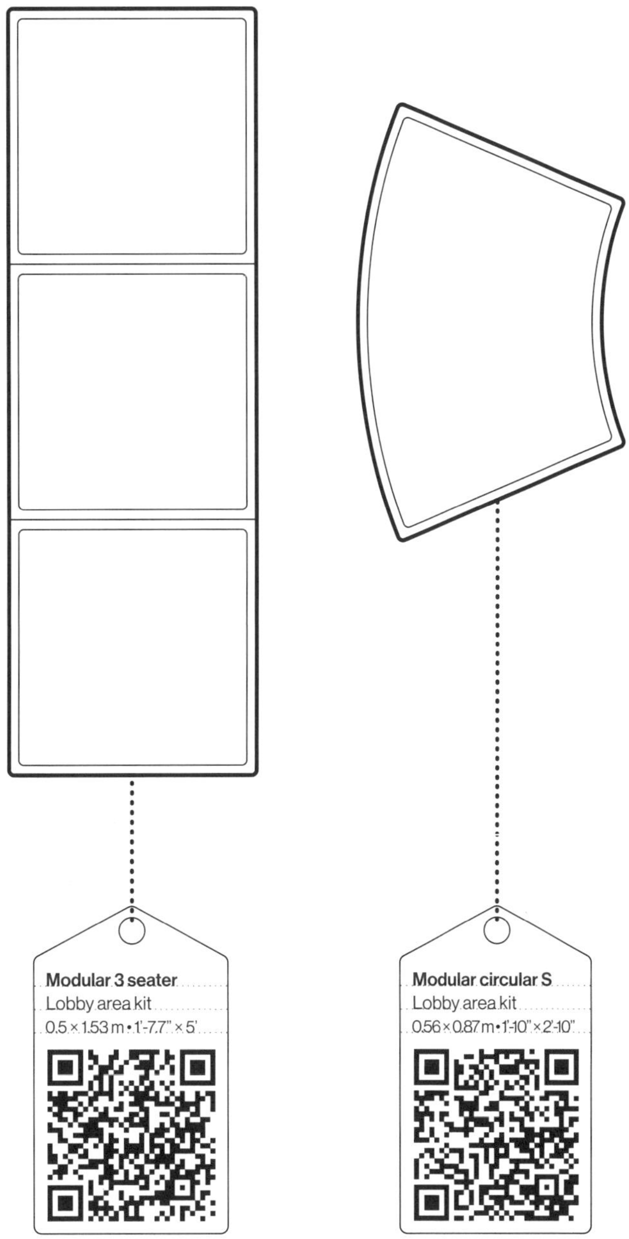
Modular 3 seater
Lobby area kit
0.5 × 1.53 m • 1'-7.7" × 5'
Modular circular S
Lobby area kit
0.56 × 0.87 m • 1'-10" × 2'-10"

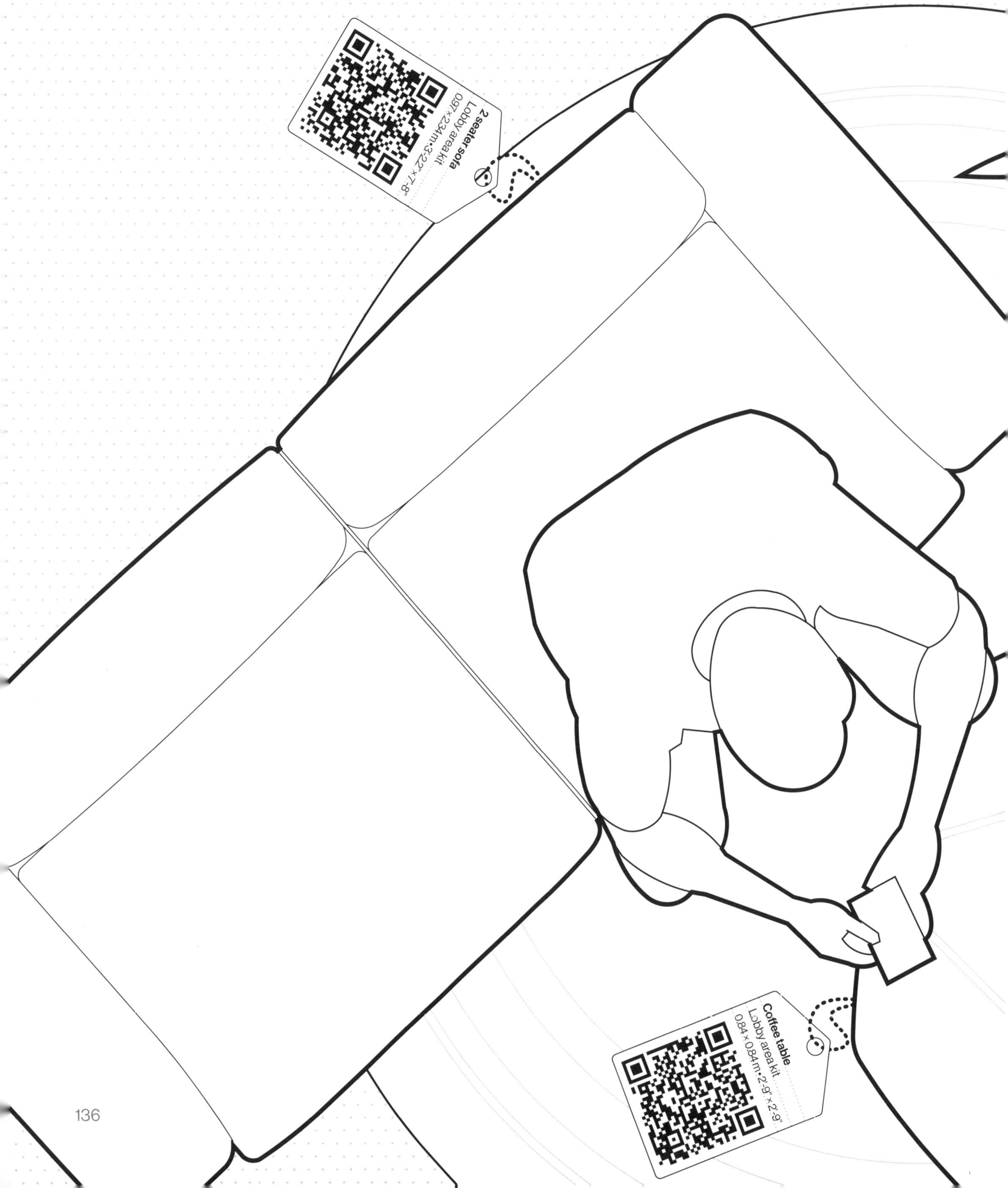
2 seater sofa
Lobby area kit
0.97 × 2.34 m • 3'-2" × 7'-8"
Coffee table
Lobby area kit
0.84 × 0.84 m • 2'-9" × 2'-9"

Round carpet S
Lobby area kit
1.5 × 1.5 m • 4'-11" × 4'-11"

Kit for a
Waiting Room

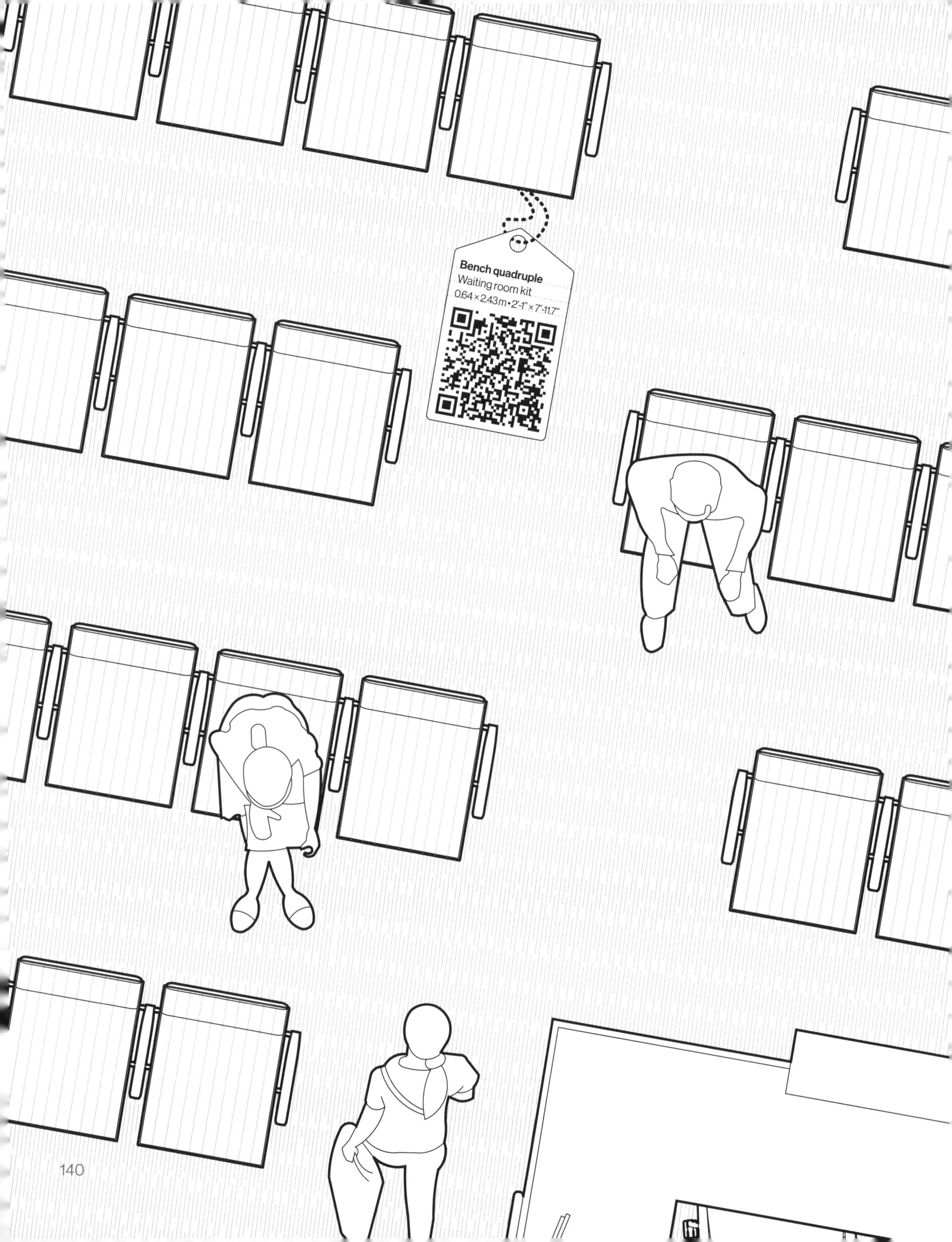

Bench quadruple
Waiting room kit
0.64 × 2.43 m • 2'-1" × 7'-11.7"

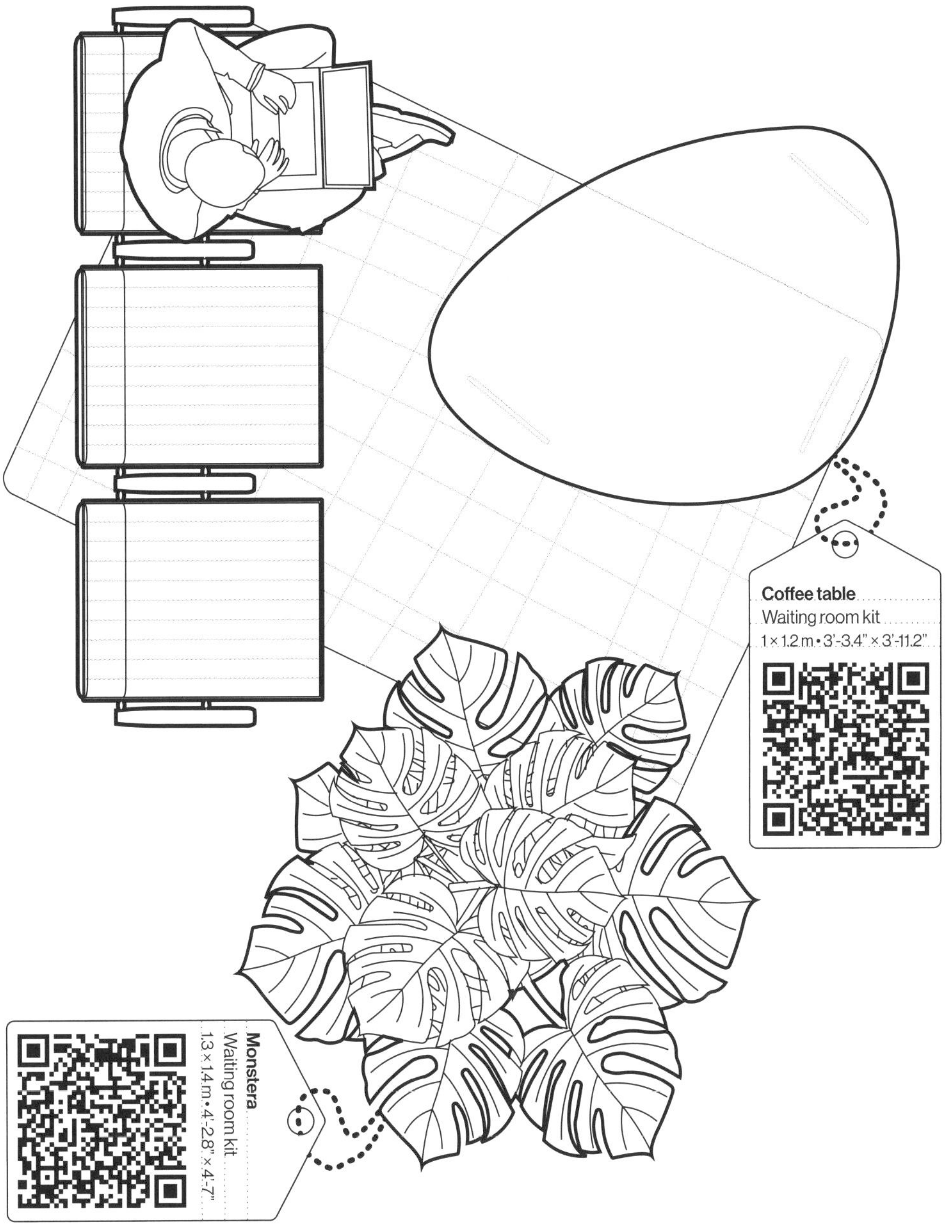
Coffee table
Waiting room kit
1 × 1.2 m • 3'-3.4" × 3'-11.2"
Monstera
Waiting room kit
1.3 × 1.4 m • 4'-2.8" × 4'-7"

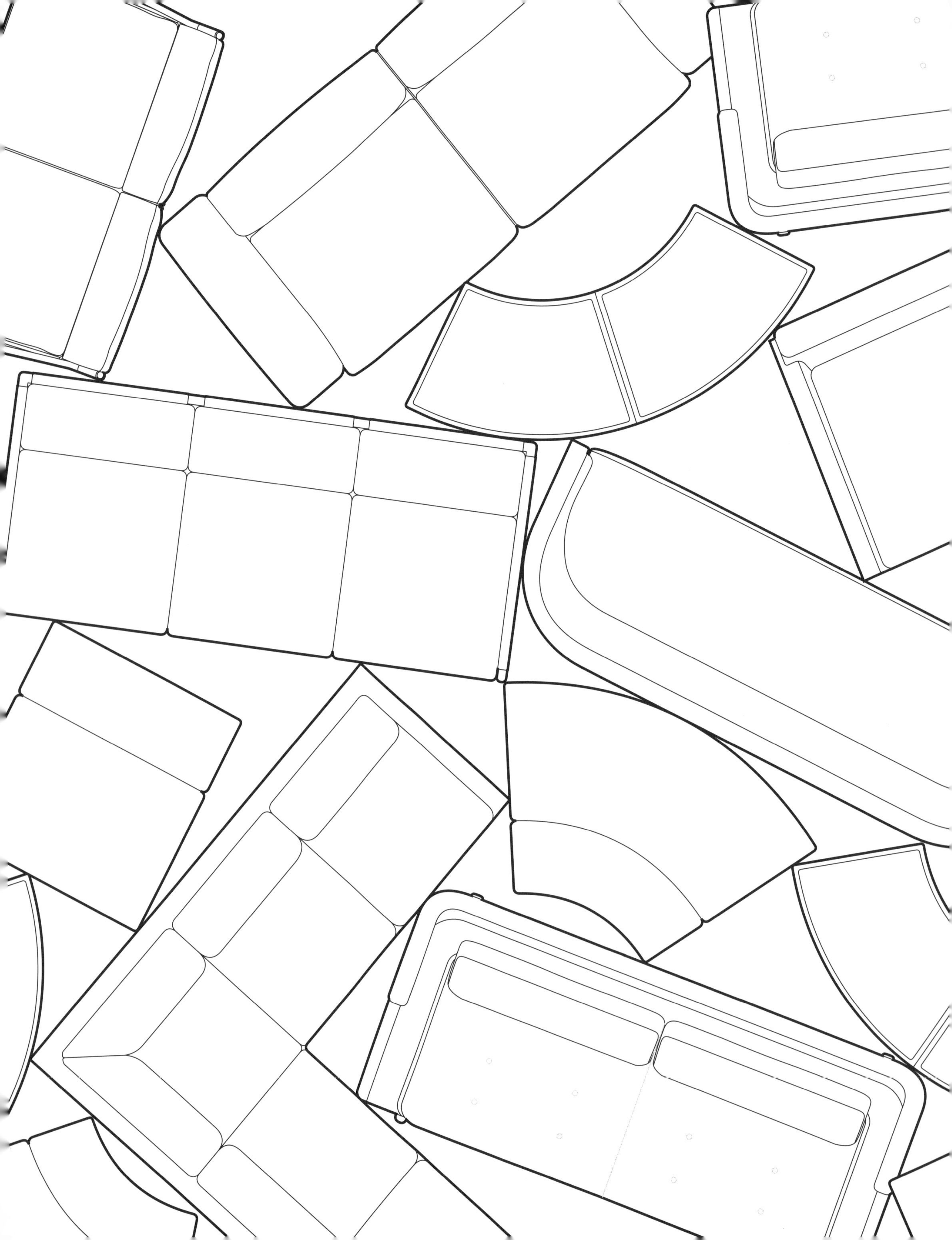

A Catalog of

Lounge Items

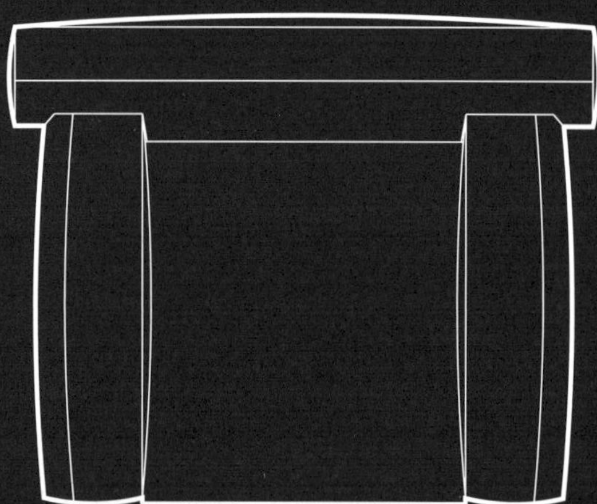

1

2

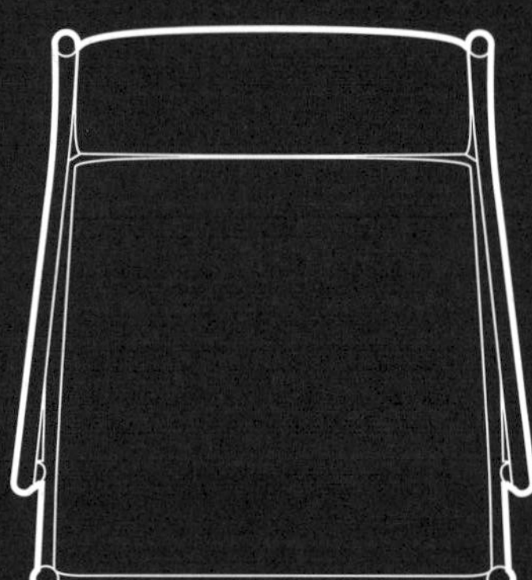

3

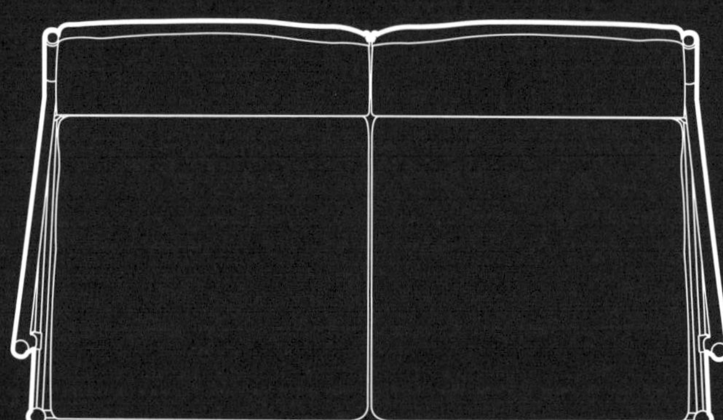

4

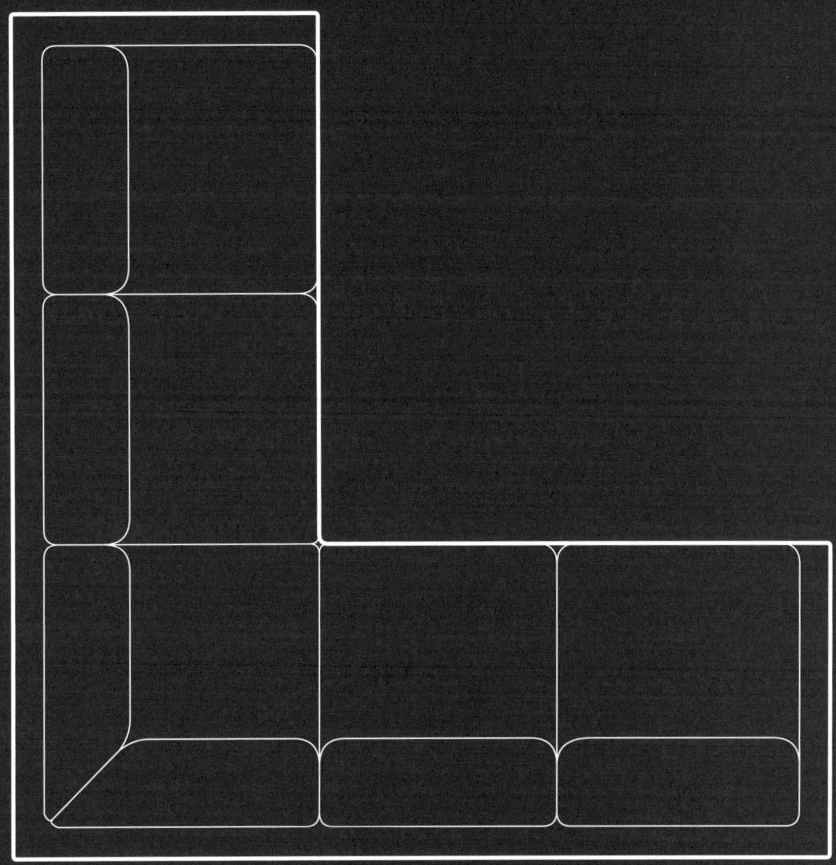

5

6

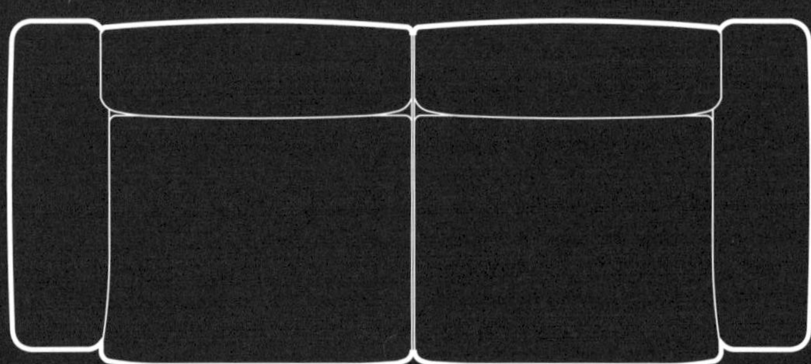

7

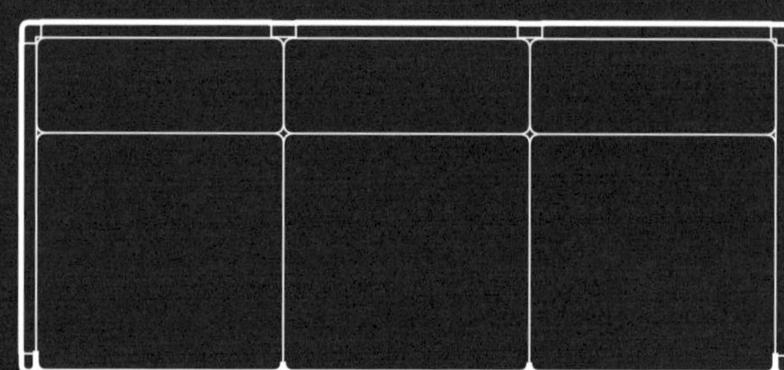

8

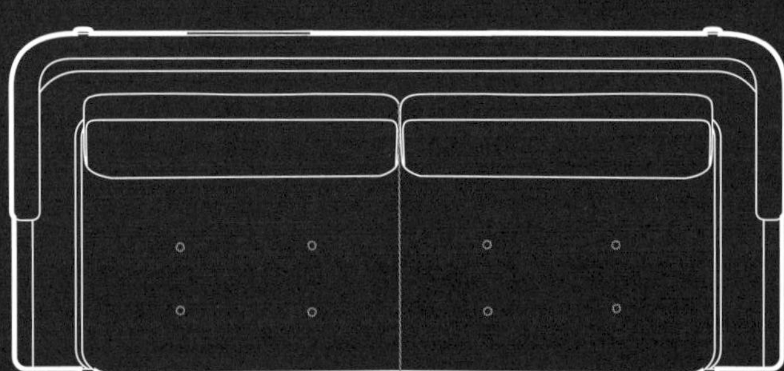

9

10

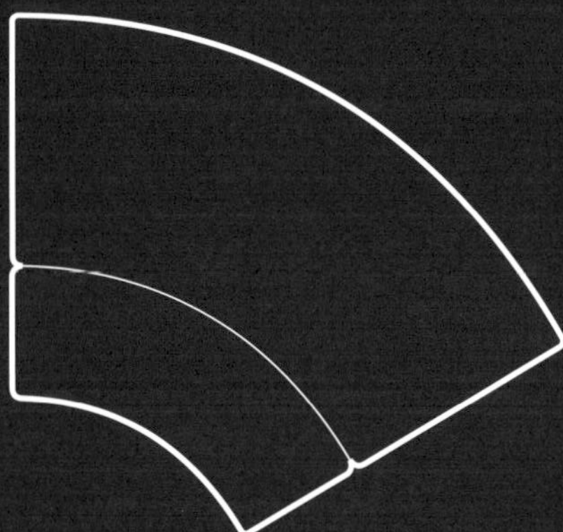

11

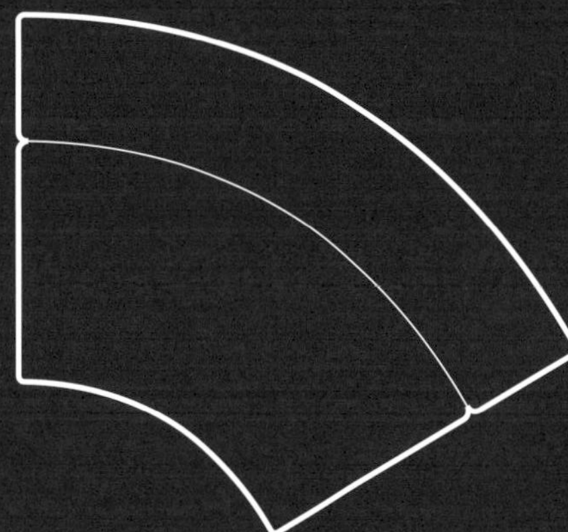

12

13

14

15

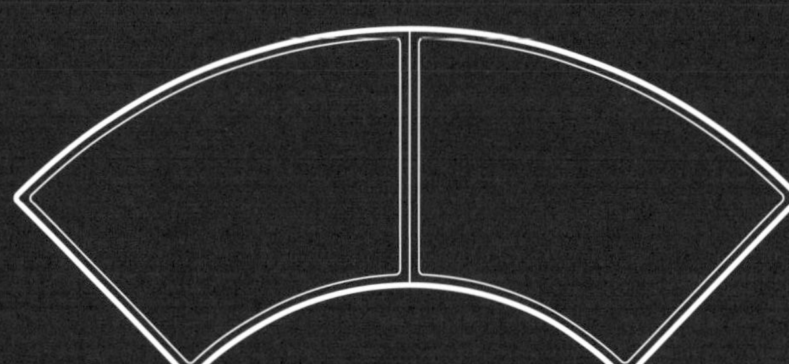

16

1. **Armchair**
Lounge items
0.8 × 1 m • 2'-7.5" × 3'-4"

2. **Armchair square**
Lounge items
0.82 × 0.97 m • 2'-8.3" × 3'-2"

3. **Armchair modern**
Lounge items
0.68 × 0.65 m • 2'-3" × 2'-1.6"

4. **Armchair modern double** • Lounge items
0.68 × 1.24 m • 2'-2.8" × 4'-1"

5. **2 seater sofa**
Lounge items
0.97 × 2.34 m • 3'-2" × 7'-8"

6. **Sofa triple**
Lounge items
0.84 × 1.9 m • 2'-9" × 6'-2.8"

7. **Alcove sofa M**
Lounge items
0.95 × 2.2 m • 3'-1.4" × 7'-2.6"

8. **Sofa alcove light**
Lounge items
0.74 × 2.14 m • 2'-5" × 7'-0.3"

9

Corner sofa basic S
Lounge items
2.4 × 2.4 m • 7'-10.5" × 7'-10.5"

10

Corner sofa basic L
Lounge items
2 × 3.2 m • 6'-6.7" × 10'-6"

11

Couch circular module • Lounge items
0.97 × 1.07 m • 3'-2" × 3'-6"

12

Couch circular module • Lounge items
1 × 1.14 m • 3'-3.4" × 3'-8.9"

13

Couch module L
Lounge items
0.72 × 1.32 m • 2'-4.3" × 4'-4"

14

Couch module S
Lounge items
0.72 × 0.66 m • 2'-4.3" × 2'-2"

15

Modular circular S
Lounge items
0.56 × 0.87 m • 1'-10" × 2'-10"

16

Modular circular M
Lounge items
0.7 × 1.62 m • 2'-3.6" × 5'-3.8"

Kit for an
Office Bathroom

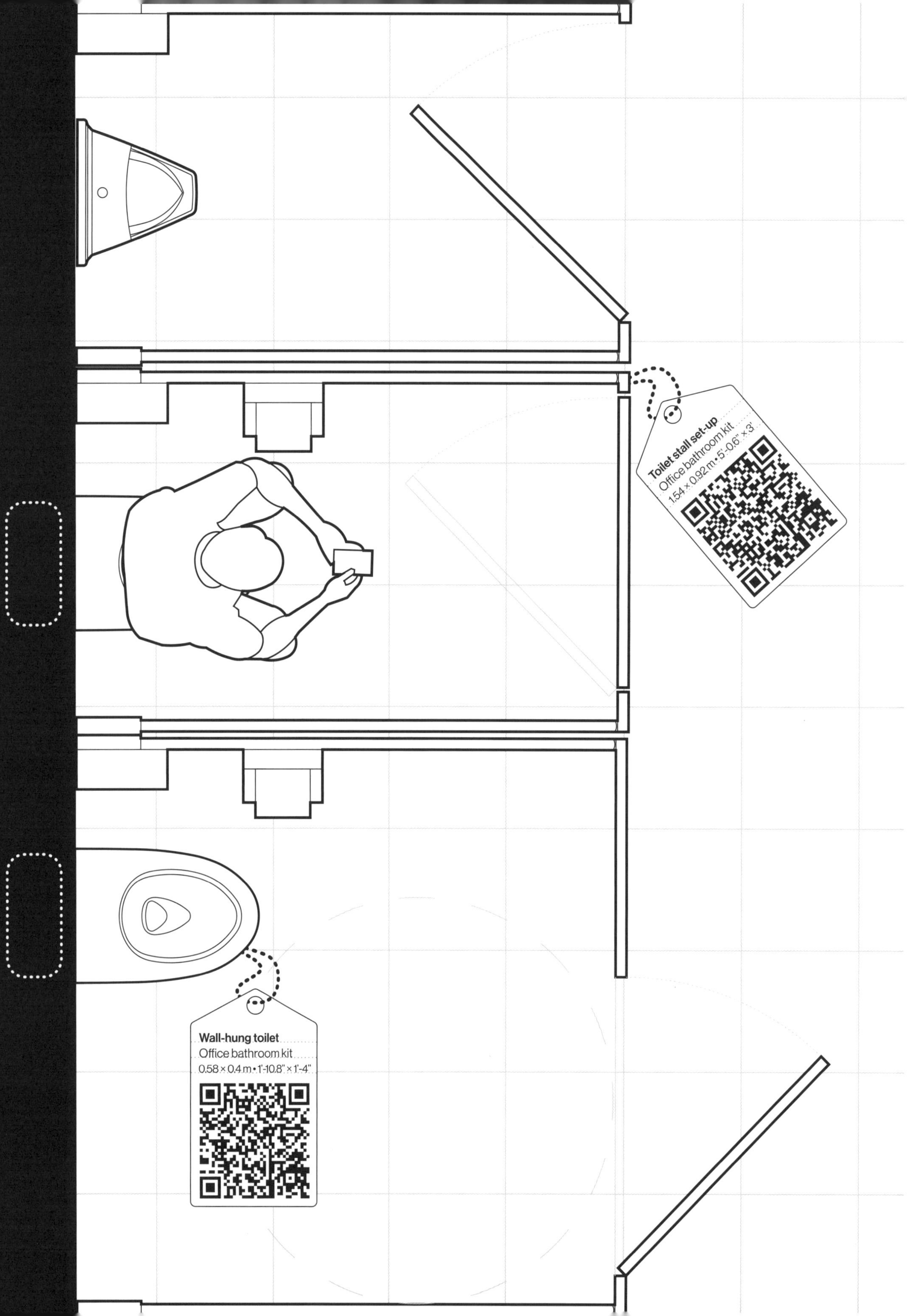
Toilet stall set-up
Office bathroom kit
1.54 × 0.92 m • 5'-0.6" × 3'
Wall-hung toilet
Office bathroom kit
0.58 × 0.4 m • 1'-10.8" × 1'-4"

Bathroom sink
Office bathroom kit
0.47 × 0.58 m • 1'-6.5" × 1'-11"

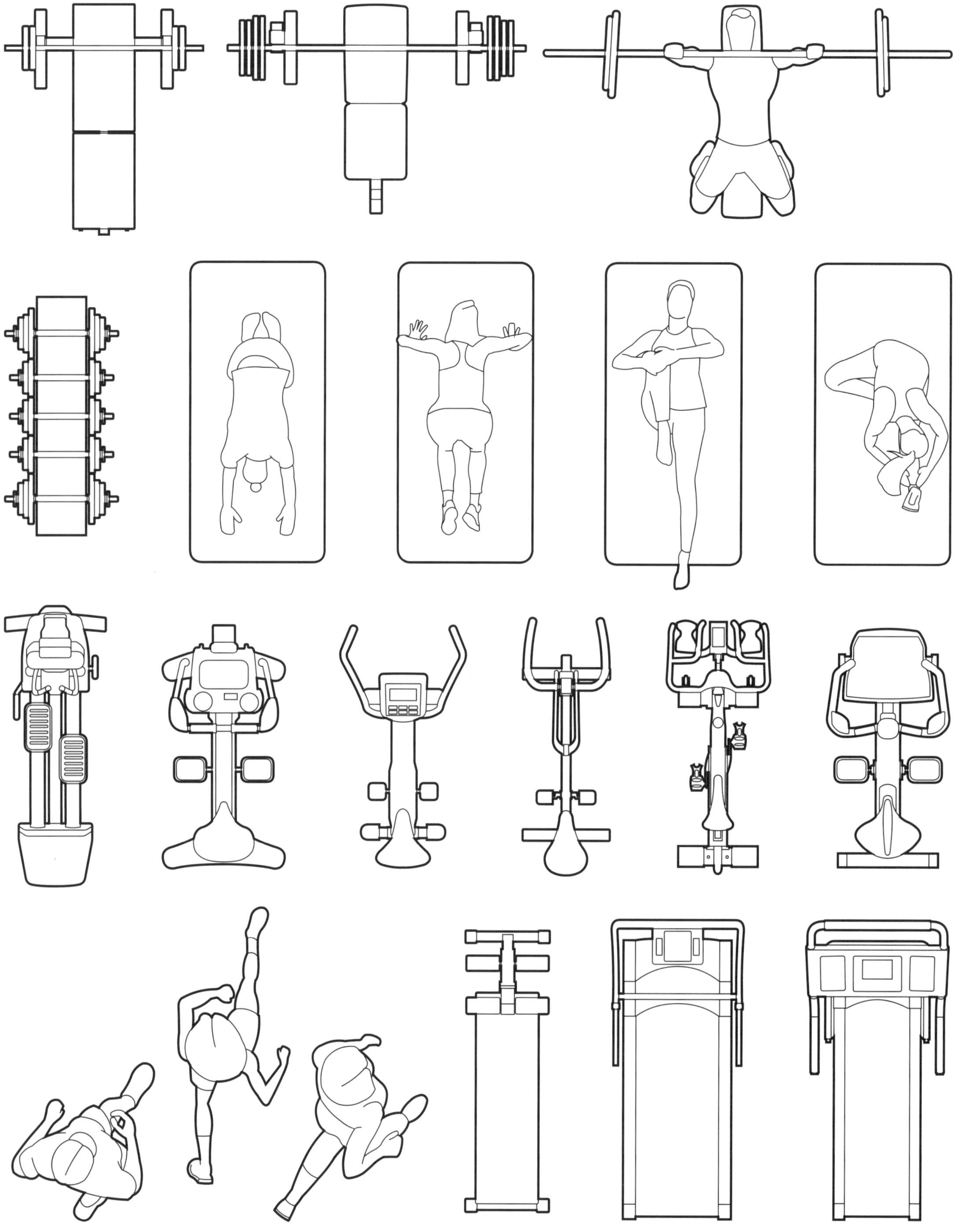

Kit for a
Gym Room

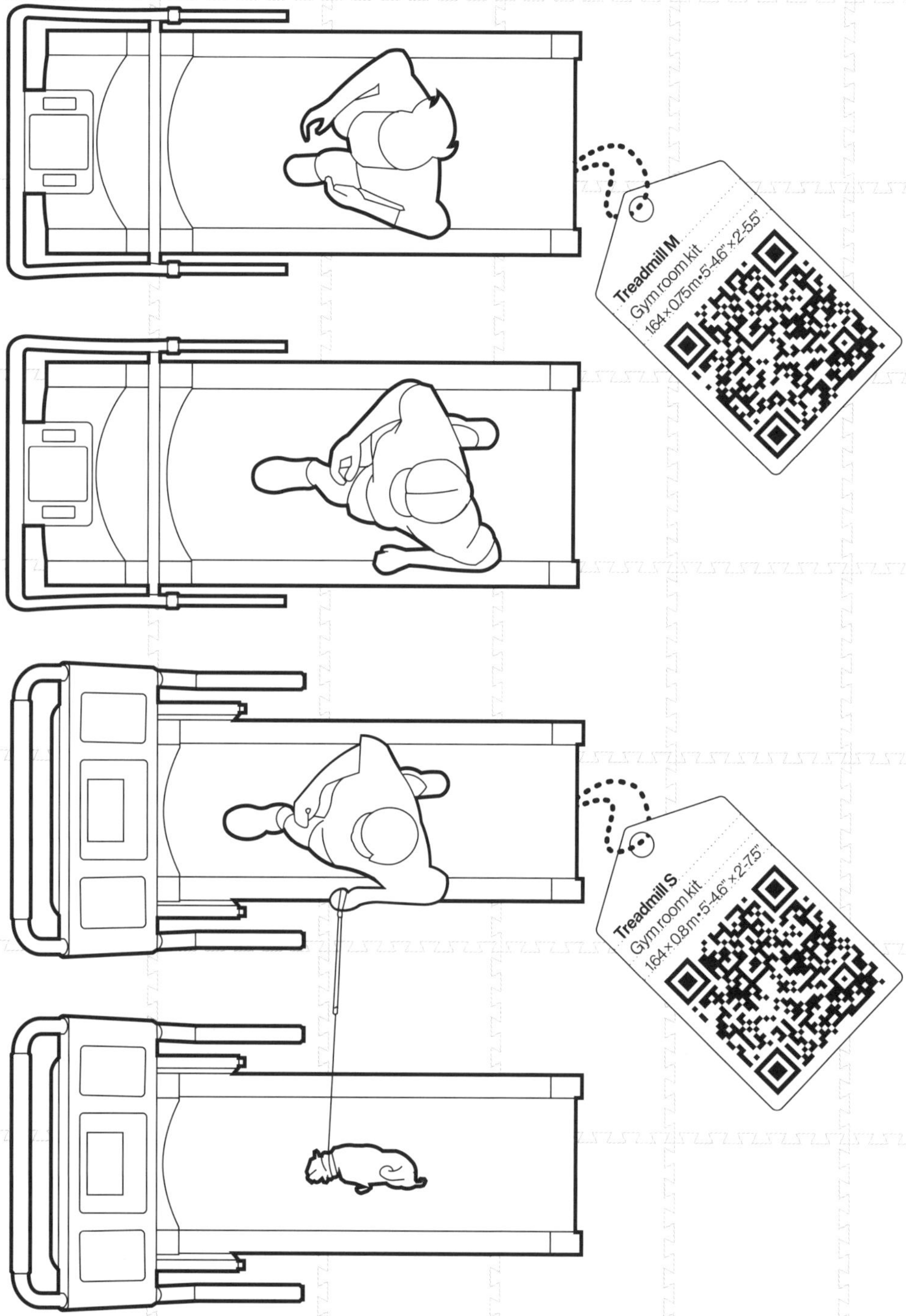
Treadmill M
Gym room kit
1.64 × 0.75 m • 5'-4.6" × 2'-5.5"
Treadmill S
Gym room kit
1.64 × 0.8 m • 5'-4.6" × 2'-7.5"

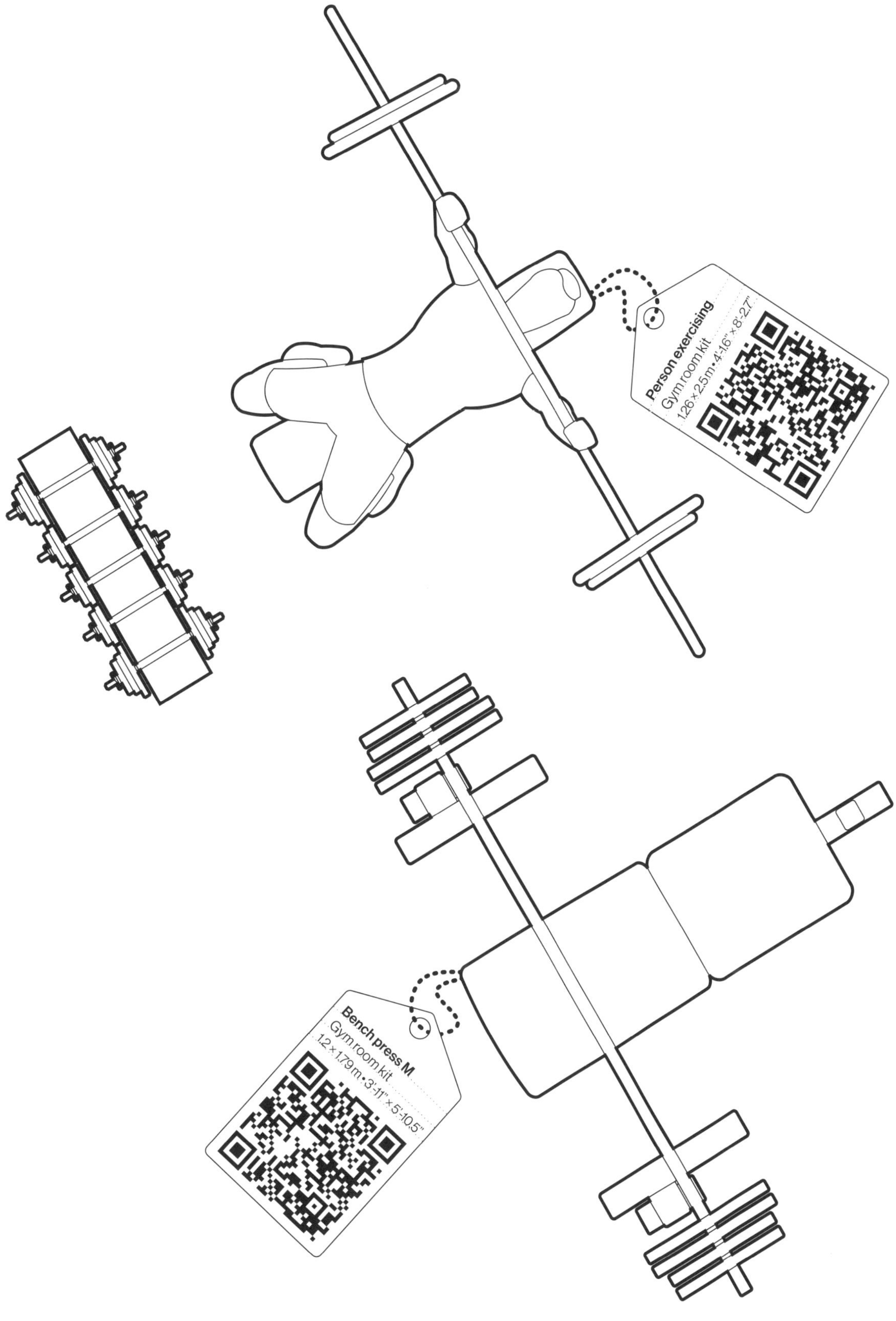
Person exercising
Gym room kit
1.26 × 2.5 m • 4'-1.6" × 8'-2.7"
Bench press M
Gym room kit
1.2 × 1.79 m • 3'-11" × 5'-10.5"

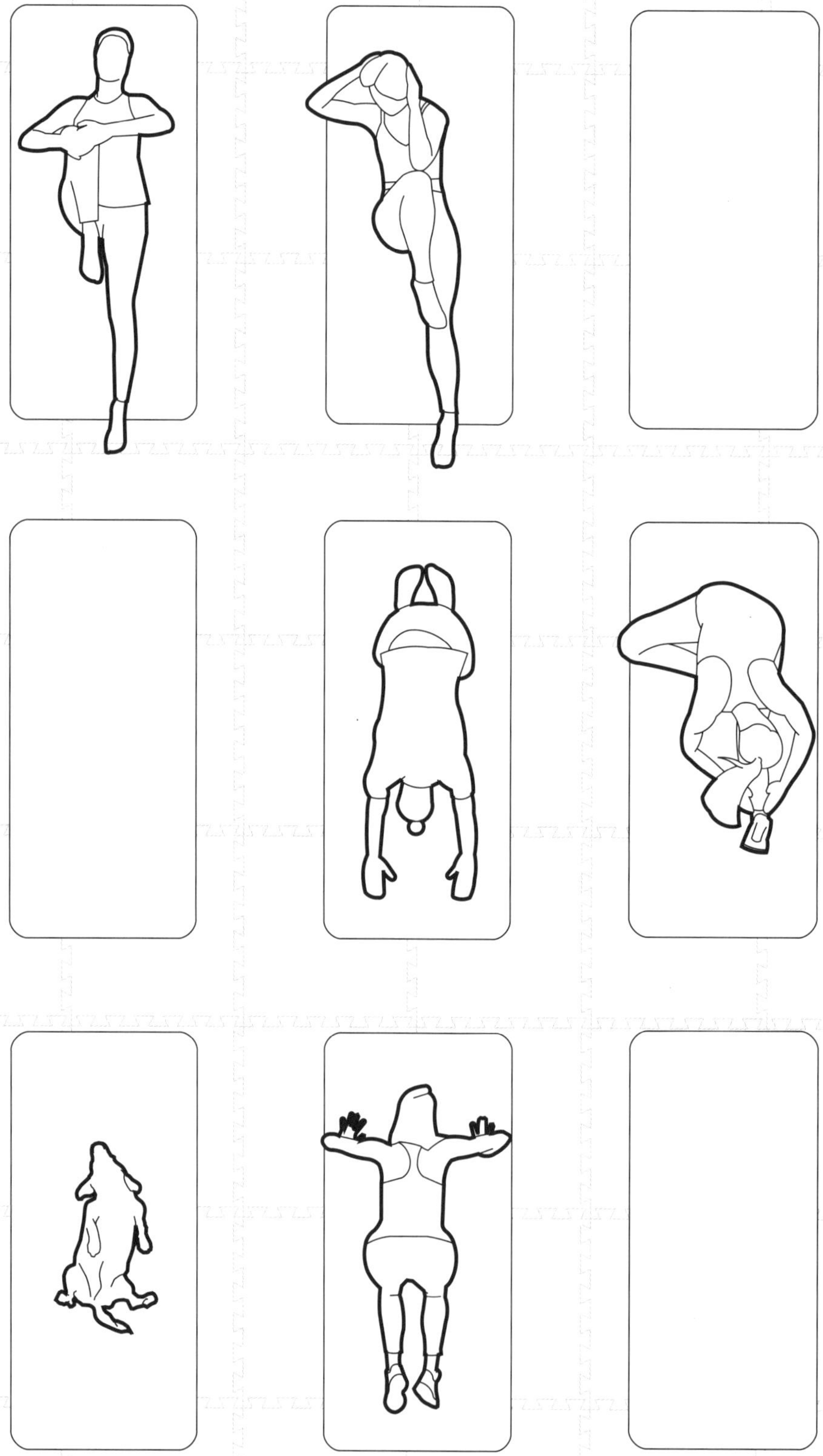

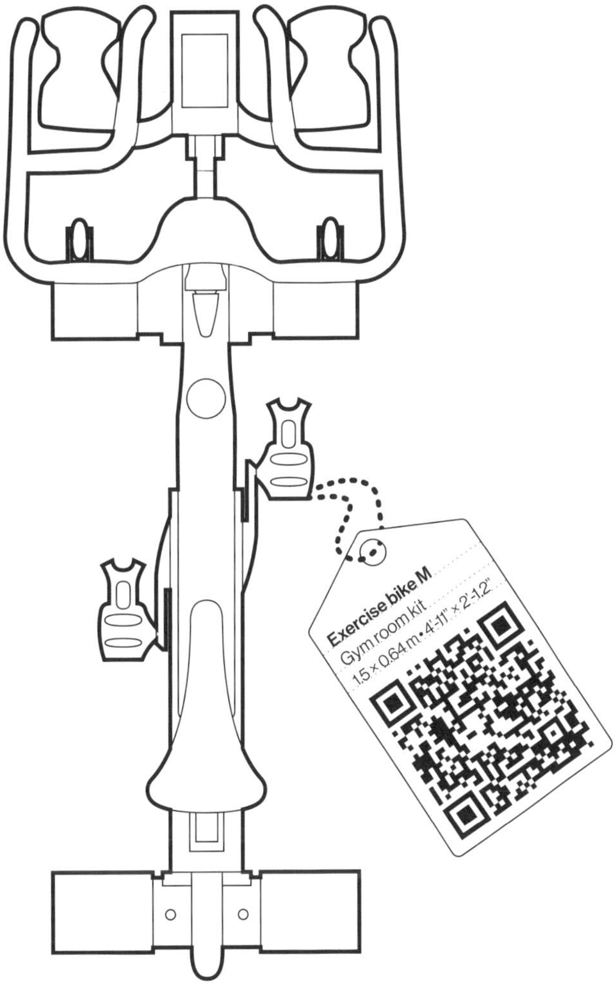
Exercise bike M
Gym room kit
1.5 × 0.64 m • 4'-11" × 2'-1.2"

Kit for a
Recreation Room

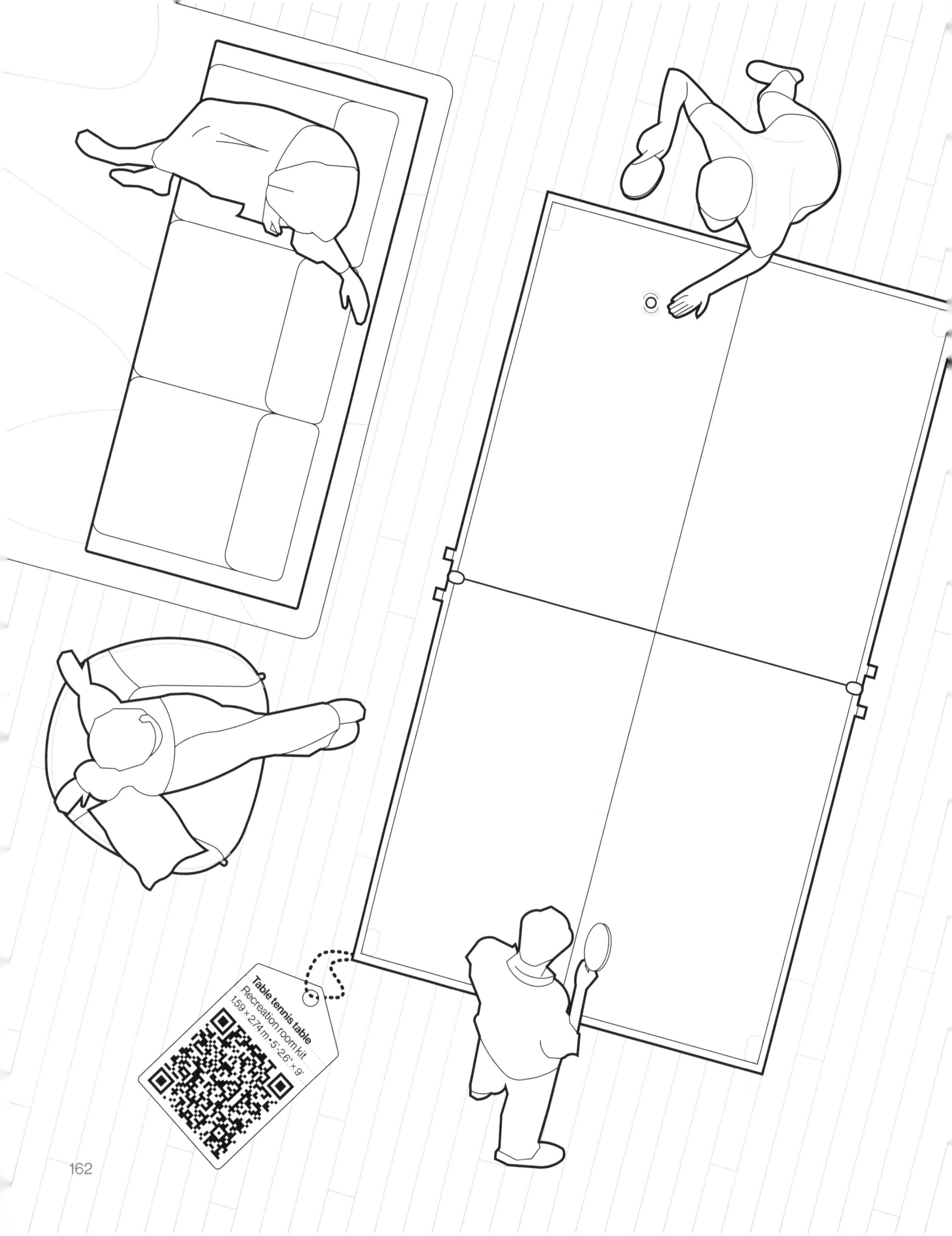
Table tennis table
Recreation room kit
1.59 × 2.74 m • 5'-2.6" × 9'

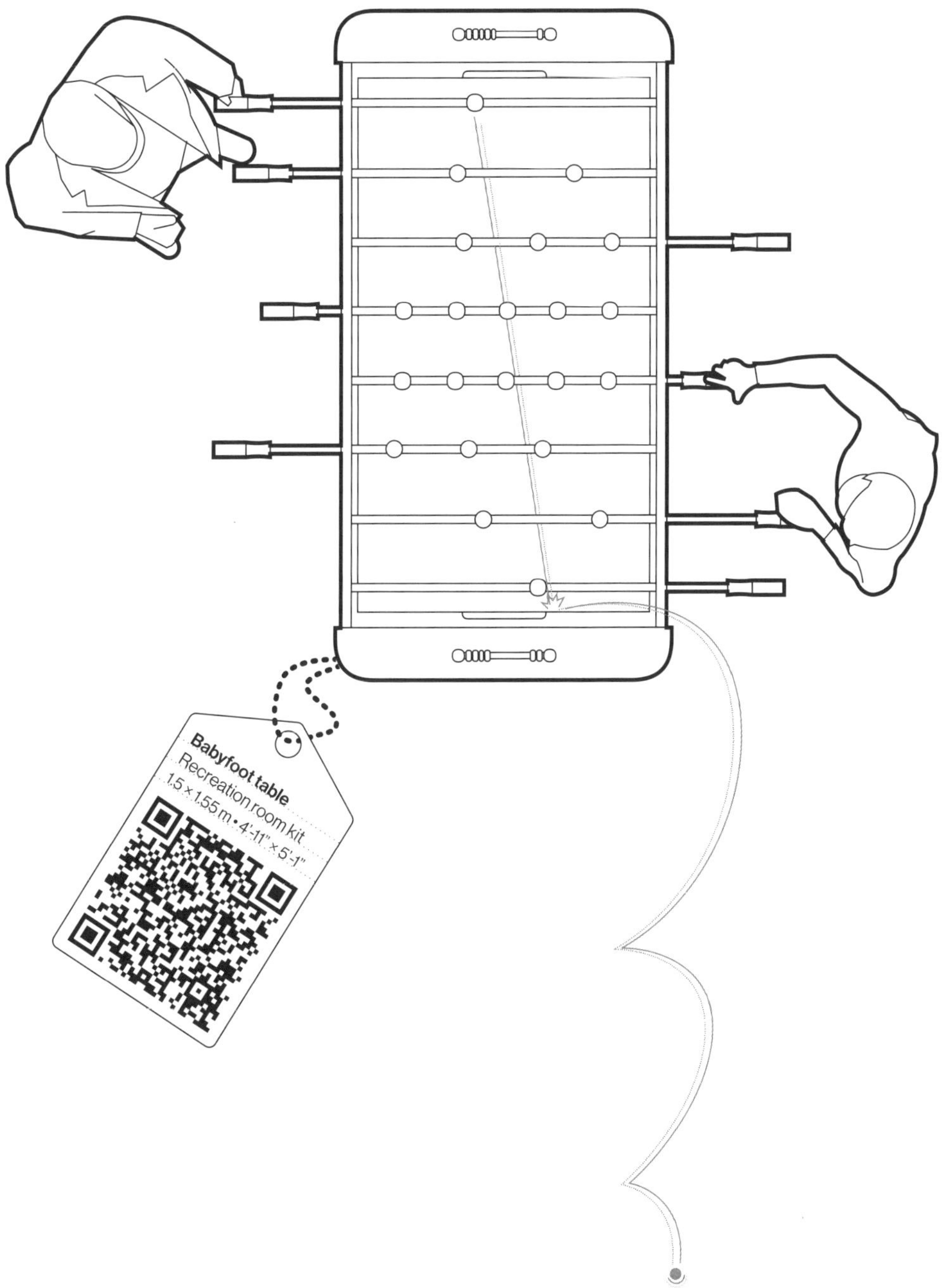
Babyfoot table
Recreation room kit
1.5 × 1.55 m • 4'-11" × 5'-1"

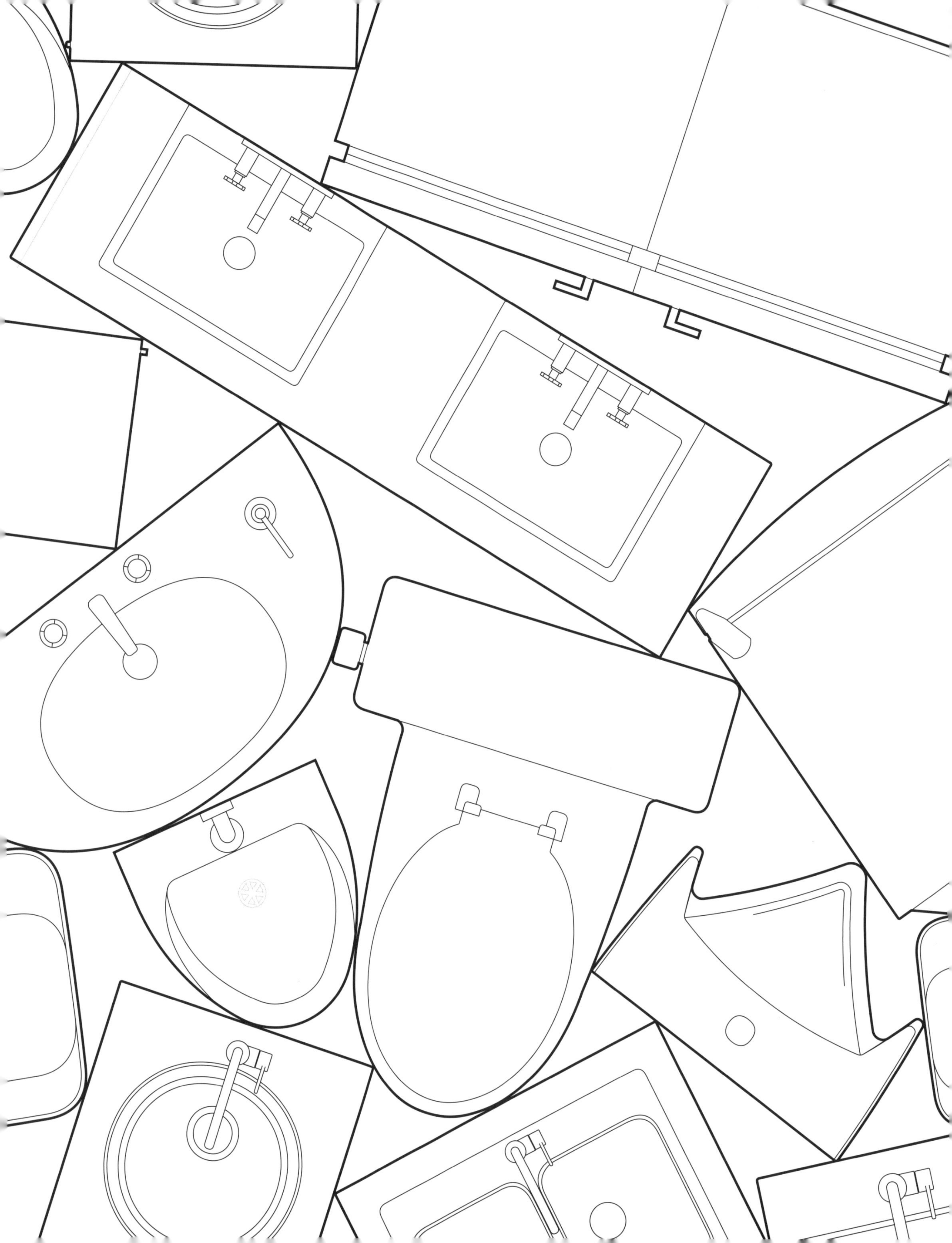

A Catalog of
Office Fixtures

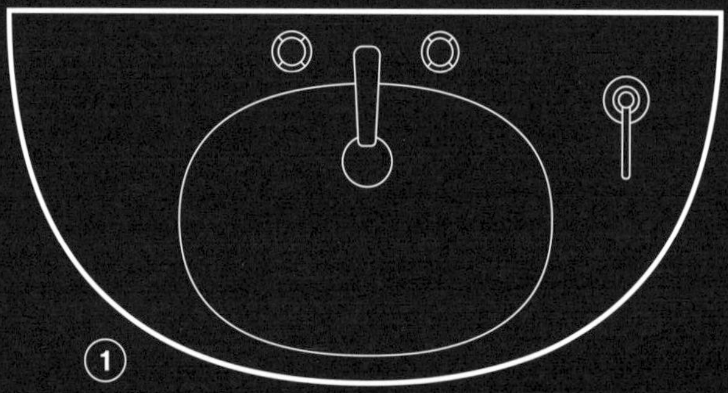

1

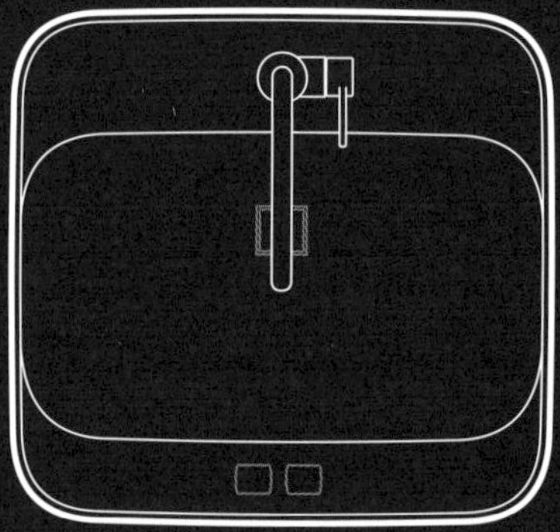

2

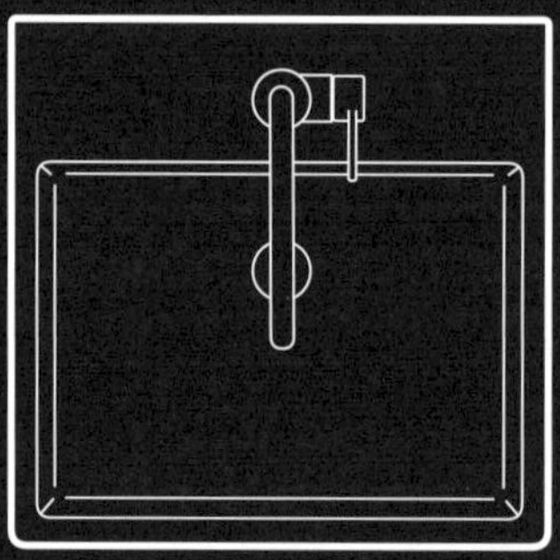

3

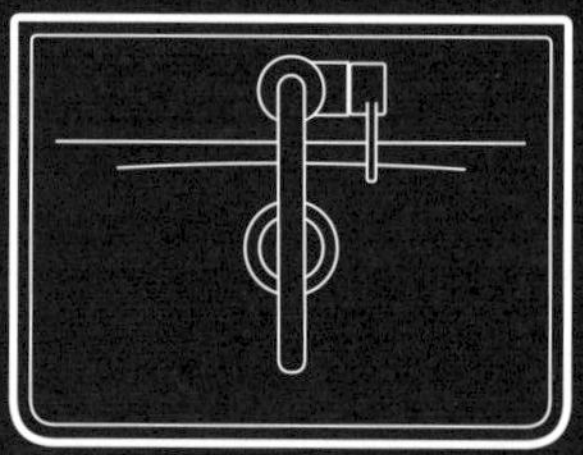

4

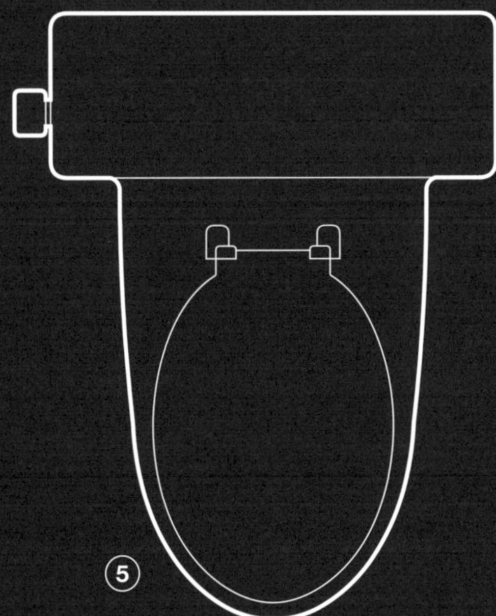

5

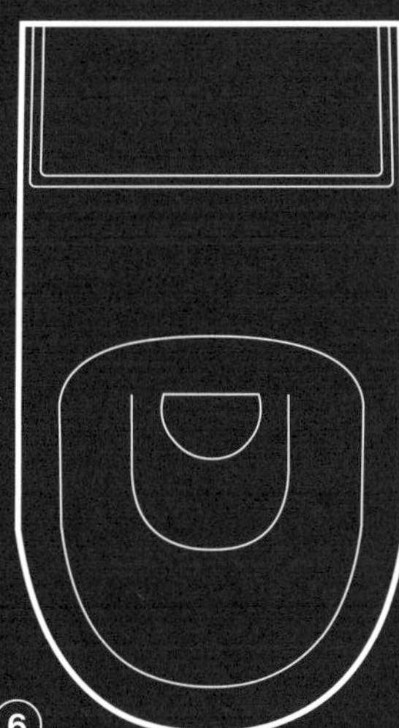

6

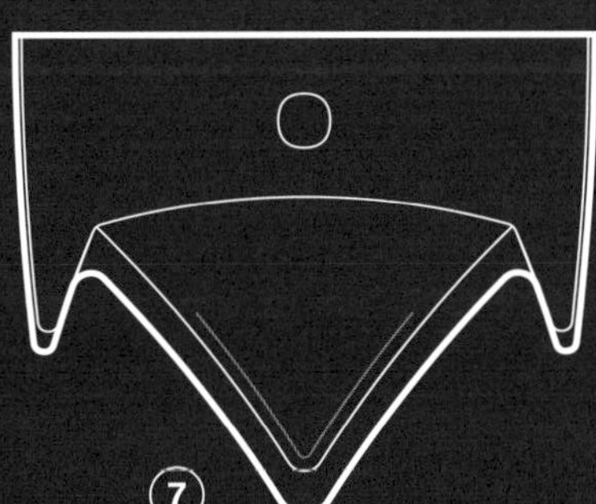

7

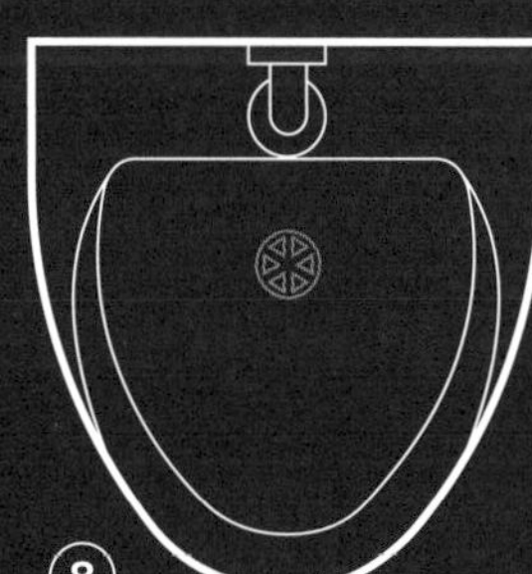

8

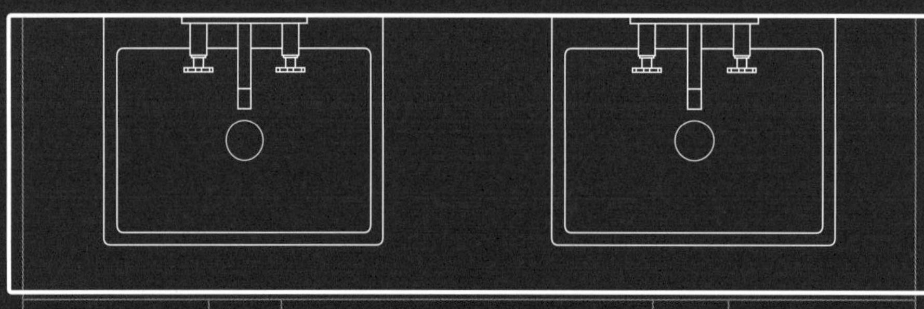

9

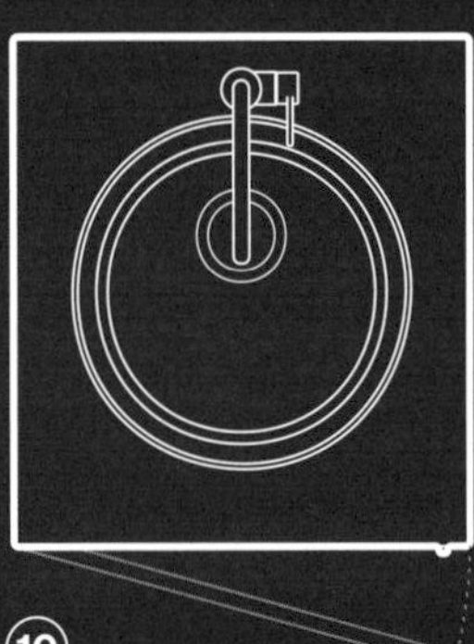

10

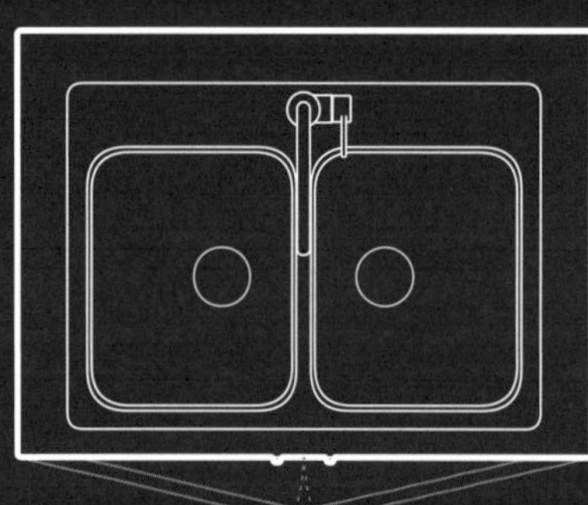

11

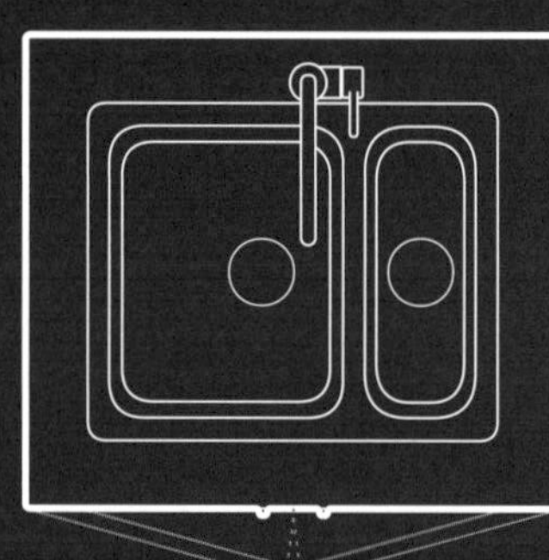

12

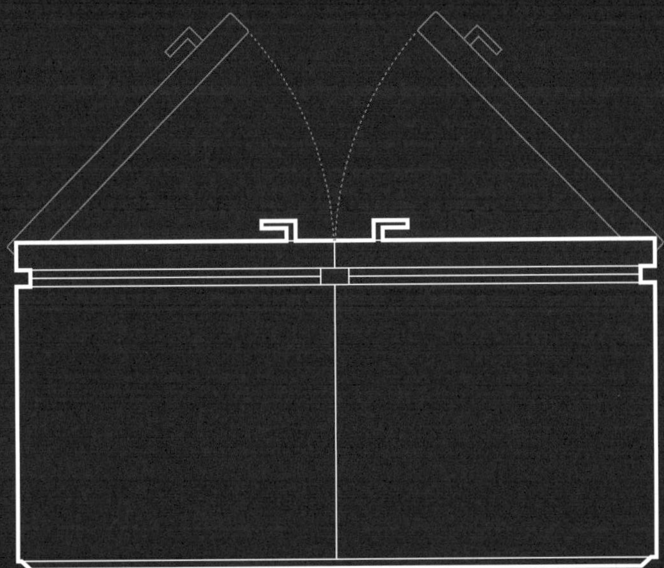

⑬

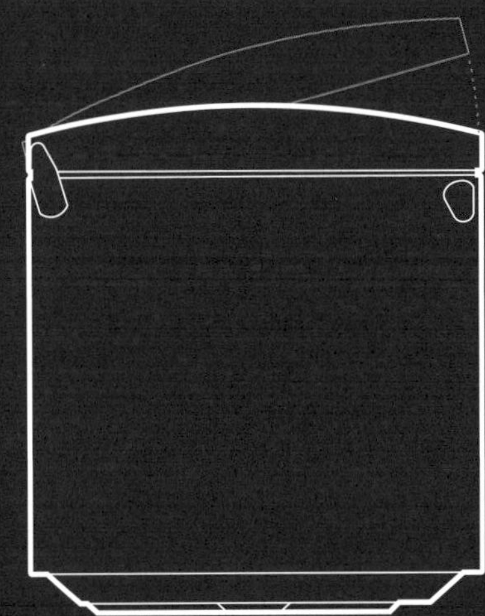

⑭

⑮

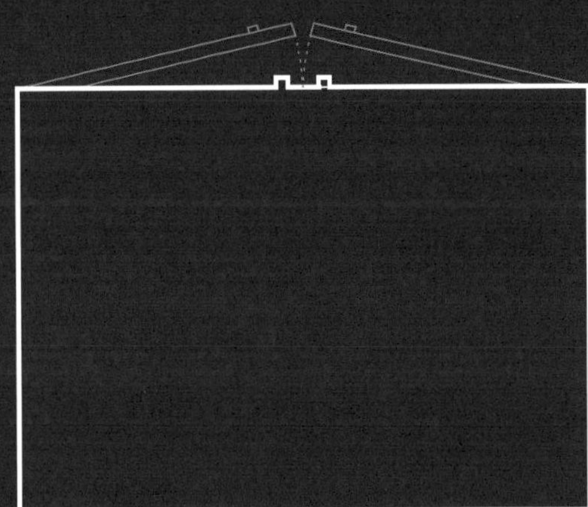

⑯

1 **Round sink**
Office fixtures
0.48 × 0.96 m • 1'-7" × 3'-1.8"

2 **Soft corner sink**
Office fixtures
0.54 × 0.58 m • 1'-9.3" × 1'-10.8"

3 **Rectangular sink S**
Office fixtures
0.47 × 0.5 m • 1'-6.5" × 1'-7.7"

4 **Square sink M**
Office fixtures
0.34 × 0.45 m • 1'-1.4" × 1'-5.7"

5 **Monoblock toilet**
Office fixtures
0.73 × 0.6 m • 2'-4.7" × 2'

6 **Extended wall-hung toilet** • Office fixtures
0.6 × 0.34 m • 2' × 1'-1.4"

7 **Urinal M**
Office fixtures
0.37 × 0.46 m • 1'-2.6" × 1'-6"

8 **Urinal XS**
Office fixtures
0.34 × 0.33 m • 1'-1.4" × 1'-1"

9
Double countertop sink L • Office fixtures
0.57 × 0.96 m • 1'-10.4" × 3'-2"

10
Circular sink
Office fixtures
0.65 × 0.61 m • 2'-1.6" × 2'

11
Double sink
Office fixtures
0.65 × 0.92 m • 2'-1.6" × 3'

12
Sink & a half
Office fixtures
0.65 × 0.76 m • 2'-1.6" × 2'-6"

13
Fridge French door S
Office fixtures
0.59 × 1.2 m • 1'-11.2" × 3'-11.2"

14
Fridge single door
Office fixtures
0.71 × 0.66 m • 2'-4" × 2'-2"

15
Casework M with door • Office fixtures
0.65 × 0.6 m • 2'-1.6" × 1'-11.6"

16
Casework L with door • Office fixtures
0.65 × 0.92 m • 2'-1.6" × 3'

For the House

Beds, Couches, Closets, Bathtubs, etc.

This next chapter addresses the housing typology. As a matter of fact, domestic spaces have undergone significant evolutions over the past decades. The aftermath of the pandemic, the densification of inner-cities, and the evolution of consumption patterns in younger generations have triggered new space-planning practices directly impacting the catalog of items that populate houses today.

To begin with, the rules of separation that applied yesterday within the living areas seem to be being called into question: for one thing, the kitchen has become the definite place for social gathering in the house. Kitchen layouts have thus evolved, offering more openness from single-wall to L-shaped, so as to better integrate with other spaces of the house. 1 p. 221 Conversely, the importance of the **dining room** is being challenged more than ever, and increasingly gets replaced by the kitchen table. Overall, the living area is finalizing a journey initiated during the last century, when the kitchen and living room boundary was lifted to offer a single continuous day zone.

The evolution of technology has also entirely 2 p. 255 overhauled the set of **appliances** and electronic devices that populated houses yesterday. **Kitchen** appliances have significantly shrunk, while desktop computers have disappeared in most cases. 3 p. 239 Screens have "flattened," and lost their box-like aspect, while freeing up space at the same time. This miniaturization of appliances and devices has significantly toned down the visual presence of electronic devices in interiors. If not miniaturized, some devices have even been removed from the domestic interior catalog. With the democratization of smartphones, for instance, fixed phones have disappeared, and with them the space dedicated to them in the household. The gradual obsolescence of the TV, caused by the shift of younger generations towards streaming platforms, has had its influence on space layout. **Couches and armchairs**, once turned 4 p. 229 towards a single wall, are getting back to circular layout, while the very idea of a living room is starting to accommodate more general and daily usages.

The pandemic has also left its mark on housing space planning. Workers have brought work back into domesticity. The need of individuals to find calm in a secluded part of the house has put the contemporary housing space plan under pressure. Either through 5 p. 225 a dedicated **home office**, or by introducing office-like furnishing in living areas, people have found ways to introduce work into their house. Conversely, the retrofitting of housing layouts to welcome work during daytime has had its impact on the catalog of typical domestic furniture.

More importantly, economic factors have significantly conditioned housing space planning over the past decades. New, more reasoned consumption patterns have found in second hand furniture ways to fill spaces more sustainably. Flea market items and antiques are an increasing presence in interiors, and are used alongside more contemporary pieces of furniture. At the same time, the emphasis on healthier interior design has also revived the public's interest in indoor greenery, adding plants 6 p. 215 to day areas (**living rooms**, etc.). To complement these trends, growing inner-city real estate prices and urban concentration have placed housing space planning under acute pressure. The importance of space optimization in current design practices 7 p. 297 has revived an interest in **storage** compactness, modular furnishing and space optimization.

Despite the winds of change that are having an impact on housing today, one timeless principle remains: the prevalence of context. Between an inner-city apartment and suburban house, the curation of rooms that constitutes the program will vary drastically. This heterogeneity of housing typologies trickles down to the catalog of items used to fill these spaces: overall, the palette of housing furniture remains fairly diverse, and differs a lot from one typology of house to the next.

That is why, in the chapter that follows, we have done our best to curate as wide a set of relevant furniture items as possible, to help designers tackle most types of housing typologies. At the same time, within each room type, new objects and dimensions have been introduced to reflect the trends and evolution explained above.

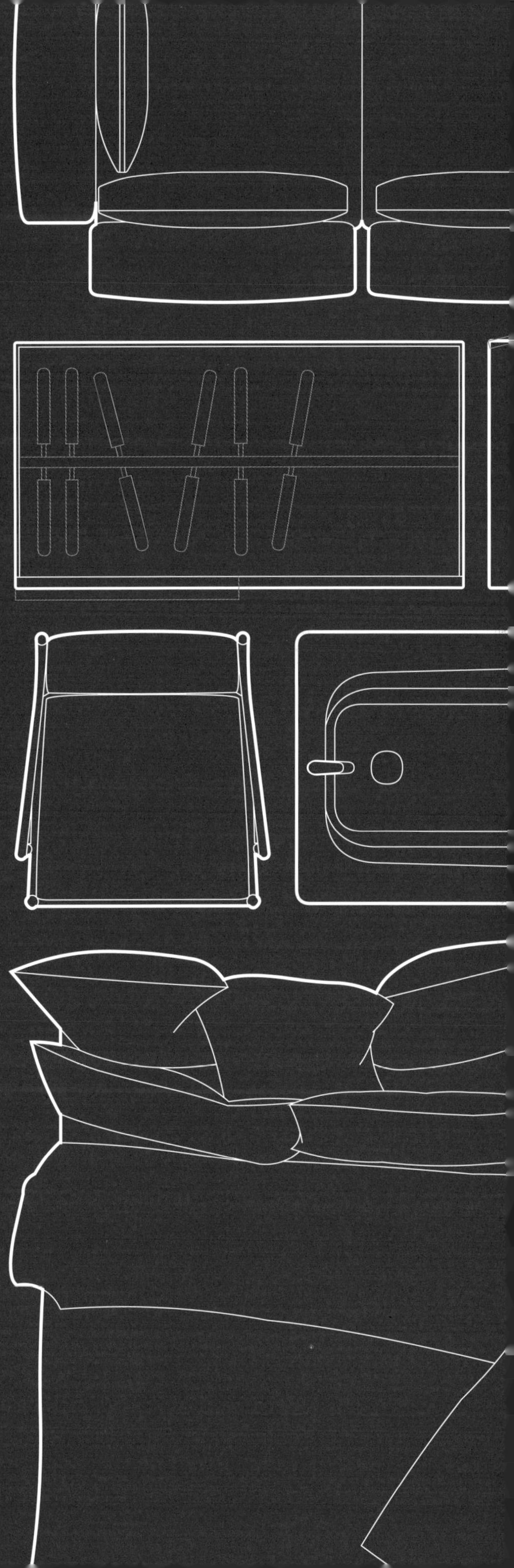

dimension
dimension
dimension
dimension
dimension
dimension
dimension
dimension
dimension
dimension
dimension
dimension
dimension
dimension
dimension
dimension
dimension
dimension
dimension
dimension
dimension
dimension
dimension

Dimensions

1 m • 3'-3"
1.5 m • 4'-11"
0.58 m • 1'-11"
2.2 m • 7'-3"
1.22 m • 4'
Single bed
Couple bed - S
Kid bed
3.29 m • 10'-9"
0.62 m • 2'-1/2"
1.9 m • 6'-3"
1.73 m • 5'-8"
0.43 m • 1'-5"
0.45 m • 1'-6"
1.95 m • 6'-5"
2.1 m • 6'-11"
Couple bed - L

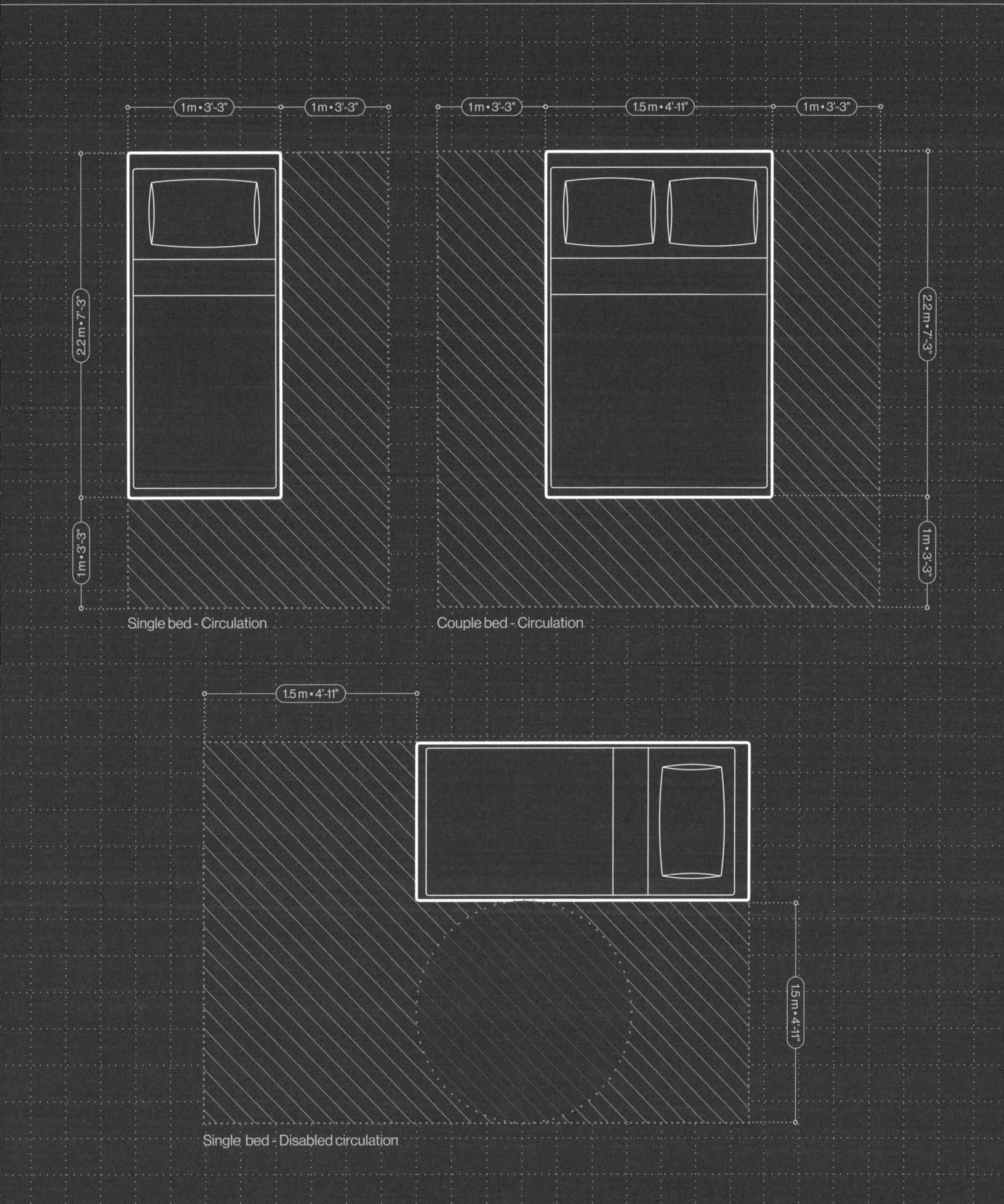
1m • 3'-3"
1m • 3'-3"
2.2m • 7'-3"
1m • 3'-3"
Single bed - Circulation
1m • 3'-3"
1.5m • 4'-11"
1m • 3'-3"
2.2m • 7'-3"
1m • 3'-3"
Couple bed - Circulation
1.5m • 4'-11"
1.5m • 4'-11"
Single bed - Disabled circulation

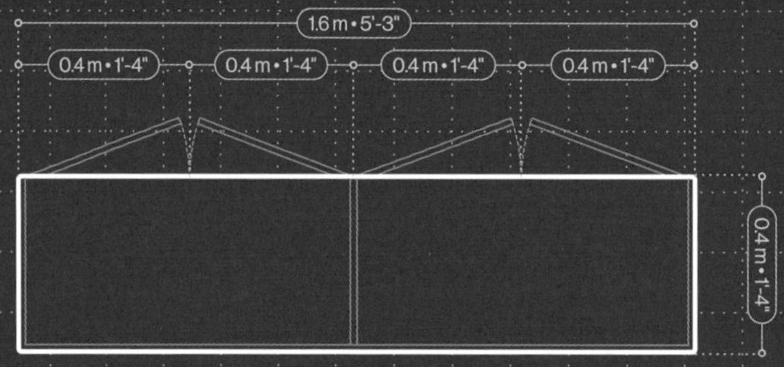

Closet - Pivot doors - S

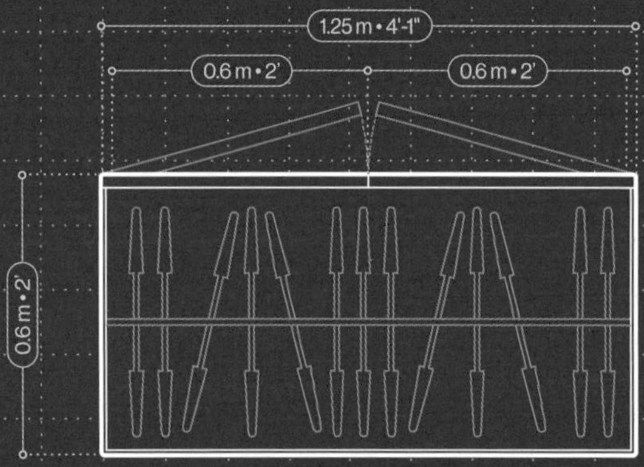

Closet - Pivot doors - M

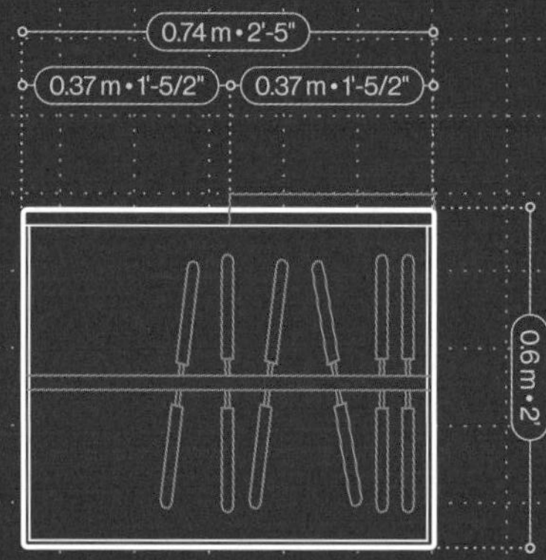

Closet - Sliding doors

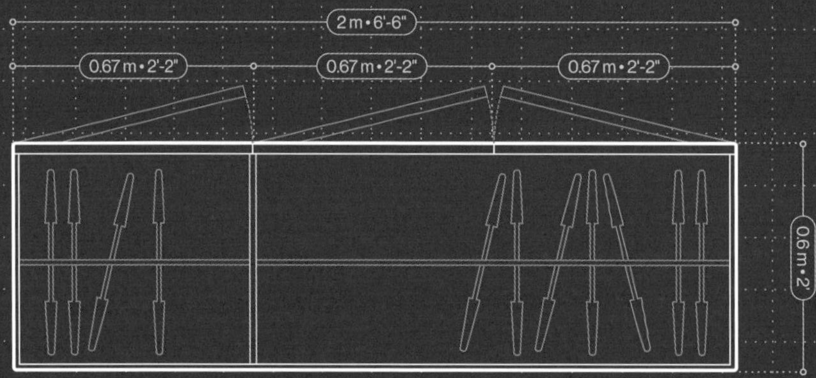

Closet - Pivot doors - L

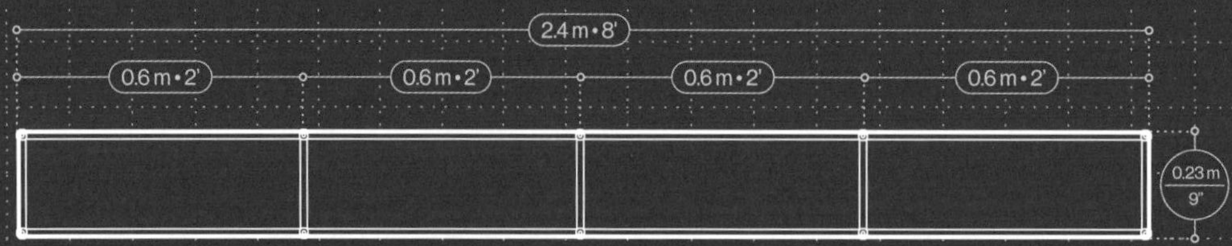

Shelf

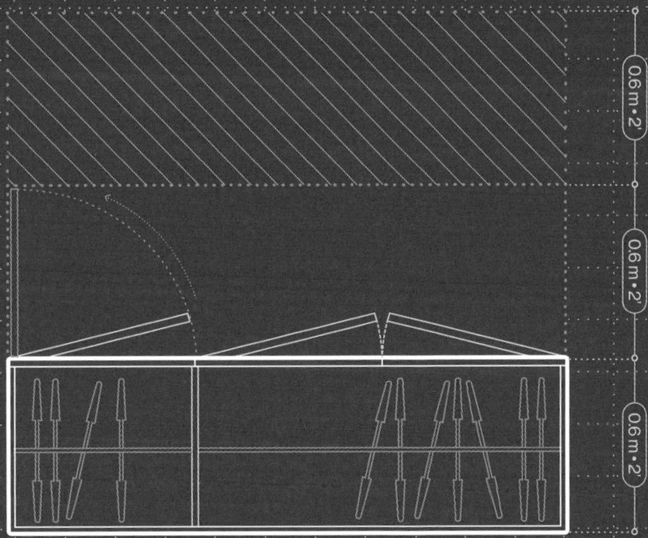

Closet - Pivot doors

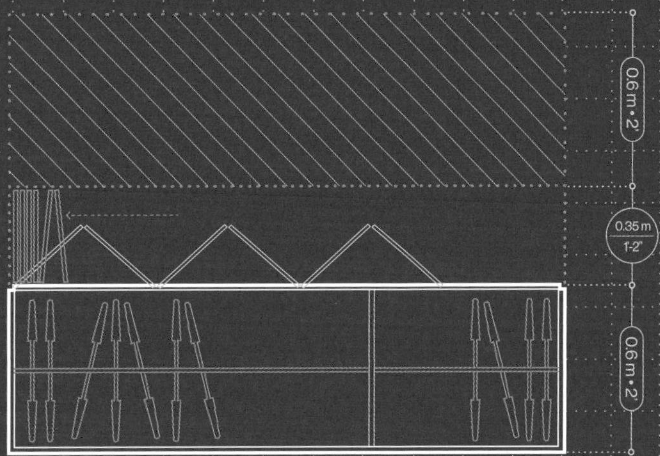

Closet - Folding doors

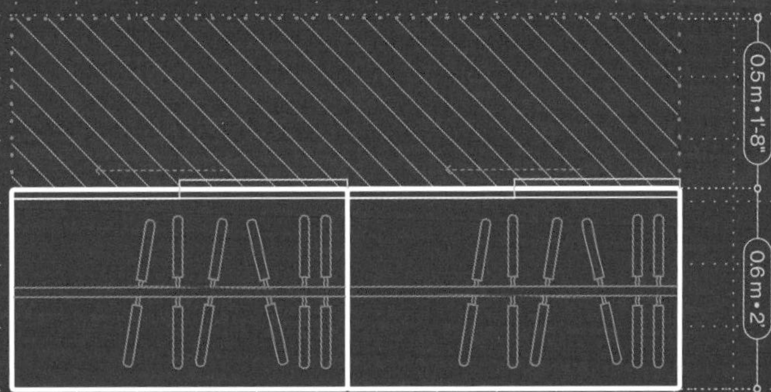

Closet - Sliding doors

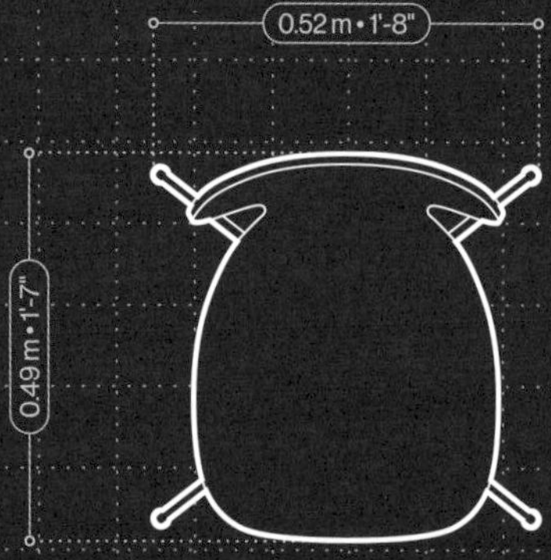

Light chair

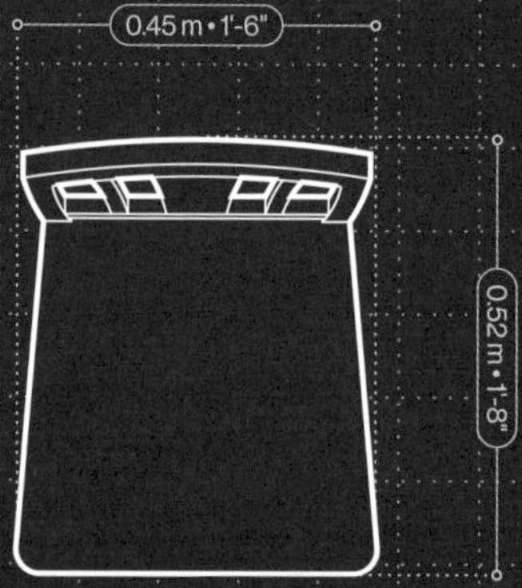

Slat chair

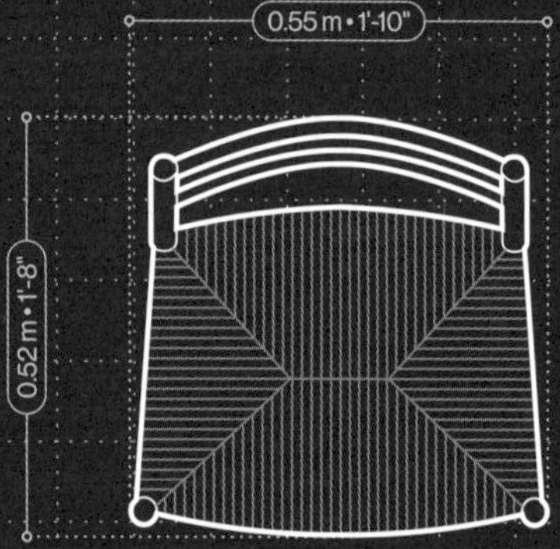

Cane chair

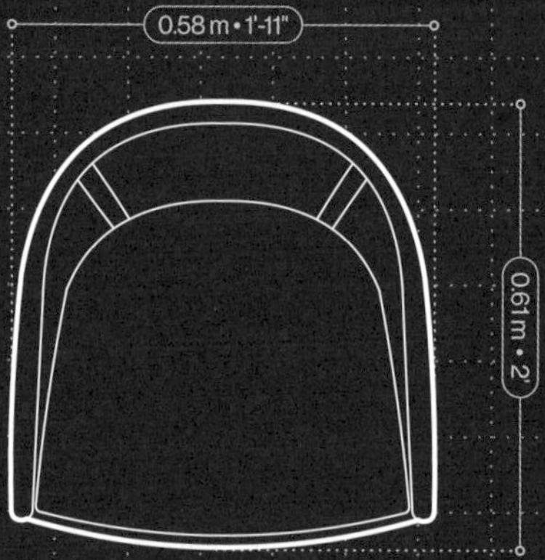

Windsor chair

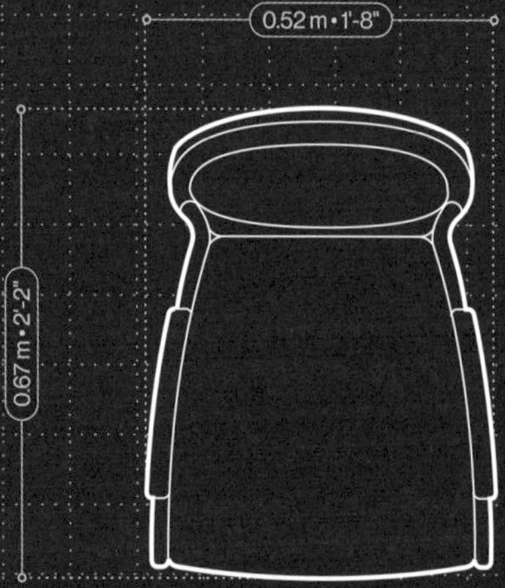

Classic chair

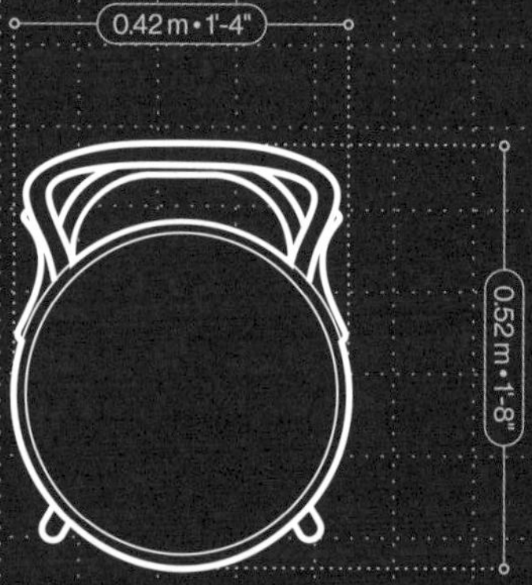

Bentwood chair

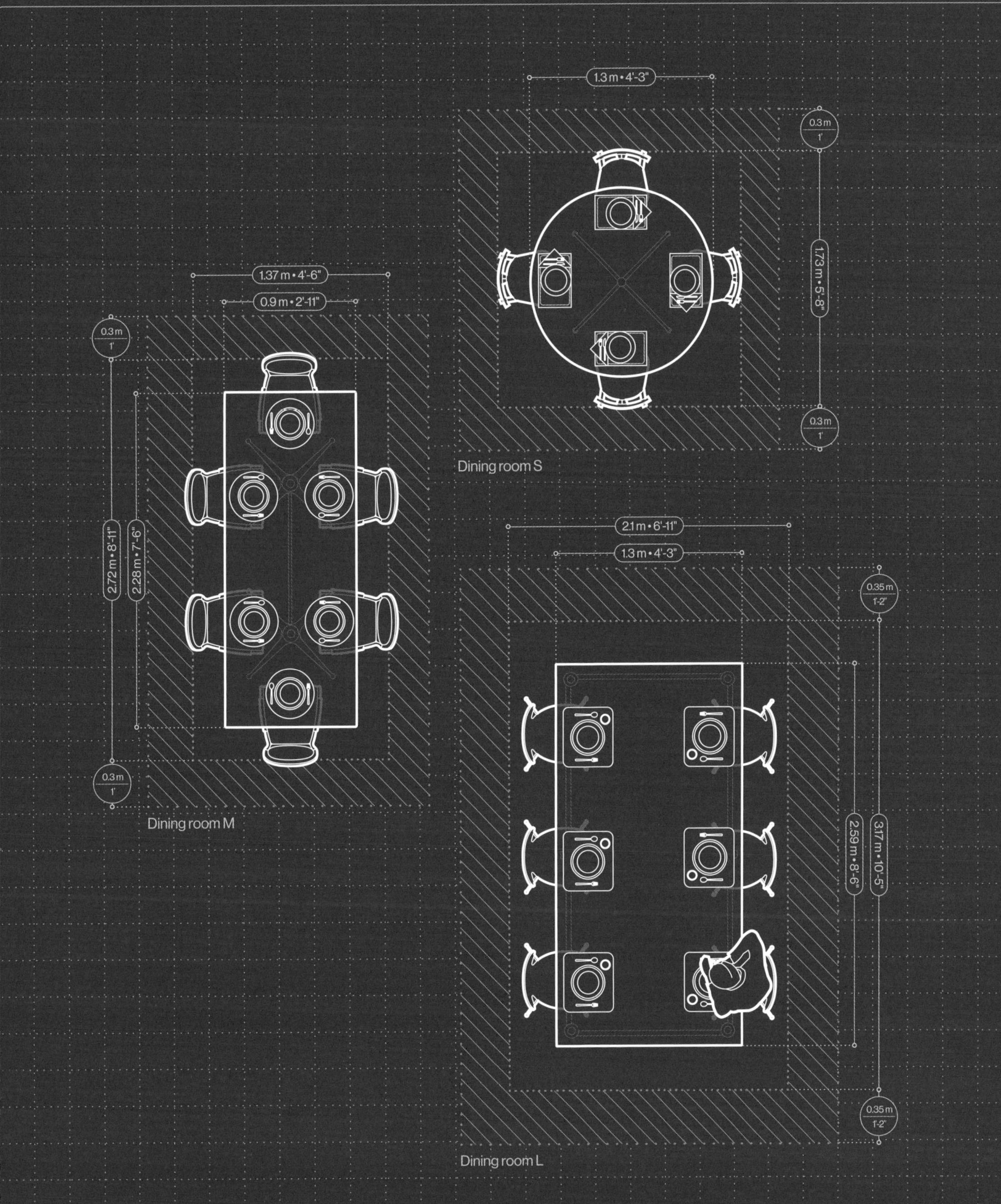

1.3 m • 4'-3"
0.3 m
1'
1.73 m • 5'-8"
0.3 m
1'
Dining room S
1.37 m • 4'-6"
0.9 m • 2'-11"
0.3 m
1'
2.72 m • 8'-11"
2.28 m • 7'-6"
0.3 m
1'
Dining room M
2.1 m • 6'-11"
1.3 m • 4'-3"
0.35 m
1'-2"
2.59 m • 8'-6"
3.17 m • 10'-5"
0.35 m
1'-2"
Dining room L

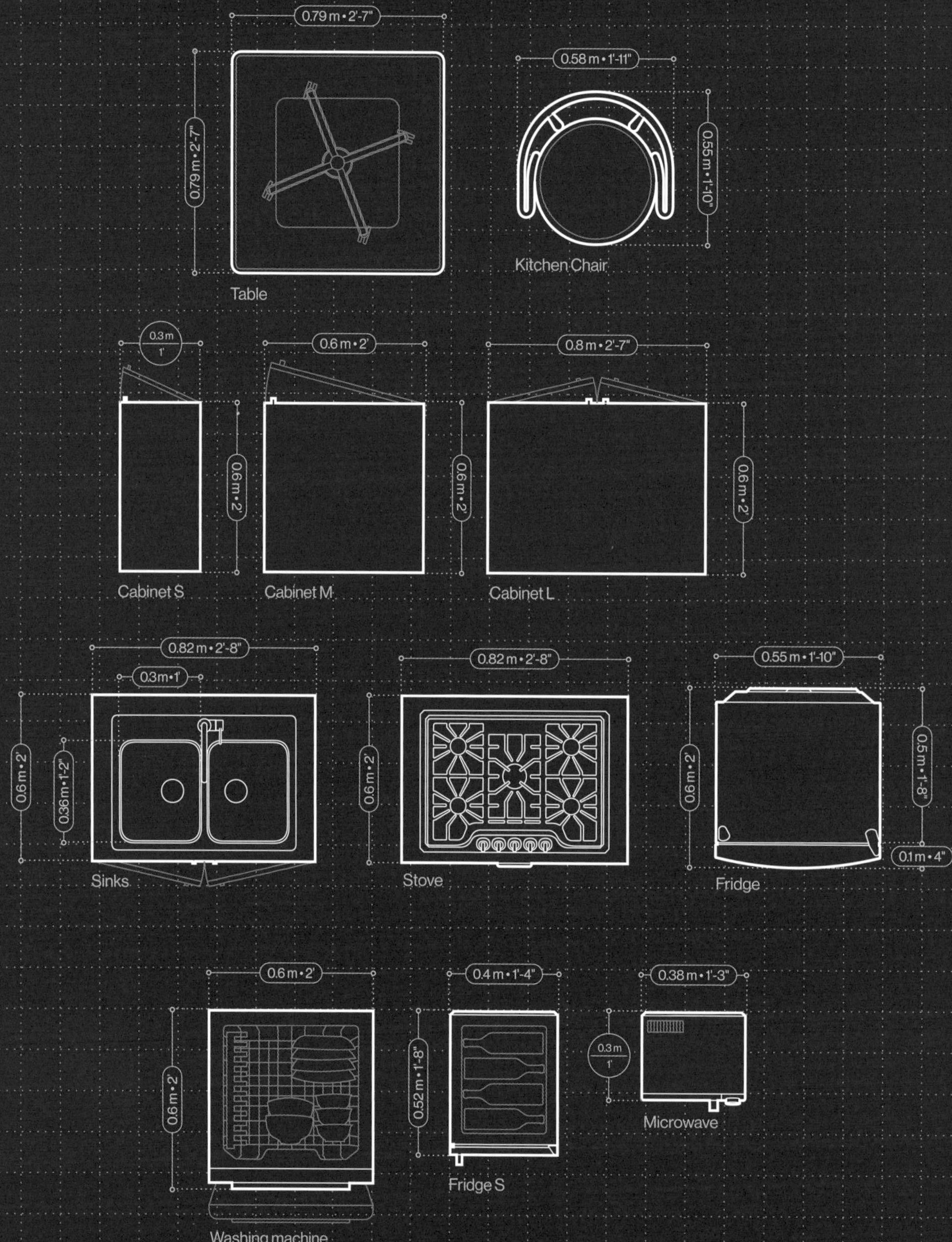

Kitchen Items

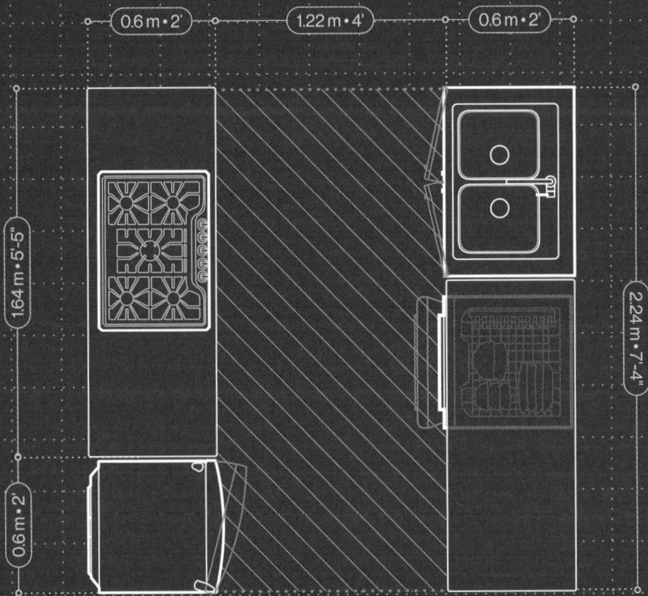

Gallery kitchen

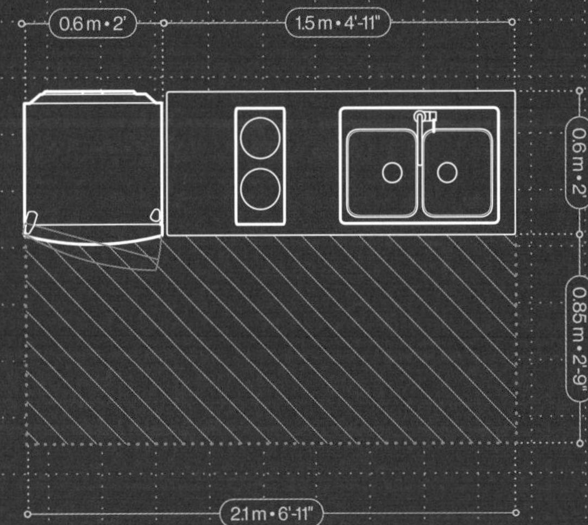

Wall kitchen

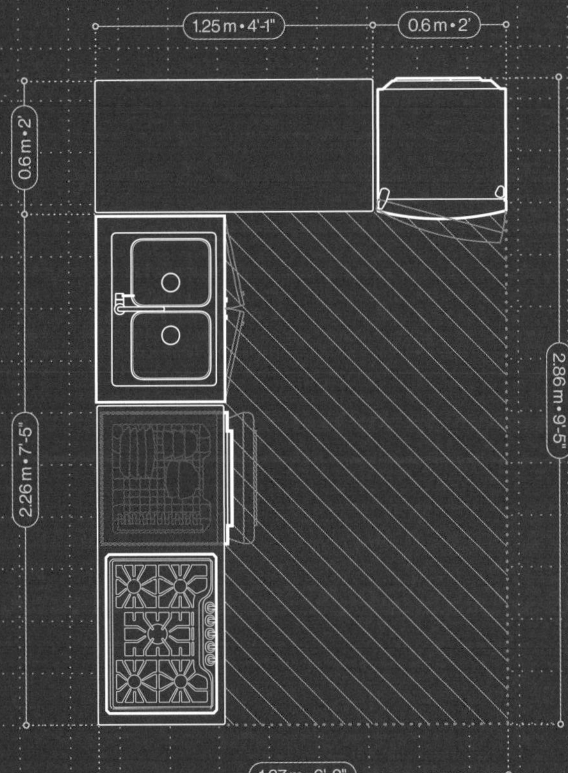

Corner kitchen

U-shaped kitchen

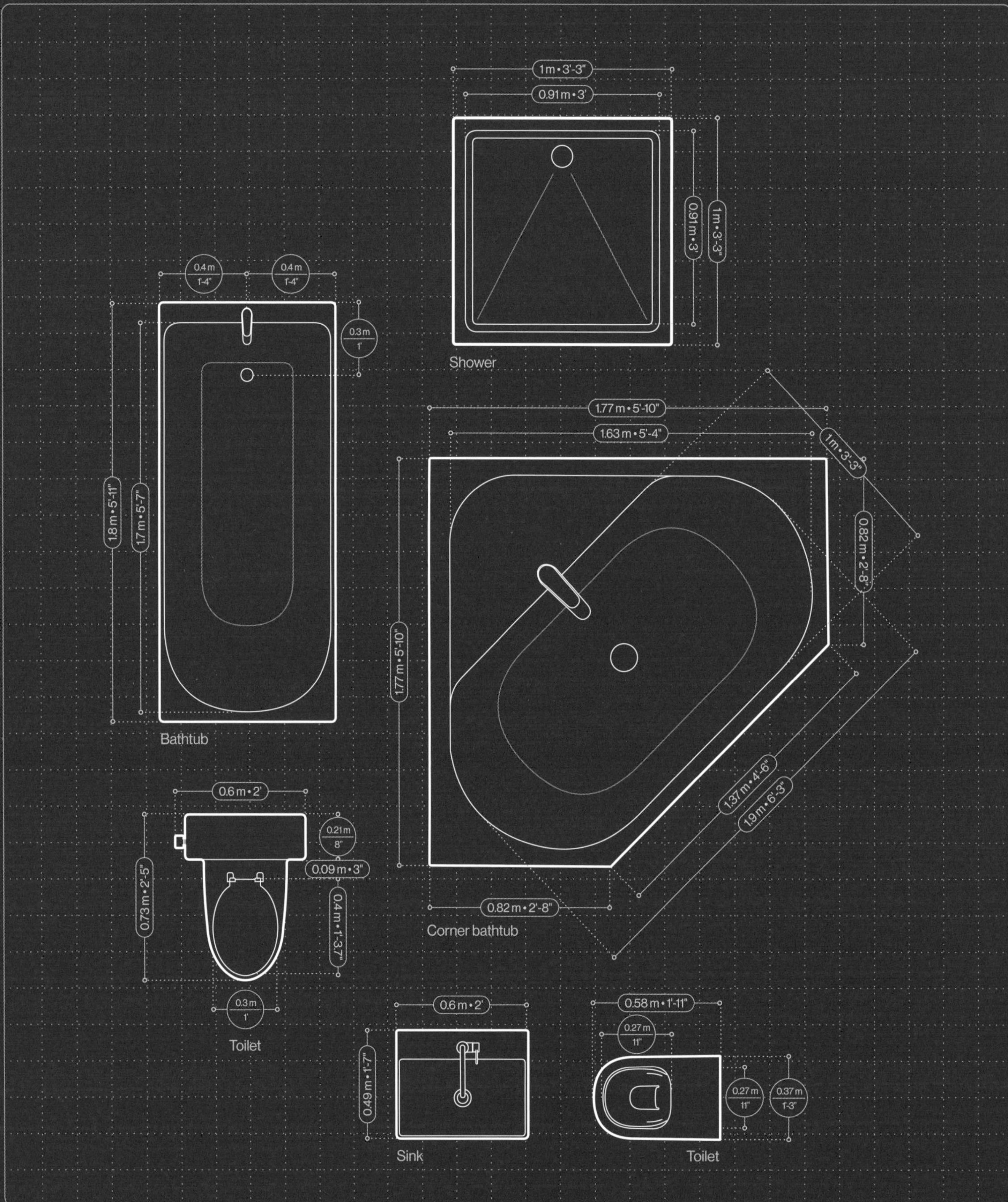

Bathroom Fixtures

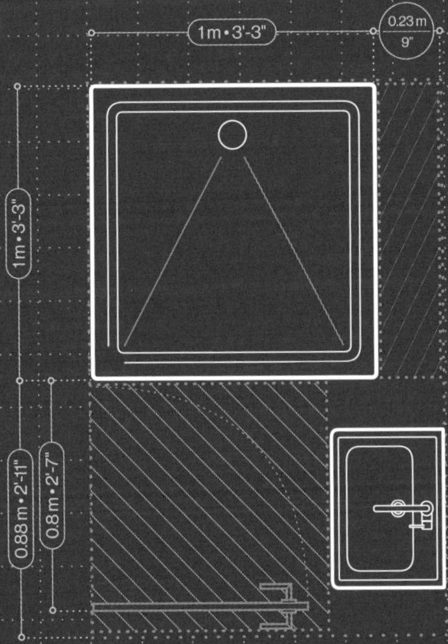

Shower room layout

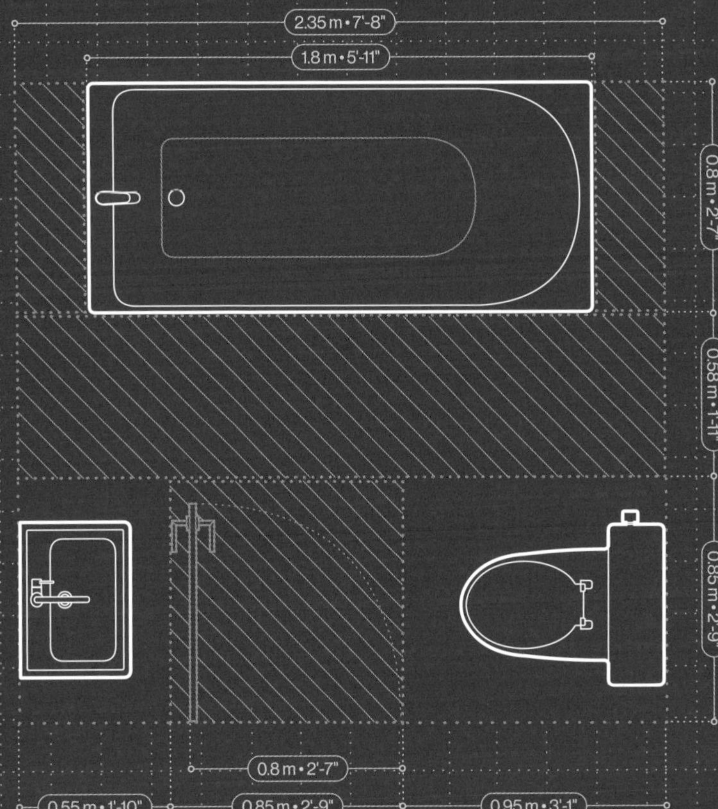

Bathroom layout

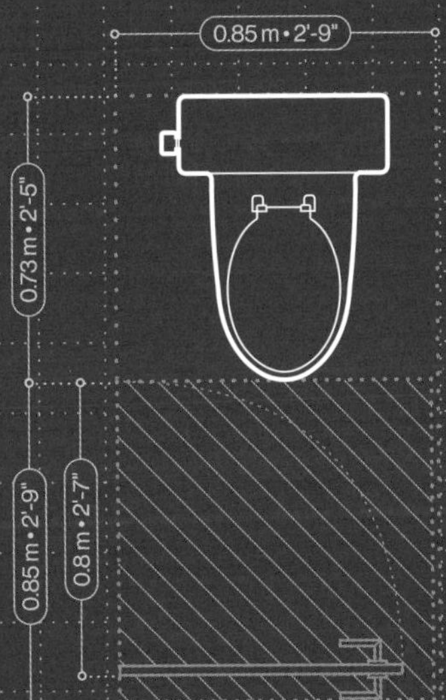

Toilet layout

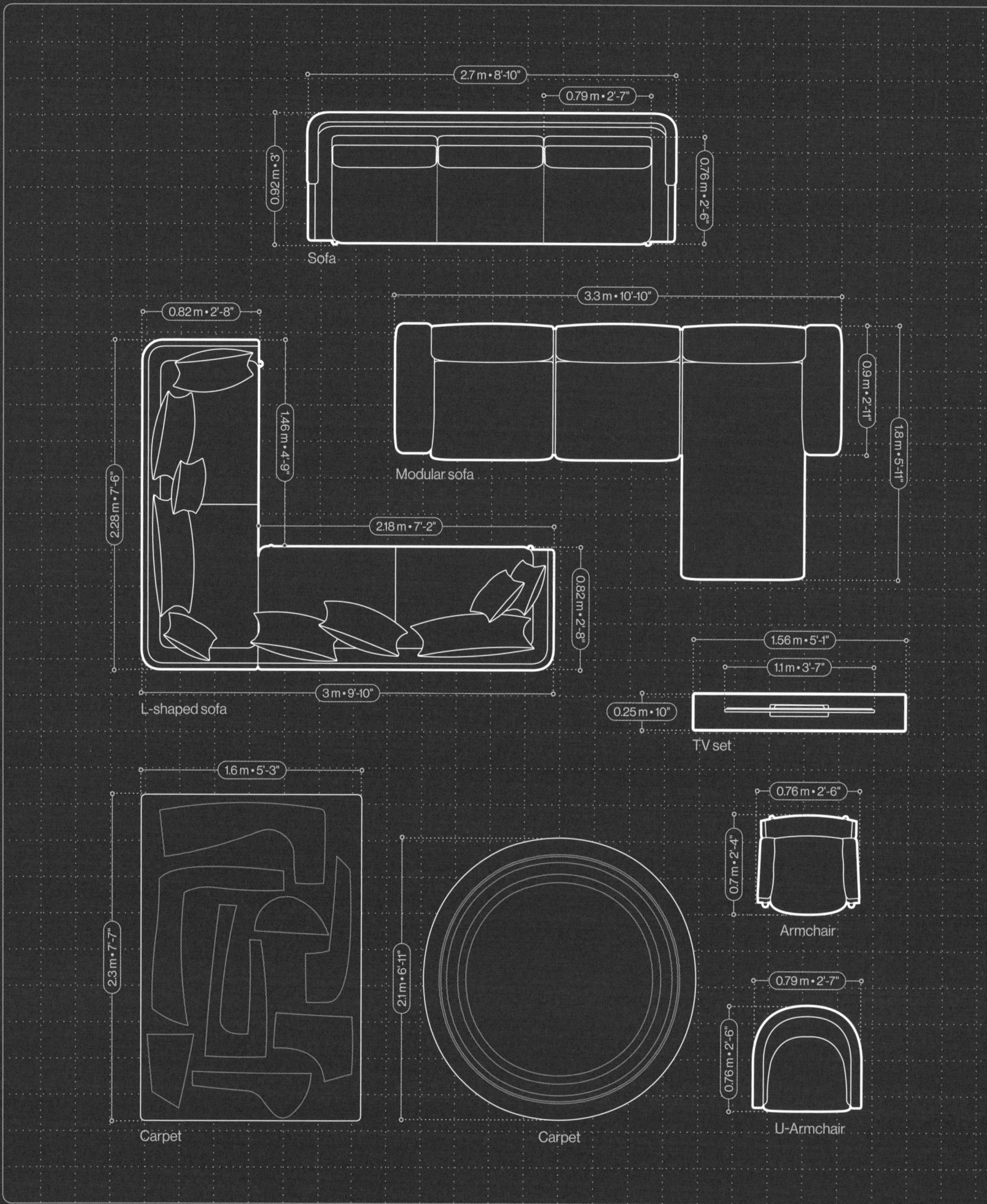
2.7 m • 8'-10"
0.79 m • 2'-7"
0.92 m • 3'
0.76 m • 2'-6"
Sofa
3.3 m • 10'-10"
0.82 m • 2'-8"
0.9 m • 2'-11"
1.8 m • 5'-11"
1.46 m • 4'-9"
Modular sofa
2.28 m • 7'-6"
2.18 m • 7'-2"
0.82 m • 2'-8"
3 m • 9'-10"
L-shaped sofa
1.56 m • 5'-1"
1.1 m • 3'-7"
0.25 m • 10"
TV set
1.6 m • 5'-3"
0.76 m • 2'-6"
0.7 m • 2'-4"
Armchair
2.3 m • 7'-7"
2.1 m • 6'-11"
0.79 m • 2'-7"
0.76 m • 2'-6"
Carpet
Carpet
U-Armchair

Seatings

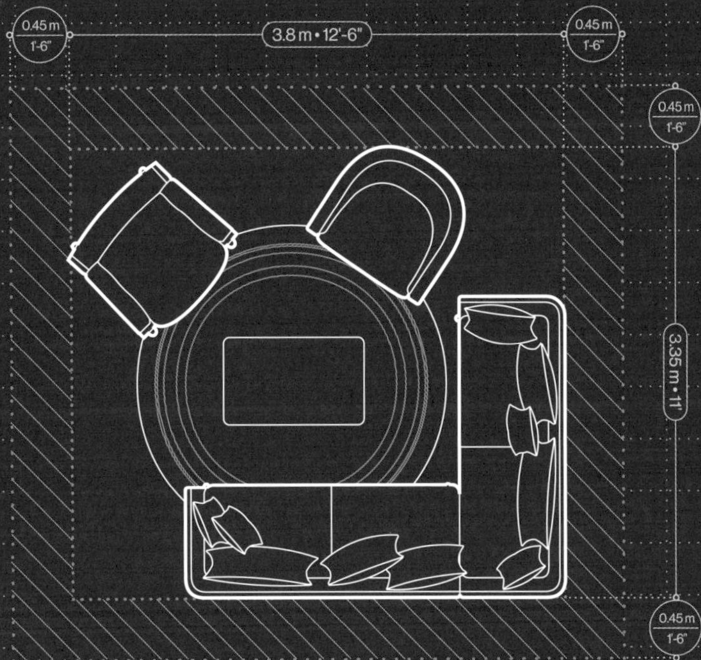

Living room - S

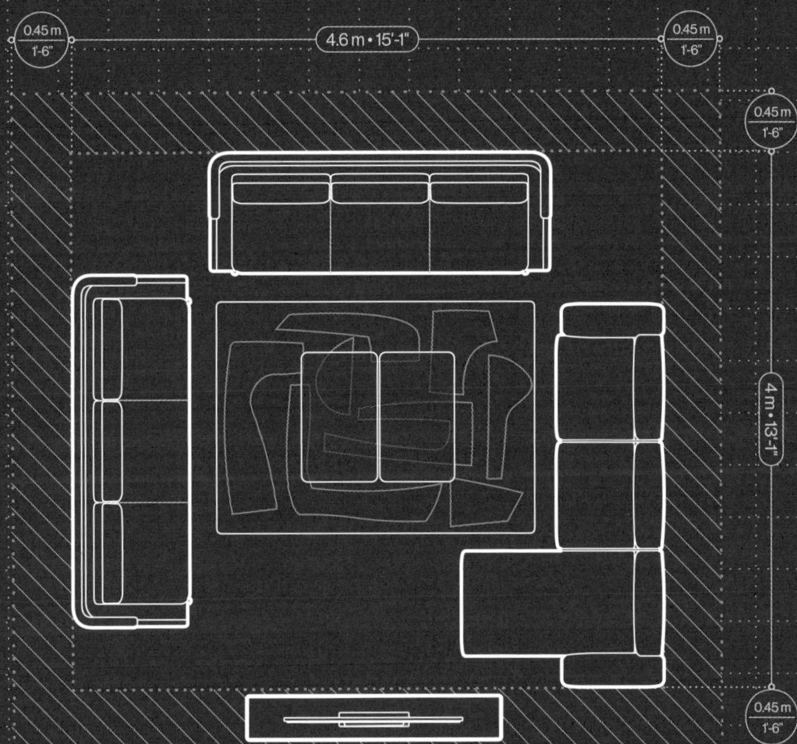

Living room - L

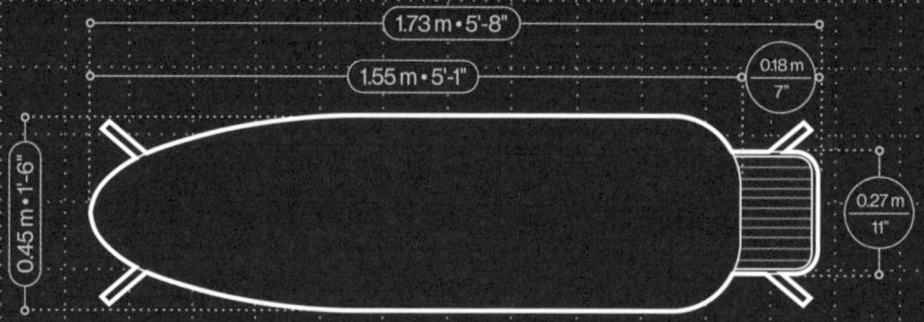

Ironing board

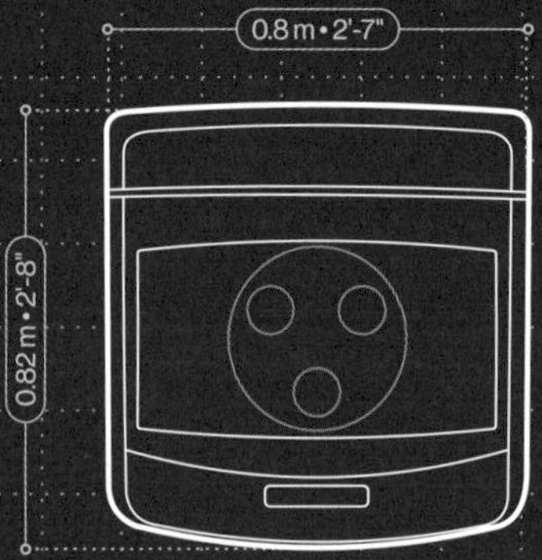

Washer

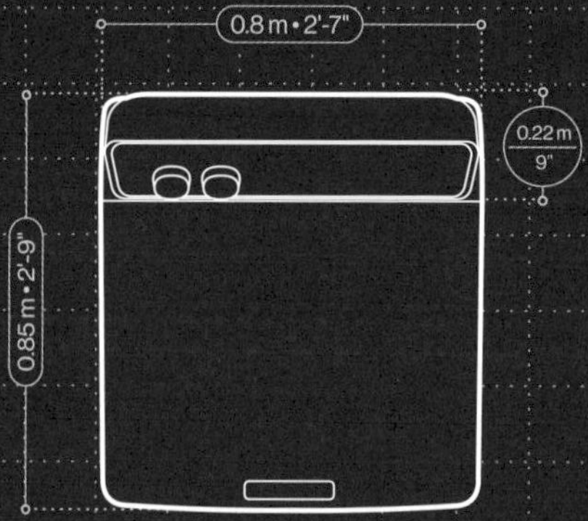

Dryer

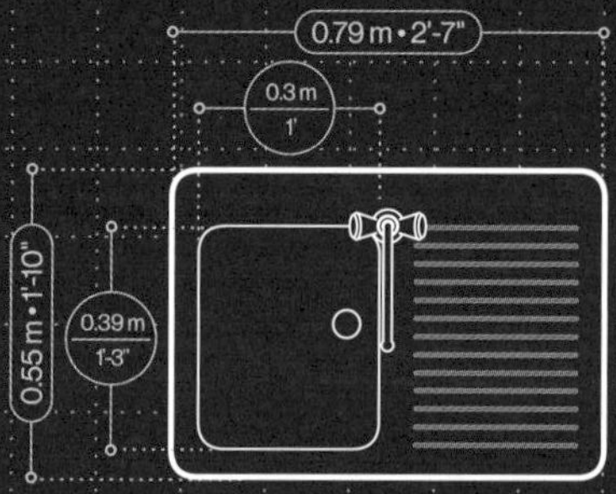

Sink

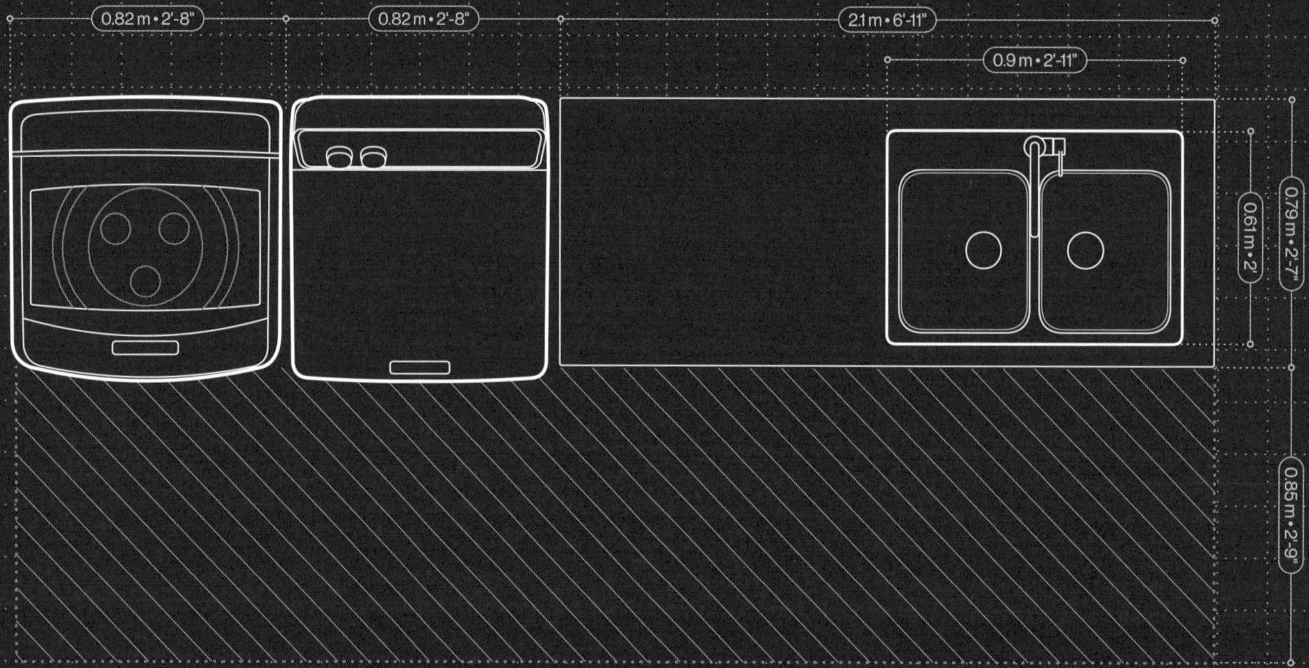

Laundry room - Layout

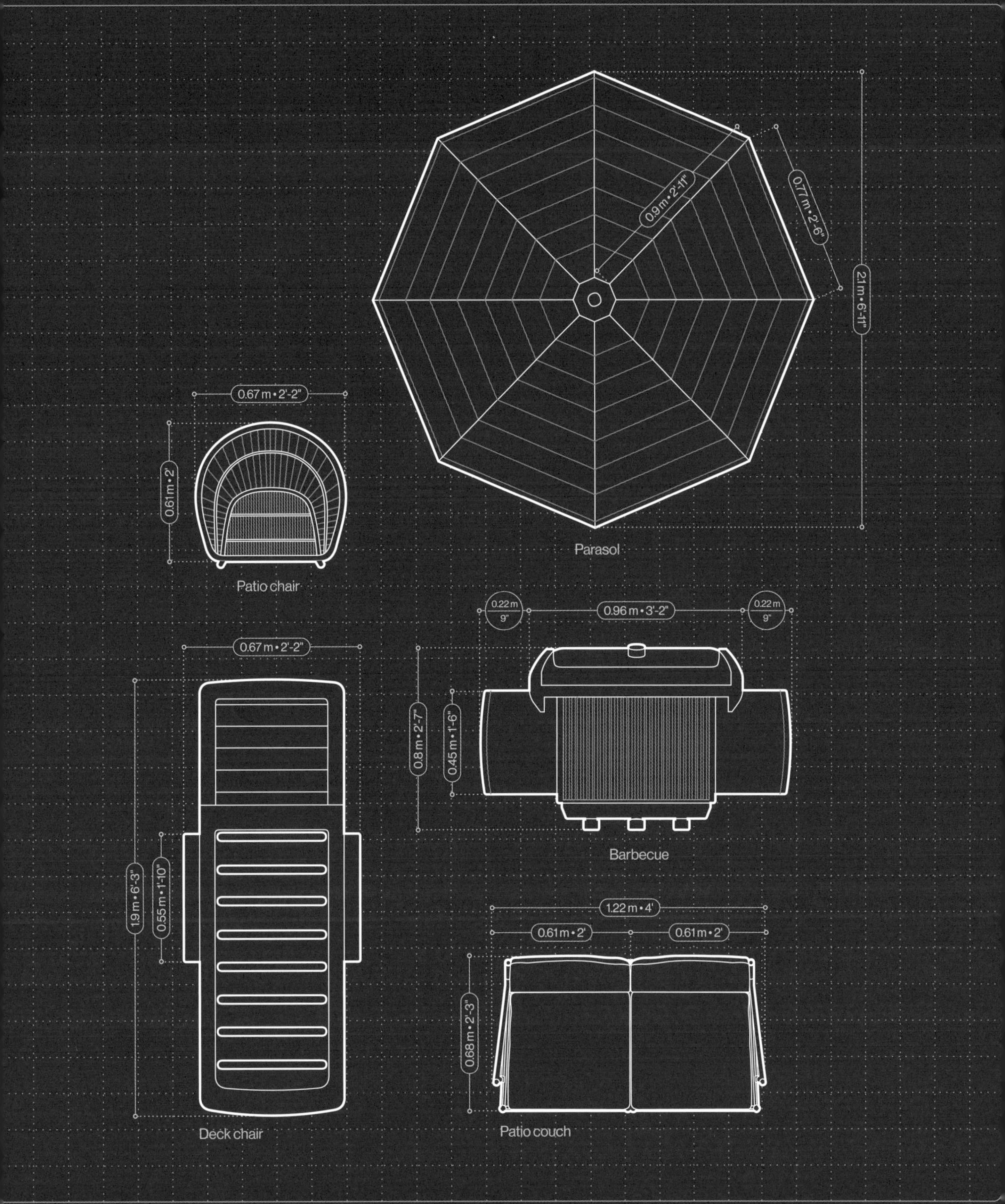
0.9 m • 2'-11"
0.77 m • 2'-6"
2.1 m • 6'-11"
Parasol
0.67 m • 2'-2"
0.61 m • 2'
Patio chair
0.22 m
9"
0.96 m • 3'-2"
0.22 m
9"
0.8 m • 2'-7"
0.45 m • 1'-6"
Barbecue
0.67 m • 2'-2"
1.9 m • 6'-3"
0.55 m • 1'-10"
Deck chair
1.22 m • 4'
0.61 m • 2'
0.61 m • 2'
0.68 m • 2'-3"
Patio couch

Kit for a

Master Bedroom

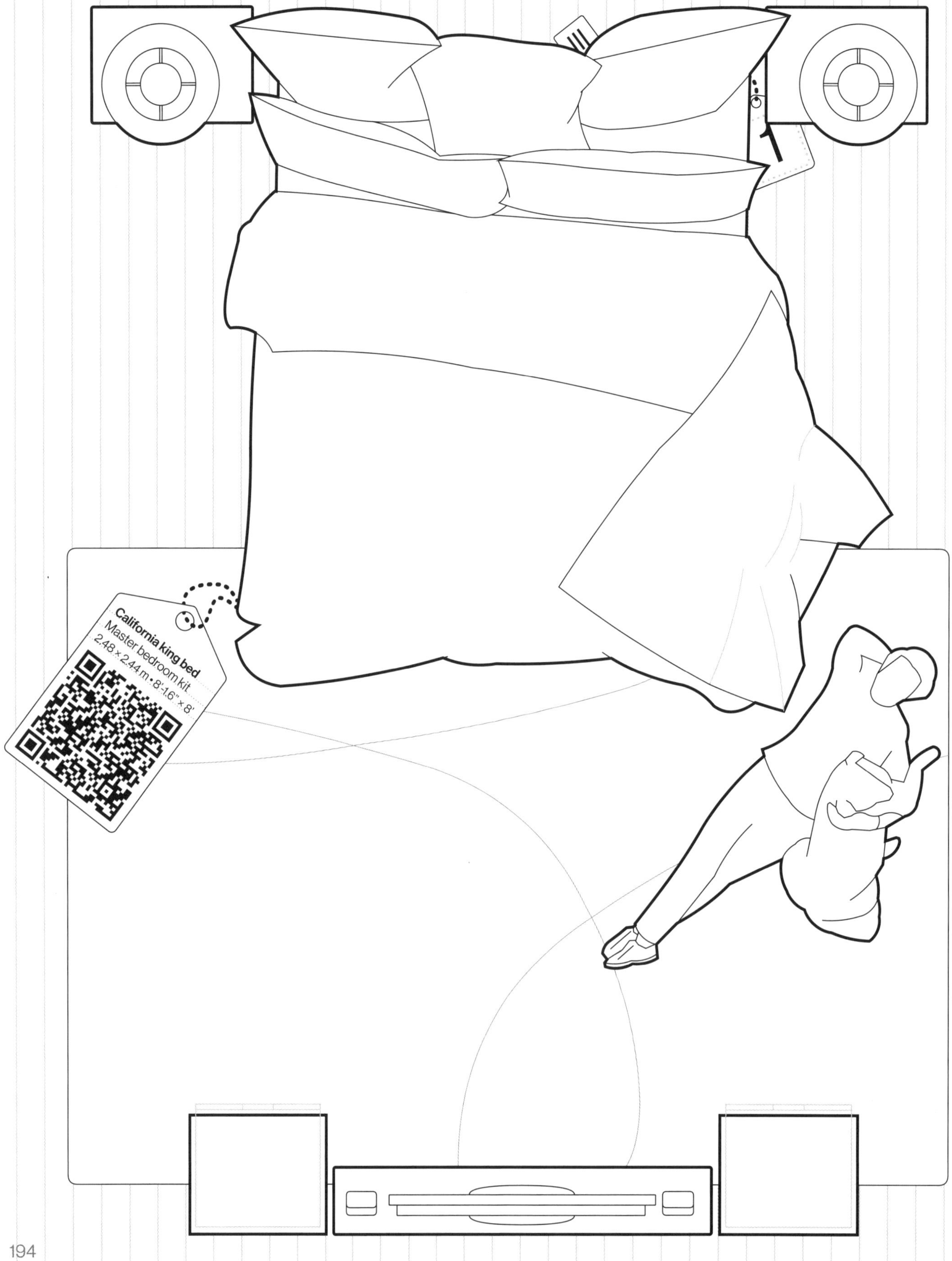
California king bed
Master bedroom kit
2.48 × 2.44 m • 8'-1.6" × 8'

Dresser large
Master bedroom kit
0.75×1.45m•2'-5.5"×4'-9"

Kit for a
Single Bedroom

Twin single
Single bedroom kit
2.1 × 1.2 m • 6'-10.7" × 3'-11.2"

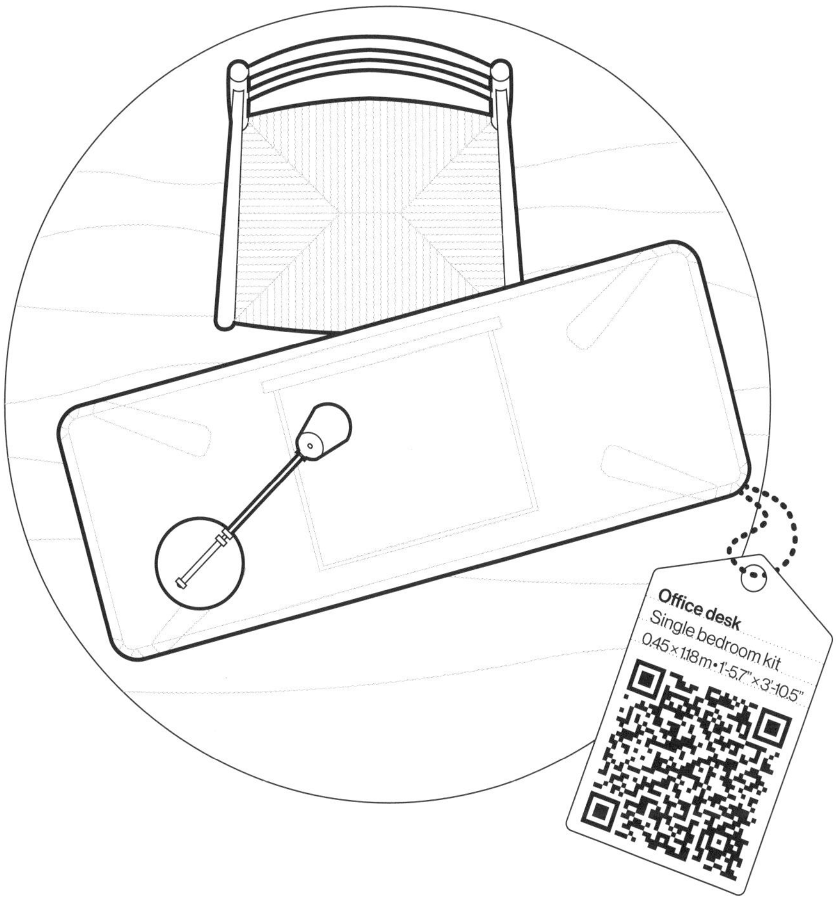
Office desk
Single bedroom kit
0.45 × 1.18 m • 1'-5.7" × 3'-10.5"

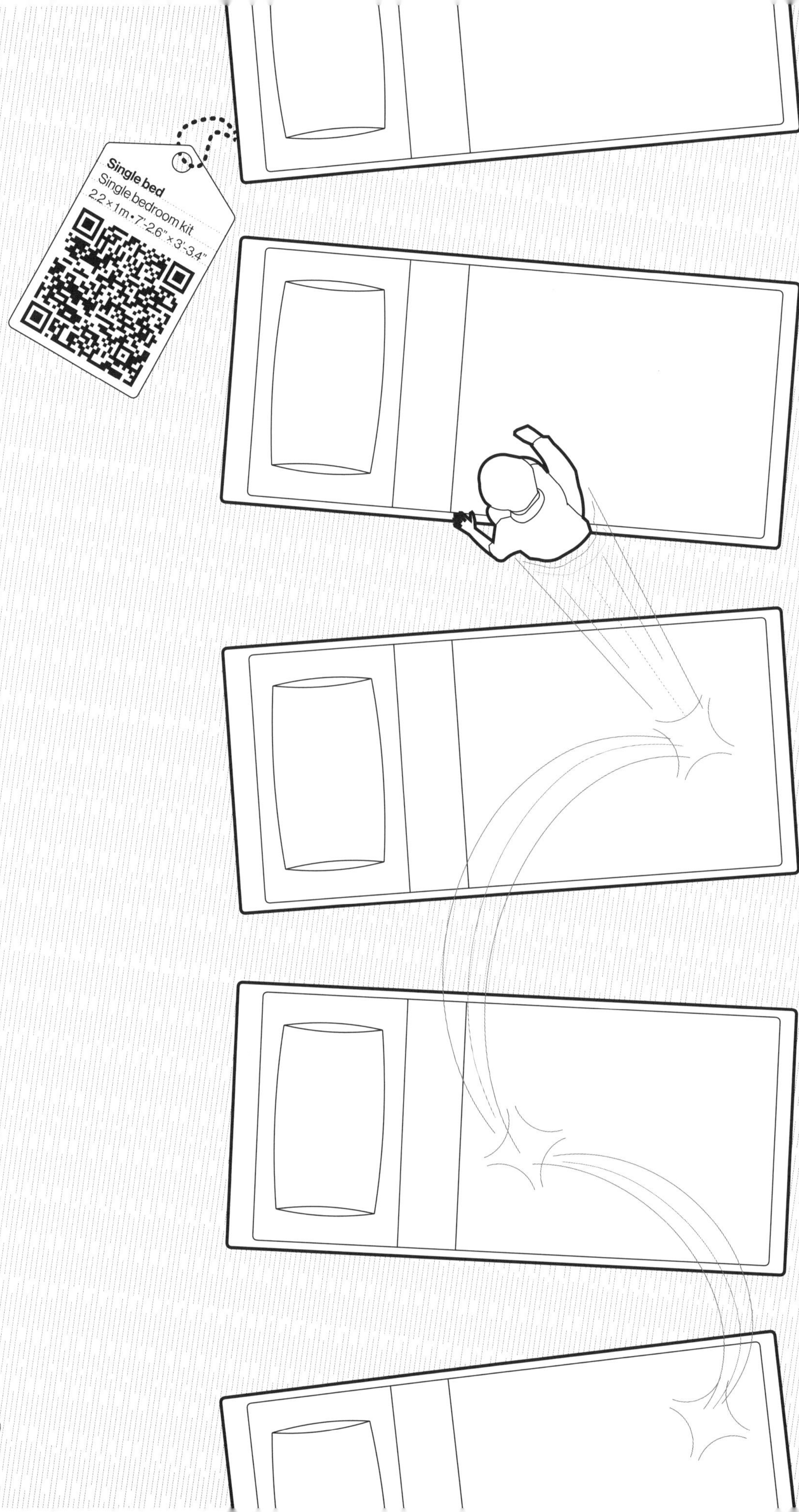
Single bed
Single bedroom kit
2.2 × 1 m • 7'-2.6" × 3'-3.4"

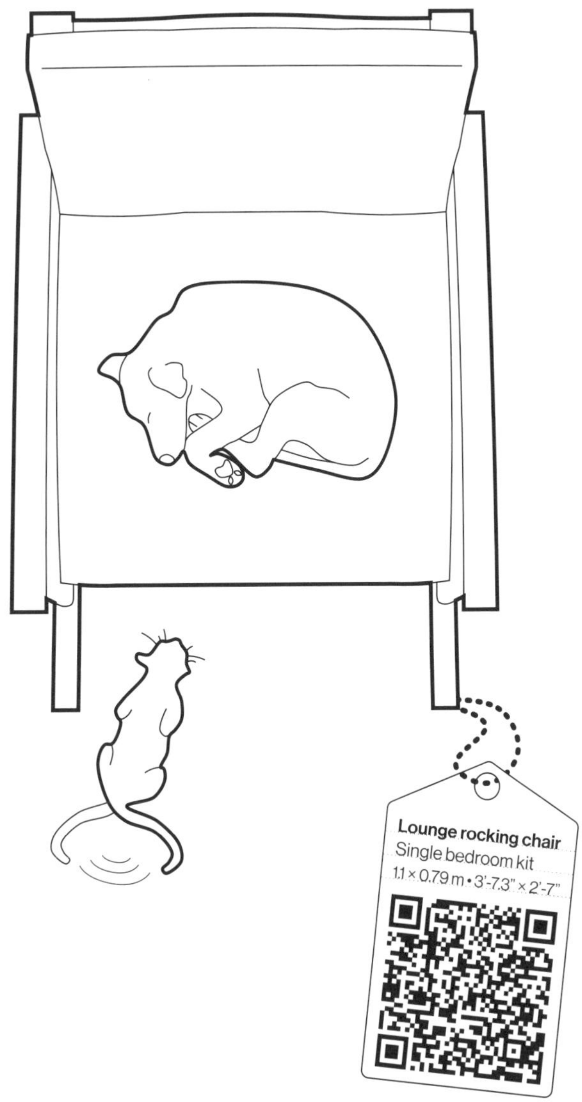
Lounge rocking chair
Single bedroom kit
1.1 × 0.79 m • 3'-7.3" × 2'-7"

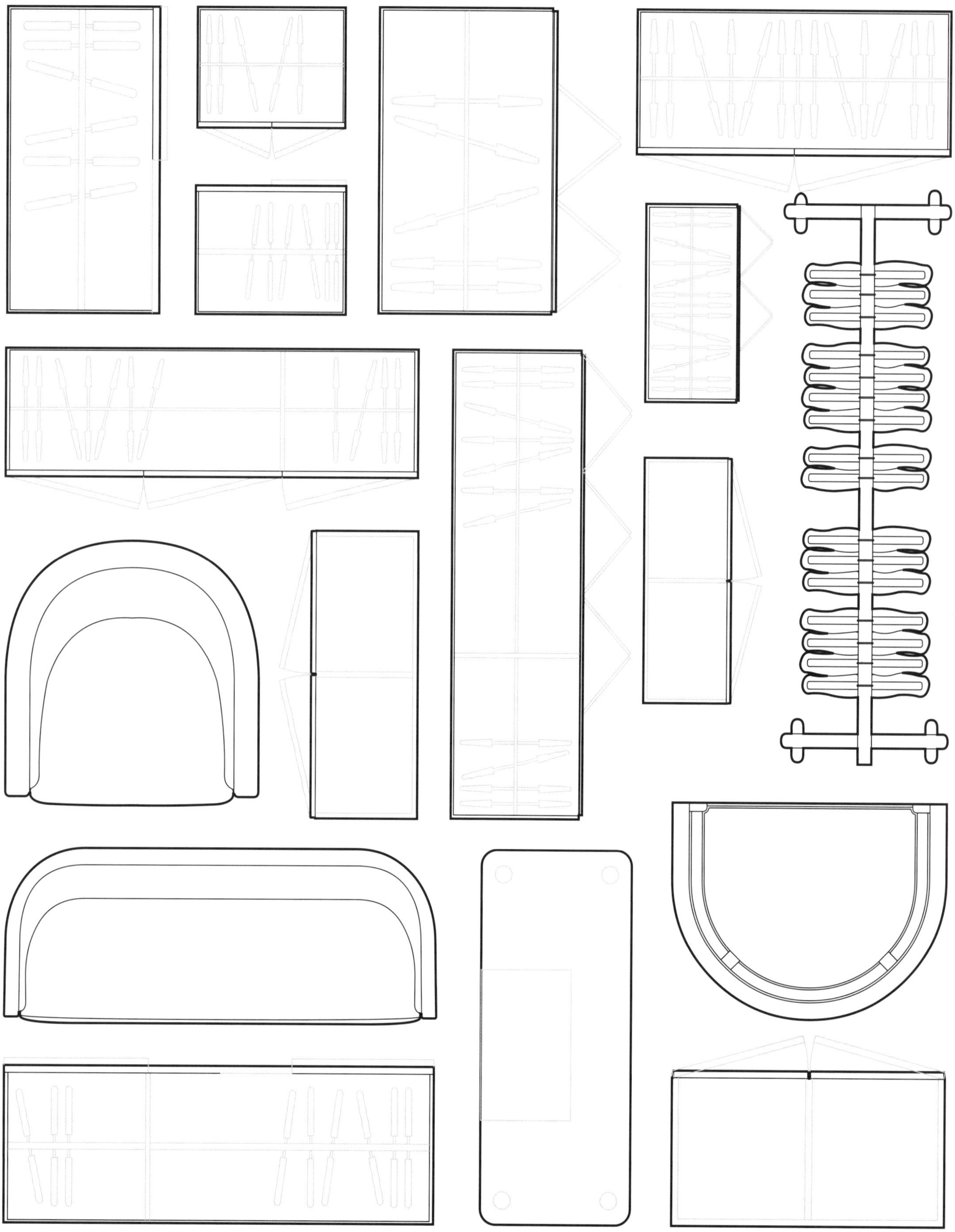

Kit for a
Dressing Room

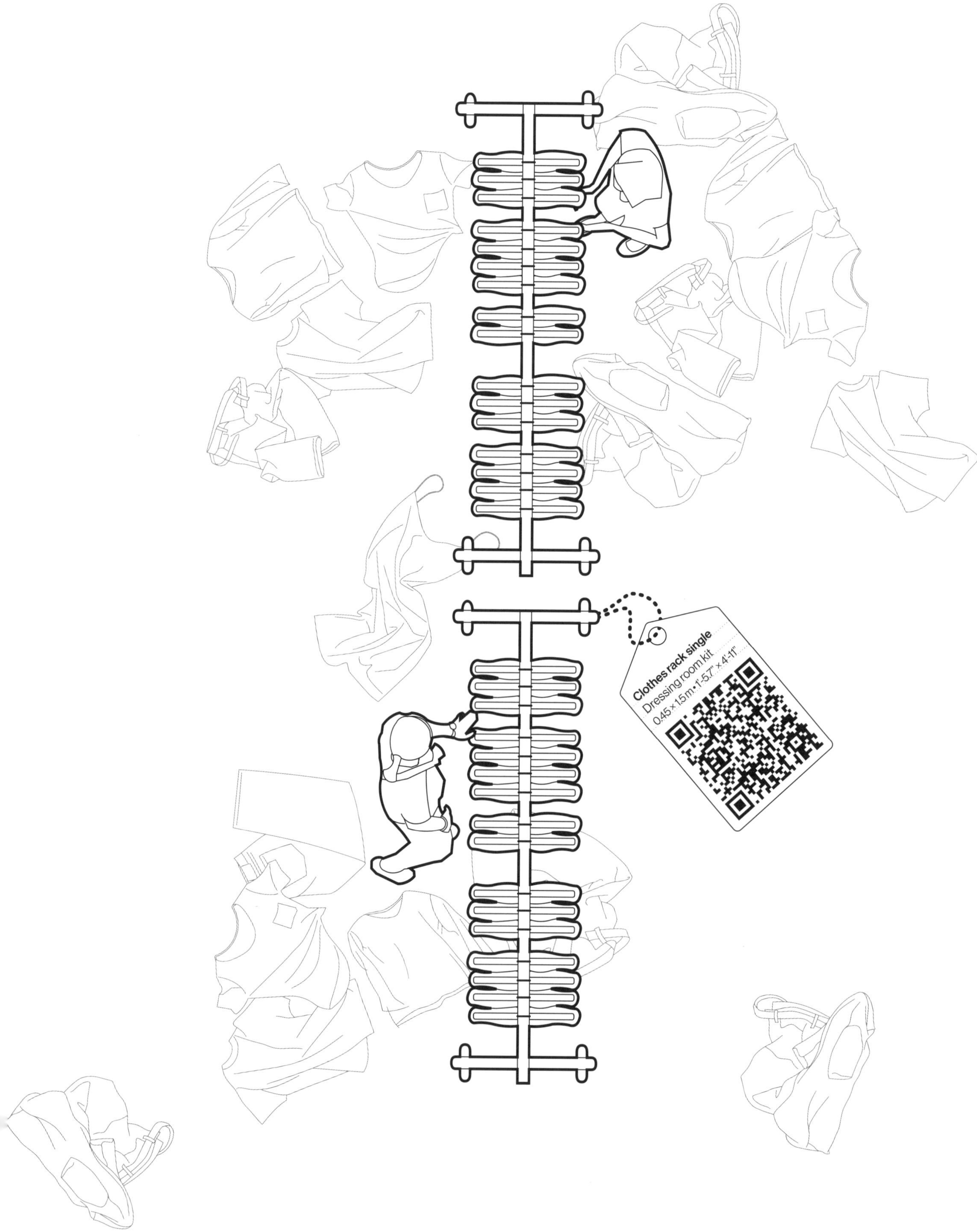
Clothes rack single
Dressing room kit
0.45 × 1.5 m • 1'-5.7" × 4'-11"

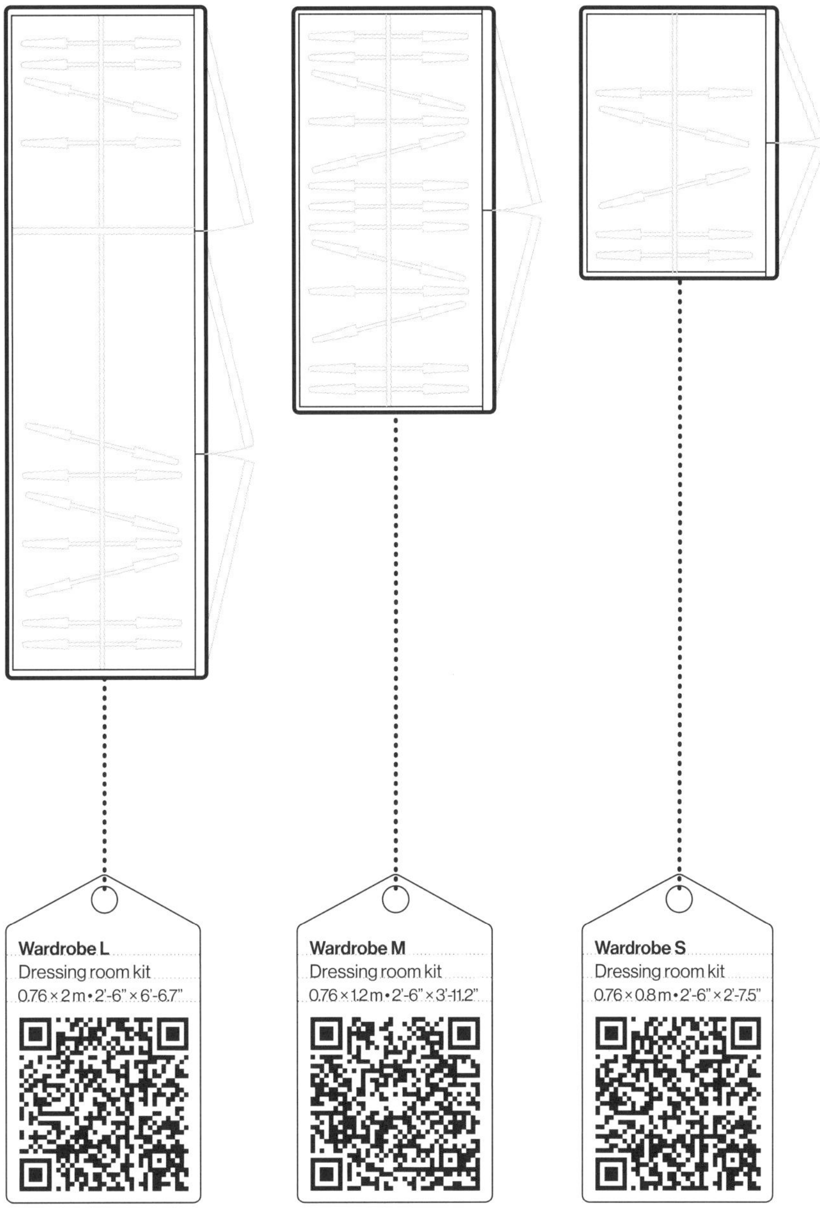
Wardrobe L
Dressing room kit
0.76 × 2 m • 2'-6" × 6'-6.7"
Wardrobe M
Dressing room kit
0.76 × 1.2 m • 2'-6" × 3'-11.2"
Wardrobe S
Dressing room kit
0.76 × 0.8 m • 2'-6" × 2'-7.5"

A Catalog of

Beds

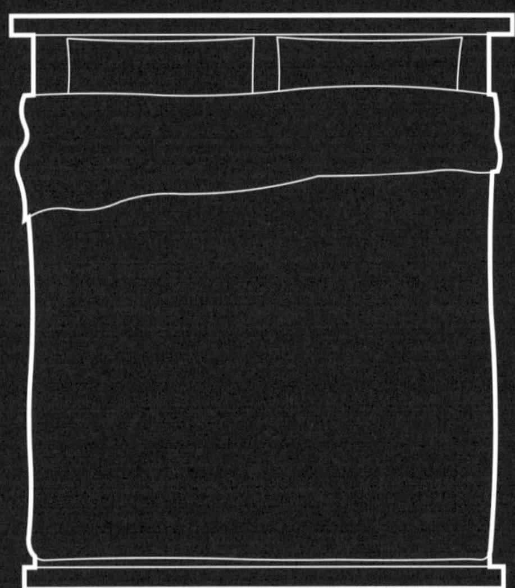

1

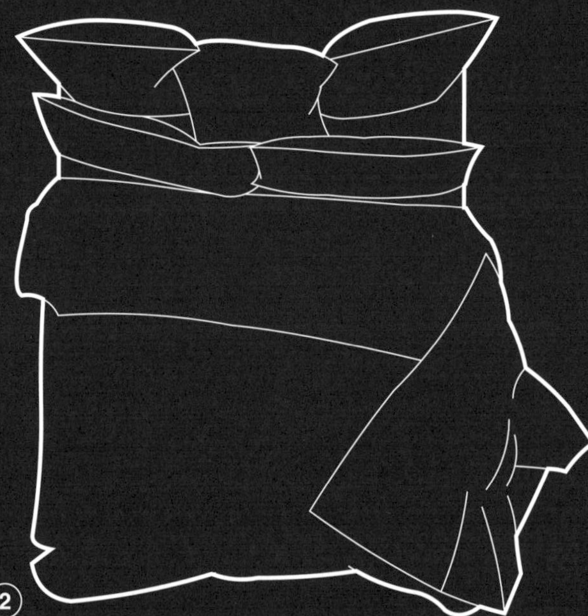

2

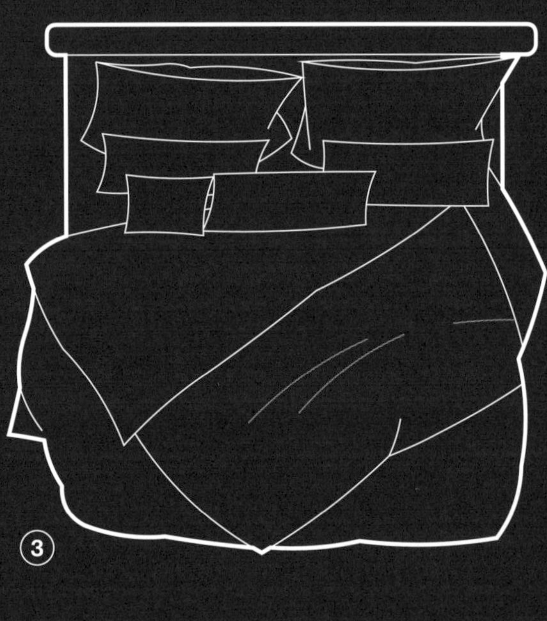

3

4

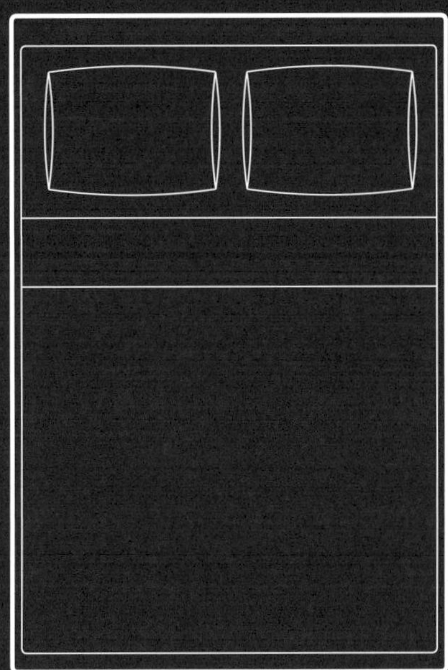

5

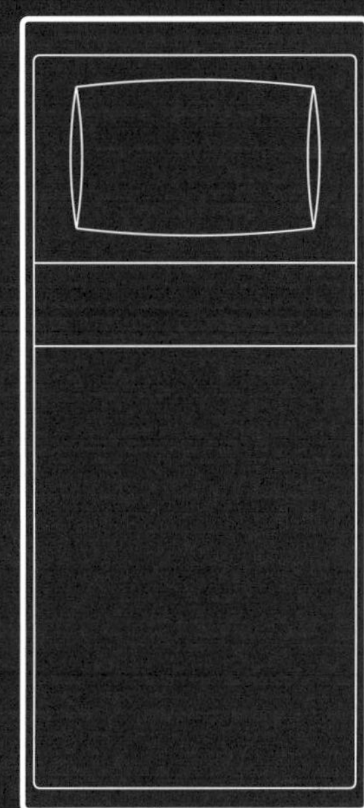

6

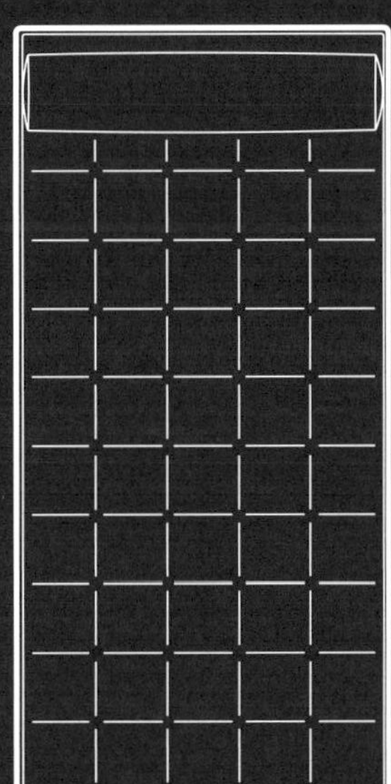

7

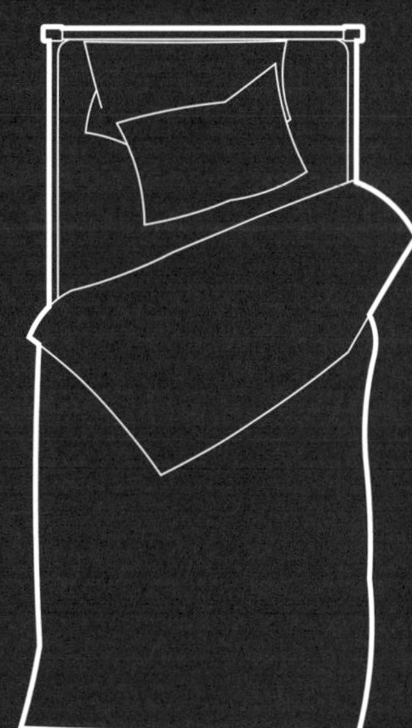

8

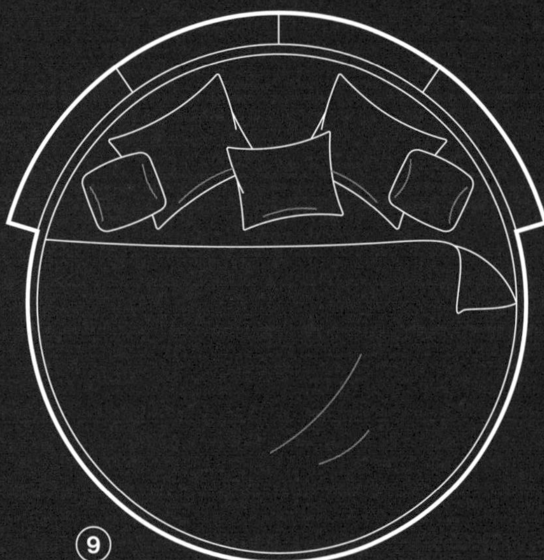

9

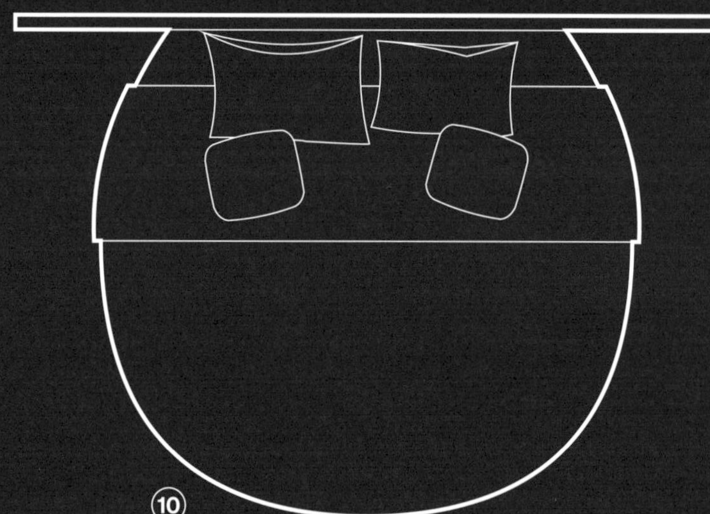

10

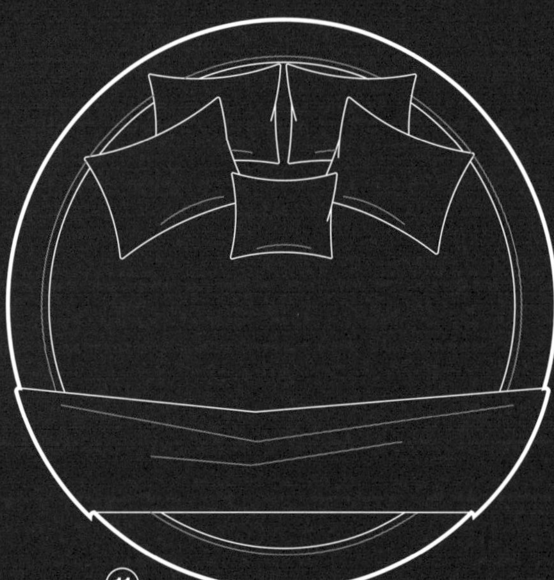

11

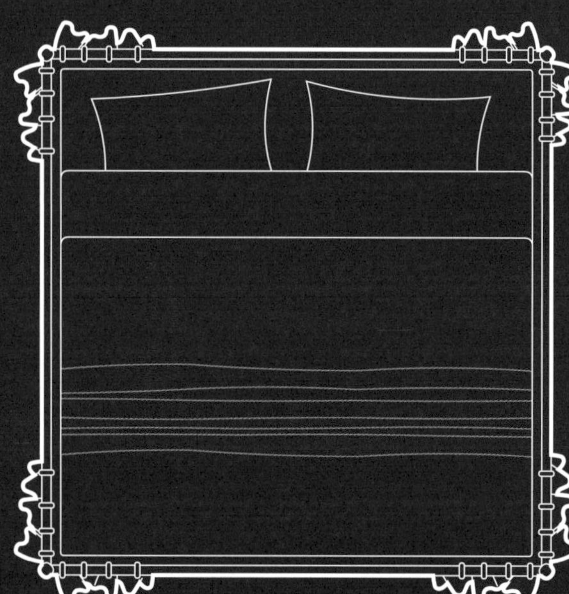

12

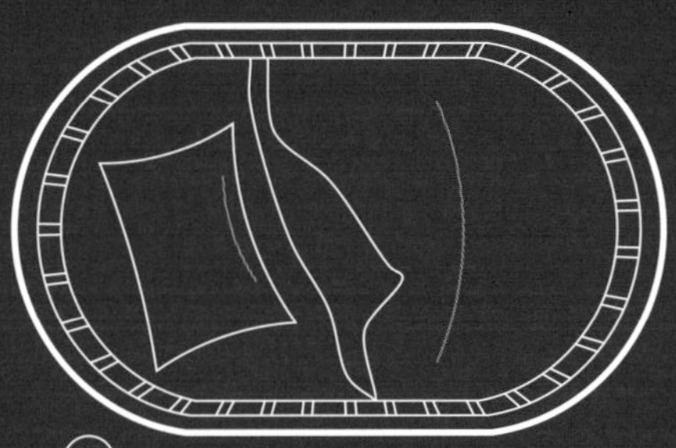

13

14

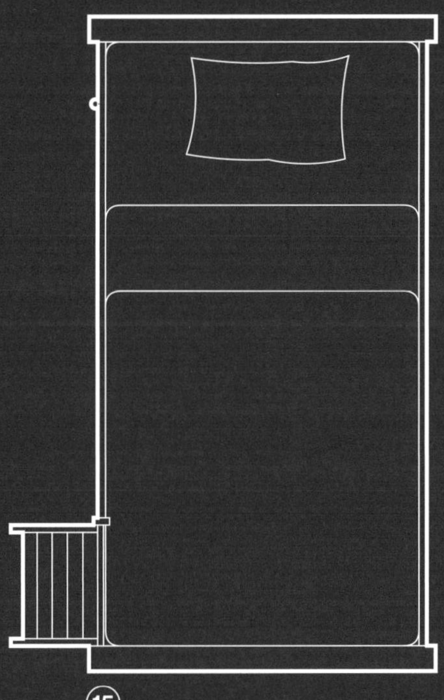

15

16

1

Double bed
Beds
2.1 × 1.9 m • 6'-10.7" × 6'-2.8"

2

California king bed
Beds
2.48 × 2.44 m • 8'-1.6" × 8'

3

Queen-size bed
Beds
2.17 × 2.3 m • 7'-1.4" × 7'-6.6"

4

Double bed with night stands • Beds
2.1 × 3.28 m • 6'-10.7" × 10'-9"

5

Double bed
Beds
2.2 × 1.5 m • 7'-2.6" × 4'-11"

6

Single bed
Beds
2.2 × 1 m • 7'-2.6" × 3'-3.4"

7

Divan
Beds
2.04 × 1.02 m • 6'-8.3" × 3'-4.2"

8

Toddler bed
Beds
2.08 × 1.22 m • 6'-9.9" × 4'

9

Round bed
Beds
2.24 × 2.27 m • 7'-4.2" × 7'-5.4"

10

Round bed with headboard • Beds
2.1 × 3.03 m • 6'-10.7" × 9'-11.3"

11

Podium round bed
Beds
2.4 × 2.4 m • 7'-10.5" × 7'-10.5"

12

Double bed canopy
Beds
2.4 × 2.4 m • 7'-10.5" × 7'-10.5"

13

Crib round
Beds
0.8 × 1.36 m • 2'-8.3" × 4'-5.5"

14

Crib L
Beds
0.94 × 1.28 m • 3'-1" × 4'-2.4"

15

Double decker
Beds
2.06 × 1.38 m • 6'-9" × 4'-6.3"

16

Double decker L
Beds
2.59 × 1.12 m • 8'-6" × 3'-8"

Kit for a Living Room

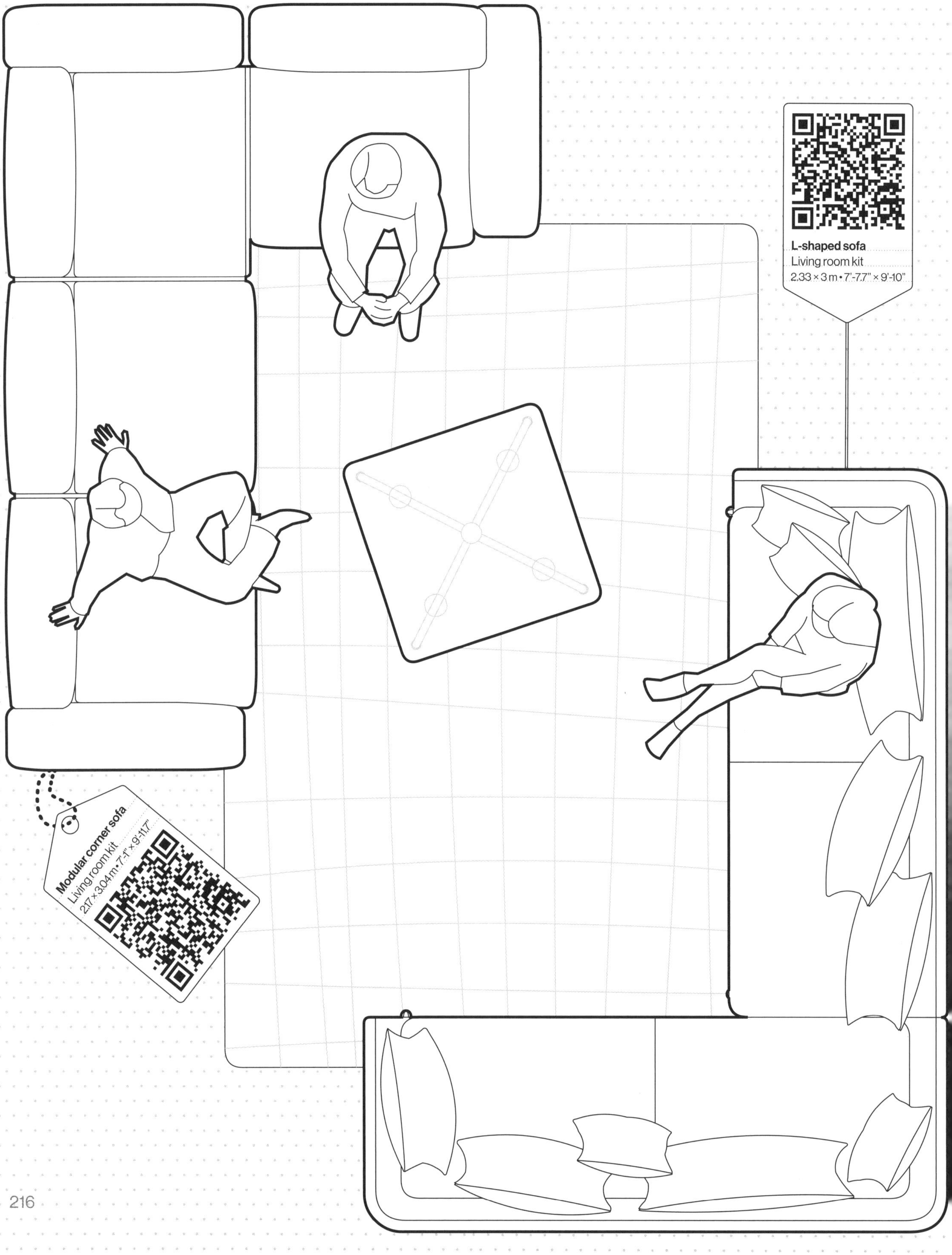
L-shaped sofa
Living room kit
2.33 × 3 m • 7'-7.7" × 9'-10"
Modular corner sofa
Living room kit
2.17 × 3.04 m • 7'-1" × 9'-11.7"

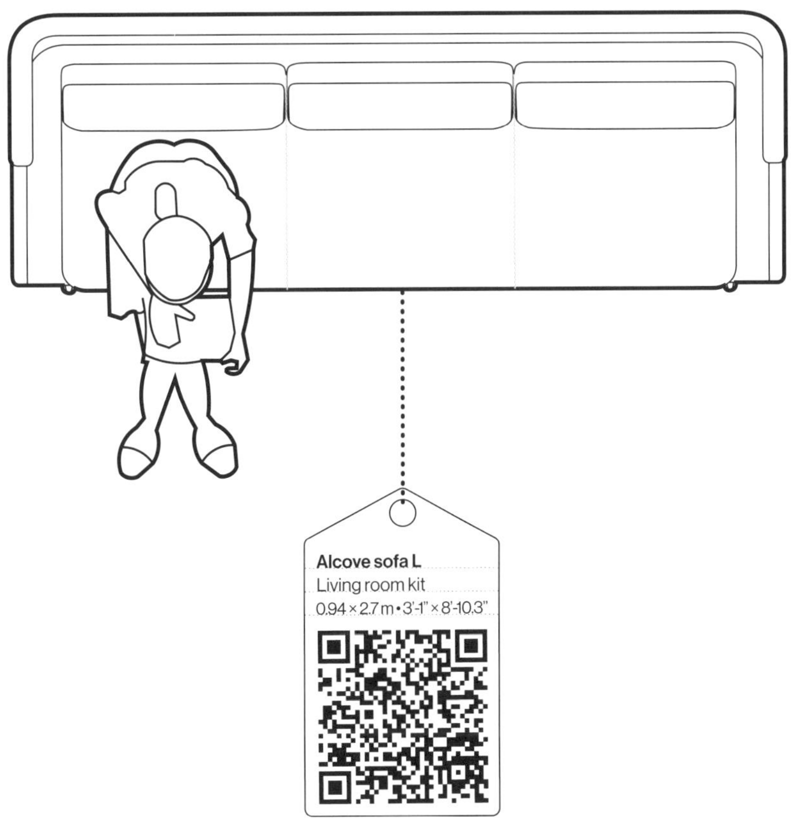
Alcove sofa L
Living room kit
0.94 × 2.7 m • 3'-1" × 8'-10.3"

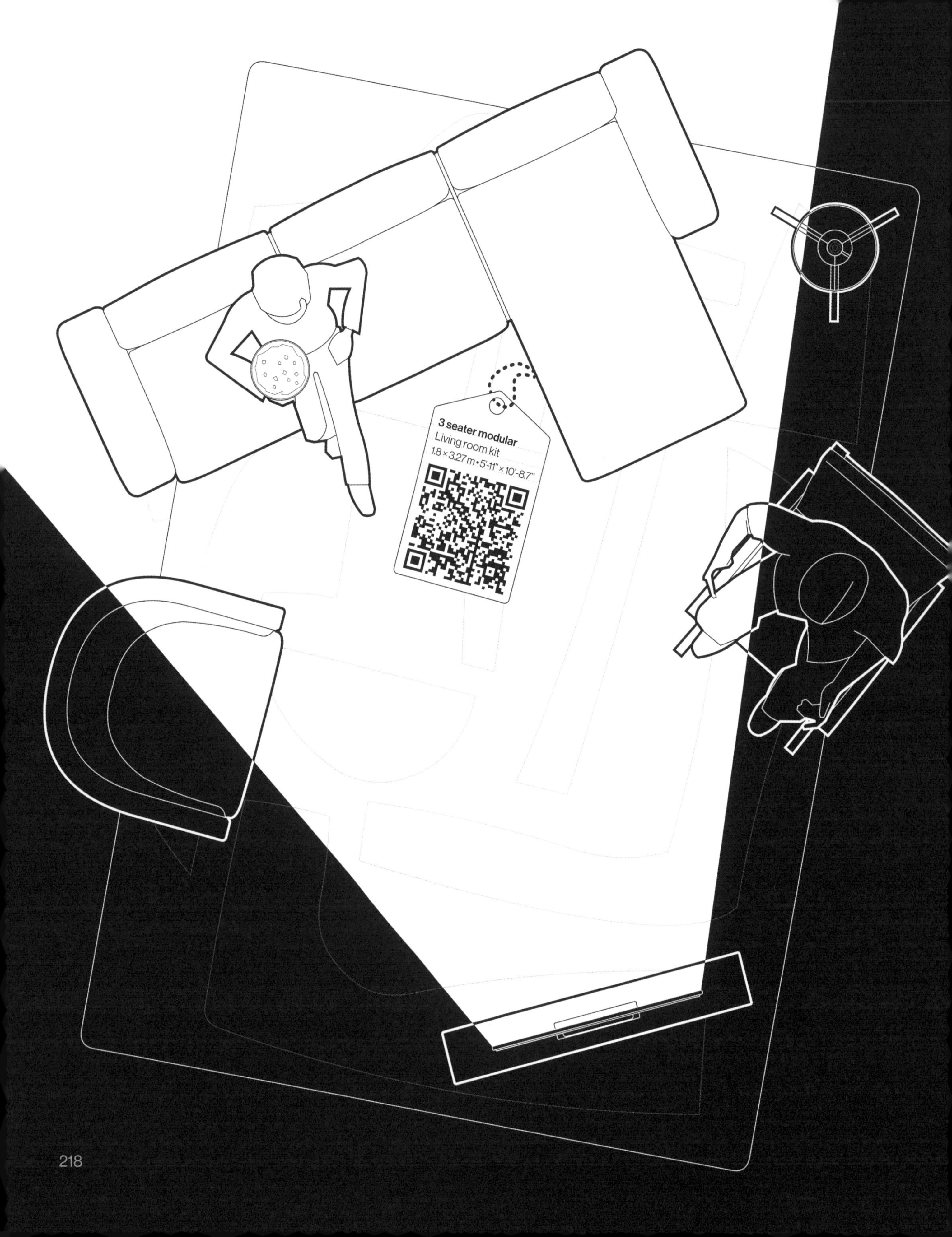
3 seater modular
Living room kit
1.8 × 3.27 m • 5'-11" × 10'-8.7"

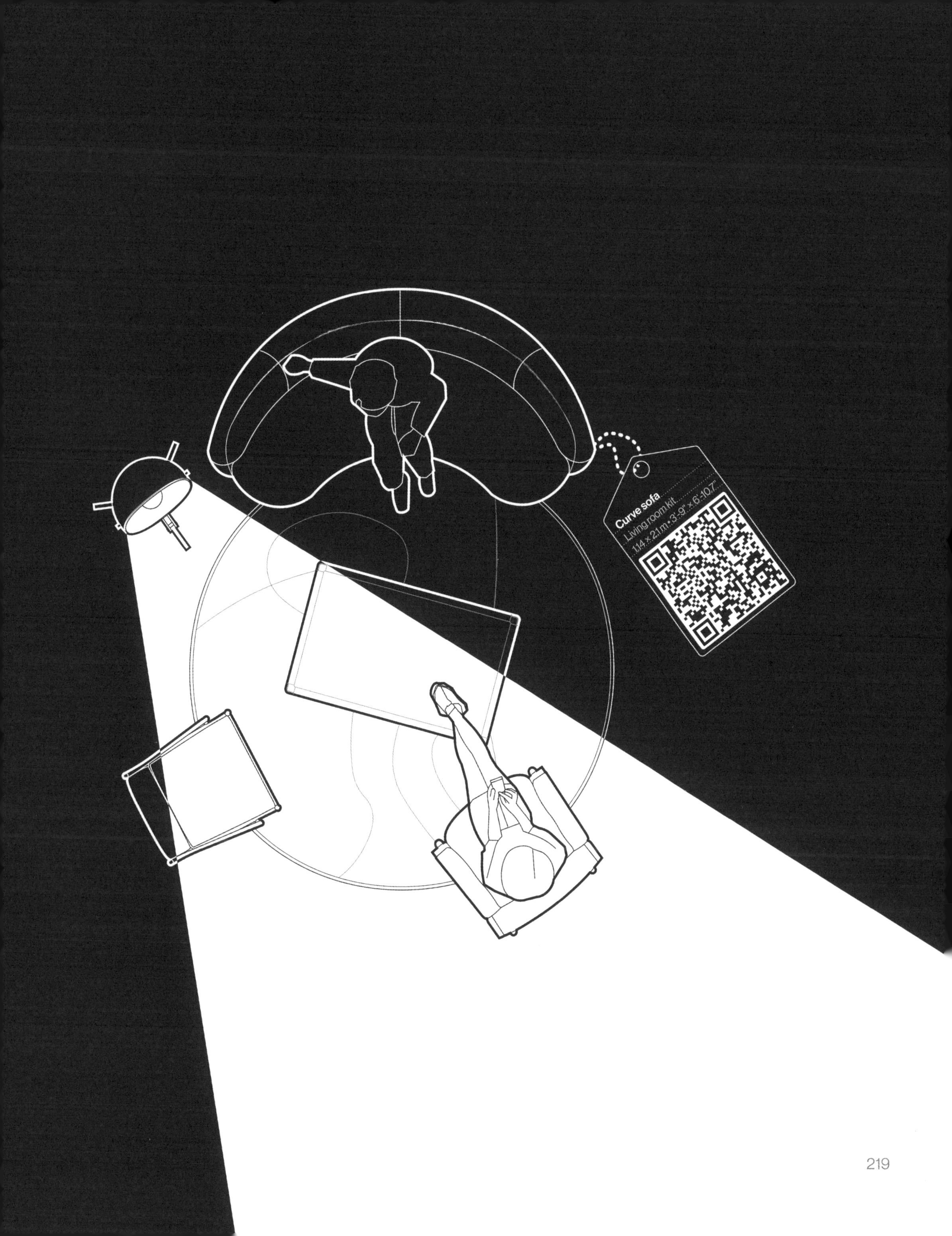
Curve sofa
Living room kit
1.14 x 2.1 m • 3'-9" x 6'-10.7"

Kit for a

Dining Room

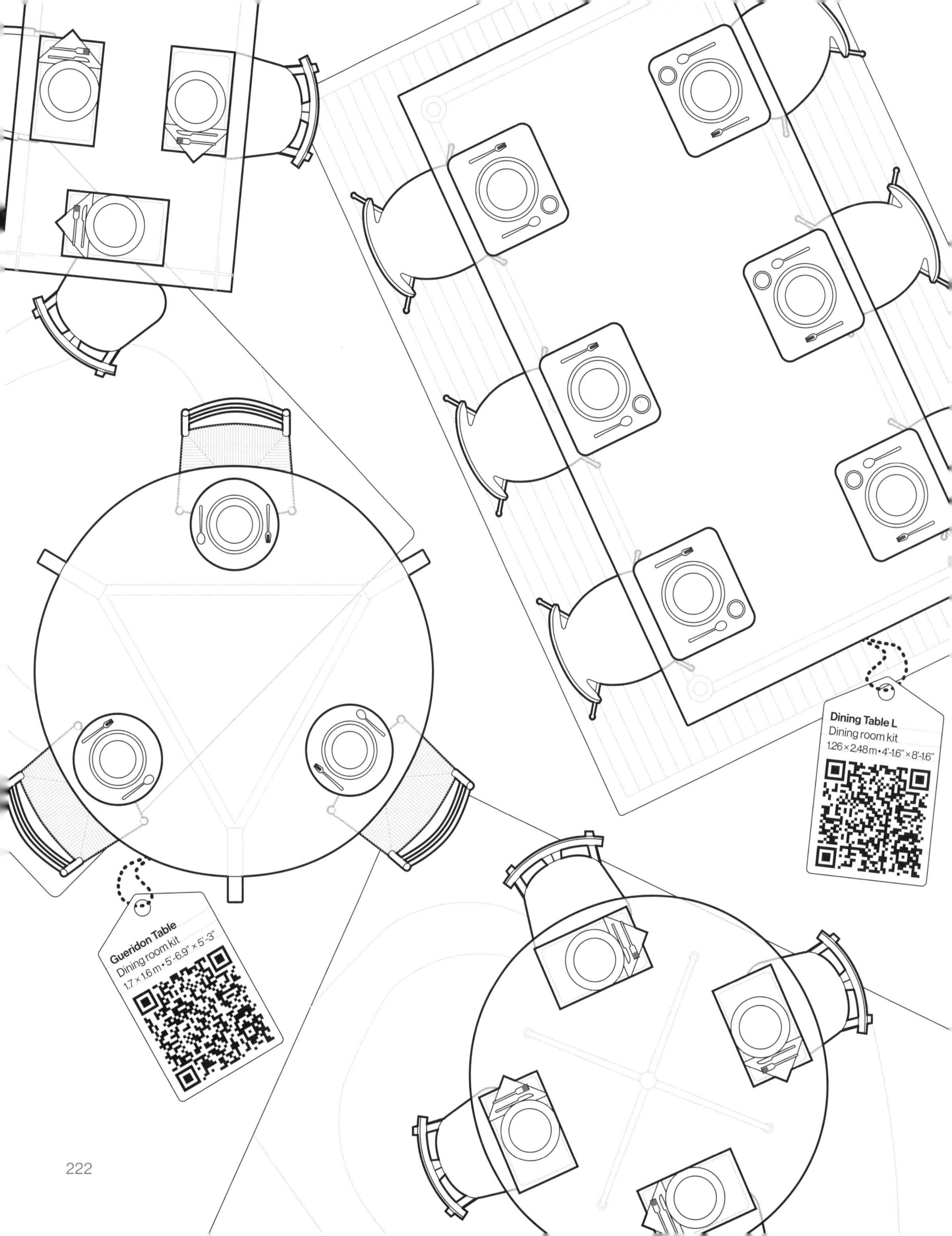
Dining Table L
Dining room kit
1.26 × 2.48 m • 4'-1.6" × 8'-1.6"
Gueridon Table
Dining room kit
1.7 × 1.6 m • 5'-6.9" × 5'-3"

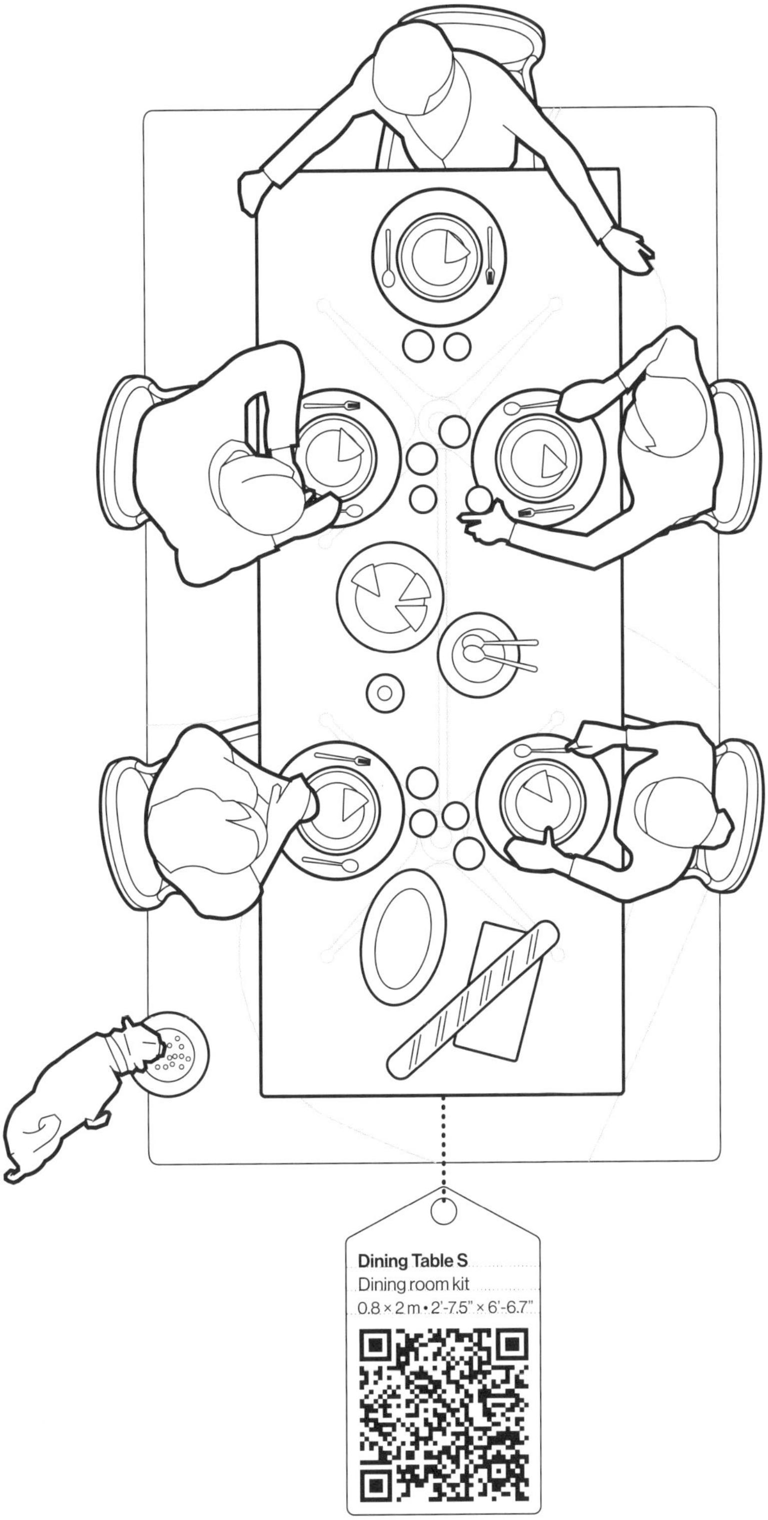
Dining Table S
Dining room kit
0.8 × 2 m • 2'-7.5" × 6'-6.7"

Kit for a
Study Room

Office desk light
Study room kit
0.61 × 1.17 m • 2' × 3'-10"

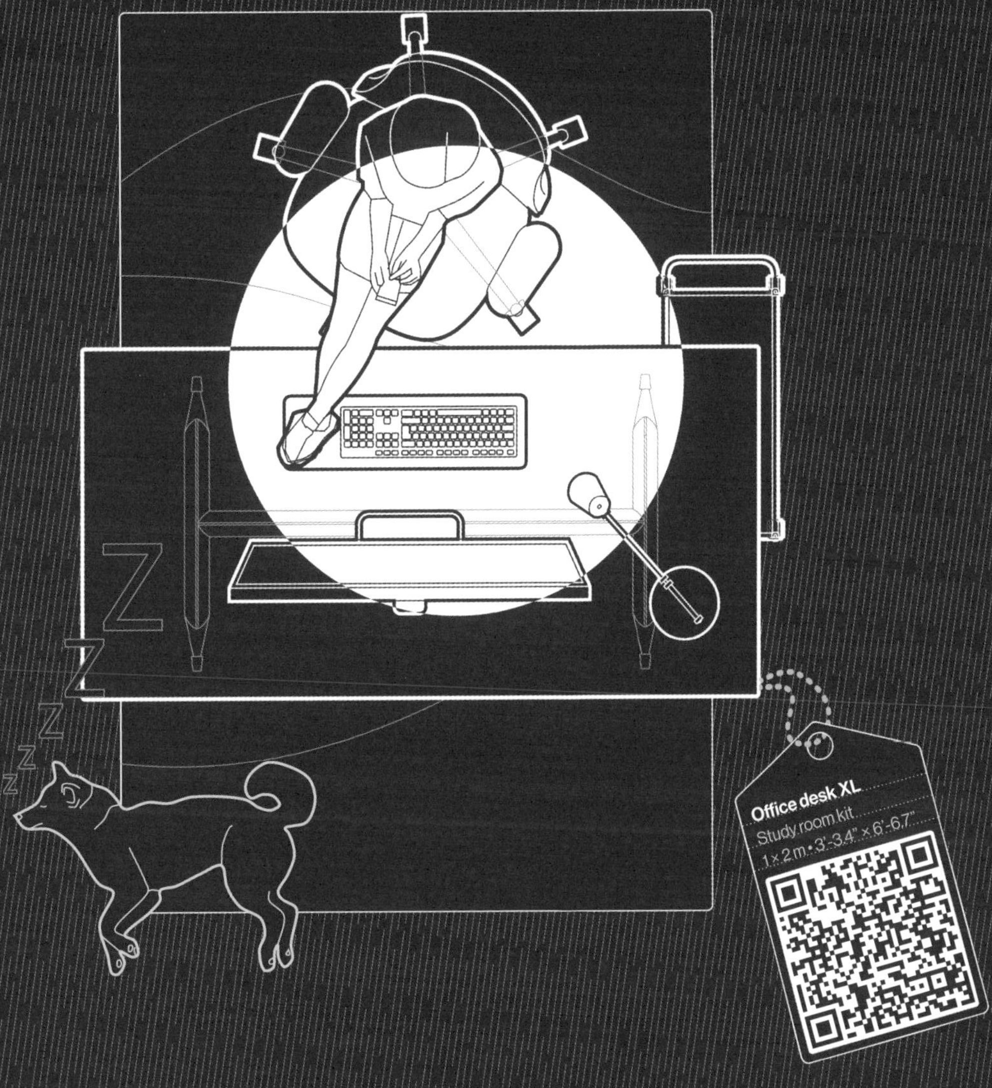
Office desk XL
Study room kit
1 × 2 m • 3'-3.4" × 6'-6.7"

A Catalog of

Seatings

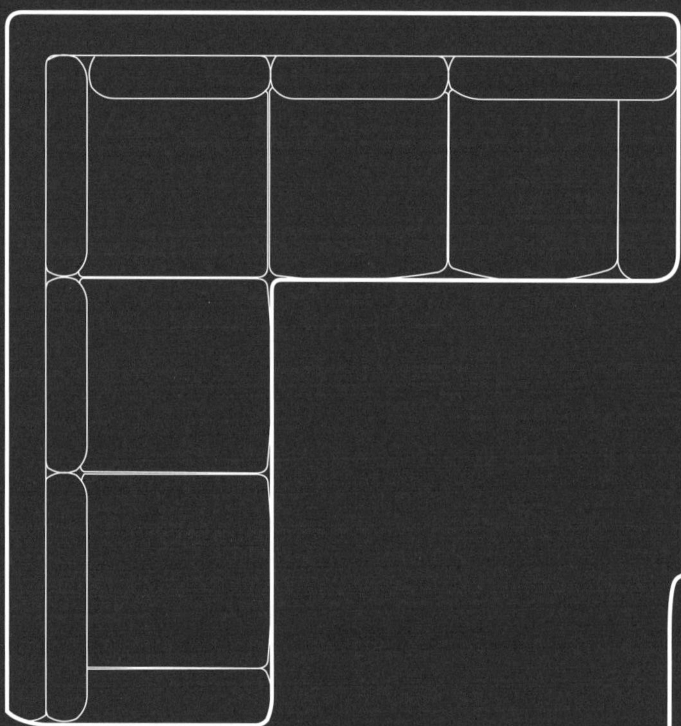

1

2

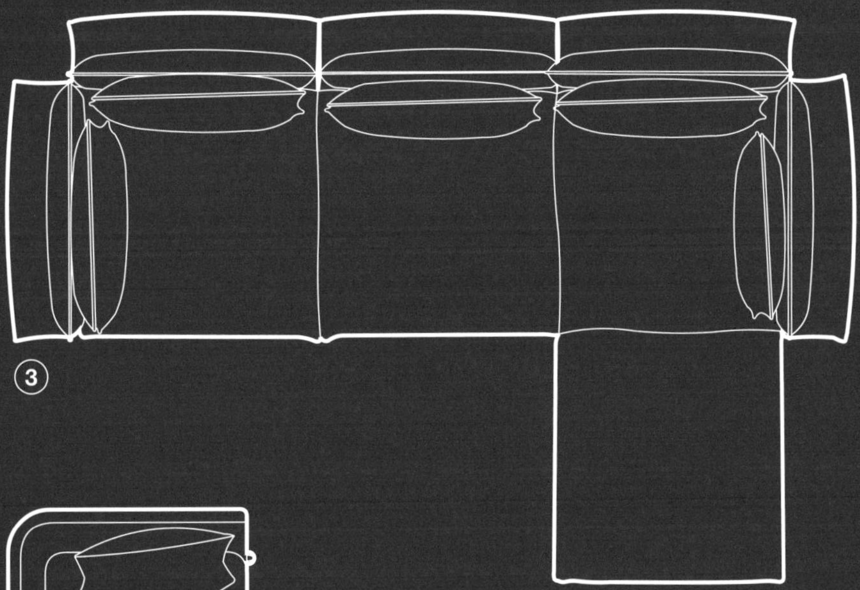

3

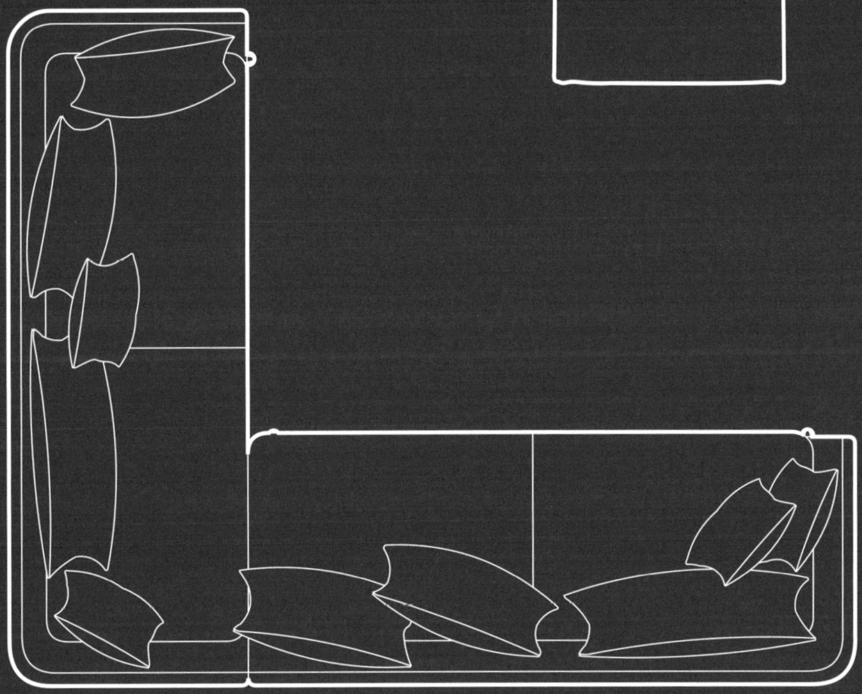

4

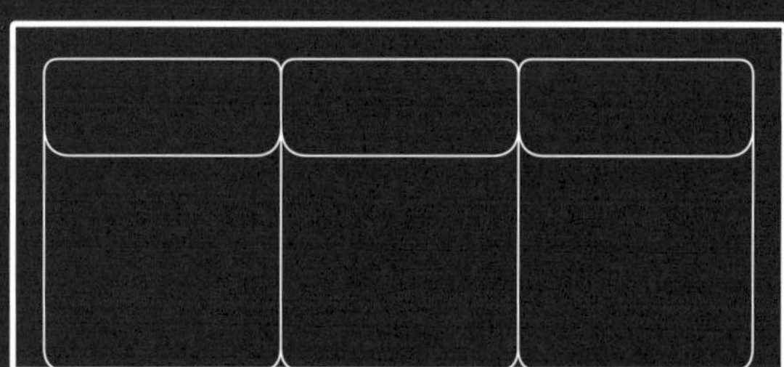

5

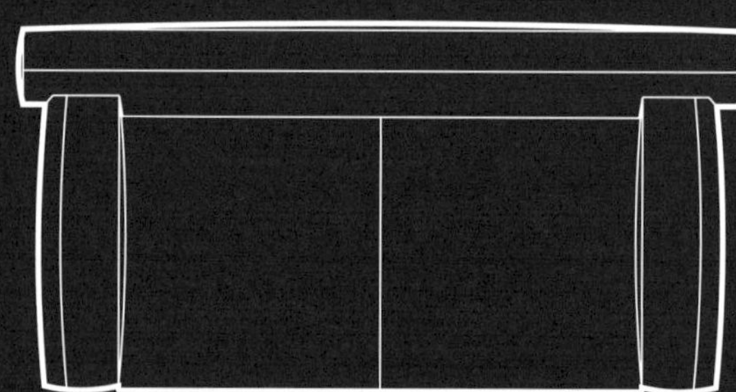

6

7

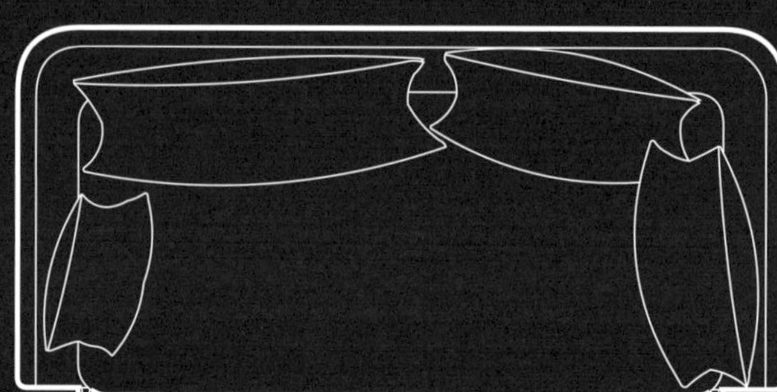

8

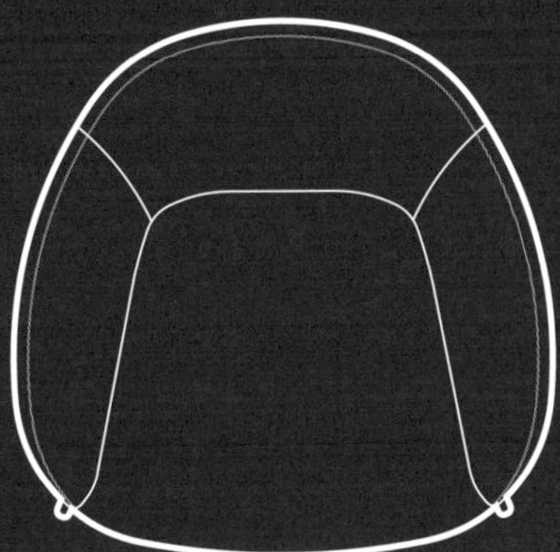

9

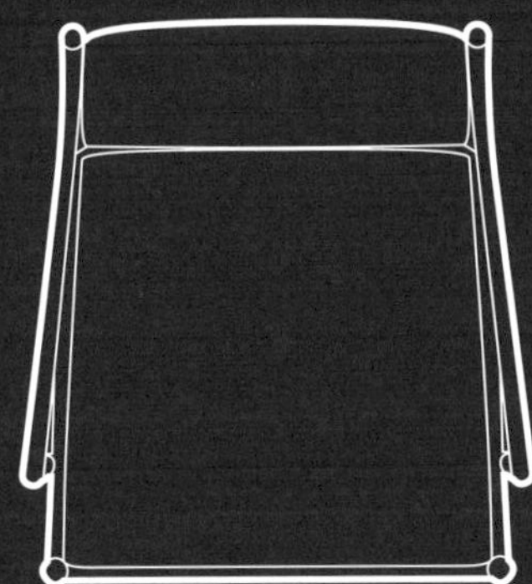

10

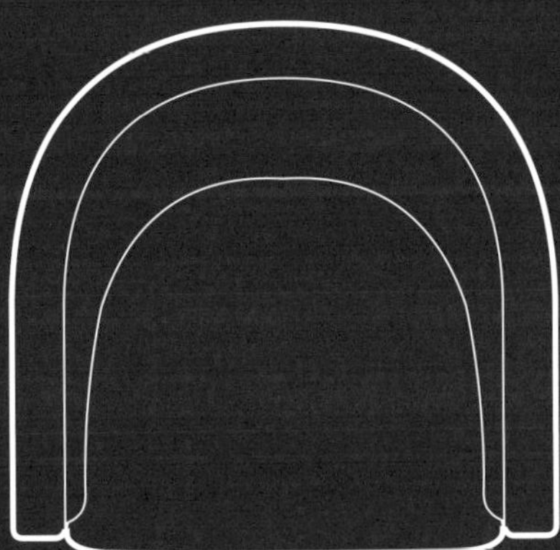

11

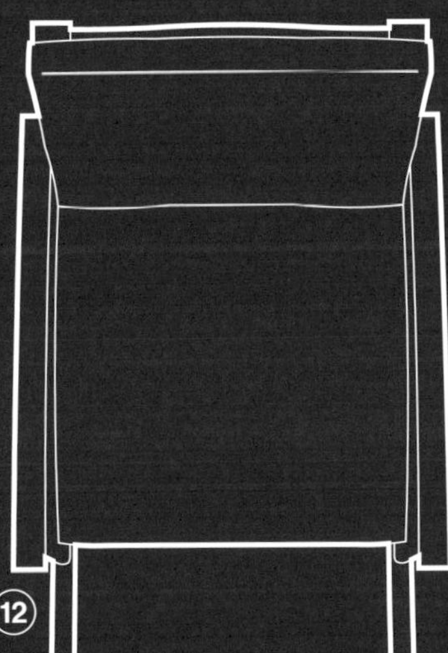

12

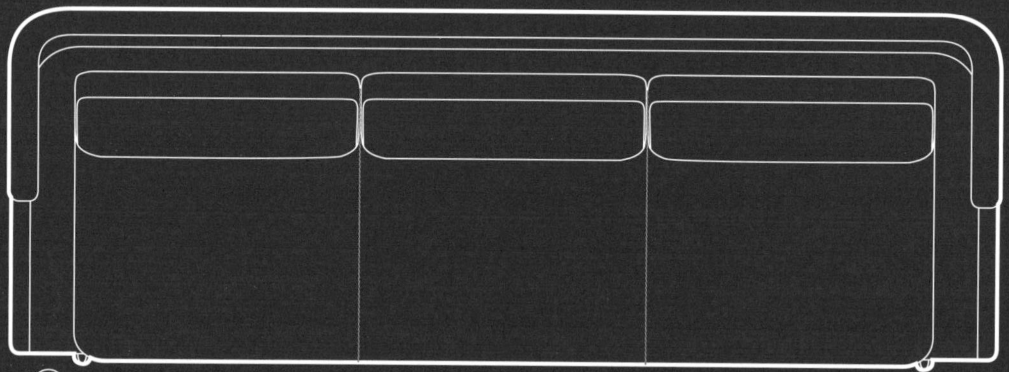

⑬

⑭

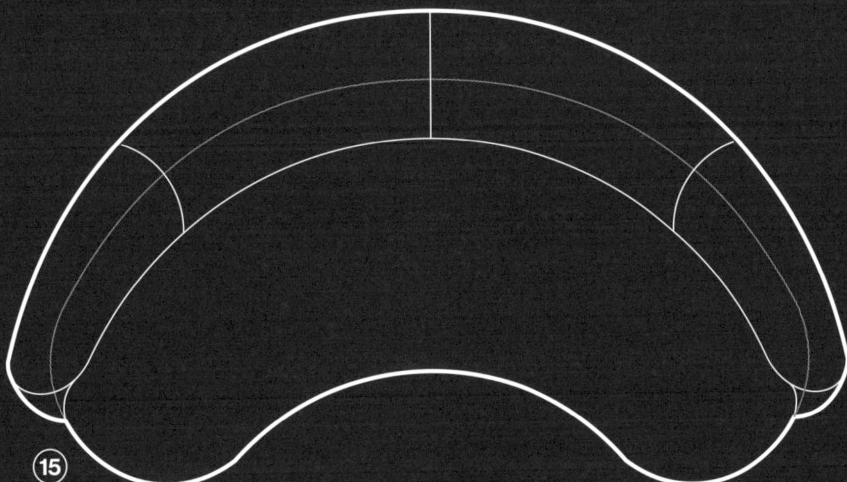

15

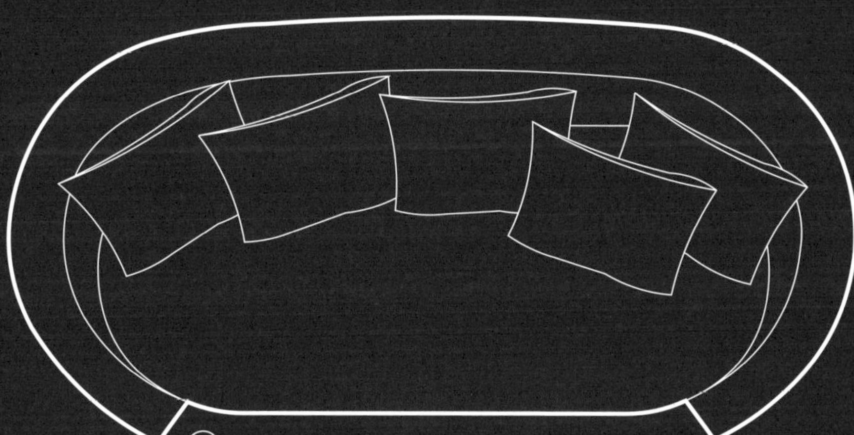

16

1

L-shaped sofa S
Seatings
2.1 × 2.14 m • 6'-10.7" × 7'

2

Modular corner sofa
Seatings
2.15 × 3.05 m • 7'-0.6" × 10'

3

L couch
Seatings
2.05 × 3.16 m • 6'-8.7" × 10'-4.4"

4

L-shaped sofa
Seatings
2.33 × 3 m • 7'-7.7" × 9'-10"

5

Sofa basic L
Seatings
0.9 × 2.1 m • 2'-11.4" × 6'-10.7"

6

Sofa S
Seatings
0.8 × 1.65 m • 2'-7.5" × 5'-5"

7

Sofa basic S
Seatings
0.9 × 1.5 m • 2'-11.4" × 4'-11"

8

Alcove sofa S
Seatings
0.88 × 1.88 m • 2'-10.6" × 6'-2"

9

Armchair alcove
Seatings
0.75 × 0.79 m • 2'-5.5" × 2'-7"

10

Armchair modern
Seatings
0.68 × 0.65 m • 2'-3" × 2'-1.6"

11

Armchair round
Seatings
0.7 × 0.74 m • 2'-3.6" × 2'-5"

12

Lounge rocking chair • Seatings
1.1 × 0.79 m • 3'-7.3" × 2'-7"

13

Alcove sofa L
Seatings
0.94 × 2.7 m • 3'-1" × 8'-10.3"

14

Couch 2-seater
Seatings
1.12 × 2.3 m • 3'-8" × 7'-6.2"

15

Curvy sofa
Seatings
1.14 × 2.1 m • 3'-9" × 6'-10.7"

16

Round sofa
Seatings
0.97 × 2 m • 3'-2.2" × 6'-6.7"

Kit for a
Kitchen

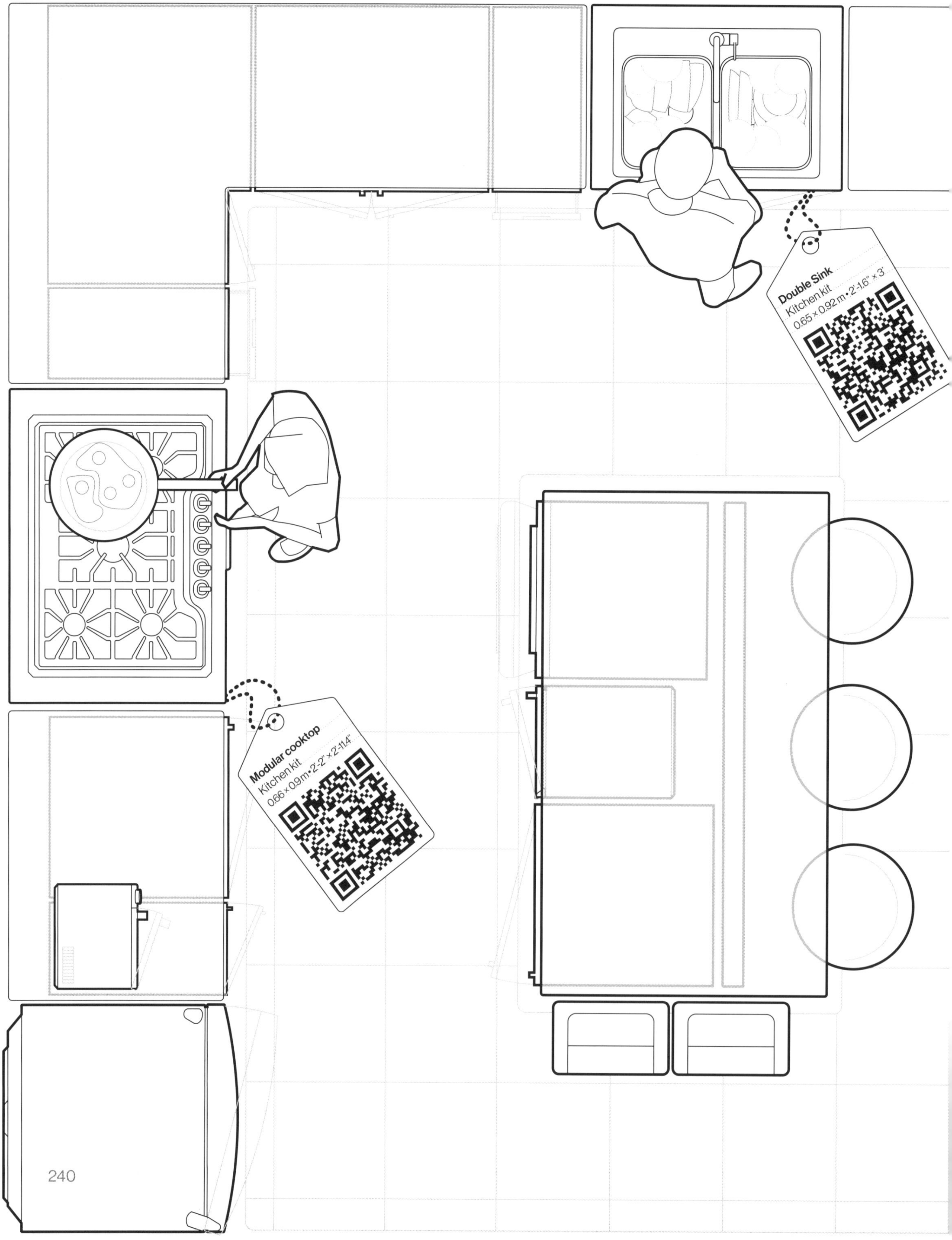
Double Sink
Kitchen kit
0.65 × 0.92 m • 2'-1.6" × 3'
Modular cooktop
Kitchen kit
0.66 × 0.9 m • 2'-2" × 2'-11.4"

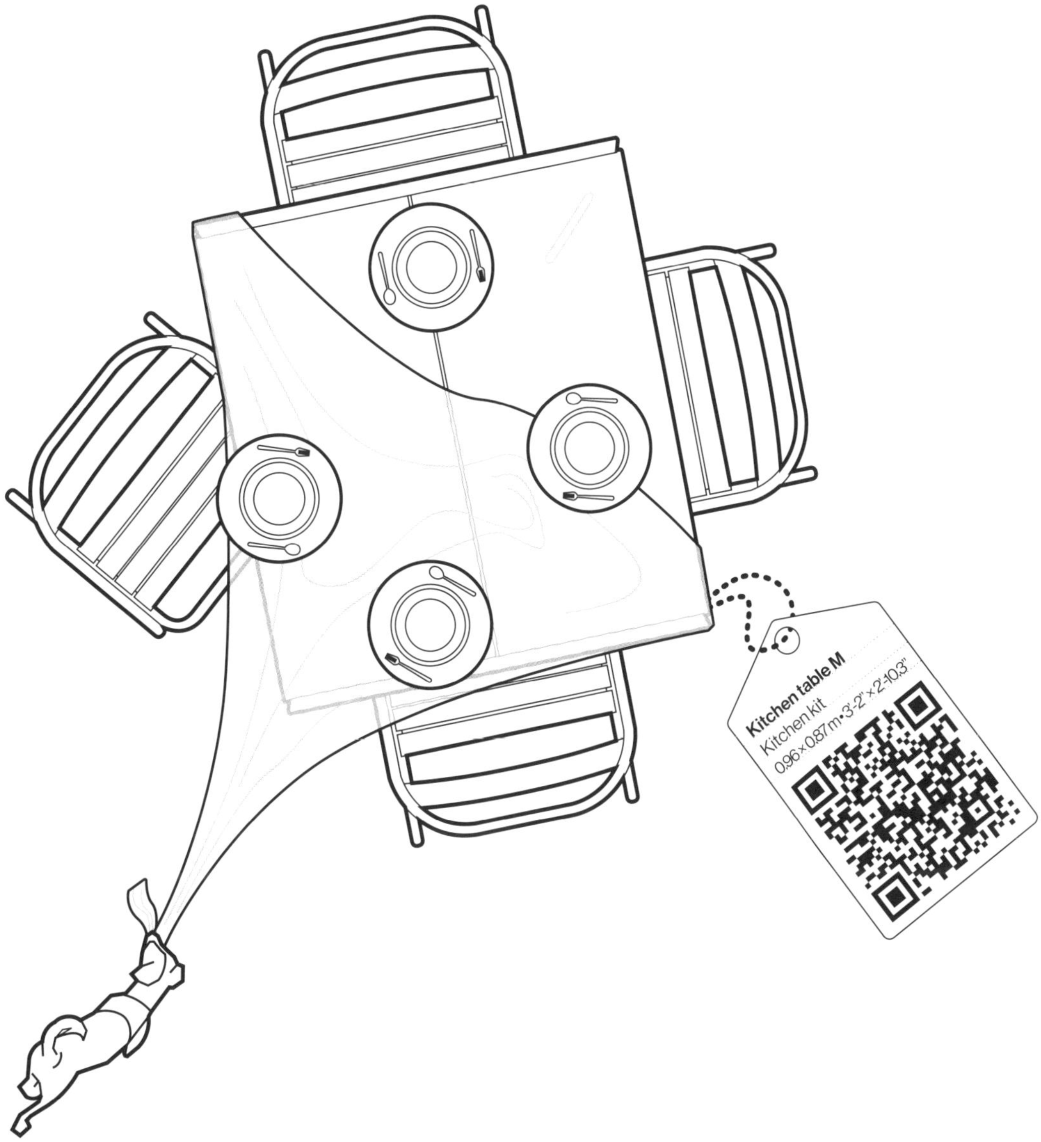
Kitchen table M
Kitchen kit
0.96 × 0.87 m • 3'-2" × 2'-10.3"

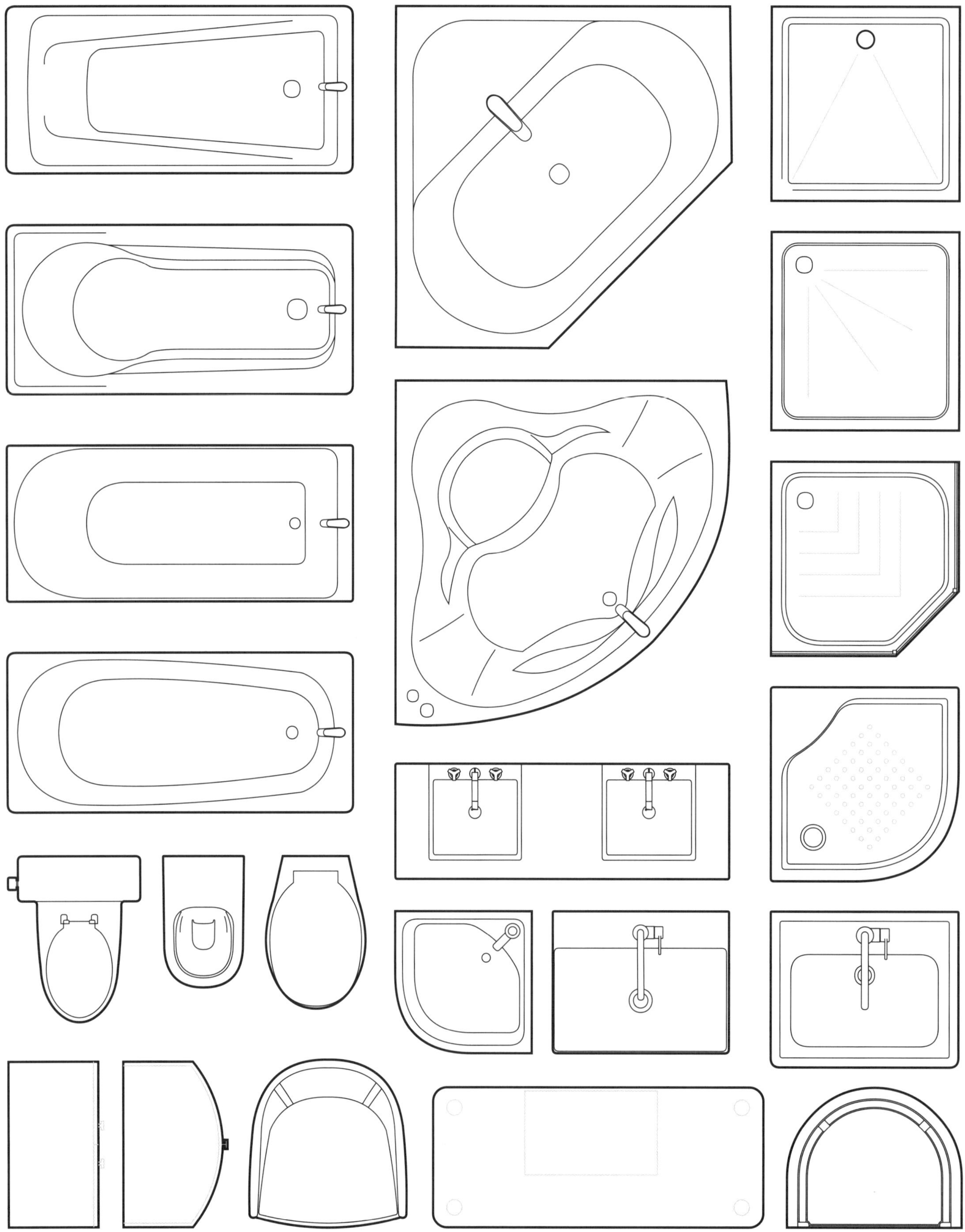

Kit for a
Bathroom

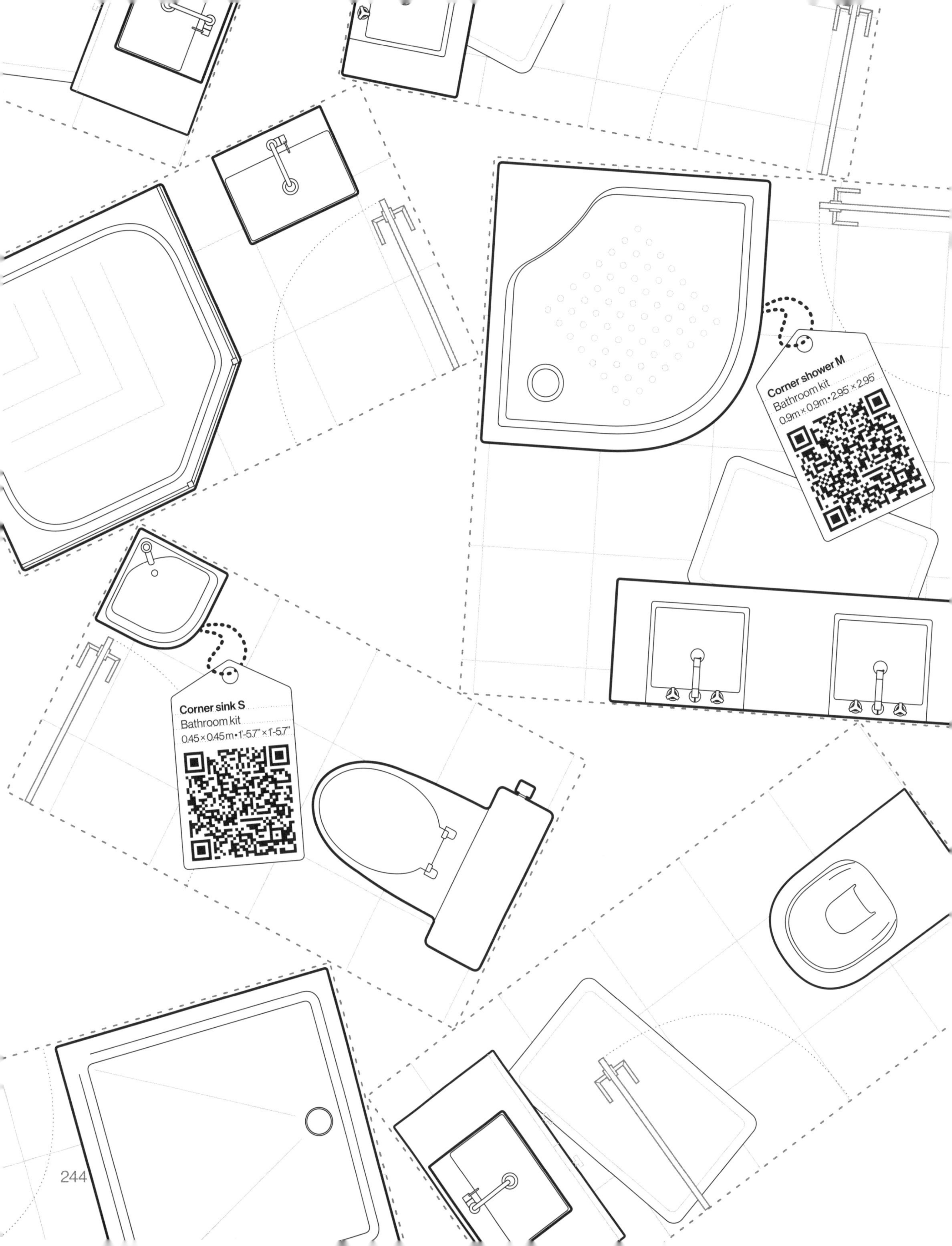
Corner shower M
Bathroom kit
0.9m × 0.9m • 2.95' × 2.95'
Corner sink S
Bathroom kit
0.45 × 0.45 m • 1'-5.7" × 1'-5.7"

Vanity round
Bathroom kit
0.57 × 0.9 m • 1'-10.4" × 2'-11.4"

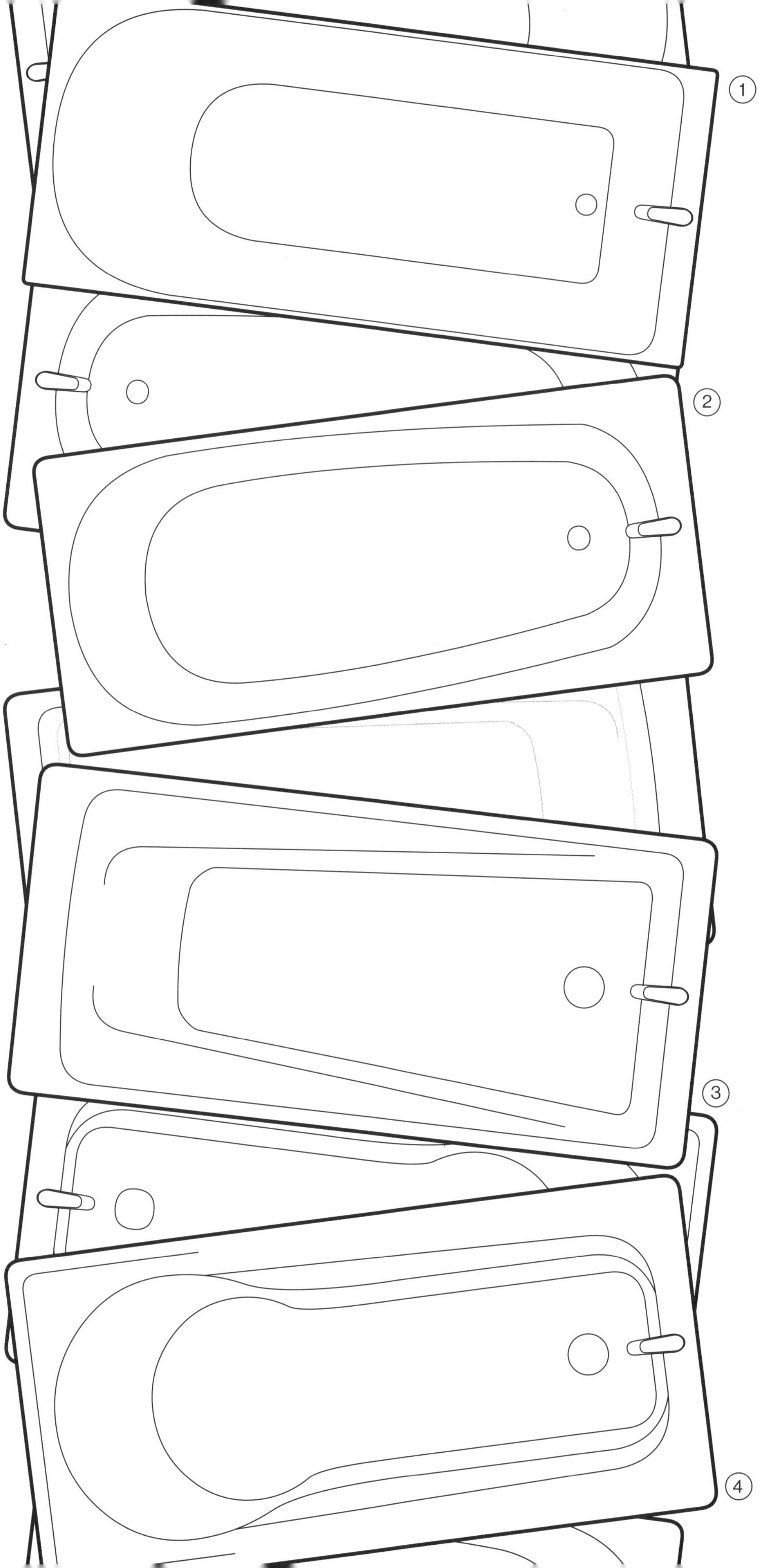

1

Alcove bathtub M
Bathroom kit
0.8 × 1.83 m • 2'-7.5" × 6'

2

Bathtub round L
Bathroom kit
0.8 × 1.8 m • 2'-7.5" × 5'-10.9"

3

Bathtub wide
Bathroom kit
0.88 × 1.9 m • 2'-10.6" × 6'-2.5"

4

Soaking bathtub L
Bathroom kit
0.89 × 1.89 m • 2'-11" × 6'-2.4"

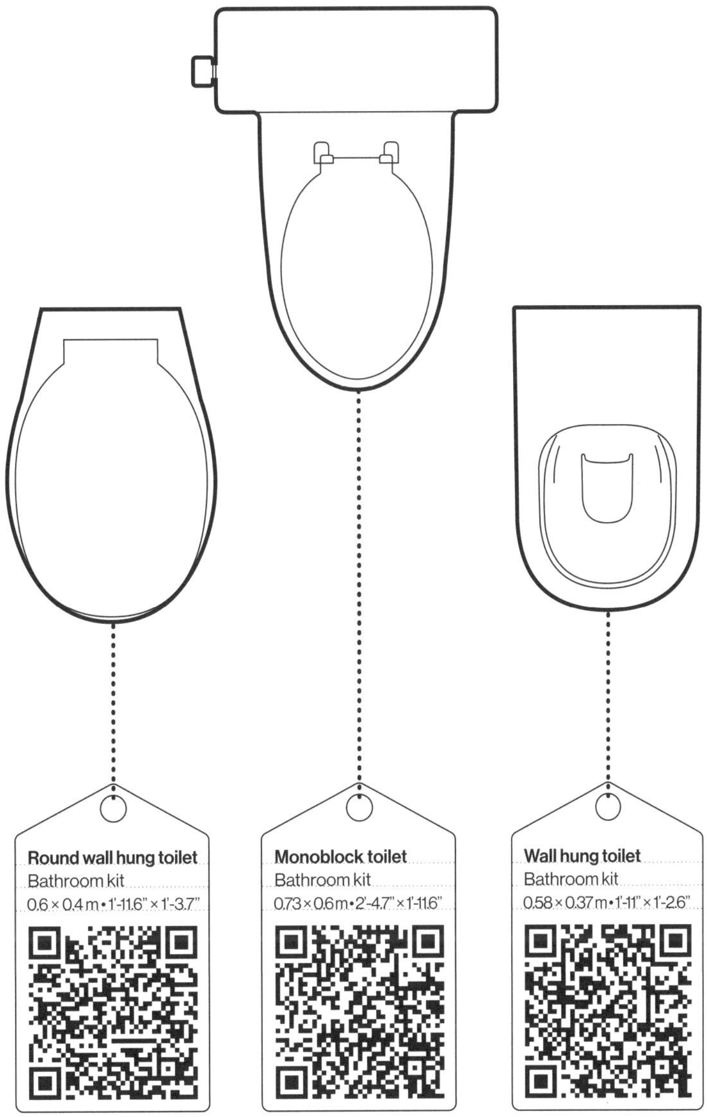
Round wall hung toilet
Bathroom kit
0.6 × 0.4 m • 1'-11.6" × 1'-3.7"
Monoblock toilet
Bathroom kit
0.73 × 0.6 m • 2'-4.7" × 1'-11.6"
Wall hung toilet
Bathroom kit
0.58 × 0.37 m • 1'-11" × 1'-2.6"

Kit for a
Washing Room

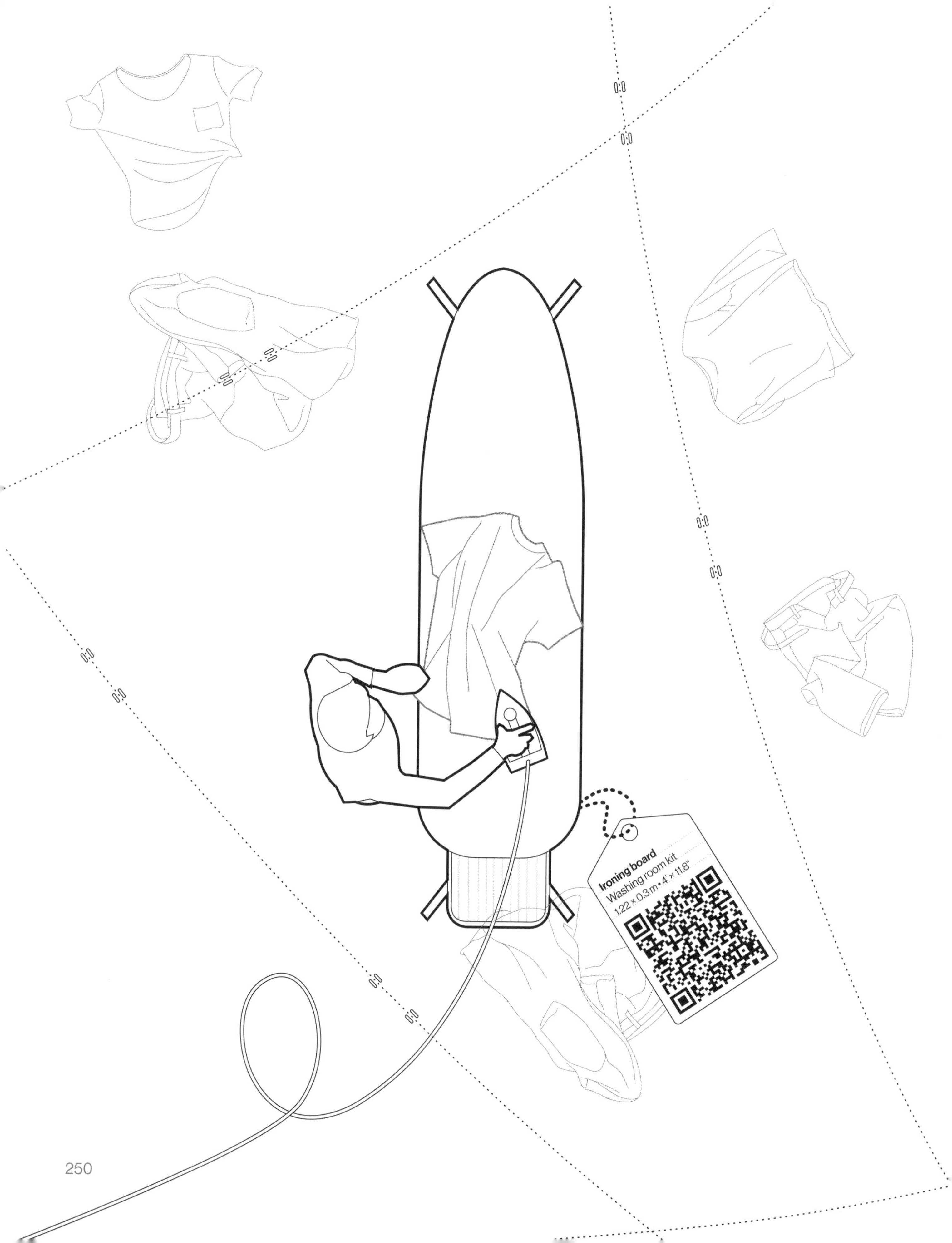
Ironing board
Washing room kit
1.22 × 0.3 m • 4' × 11.8"

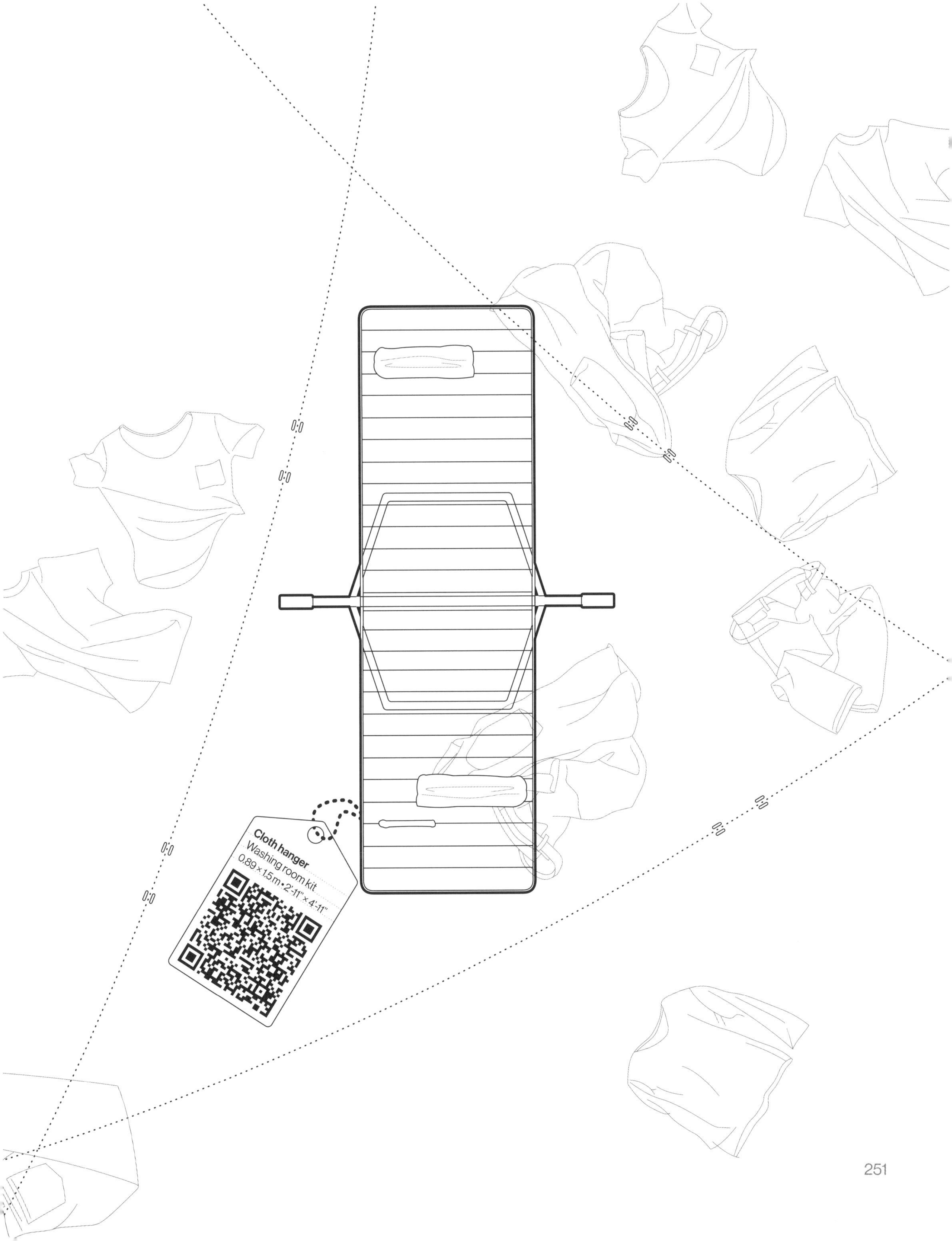
Cloth hanger
Washing room kit
0,89 × 1,5 m • 2'-11" × 4'-11"

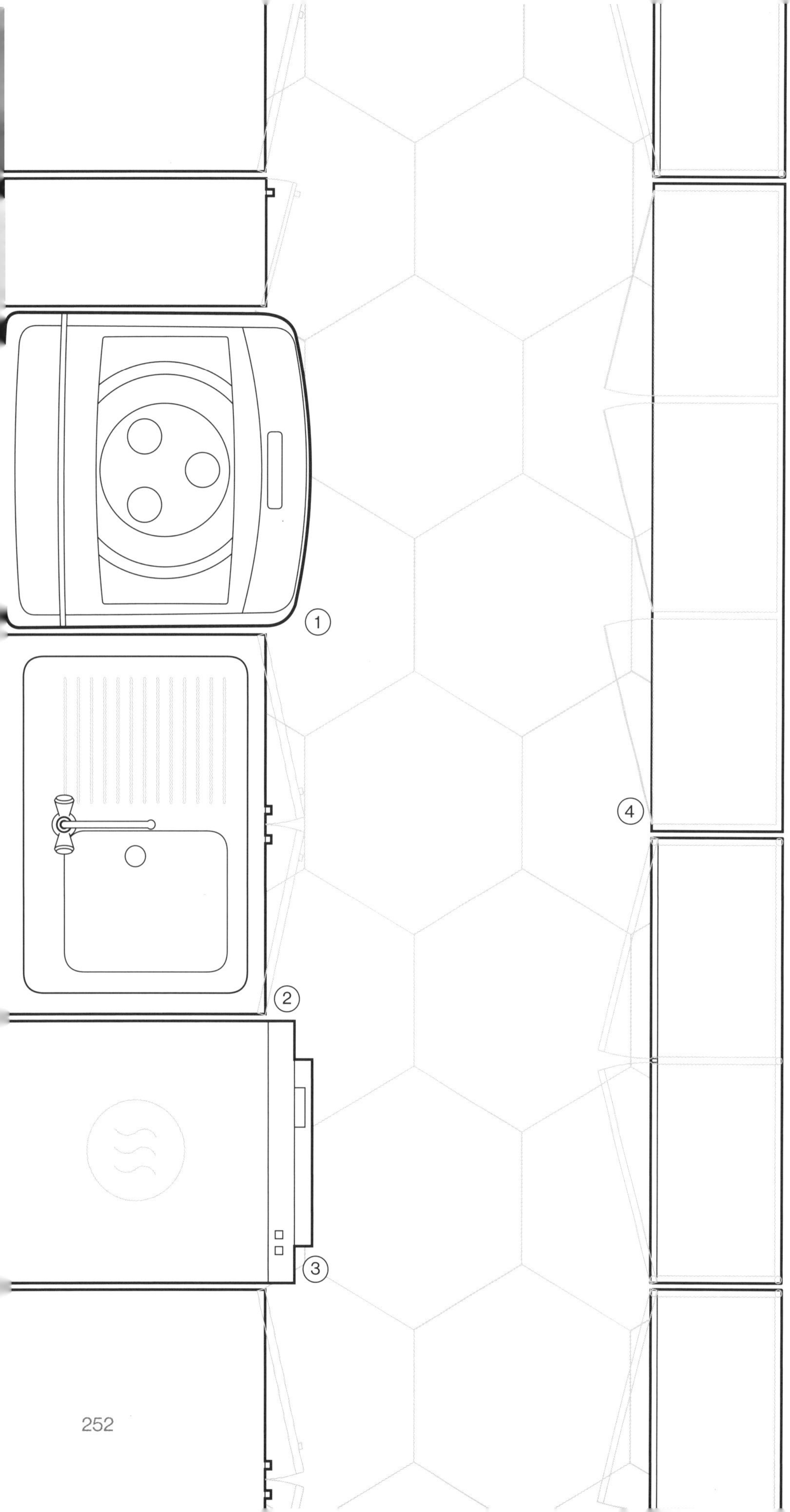

1

Washing machine
Washing room kit
0.82 × 0.8 m • 2'-8.3" × 2'-7.5"

2

Casework L with doors
Washing room kit
0.65 × 0.92 m • 2'-1.6" × 3'

3

Dryer
Washing room kit
0.84 × 0.7 m • 2'-9" × 2'-3.6"

4

Closet 3 doors
Washing room kit
0.55 × 1.8 m • 1'-9.7" × 5'-11"

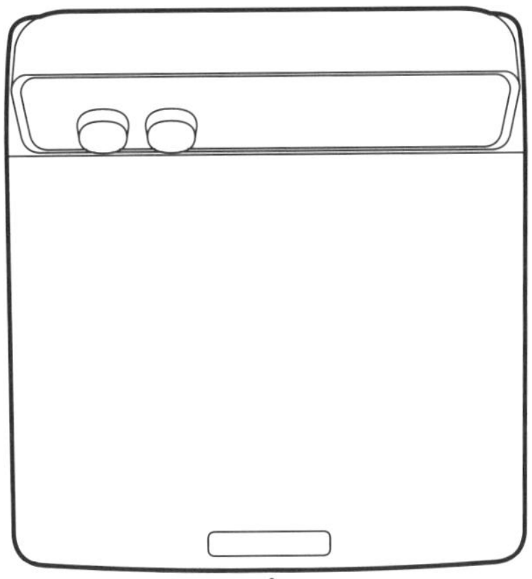

Washing machine
Washing room kit
0.84 × 0.8 m • 2'-9" × 2'-7.5"

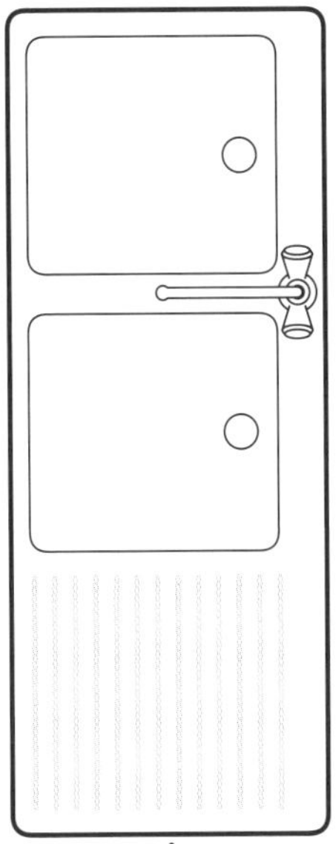

Kitchen sink double
Washing room kit
0.5 × 1.25 m • 1'-7.7" × 4'-1"

A Catalog of

Appliances

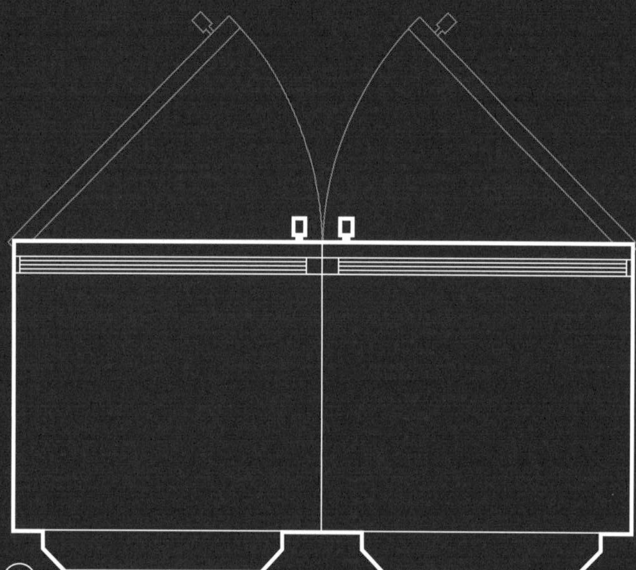

①

②

③

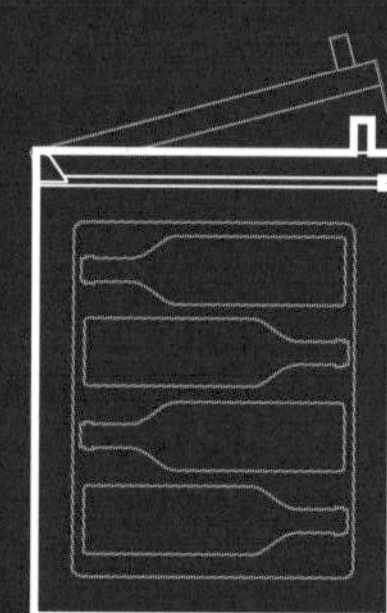

④

⑤

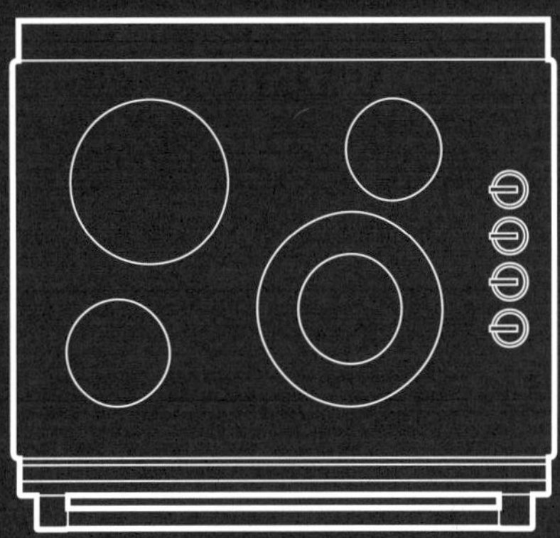

⑥

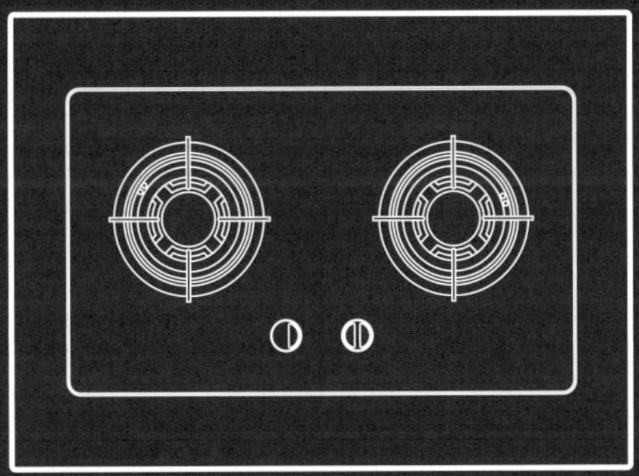

⑦

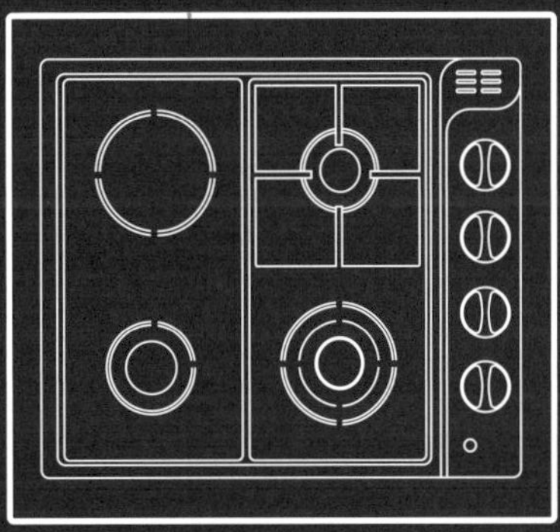

⑧

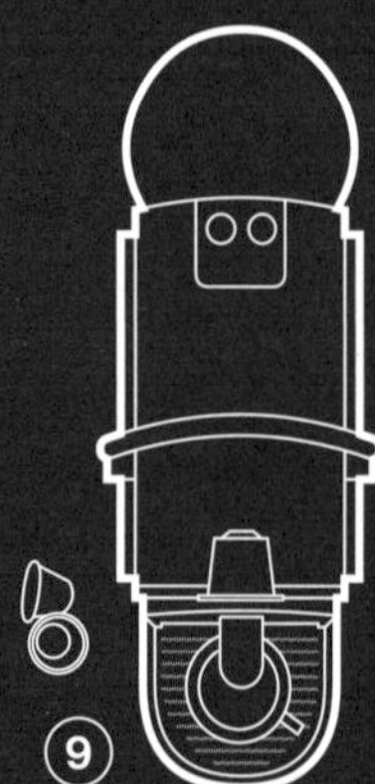

9

10

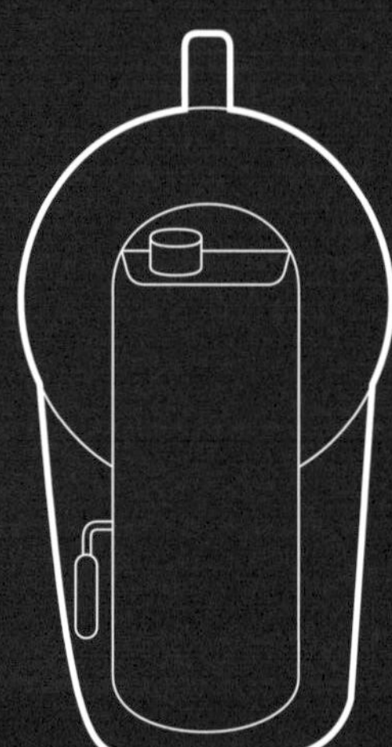

11

12

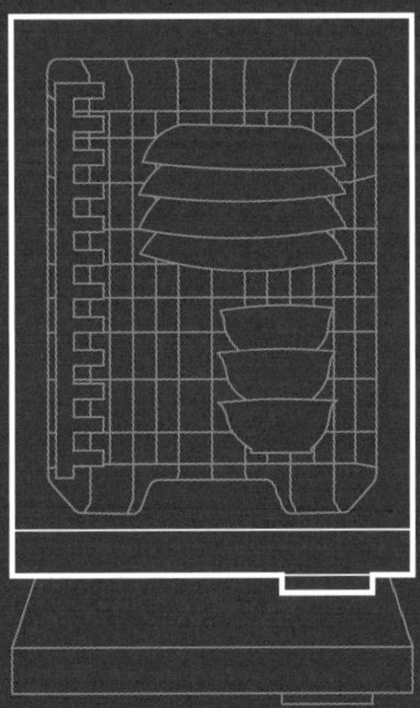

13

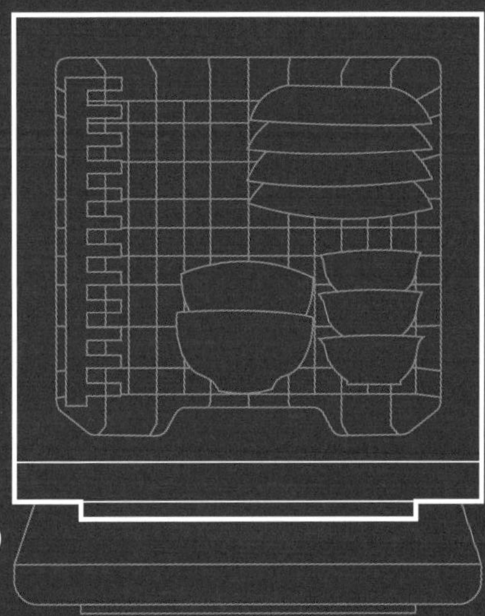

14

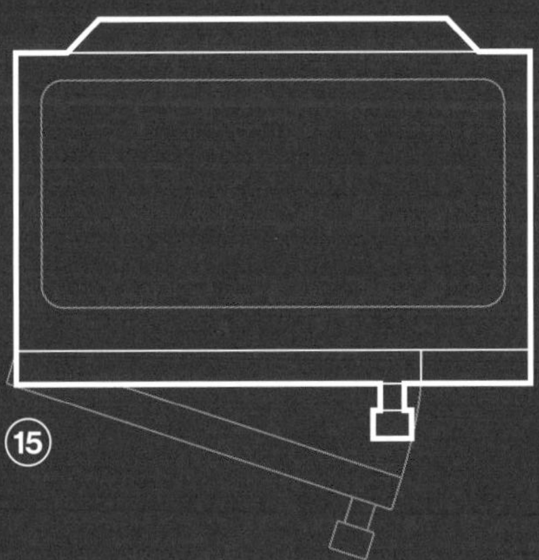

15

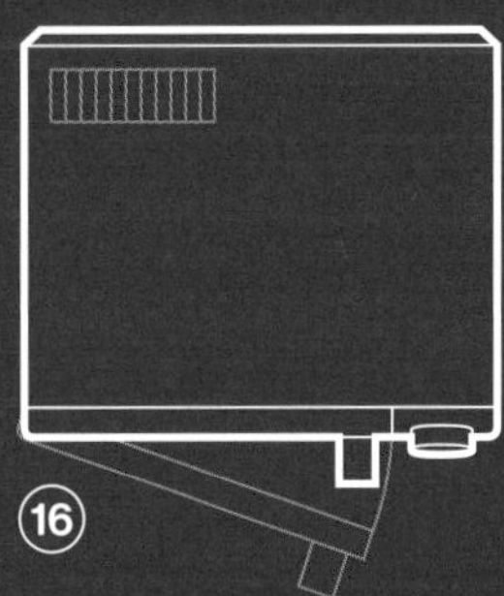

16

1

Fridge French door L
Appliances
0.72 × 1.4 m • 2'-4.3" × 4'-7"

2

Mini bar water L
Appliances
0.5 × 0.5 m • 1'-7.7" × 1'-7.7"

3

Fridge basic
Appliances
0.77 × 0.77 m • 2'-6.3" × 2'-6.3"

4

Mini bar rectangular
Appliances
0.5 × 0.4 m • 1'-7.7" × 1'-3.7"

5

Modular cooktop
Appliances
0.66 × 0.9 m • 2'-2" × 2'-11.4"

6

Electric stove L
Appliances
0.7 × 0.78 m • 2'-3.6" × 2'-6.7"

7

Compact gas cooktop • Appliances
0.65 × 0.9 m • 2'-1.6" × 2'-11.4"

8

Hybrid cooktop
Appliances
0.65 × 0.74 m • 2'-1.6" × 2'-5"

9

Coffee machine S
Appliances
0.3 × 0.11 m • 11.8" × 4.3"

10

Coffee machine L
Appliances
0.32 × 0.25 m • 1'-0.6" × 9.8"

11

Mixer L
Appliances
0.24 × 0.45 m • 9.4" × 1'-5.7"

12

Mixer S
Appliances
0.18 × 0.35 m • 7" × 1'-1.8"

13

Dishwasher M
Appliances
0.63 × 0.45 m • 2'-1" × 1'-5.7"

14

Dishwasher L
Appliances
0.63 × 0.6 m • 2'-1" × 1'-11.6"

15

Microwave L
Appliances
0.4 × 0.58 m • 1'-3.7" × 1'-11"

16

Microwave S
Appliances
0.33 × 0.38 m • 1'-1" × 1'-3"

Kit for a
Kid's Bedroom

Toddler bed
Kid bedroom kit
2.08 × 1.22 m • 6'-9.9" × 4'

Crib L
Kid bedroom kit
0.94 × 1.28 m • 3'-1" × 4'-2.4"

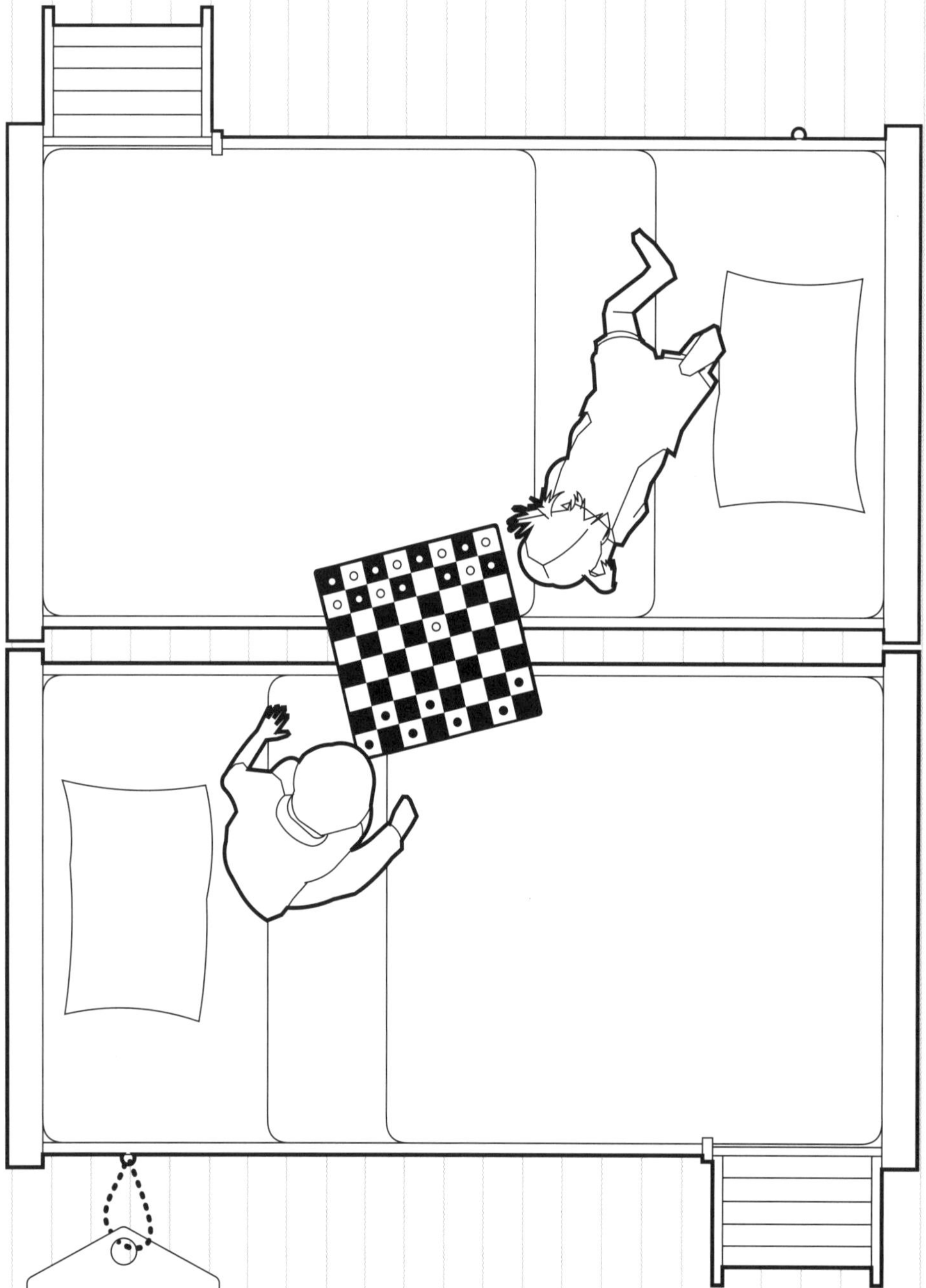

Double decker
Kid bedroom kit
2.06 × 1.38 m • 6'-9" × 4'-6.3"

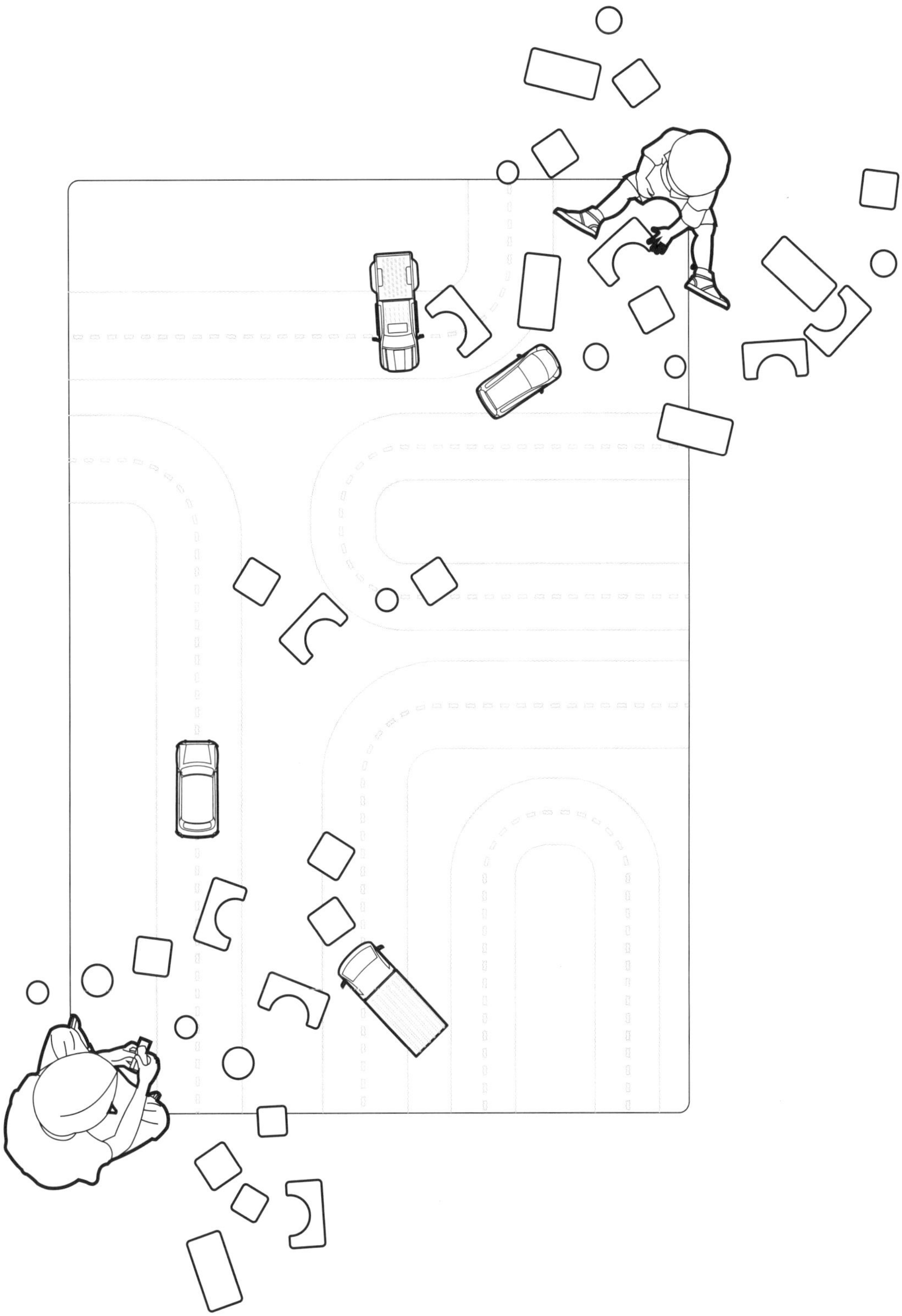

Kit for a
Game Room

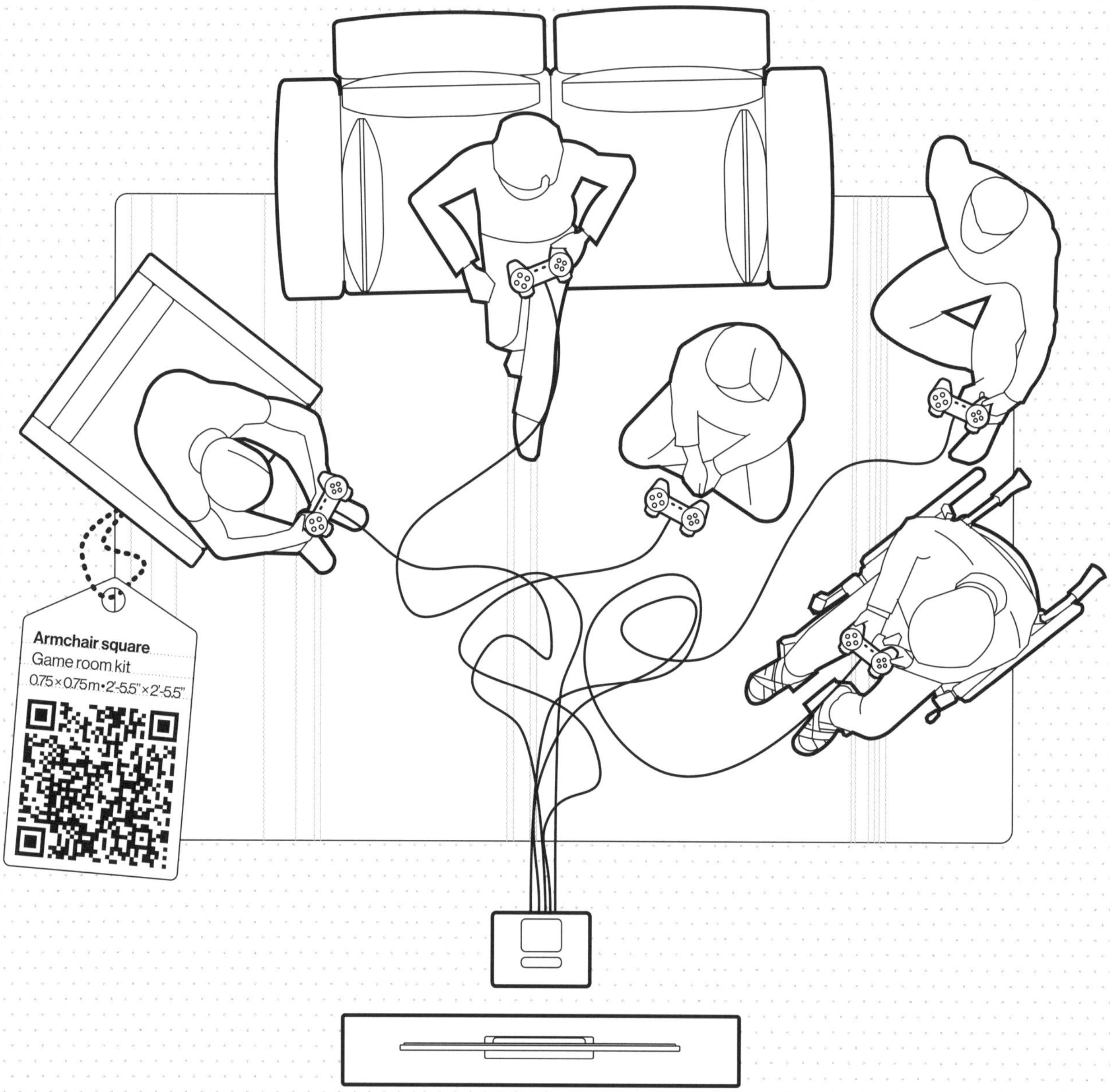
Armchair square
Game room kit
0.75×0.75m•2'-5.5"×2'-5.5"

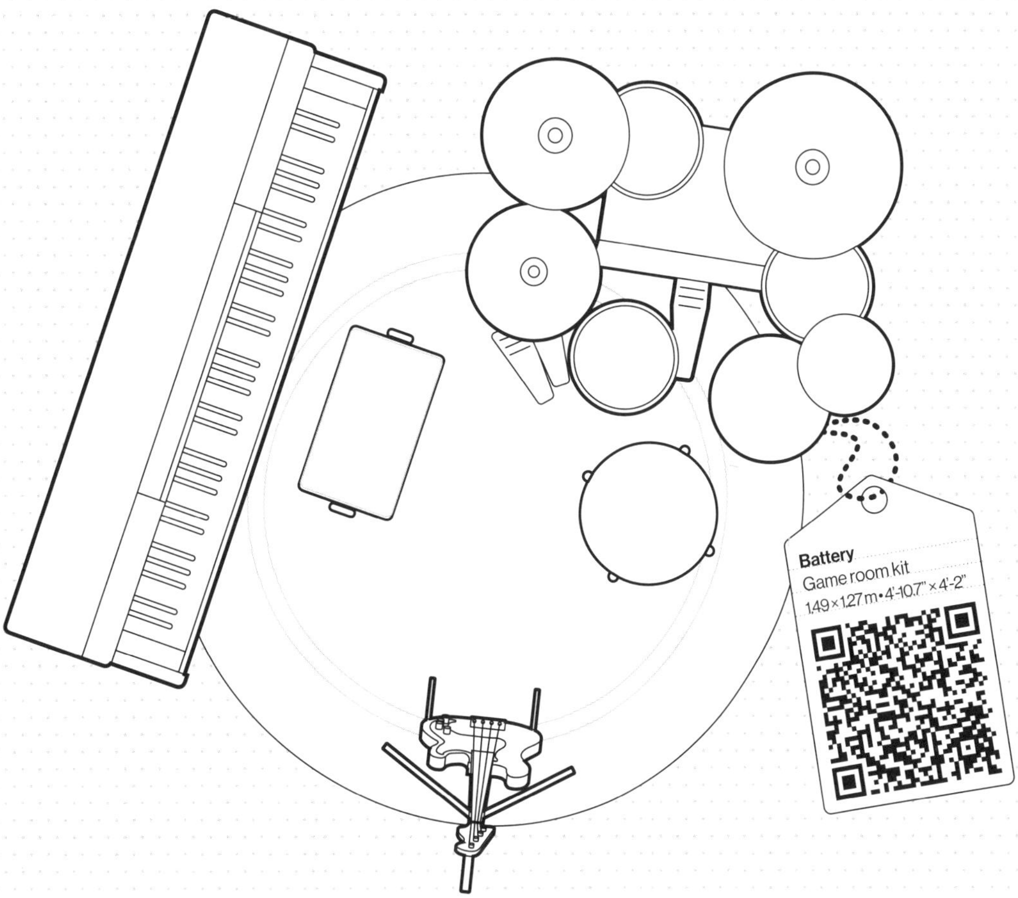
Battery
Game room kit
1.49 × 1.27 m • 4'-10.7" × 4'-2"

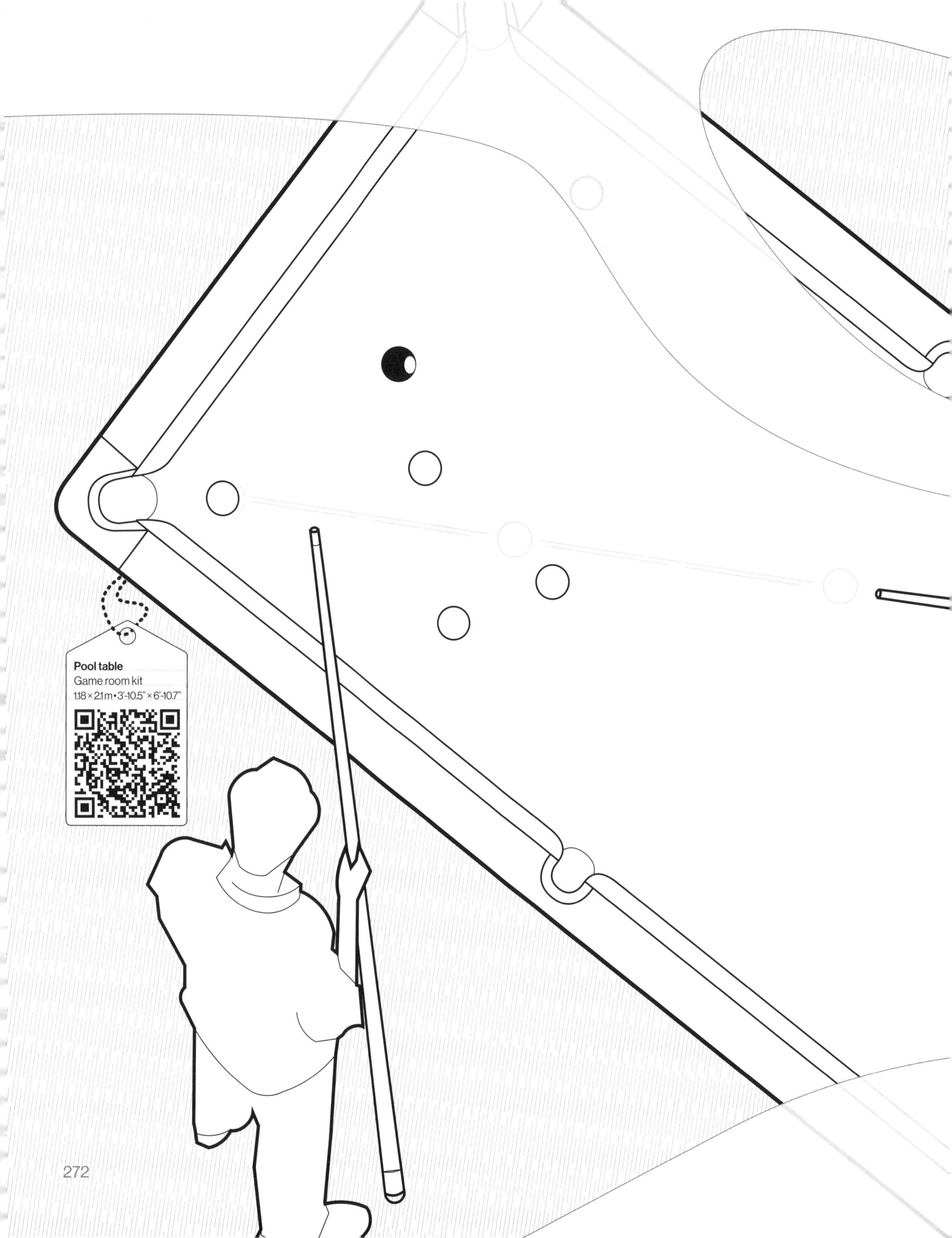
Pool table
Game room kit
1.18 × 2.1 m • 3'-10.5" × 6'-10.7"

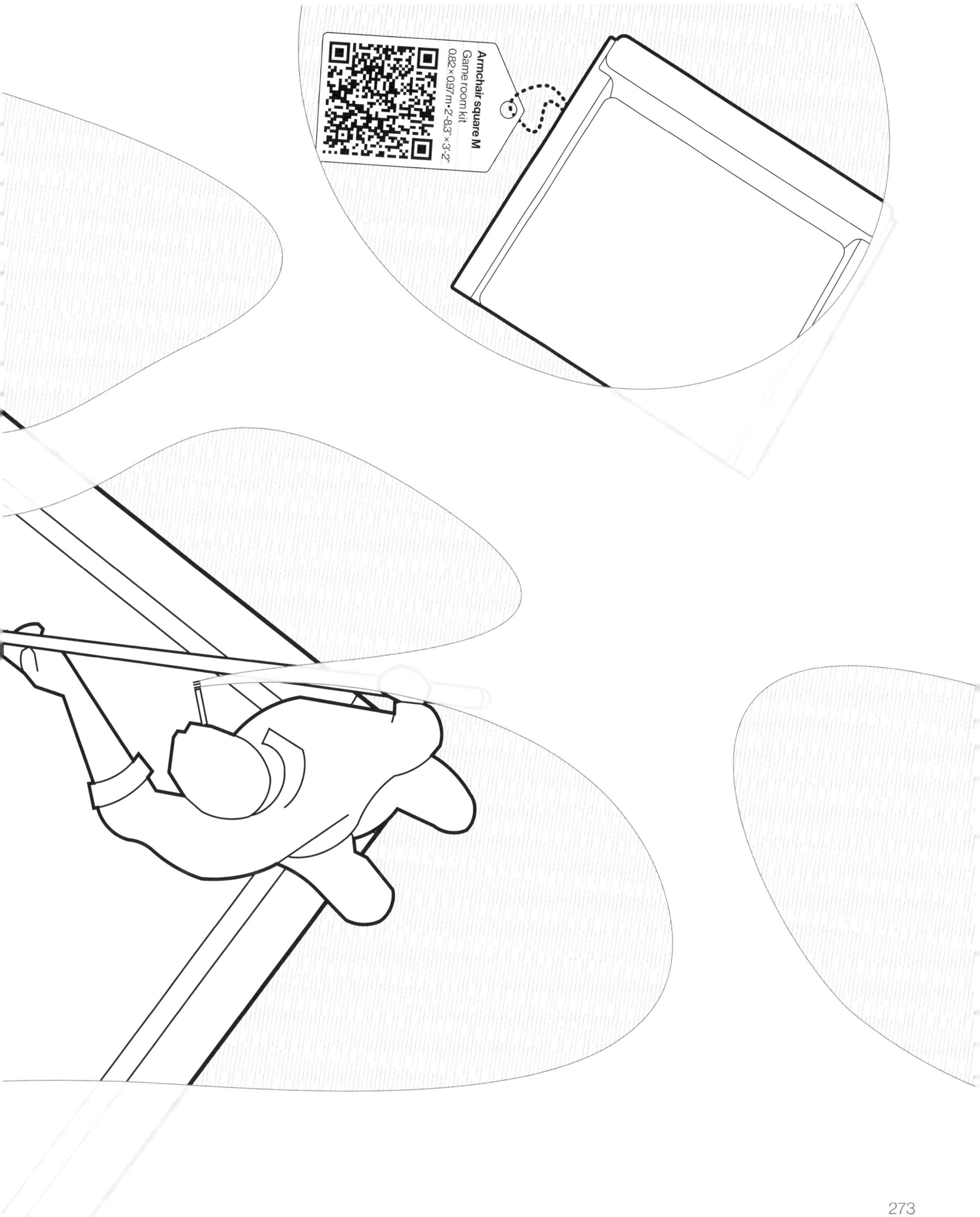
Armchair square M
Game room kit
0.82×0.97 m•2'-8.3"×3'-2"

Kit for a
Library Room

Shelving 5-section
Library room kit
0.39 × 1.85 m • 1'-3.4" × 6'-1"

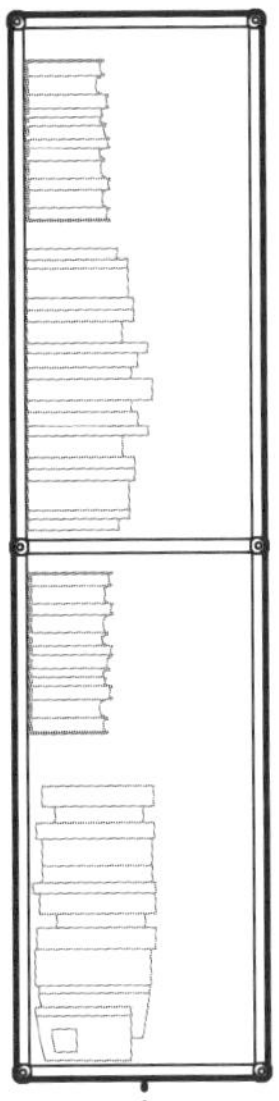

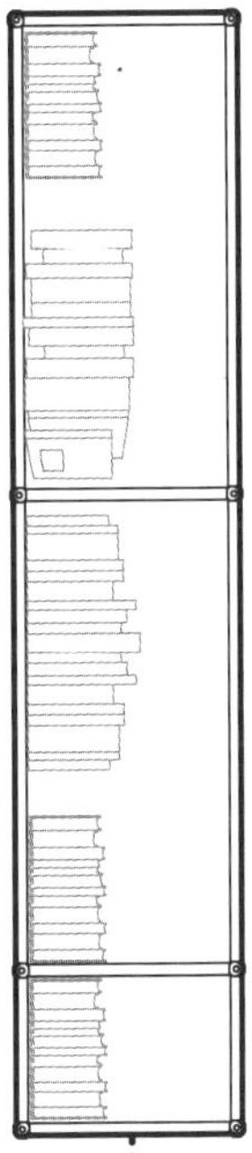

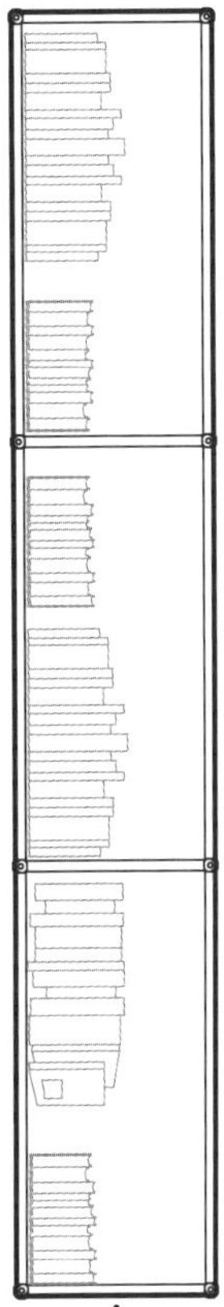

Shelving 2-section
Library room kit
0.37 × 1.52 m • 1'-2.6" × 5'

Shelving 2.5-section
Library room kit
0.37 × 1.77 m • 1'-2.6" × 5'-9.7"

Shelving 3-section
Library room kit
0.37 × 2.27 m • 1'-2.6" × 7'-5.4"

1
Sofa triple
Library room kit
0.84 × 1.9 m • 2'-9" × 6'-2.8"
2
Swing-arm desk lamp
Library room kit
0.22 × 0.89 m • 8.7" × 2'-11"
1
2

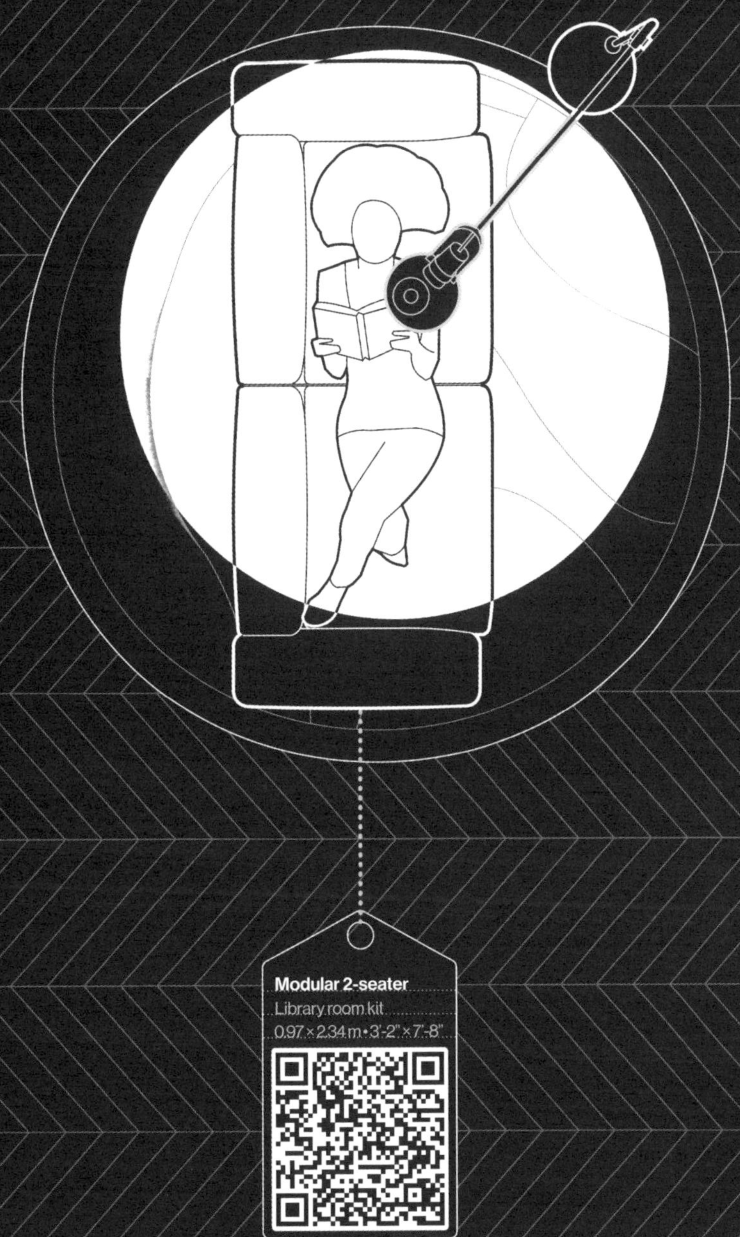
Modular 2-seater
Library room kit
0.97 × 2.34 m • 3'-2" × 7'-8"

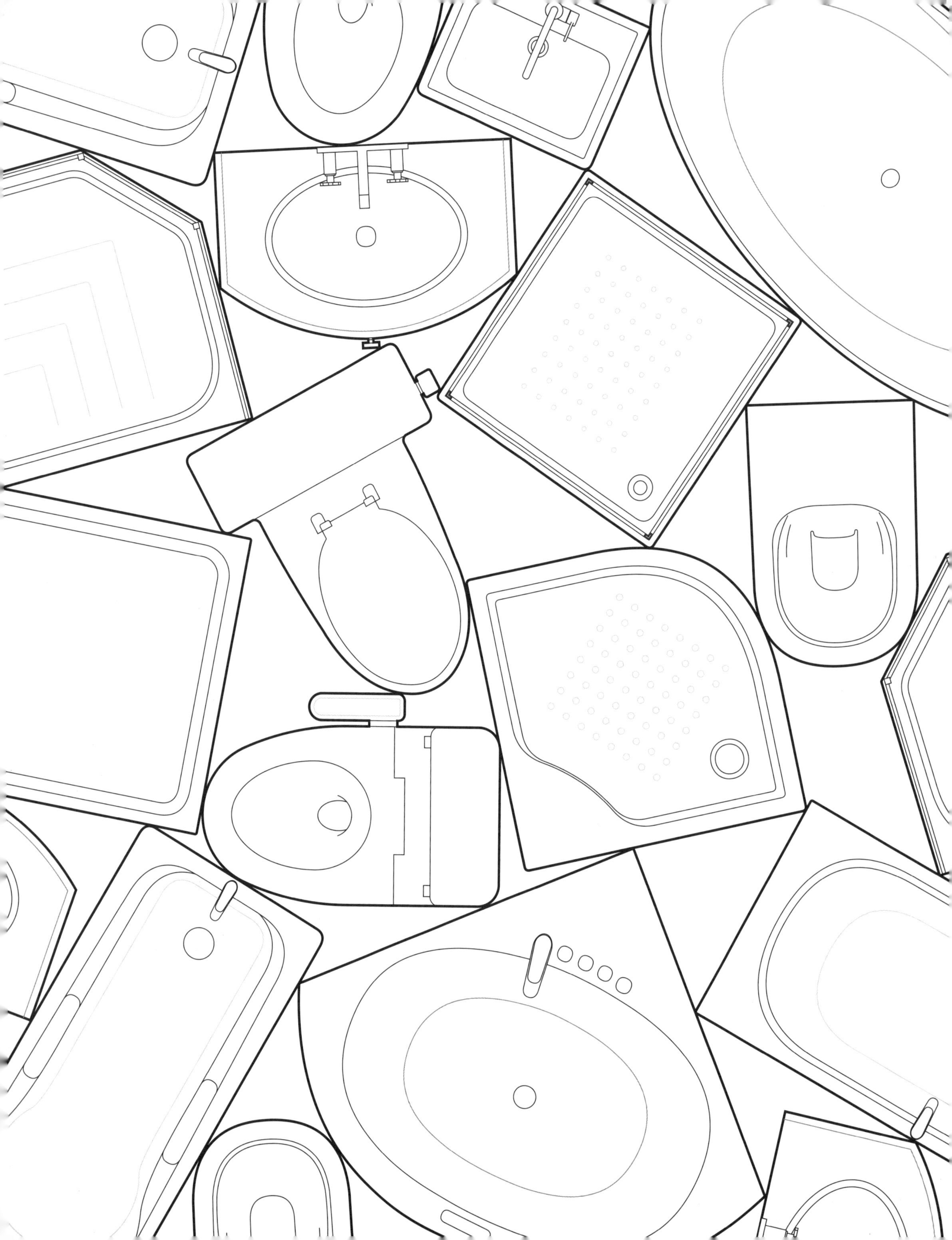

A Catalog of

Housing Fixtures

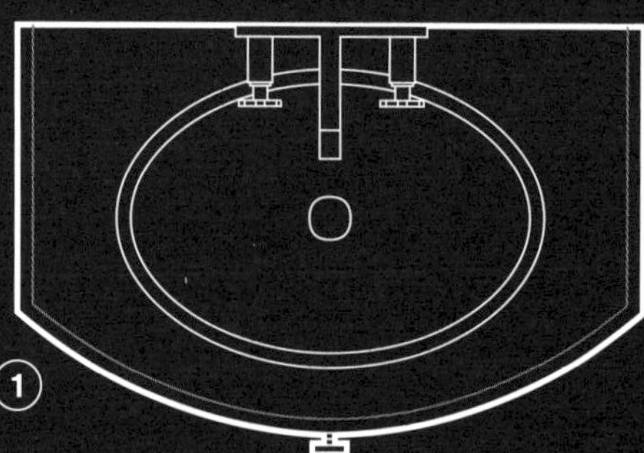

1

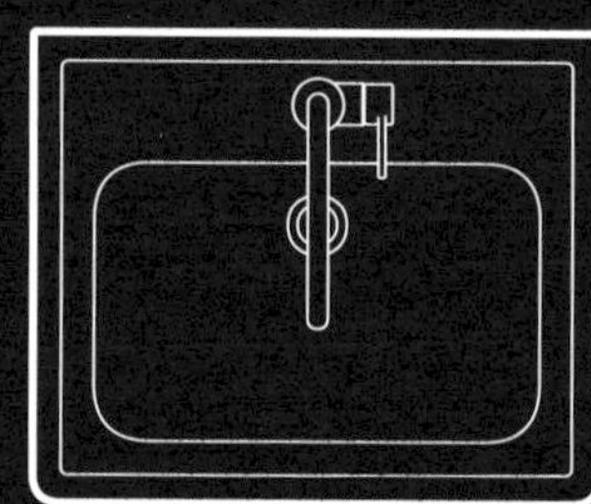

2

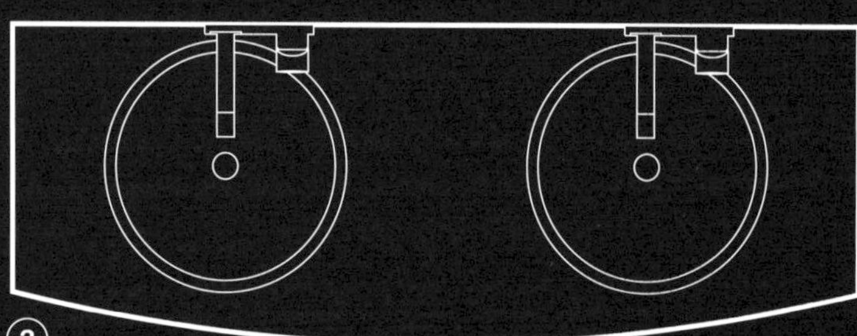

3

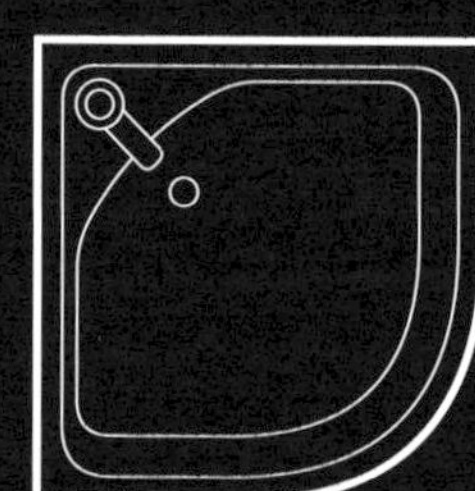

4

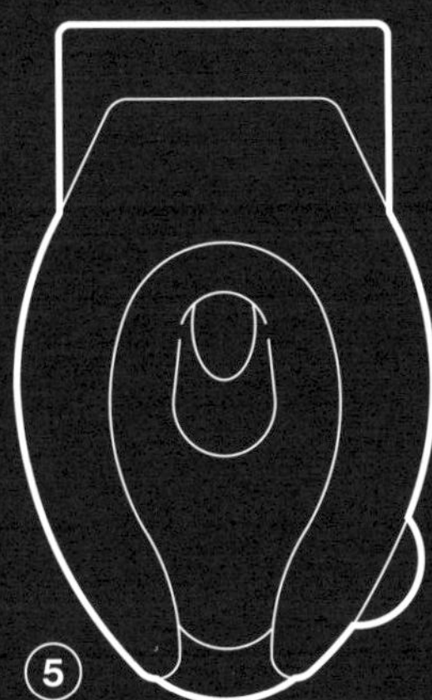

5

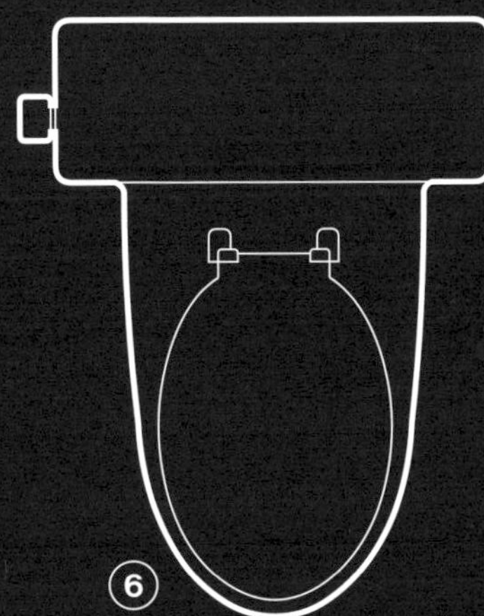

6

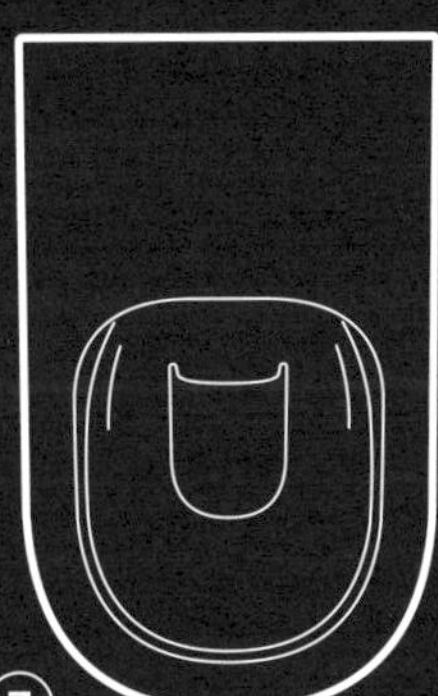

7

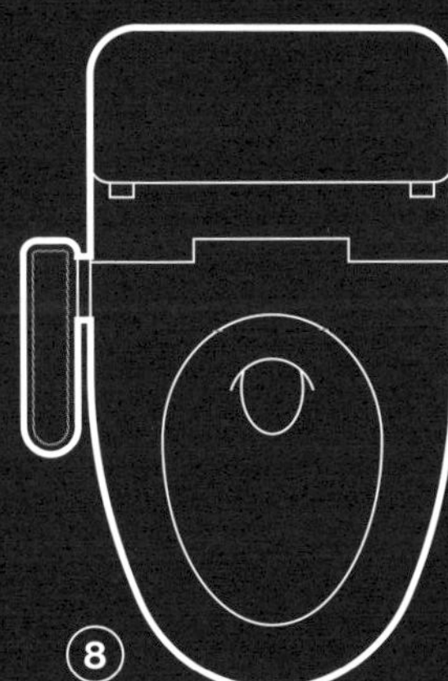

8

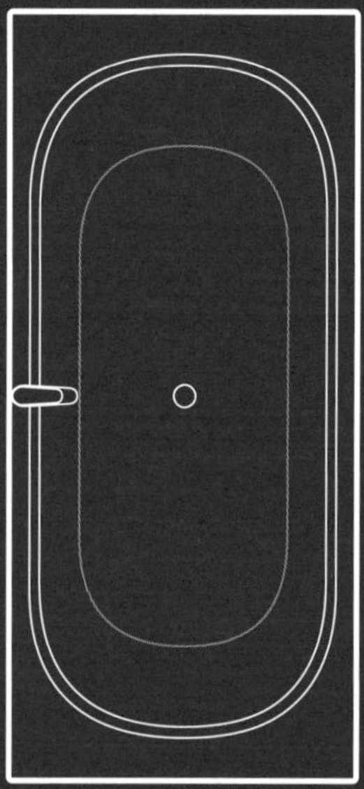

9

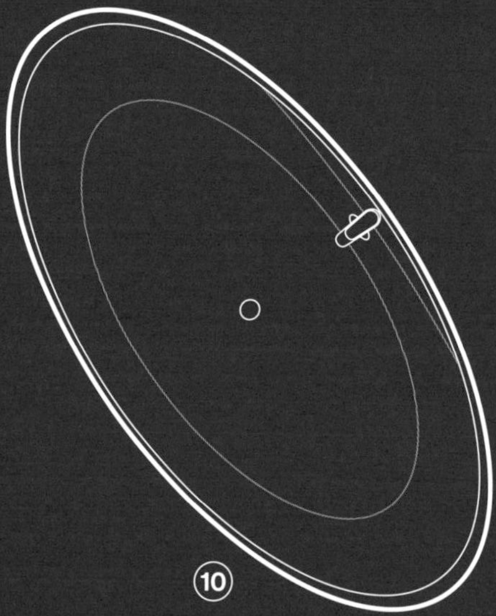

10

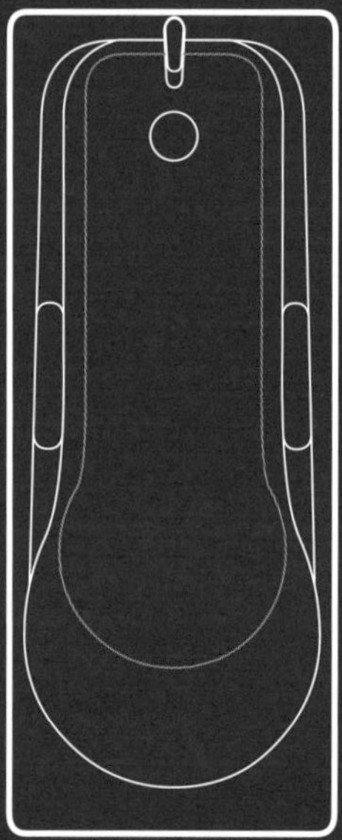

11

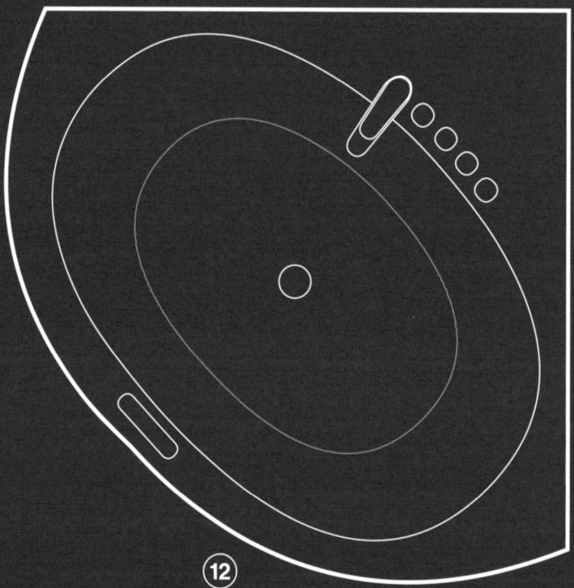

12

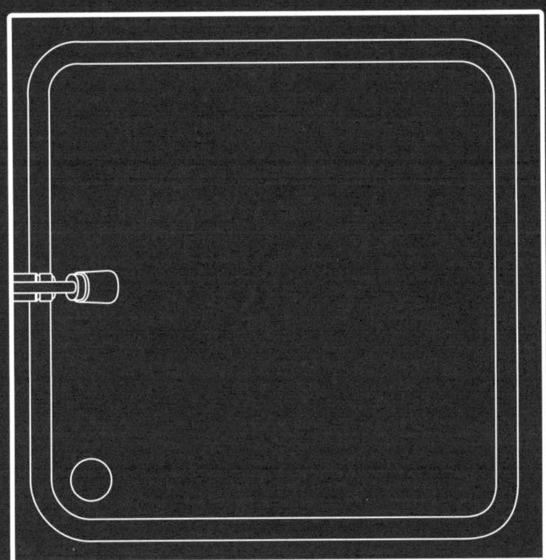

⑬

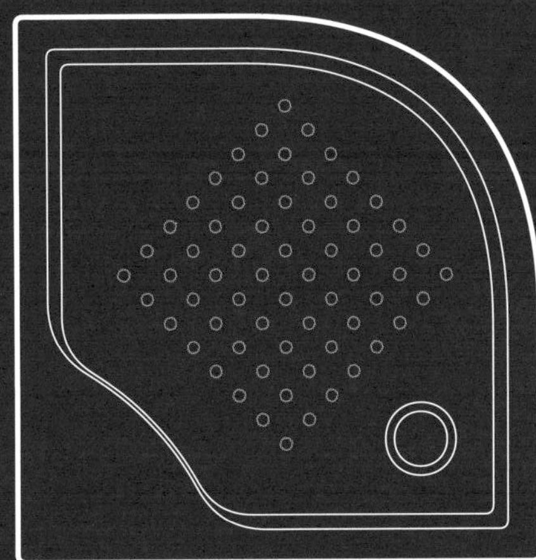

⑭

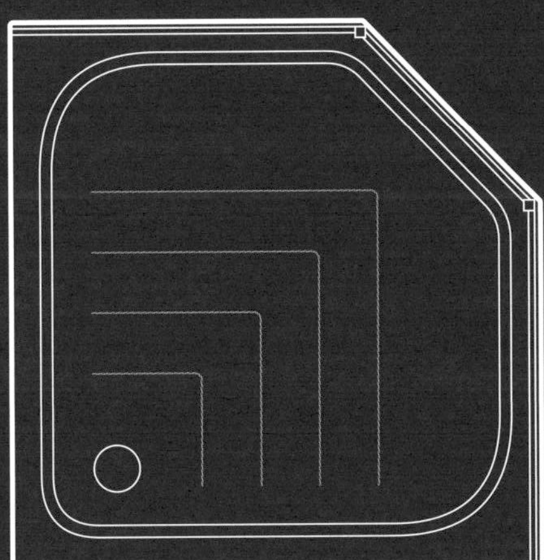

⑮

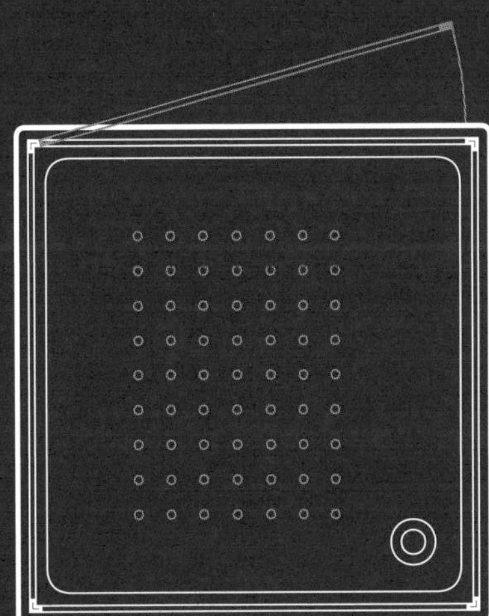

⑯

1

Countertop sink oval
Housing fixtures
0.57 × 0.88 m • 1'-10" × 2'-11"

2

Bathroom sink
Housing fixtures
0.47 × 0.58 m • 1'-6.5" × 1'-11"

3

Double countertop sink S • Housing fixtures
0.5 × 1.4 m • 1'-7.7" × 4'-7"

4

Corner sink S
Housing fixtures
0.45 × 0.45 m • 1'-5.7" × 1'-5.7"

5

Accessible toilet
Housing fixtures
0.7 × 0.44 m • 2'-3.6" × 1'-5.3"

6

Monoblock toilet
Housing fixtures
0.73 × 0.6 m • 2'-4.7" × 1'-11.6"

7

Wall hung toilet
Housing fixtures
0.58 × 0.37 m • 1'-11" × 1'-2.6"

8

Smart toilet S
Housing fixtures
0.69 × 0.47 m • 2'-3" × 1'-6.5"

9

Alcove round bathtub
Housing fixtures
0.85 × 1.8 m • 2'-9.5" × 5'-11"

10

Oval freestanding tub
Housing fixtures
1.06 × 2.13 m • 3'-5.7" × 7'

11

Soaking bathtub S
Housing fixtures
0.78 × 1.88 m • 2'-6.7" × 6'-2"

12

Corner round tub
Housing fixtures
1.97 × 1.94 m • 6'-5.6" × 6'-4.4"

13

Shower M
Housing fixtures
1 × 1 m • 3'-3.4" × 3'-3.4"

14

Corner shower M
Housing fixtures
0.9 × 0.9 m • 2'-11.4" × 2'-11.4"

15

Angle corner shower
Housing fixtures
0.9 × 0.9 m • 2'-11.4" × 2'-11.4"

16

Shower with door S
Housing fixtures
0.8 × 0.8 m • 2'-7.5" × 2'-7.5"

Kit for a
Patio

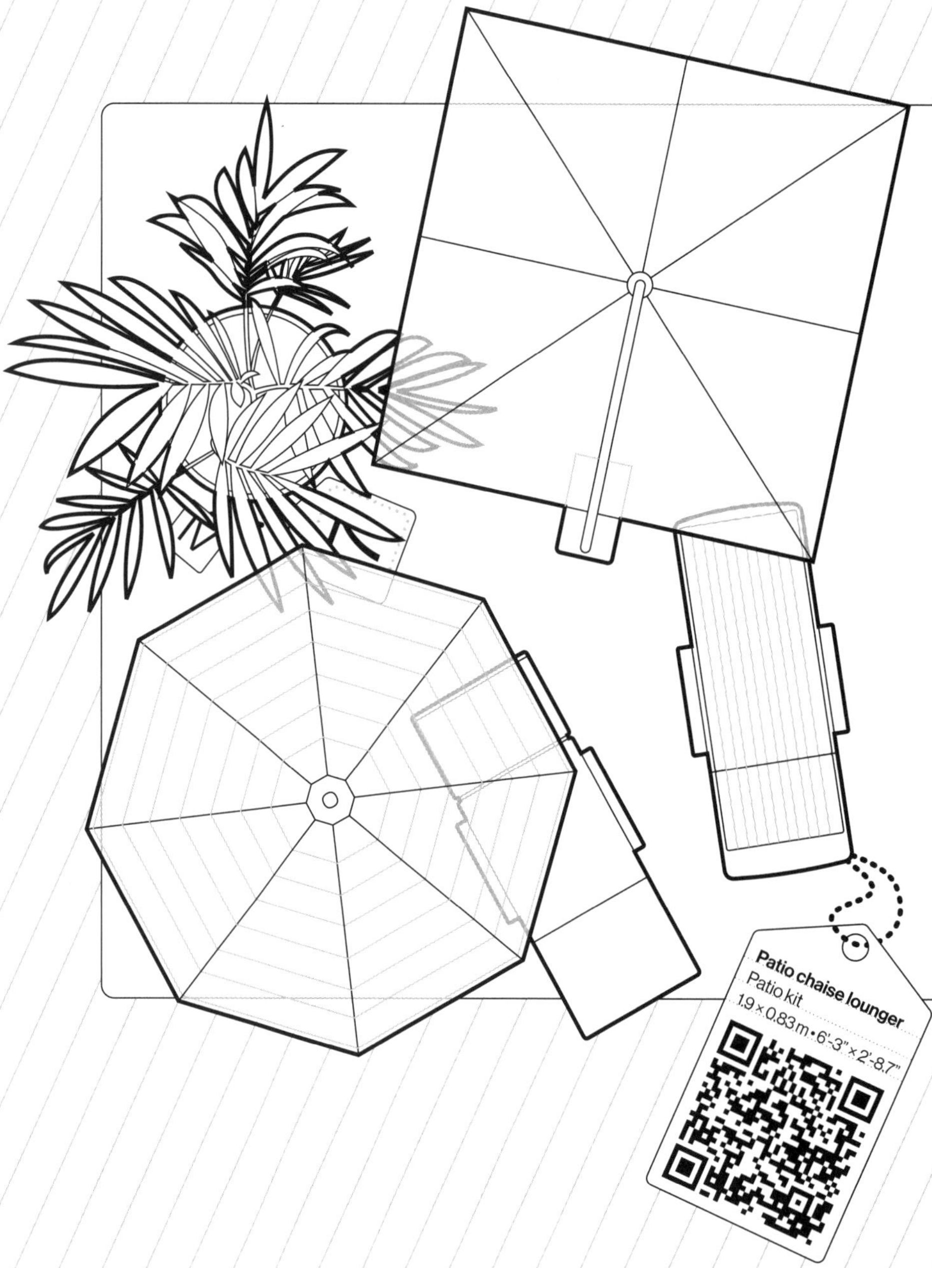
Patio chaise lounger
Patio kit
1.9 × 0.83 m • 6'-3" × 2'-8.7"

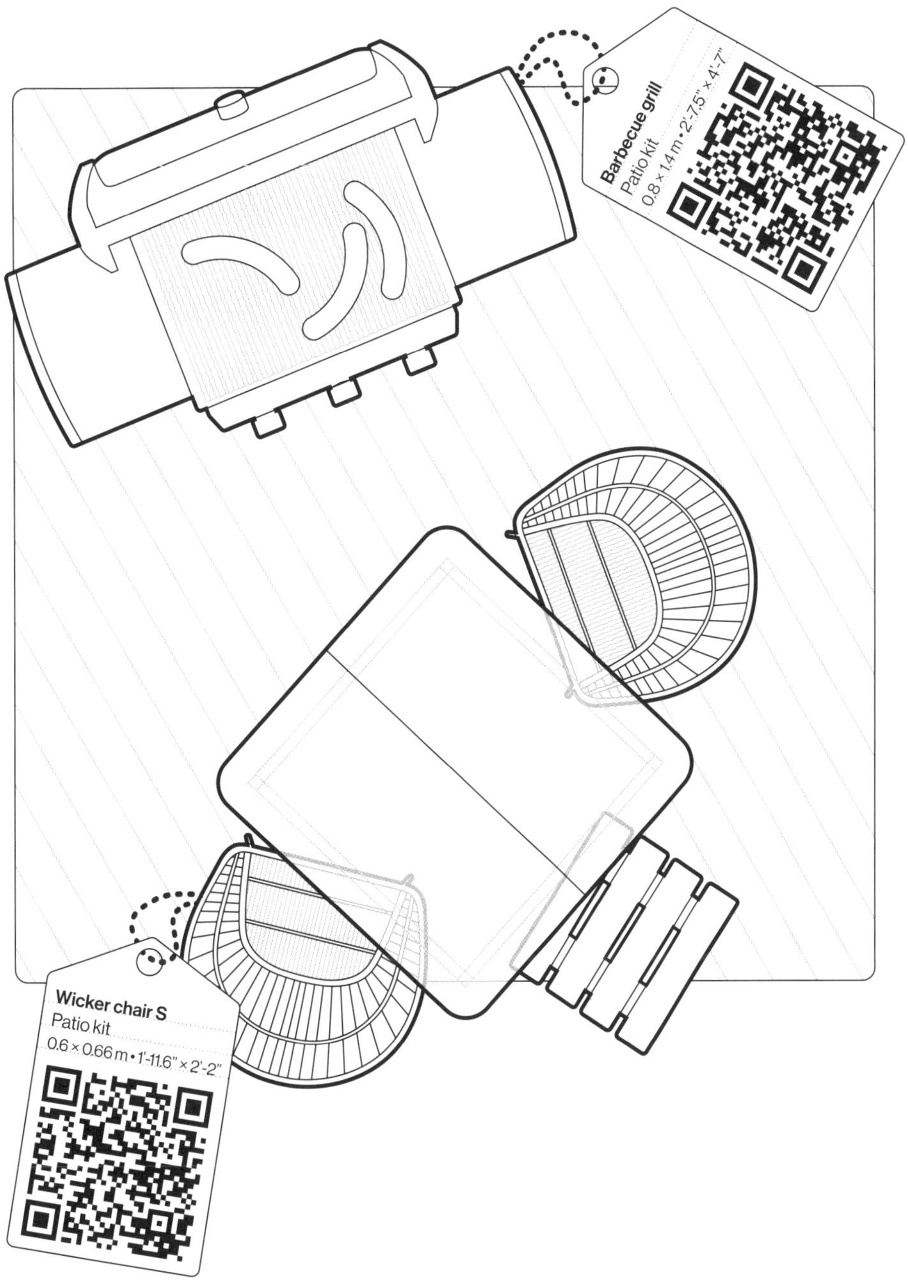
Barbecue grill
Patio kit
0.8 × 1.4 m • 2'-7.5" × 4'-7"
Wicker chair S
Patio kit
0.6 × 0.66 m • 1'-11.6" × 2'-2"

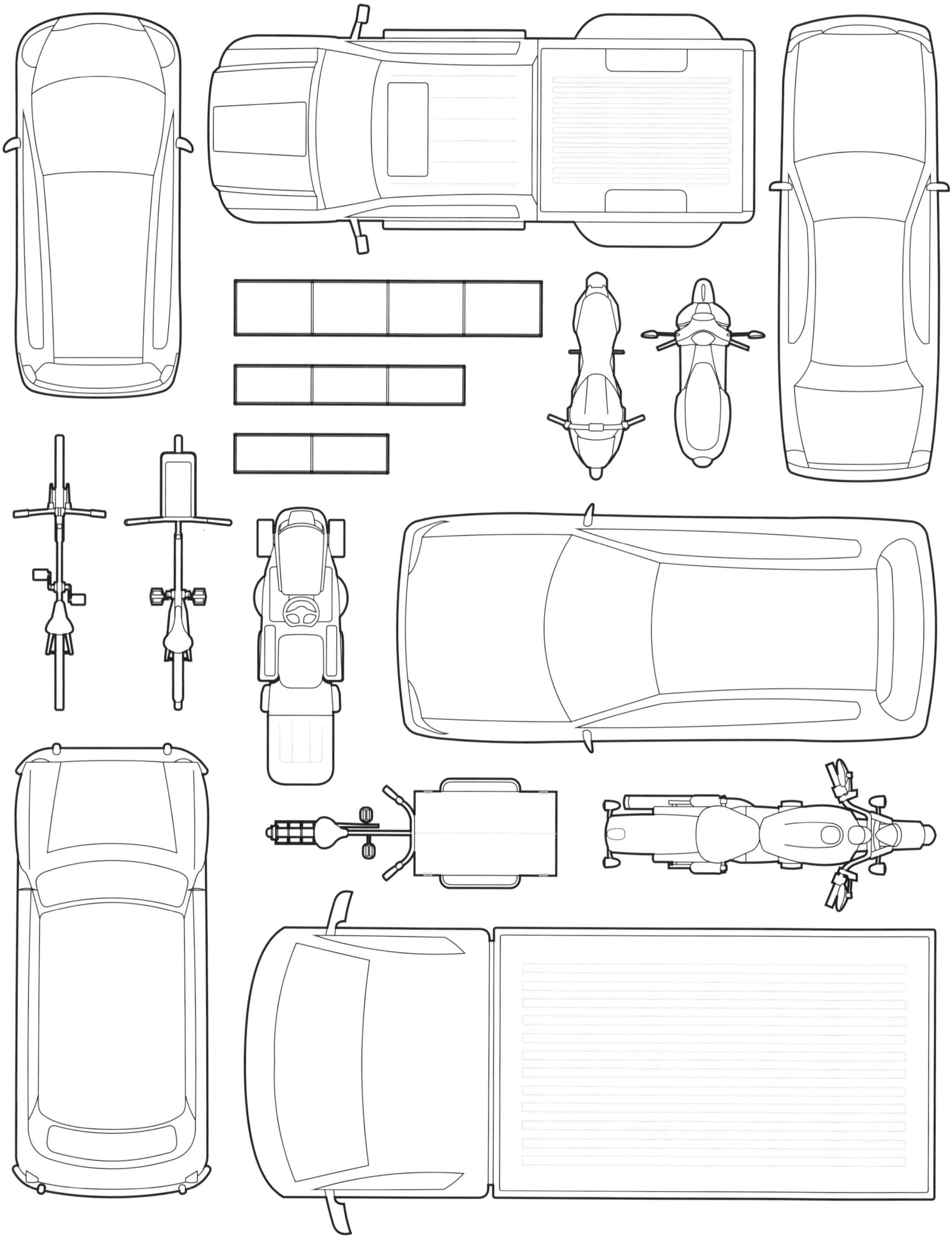

Kit for a
Garage

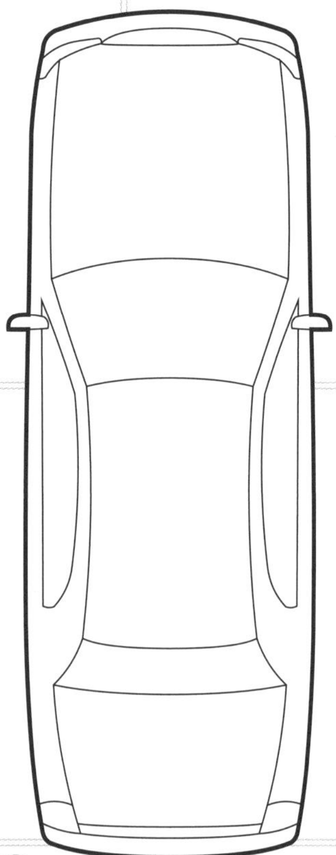

①

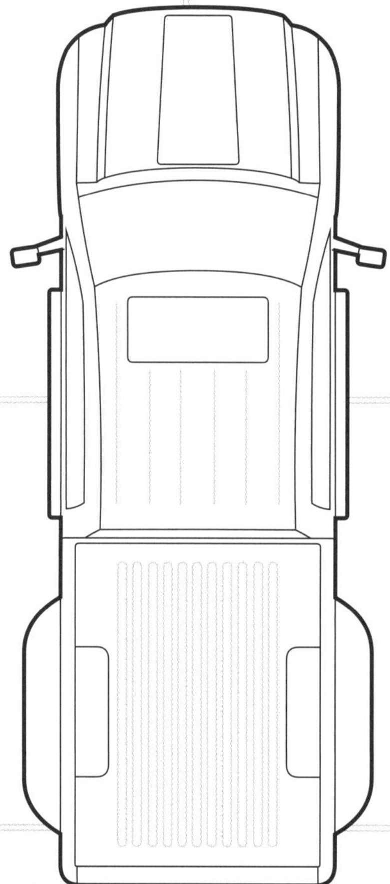

②

③

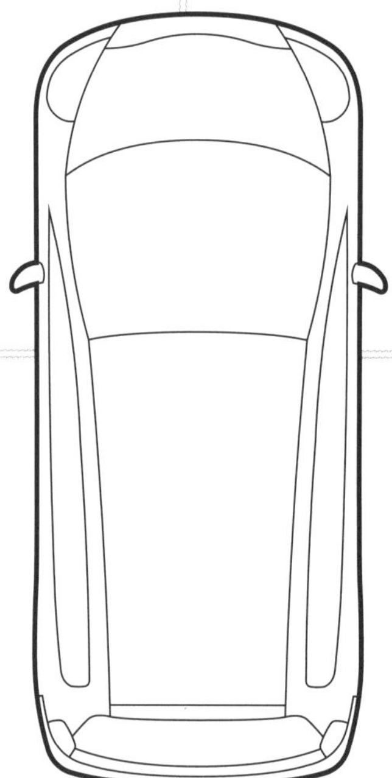

④

①
Sedan car S
Garage kit
4.58 × 1.82 m • 15' × 5'-11.7"

②
Pickup car
Garage kit
5.3 × 2.33 m • 17'-4.7" × 7'-7.7"

③
Mini car
Garage kit
4 × 1.8 m • 13'-1.5" × 5'-11"

④
Compact hatchback
Garage kit
4 × 2.02 m • 13'-1.5" × 6'-7.5"

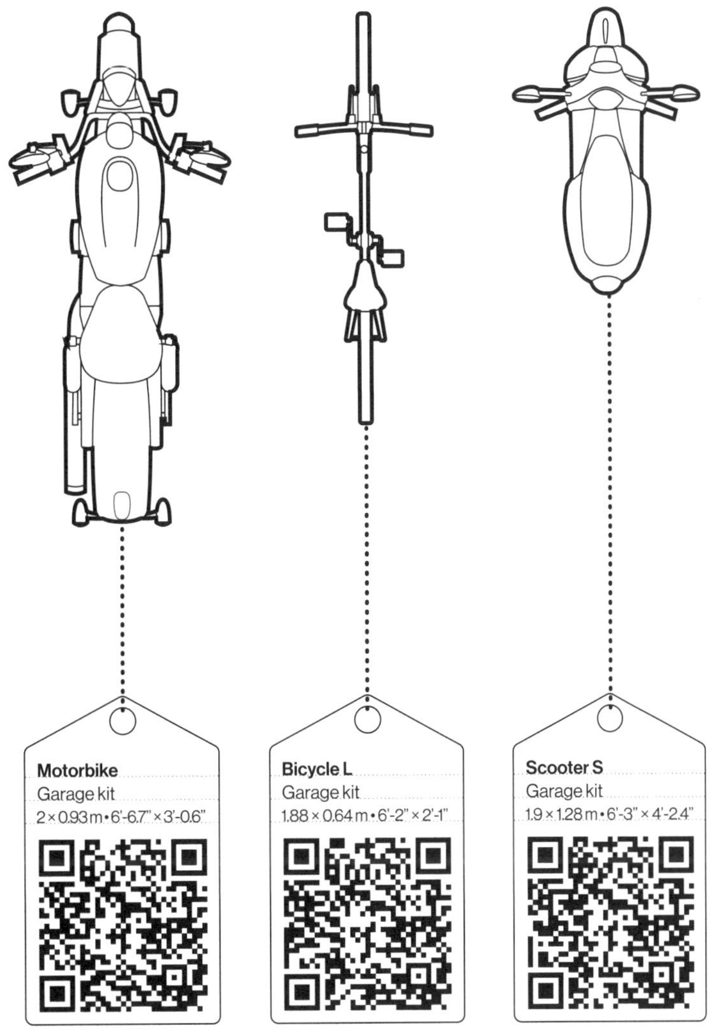
Motorbike
Garage kit
2 × 0.93 m • 6'-6.7" × 3'-0.6"
Bicycle L
Garage kit
1.88 × 0.64 m • 6'-2" × 2'-1"
Scooter S
Garage kit
1.9 × 1.28 m • 6'-3" × 4'-2.4"

A Catalog of

Storages

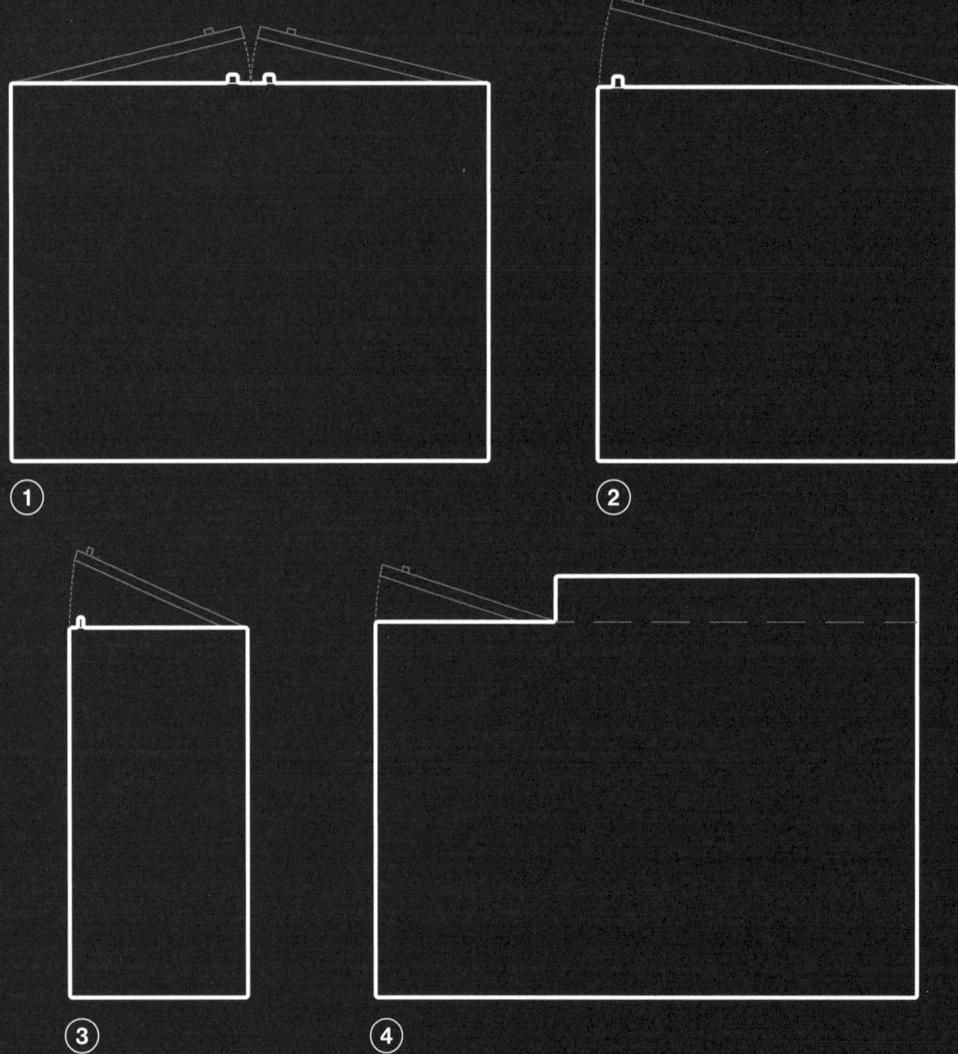
1
2
3
4

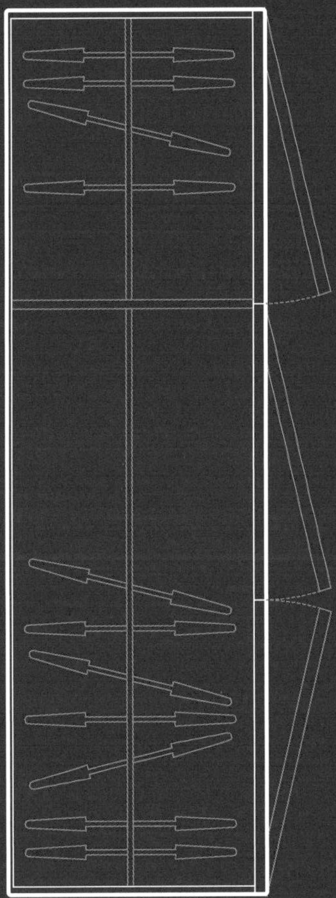

⑤

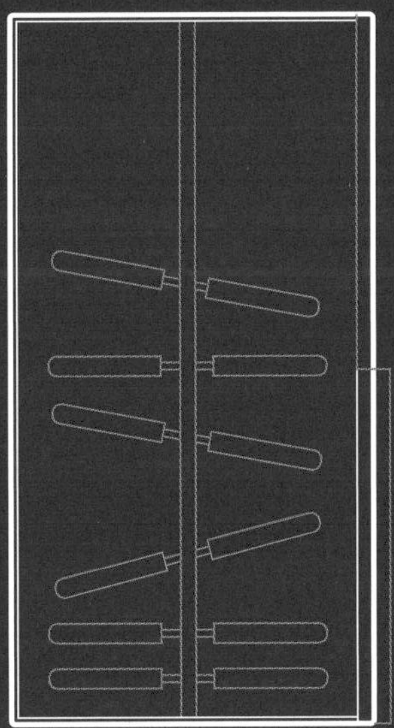

⑥

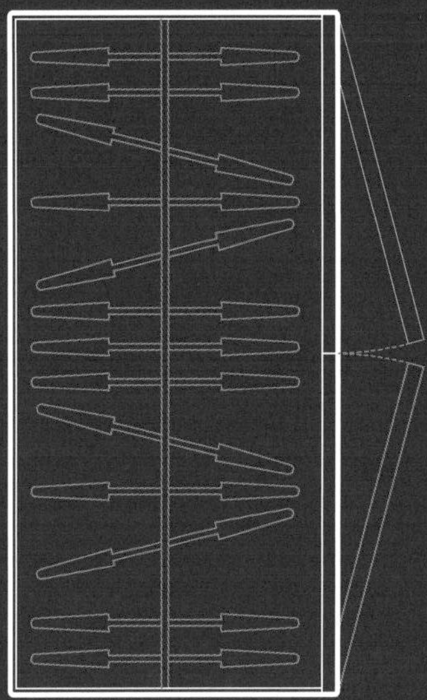

⑦

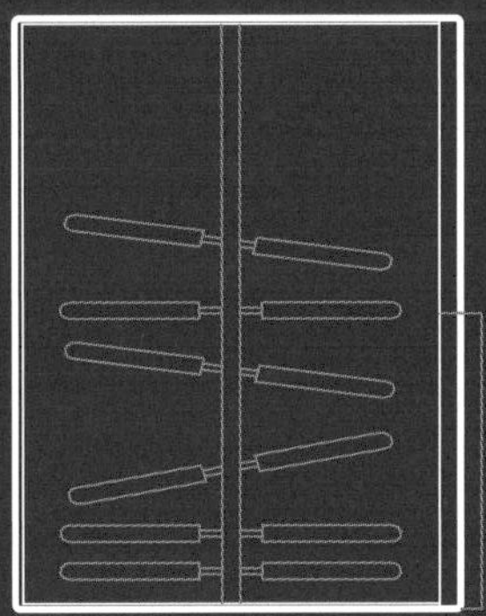

⑧

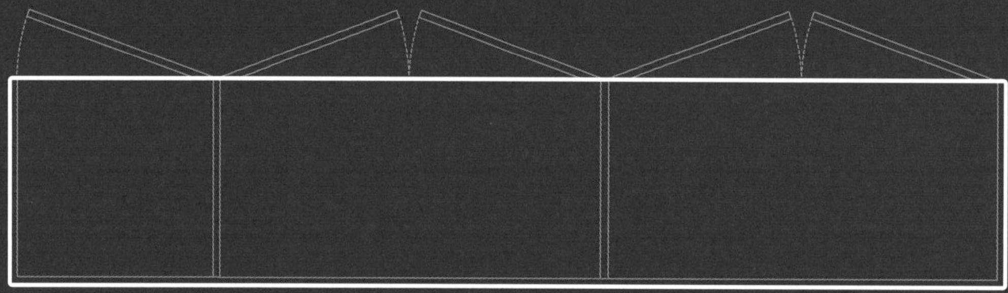

9

10

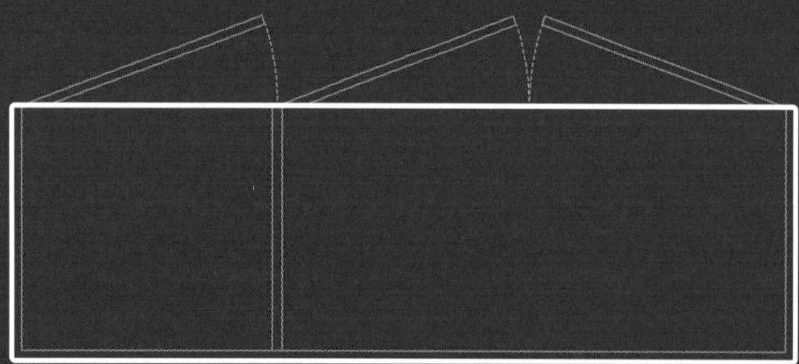

11

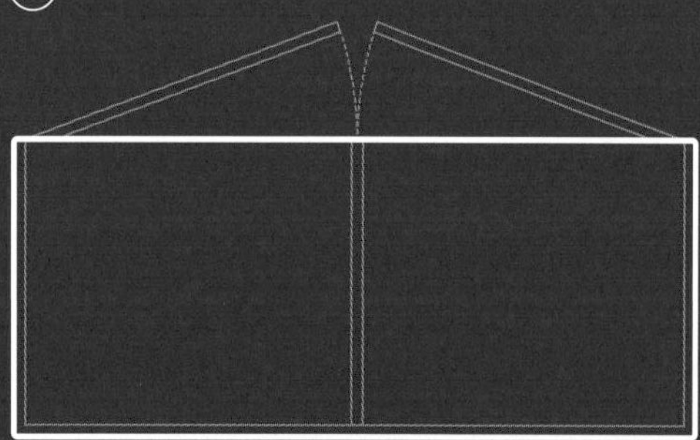

12

13
14
15
16

1. **Casework L with doors** • Storages
0.6 × 0.8 m • 1'-11.6" × 2'-7.5"

2. **Office chair**
Storages
0.6 × 0.59 m • 1'-11.6" × 1'-11"

3. **Casework M with door** • Storages
0.6 × 0.3 m • 1'-11.6" × 11.8"

4. **Casework S with door** • Storages
0.67 × 0.9 m • 2'-2.4" × 2'-11.4"

5. **Wardrobe L**
Storages
2 × 0.6 m • 6'-6.7" × 1'-11.6"

6. **Wardrobe sliding doors** • Storages
1.2 × 0.6 m • 3'-11.2" × 1'-11.6"

7. **Wardrobe M**
Storages
1.2 × 0.6 m • 3'-11.2" × 1'-11.6"

8. **Wardrobe sliding doors** • Storages
0.8 × 0.6 m • 2'-7.5" × 1'-11.6"

9

Sideboard XL
Storages
0.5 × 2.5 m • 1'-7.7" × 8'-2.4"

10

Sideboard L
Storages
0.5 × 2 m • 1'-7.7" × 6'-6.7"

11

Sideboard M
Storages
0.5 × 1.6 m • 1'-7.7" × 5'-3"

12

Sideboard S
Storages
0.5 × 1.2 m • 1'-7.7" × 3'-11"

13

Shelving 5-section
Storages
0.37 × 3.77 m • 1'-2.6" × 12'-4"

14

Shelving 4-section
Storages
0.27 × 3.02 m • 10.6" × 9'-11"

15

Shelving 3-section
Storages
0.27 × 2.27 m • 10.6" × 7'-5.4"

16

Shelving 2-section
Storages
0.27 × 1.52 m • 10.6" × 4'-11.8"

For the Outdoor

Sport fields, Roads, Animals, etc.

This final chapter of the Sourcebook concludes on the wild variety of outdoor spaces that today constitute our cities, from roadways, to sport venues and leisure. If planning and designing the urban realm is often part of architects' interventions, it remains a challenging side of architectural design, heavily conditioned by the standard dimensions of items and spaces that shape the urban outdoor.

In the midst of rapidly densifying city centers and with the increasing importance of sustainability, this exercise has in fact significantly evolved; likewise, the catalog of items provided in this chapter hopes to reflect the evolution that outdoor public spaces have undergone.

Public outdoor spaces in cities have found in this decade a renewed interest. The recent pandemic made policymakers vividly aware of the importance of such places for promoting physical activity, a sense of belonging to city dwellers and generally decompressing increasingly packed urban centers. With that in mind, green spaces such as **public parks** 1 p. 397 have been reinvested in by institutional stakeholders, while private developments have placed an emphasis on providing **communal gardens** 2 p. 411 as part of new projects.

Sport has also been a recurring theme for urban design. Consequently, the past decades have seen sport facilities being much more tightly woven within the urban fabric, across most major cities. **Sport courts** 3 p. 333 as well as fitness equipment have been disseminated around public parks, or built close to areas of affluence.

Larger pieces of infrastructure, from **stadiums** 4 p. 327 to public swimming pools, have also allowed city dwellers to be served with increasingly rich sport options. Taking advantage of the many buffers cities have to offer, **skate parks** 5 p. 391 or even **playgrounds** 6 p. 385 today contribute to the general strategy of municipalities to inject more leisure spaces within urban centers.

This offering of outdoor public spaces sits on top of a more prosaic layer of road infrastructures. The past decades have in fact seen many updates to this rather pragmatic facet 7 p. 321 of the urban fabric: the introduction of **bike lanes**, the displacement or concealing of large 8 p. 365 **parking** garages, the burying of high-speed roads close to city centers, the multiplication of pedestrian streetways have corresponded to dwellers' wish for calmer, less busy neighborhoods.

In conjunction with these updates, municipalities around the globe have sought to diver- 9 p. 371 sify their public **transport** offering; from bus and subway to public bike services or electric scooters. The overhaul of roadways and the diversification of public transportation modes together speak to the magnitude of the change that has happened to urban mobility over the past decades.

This evolution has come hand-in-hand with two additional noticeable trends: the extensive use of vegetation along most important circulation paths, and the dissemination of ad hoc street furnishing. Beside providing shade, 10 p. 423 the inception of **trees** and plants along the main streets of cities has had the effect of taming the otherwise rather mineral landscape of dense urban centers.

At the same time, the municipalities of large metropolises have extensively leveraged the use of 11 p. 403 **street furnishing** to invite city dwellers to actively use the public space. More inviting, more green: our cities have undergone a striking update in the way streets and walkways cater to pedestrians.

All these changes have had an actual impact on the urban fabric over the past decades. Together, they have reshaped in part the catalog of items usually considered for designing our cities. From the urban furniture, to the roads and streets, to the very type of transportation people use every day, the library of things that populate our cities has undergone a significant reset.

With this upcoming chapter, we hope to bring to this catalog a much-needed update, as we touch upon most of the typologies necessary for planning public outdoor spaces.

For the Outdoor

dimension
dimension
dimension
dimension
dimension
dimension
dimension
dimension
dimension
dimension
dimension
dimension
dimension
dimension
dimension
dimension
dimension
dimension
dimension
dimension
dimension
dimension
dimension
dimension
9
7
8
6
4
5
3
2
1

Dimensions

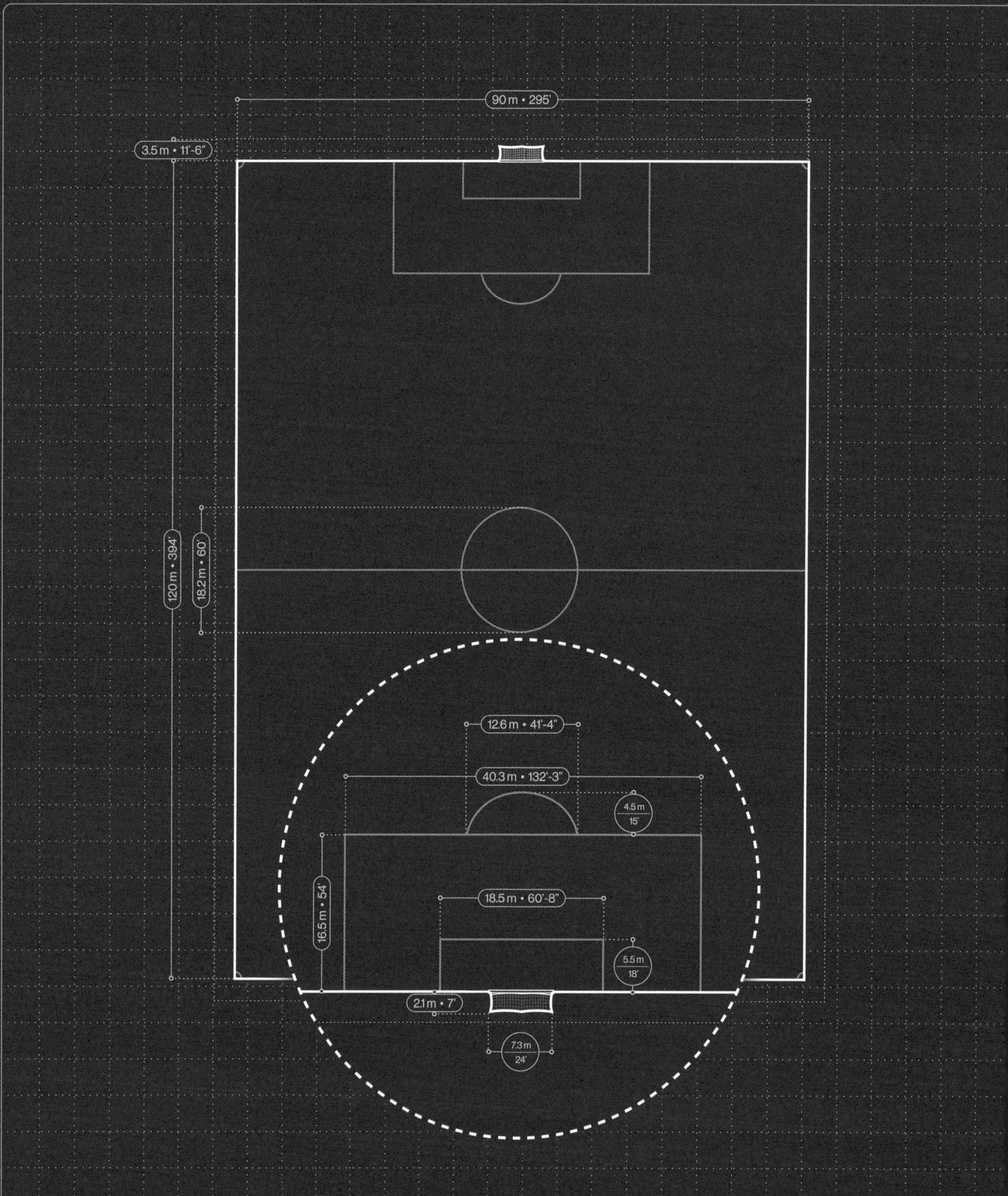
90 m • 295'
3.5 m • 11'-6"
120 m • 394'
18.2 m • 60'
12.6 m • 41'-4"
40.3 m • 132'-3"
4.5 m
15'
16.5 m • 54'
18.5 m • 60'-8"
5.5 m
18'
2.1 m • 7'
7.3 m
24'

Football

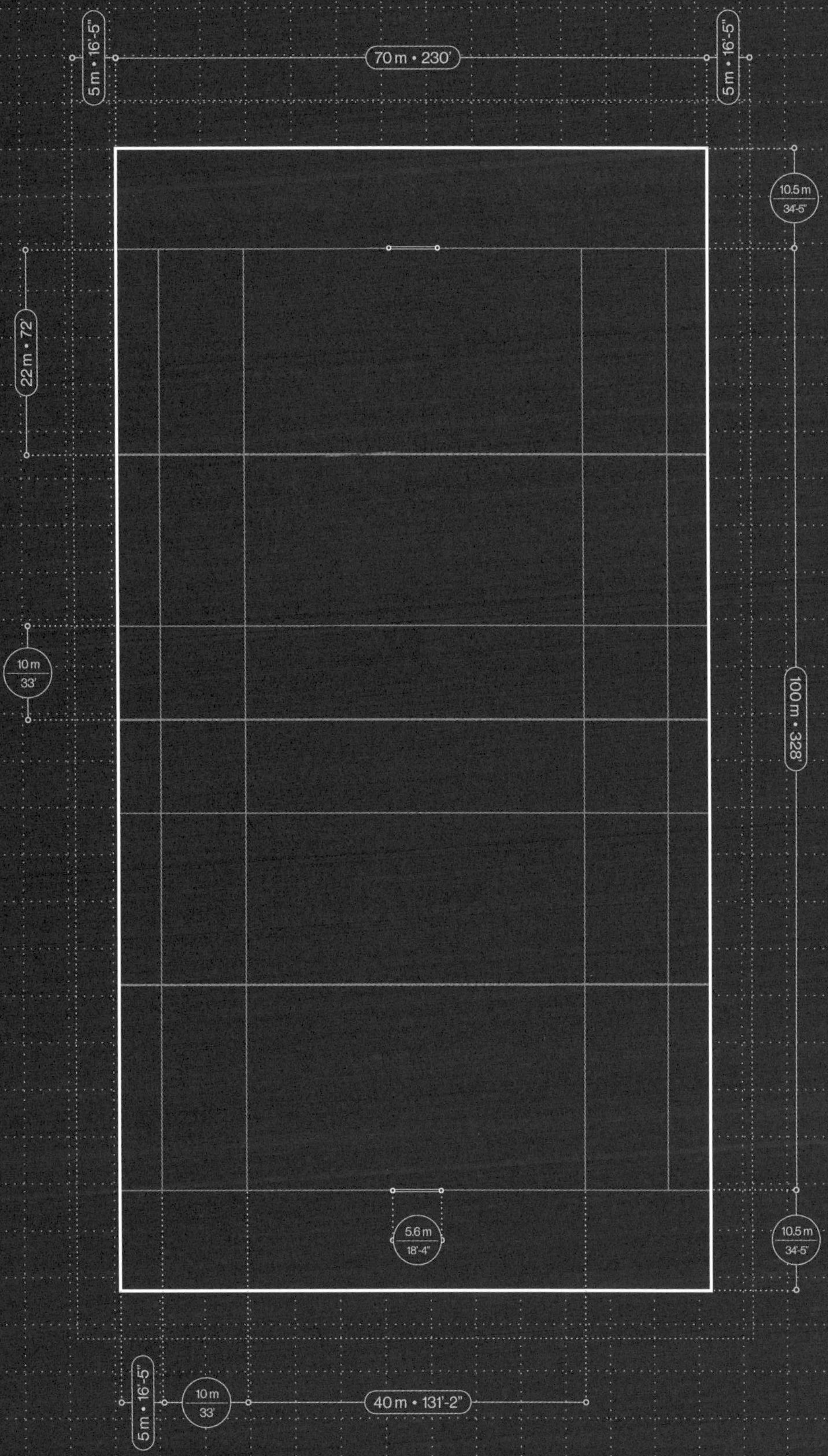

5 m • 16'-5"
70 m • 230'
5 m • 16'-5"
10.5 m
34'-5'
22 m • 72'
10 m
33'
100 m • 328'
5.6 m
18'-4"
10.5 m
34'-5'
5 m • 16'-5"
10 m
33'
40 m • 131'-2"

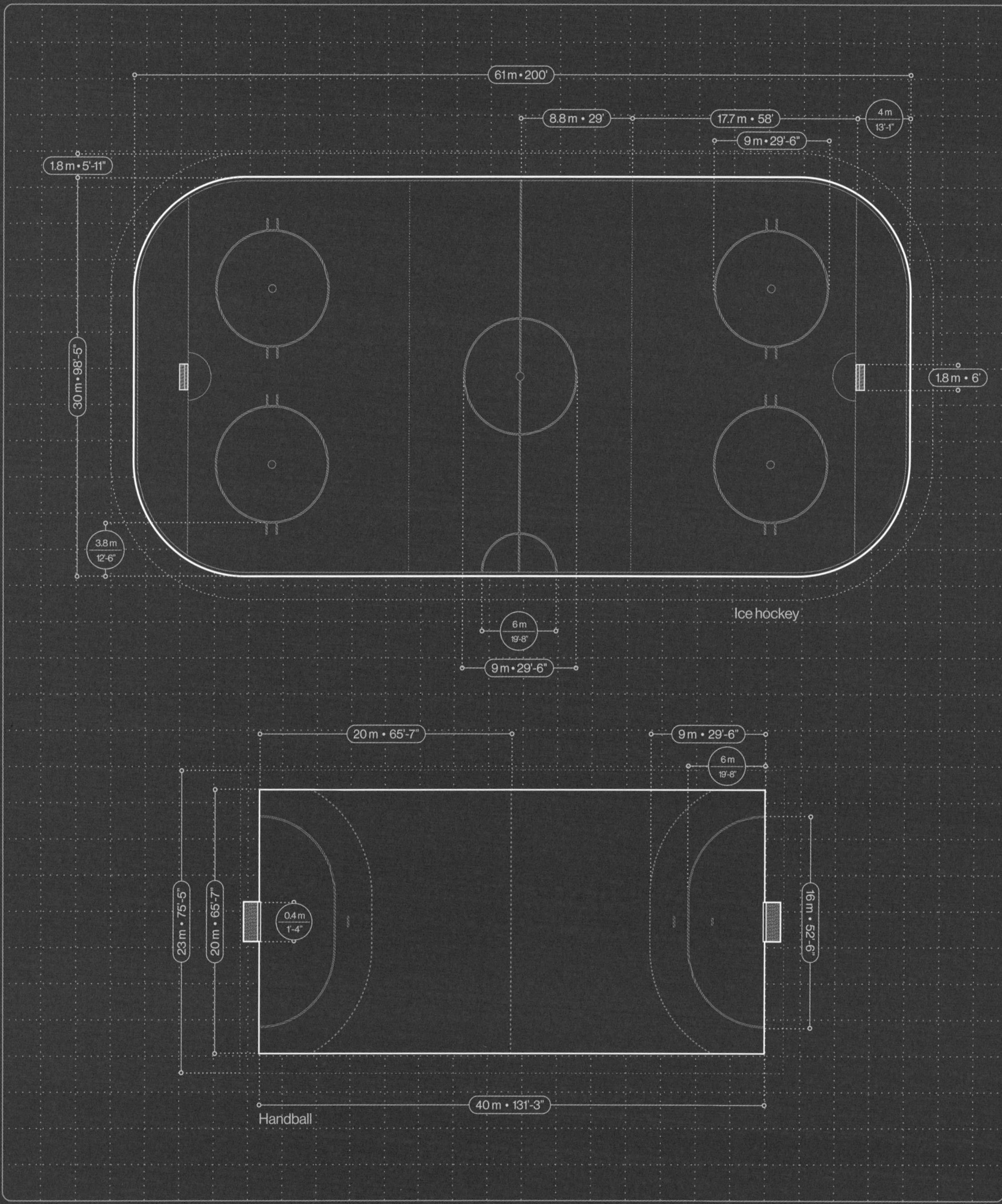

Hockey / Handball

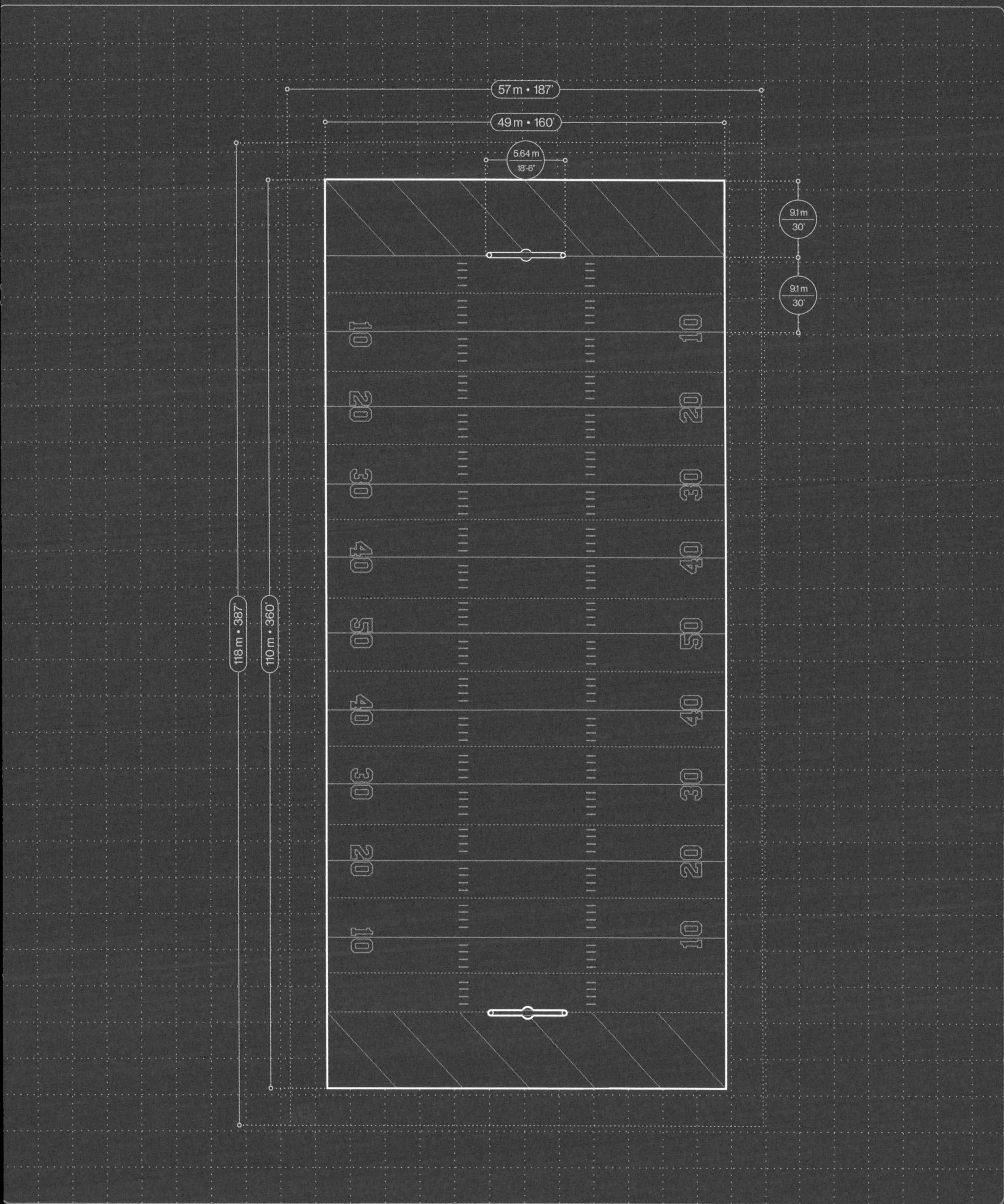
57 m • 187'
49 m • 160'
5.64 m
18'-6"
9.1 m
30'
9.1 m
30'
118 m • 387'
110 m • 360'
10
20
30
40
50
40
30
20
10

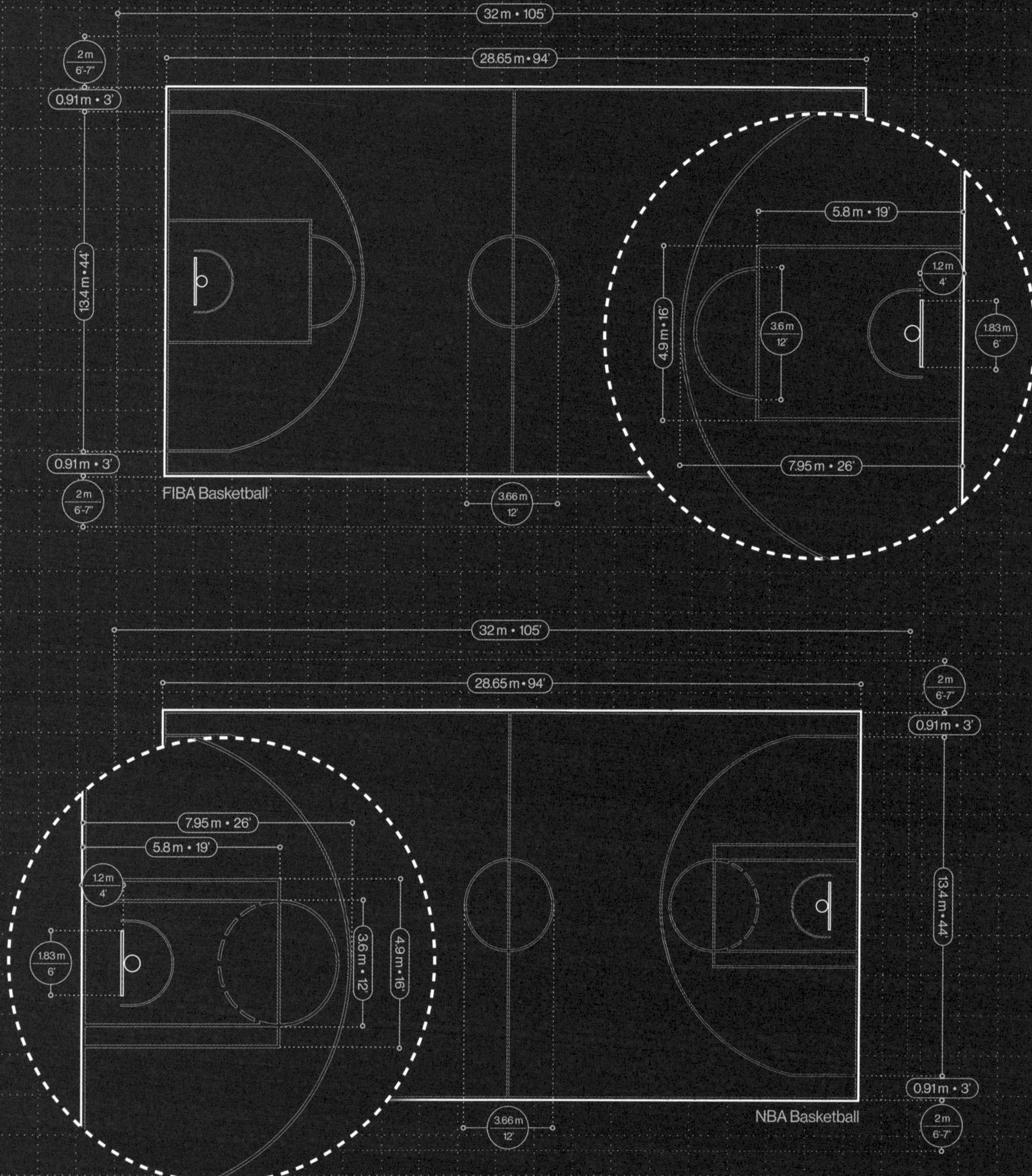
32 m • 105'
28.65 m • 94'
2 m
6'-7"
0.91 m • 3'
13.4 m • 44'
5.8 m • 19'
1.2 m
4'
4.9 m • 16'
3.6 m
12'
1.83 m
6'
7.95 m • 26'
3.66 m
12'
FIBA Basketball
NBA Basketball
3.6 m • 12'
4.9 m • 16'

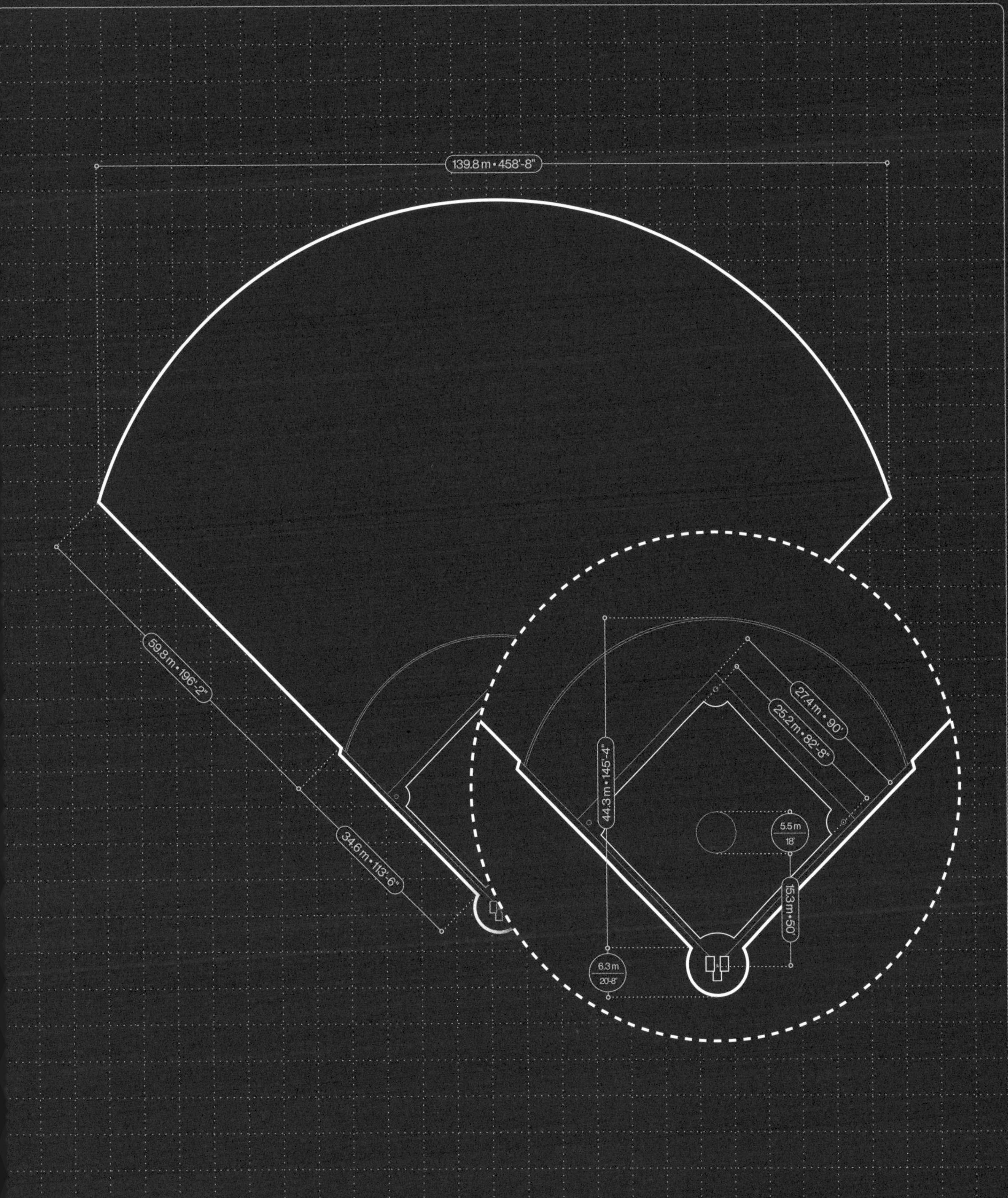

139.8 m • 458'-8"
59.8 m • 196'-2"
34.6 m • 113'-6"
27.4 m • 90'
25.2 m • 82'-8"
44.3 m • 145'-4"
5.5 m
18'
15.3 m • 50'
6.3 m
20-8"

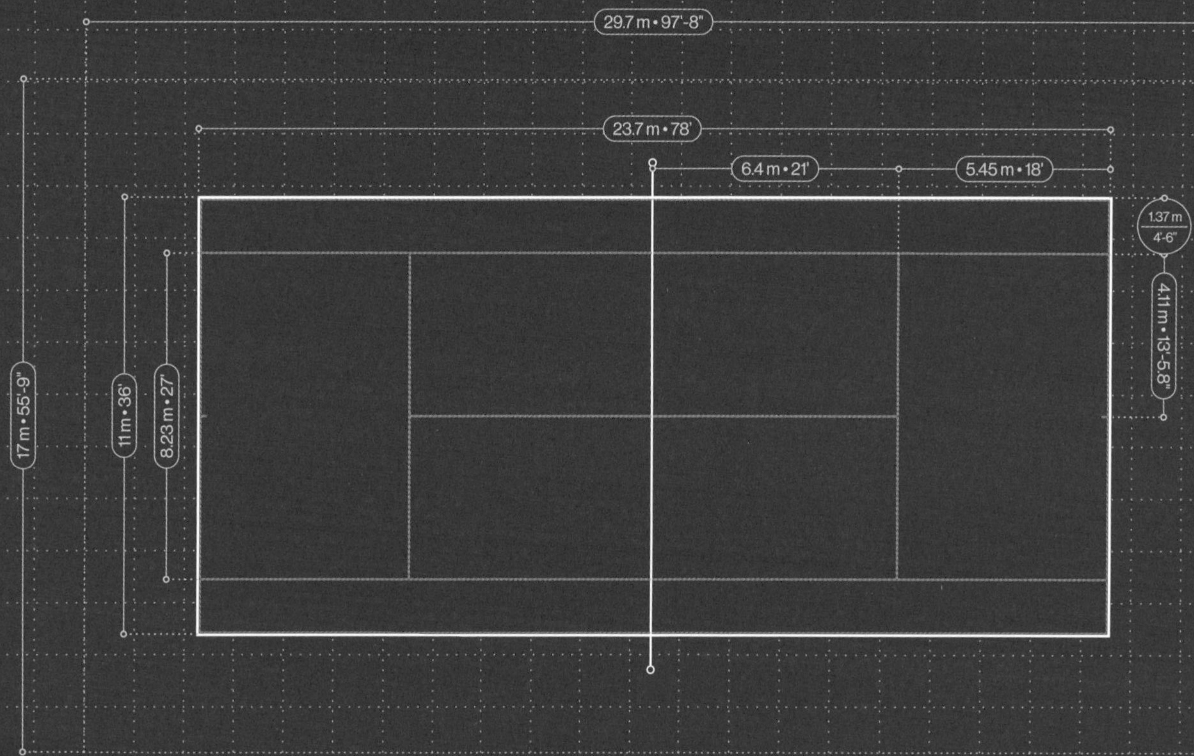

Tennis

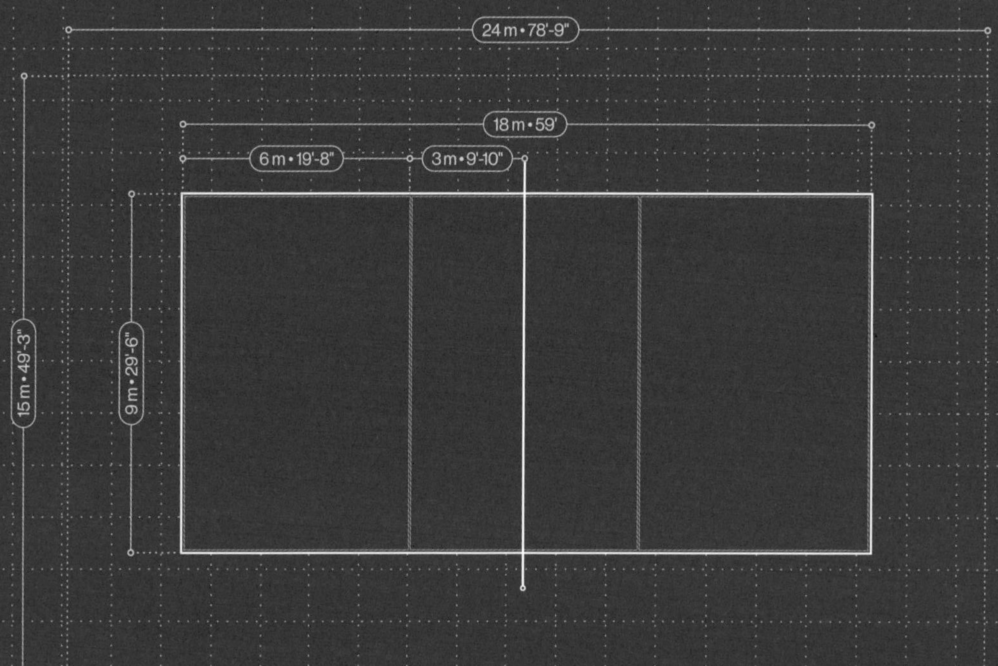

Volleyball

Tennis / Volleyball

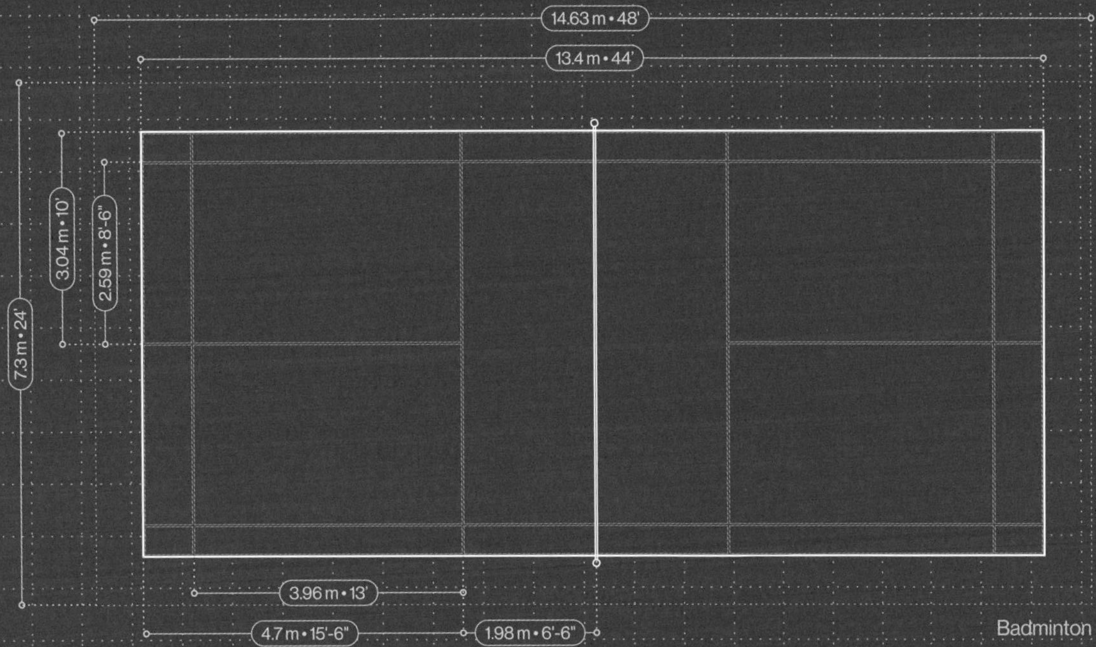

14.63 m • 48'
13.4 m • 44'
7.3 m • 24'
3.04 m • 10'
2.59 m • 8'-6"
3.96 m • 13'
4.7 m • 15'-6"
1.98 m • 6'-6"
Badminton

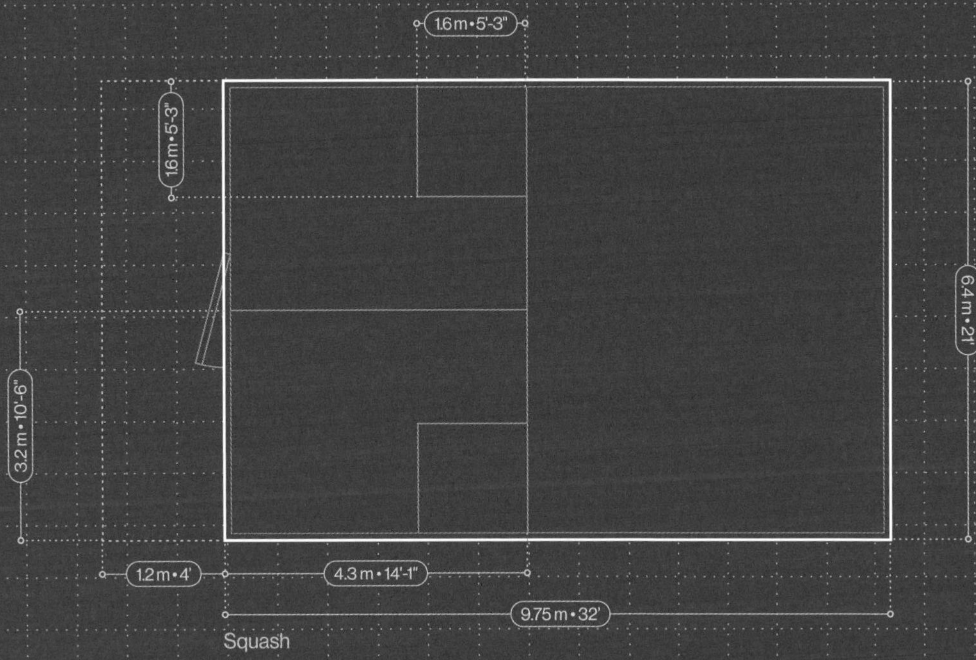

1.6 m • 5'-3"
1.6 m • 5'-3"
6.4 m • 21'
3.2 m • 10'-6"
1.2 m • 4'
4.3 m • 14'-1"
9.75 m • 32'
Squash

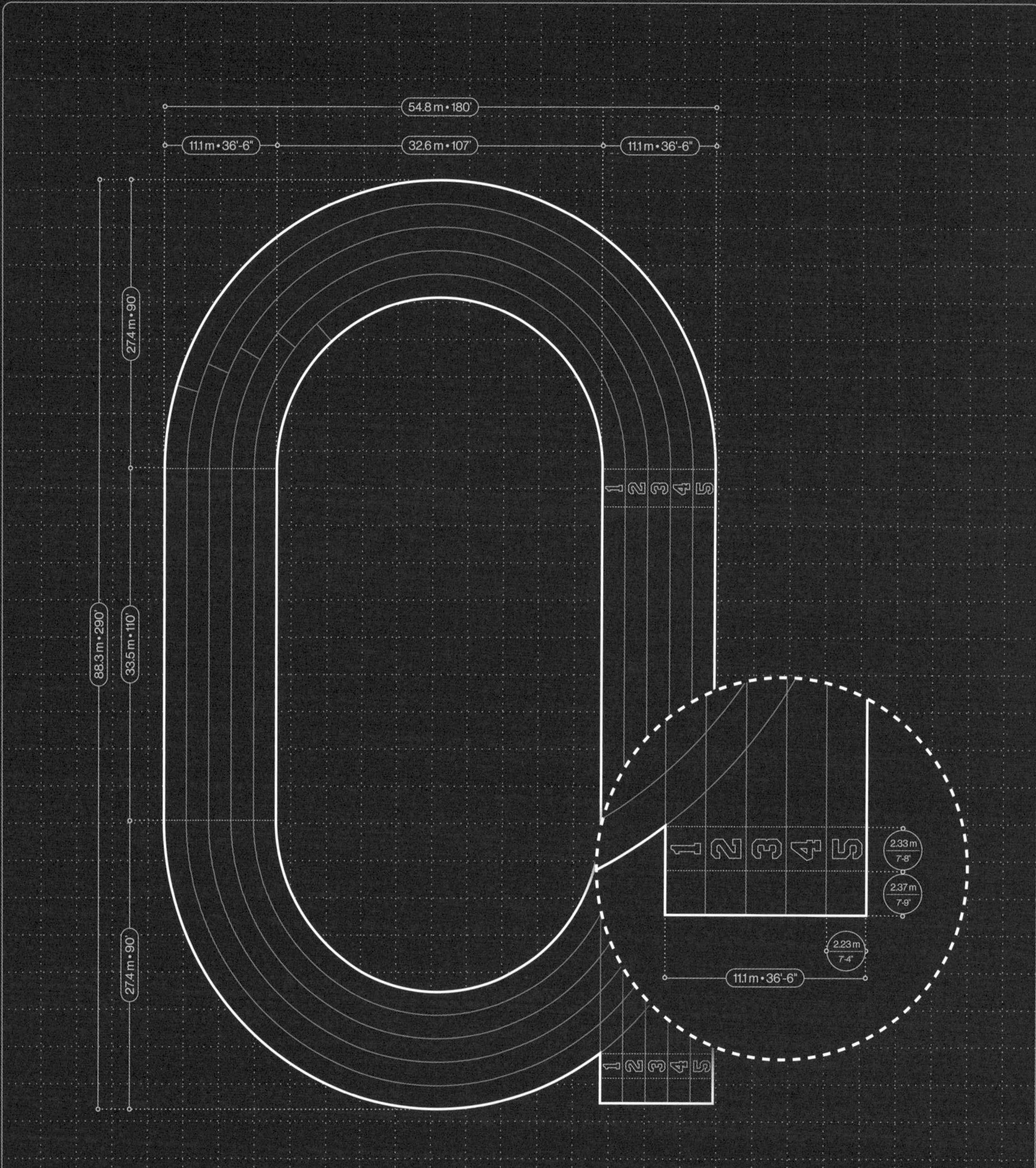

Racing Track

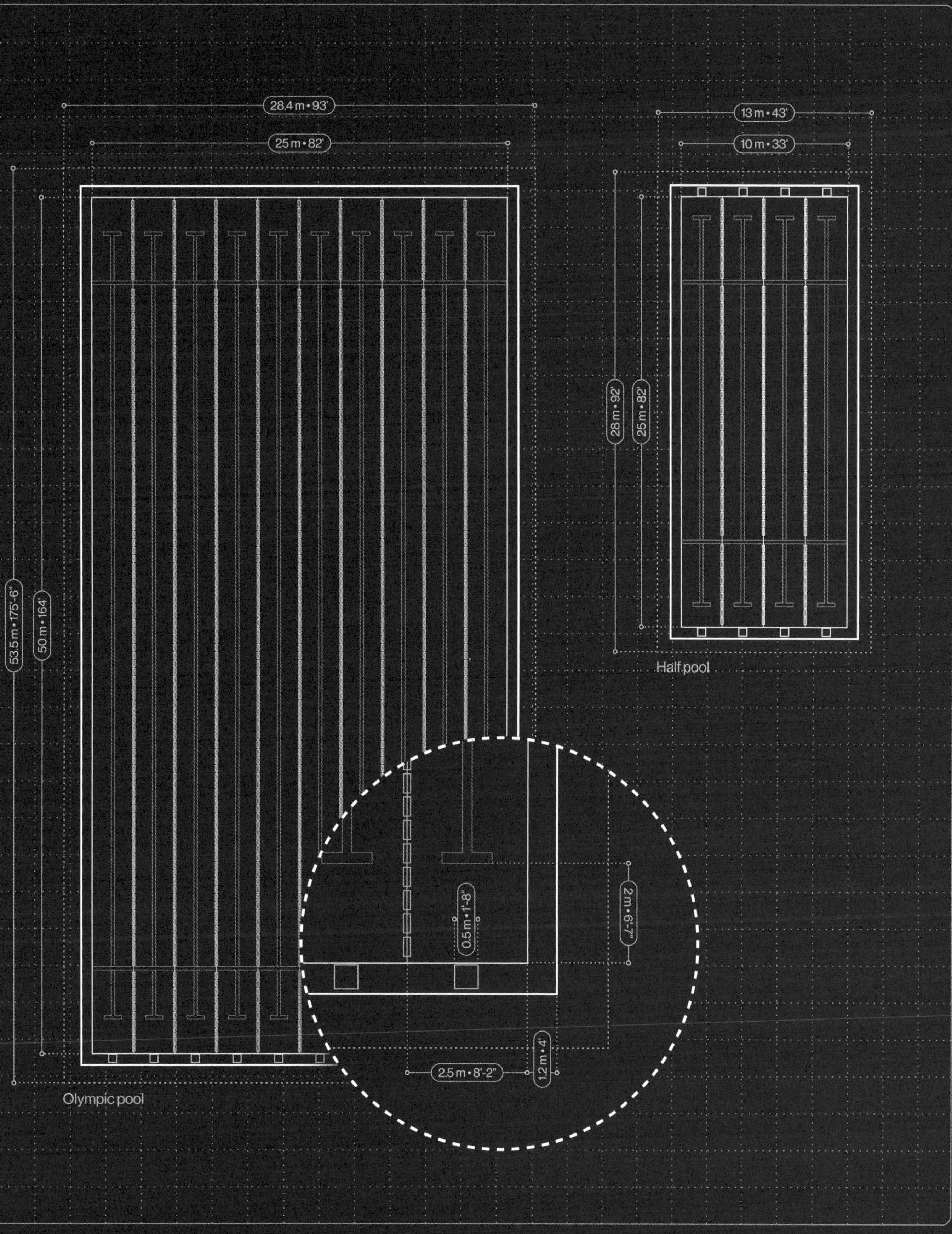
28.4 m • 93'
25 m • 82'
13 m • 43'
10 m • 33'
53.5 m • 175'-6"
50 m • 164'
28 m • 92'
25 m • 82'
Half pool
0.5 m • 1'-8"
2 m • 6'-7"
1.2 m • 4'
2.5 m • 8'-2"
Olympic pool

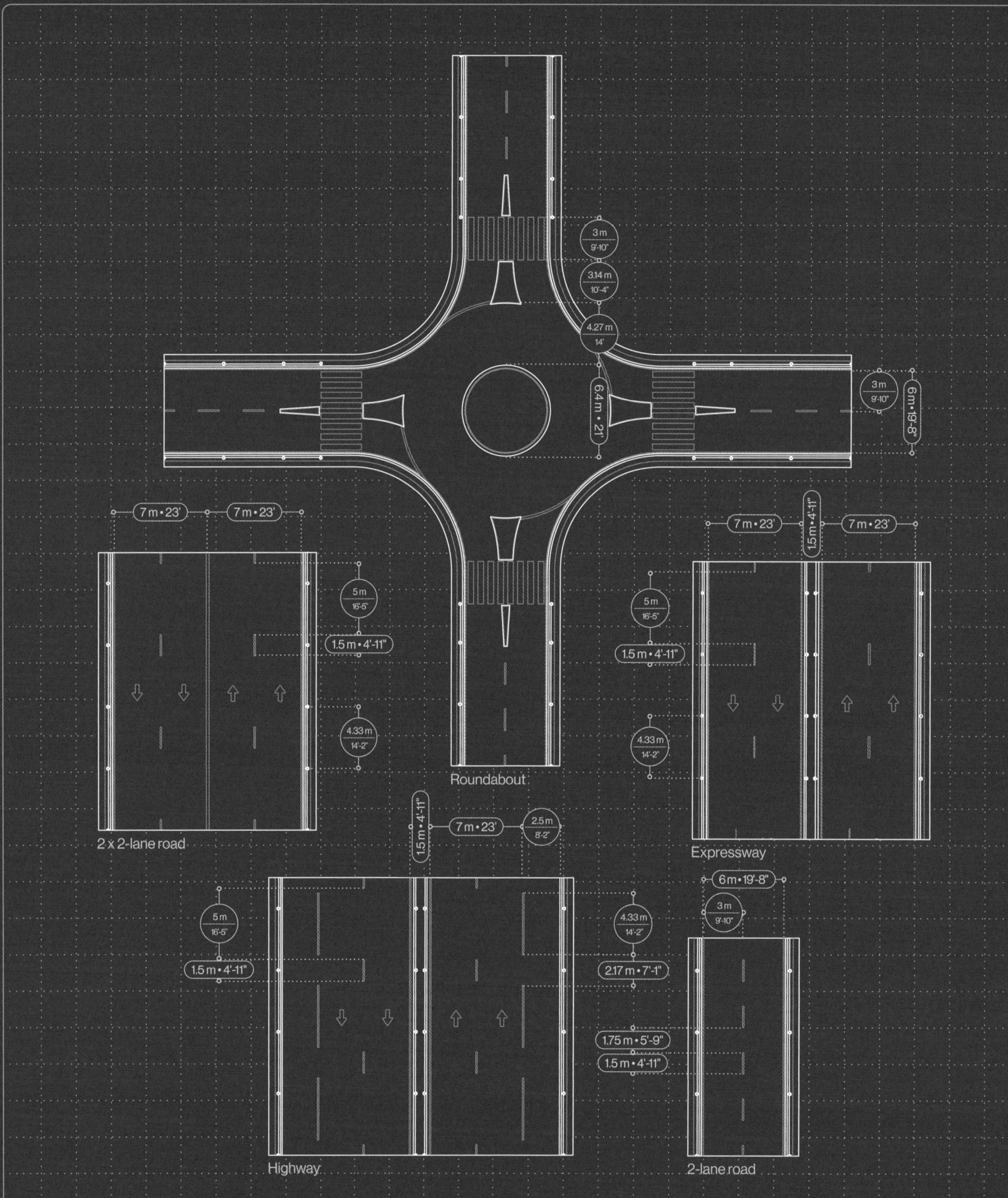

Roundabout
3 m
9'-10"
3.14 m
10'-4"
4.27 m
14'
6.4 m • 21'
3 m
9'-10"
6 m • 19'-8"
2 x 2-lane road
7 m • 23'
7 m • 23'
5 m
16'-5'
1.5 m • 4'-11"
4.33 m
14'-2'
Expressway
7 m • 23'
1.5 m • 4'-11"
7 m • 23'
5 m
16'-5'
1.5 m • 4'-11"
4.33 m
14'-2'
Highway
1.5 m • 4'-11"
7 m • 23'
2.5 m
8'-2'
5 m
16'-5'
1.5 m • 4'-11"
4.33 m
14'-2'
2.17 m • 7'-1"
1.75 m • 5'-9"
1.5 m • 4'-11"
2-lane road
6 m • 19'-8"
3 m
9'-10"

One-way street - Bike lane

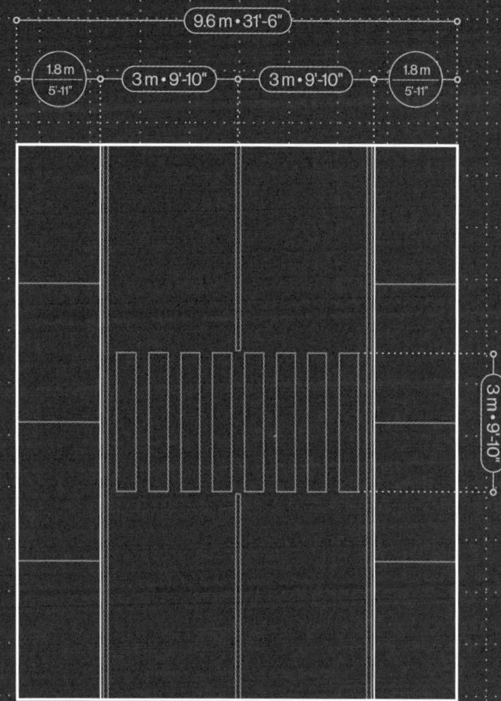

Two-way street

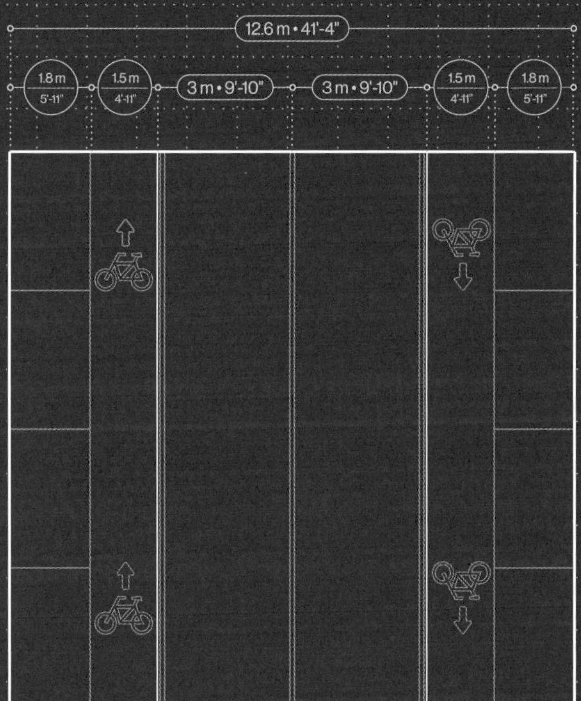

Two-way street - Bike lanes

One-way street

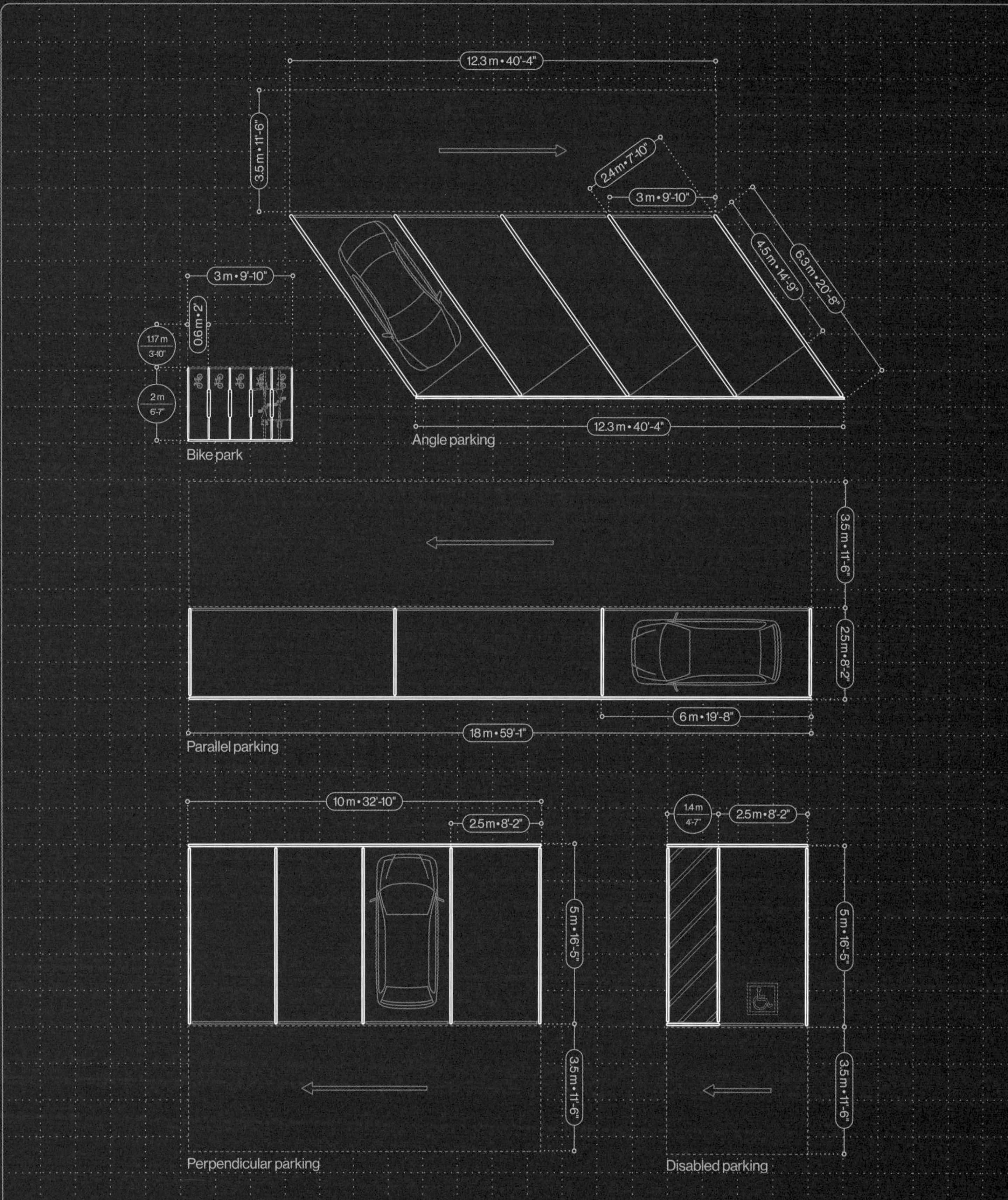
12.3 m • 40'-4"
3.5 m • 11'-6"
2.4 m • 7'-10"
3 m • 9'-10"
4.5 m • 14'-9"
6.3 m • 20'-8"
3 m • 9'-10"
0.6 m • 2'
1.17 m
3'-10'
2 m
6'-7'
12.3 m • 40'-4"
Angle parking
Bike park
3.5 m • 11'-6"
2.5 m • 8'-2"
6 m • 19'-8"
18 m • 59'-1"
Parallel parking
10 m • 32'-10"
2.5 m • 8'-2"
5 m • 16'-5"
3.5 m • 11'-6"
Perpendicular parking
1.4 m
4'-7'
2.5 m • 8'-2"
5 m • 16'-5"
3.5 m • 11'-6"
Disabled parking

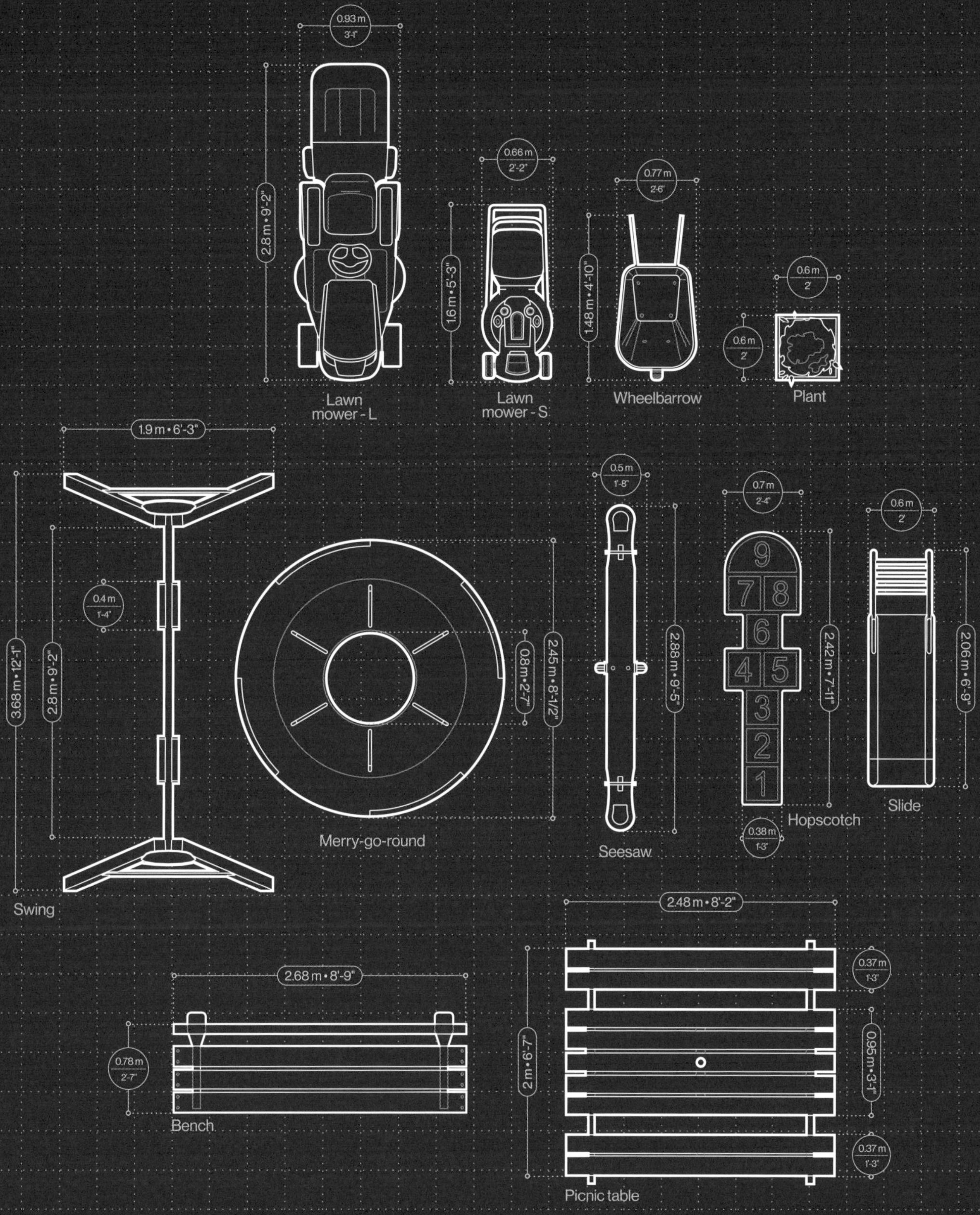

Lawn mower - L
0.93 m
3'-1"
2.8 m • 9'-2"
Lawn mower - S
0.66 m
2'-2"
1.6 m • 5'-3"
Wheelbarrow
0.77 m
2'-6"
1.48 m • 4'-10"
Plant
0.6 m
2'
0.6 m
2'
Swing
1.9 m • 6'-3"
3.68 m • 12'-1"
2.8 m • 9'-2"
0.4 m
1'-4"
Merry-go-round
0.8 m • 2'-7"
2.45 m • 8'-1/2"
Seesaw
0.5 m
1'-8"
2.88 m • 9'-5"
Hopscotch
0.7 m
2'-4"
2.42 m • 7'-11"
0.38 m
1'-3'
Slide
0.6 m
2'
2.06 m • 6'-9"
Bench
2.68 m • 8'-9"
0.78 m
2'-7"
Picnic table
2.48 m • 8'-2"
2 m • 6'-7"
0.37 m
1'-3'
0.95 m • 3'-1"
0.37 m
1'-3'

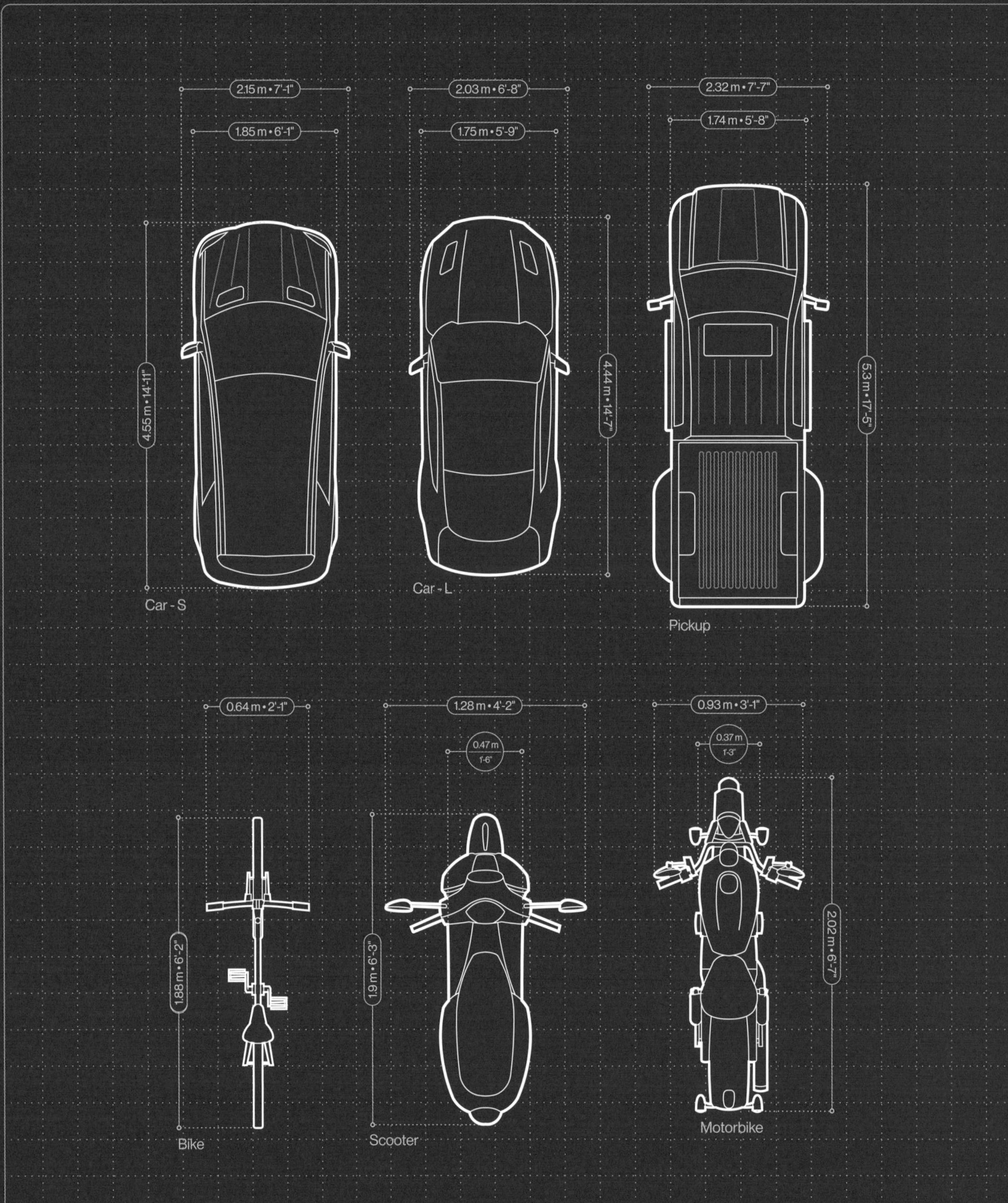

 Private Transportation

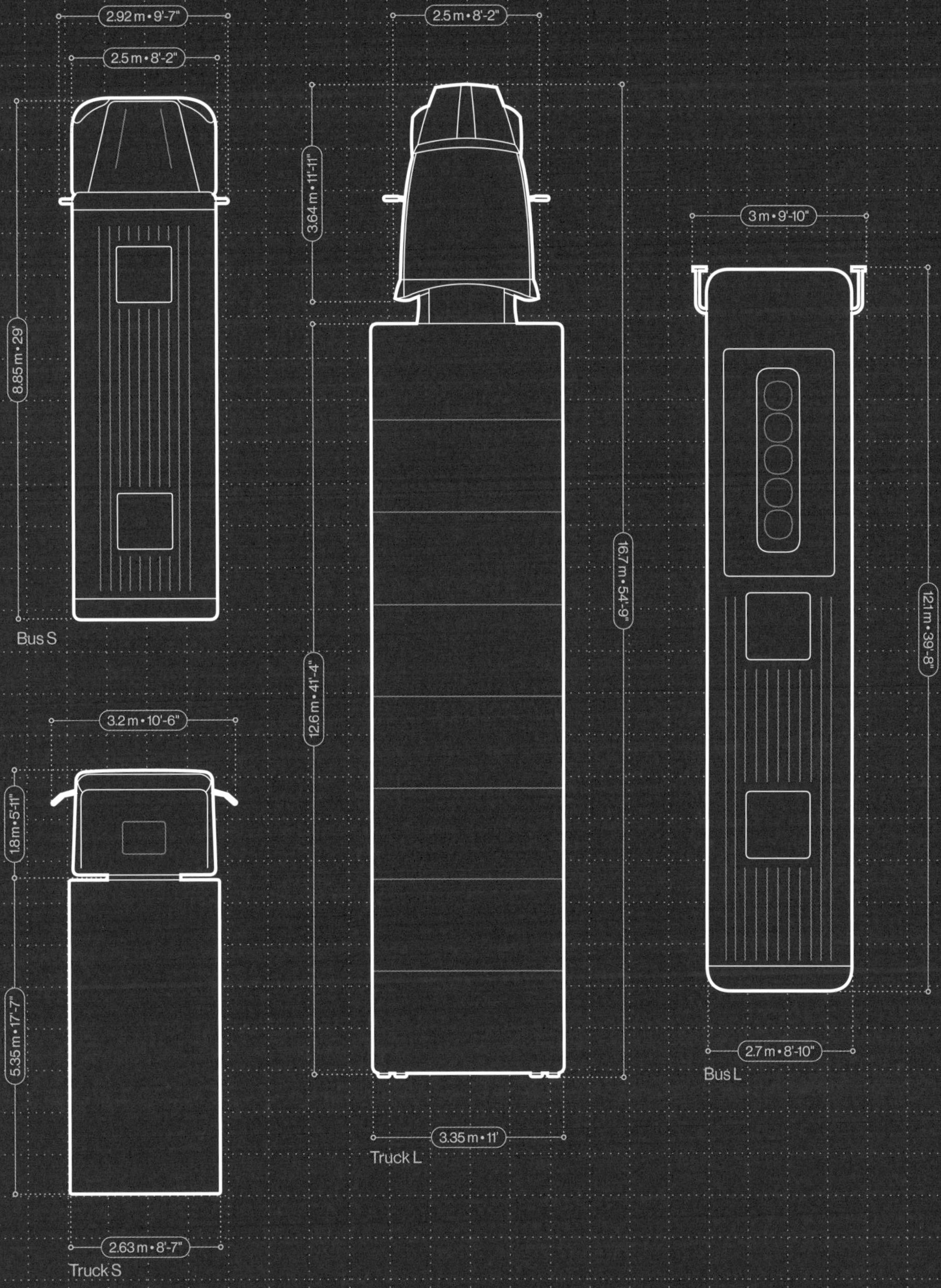
2.92 m • 9'-7"
2.5 m • 8'-2"
8.85 m • 29'
Bus S
3.2 m • 10'-6"
1.8 m • 5'-11"
5.35 m • 17'-7"
2.63 m • 8'-7"
Truck S
2.5 m • 8'-2"
3.64 m • 11'-11"
12.6 m • 41'-4"
16.7 m • 54'-9"
3.35 m • 11'
Truck L
3 m • 9'-10"
12.1 m • 39'-8"
2.7 m • 8'-10"
Bus L

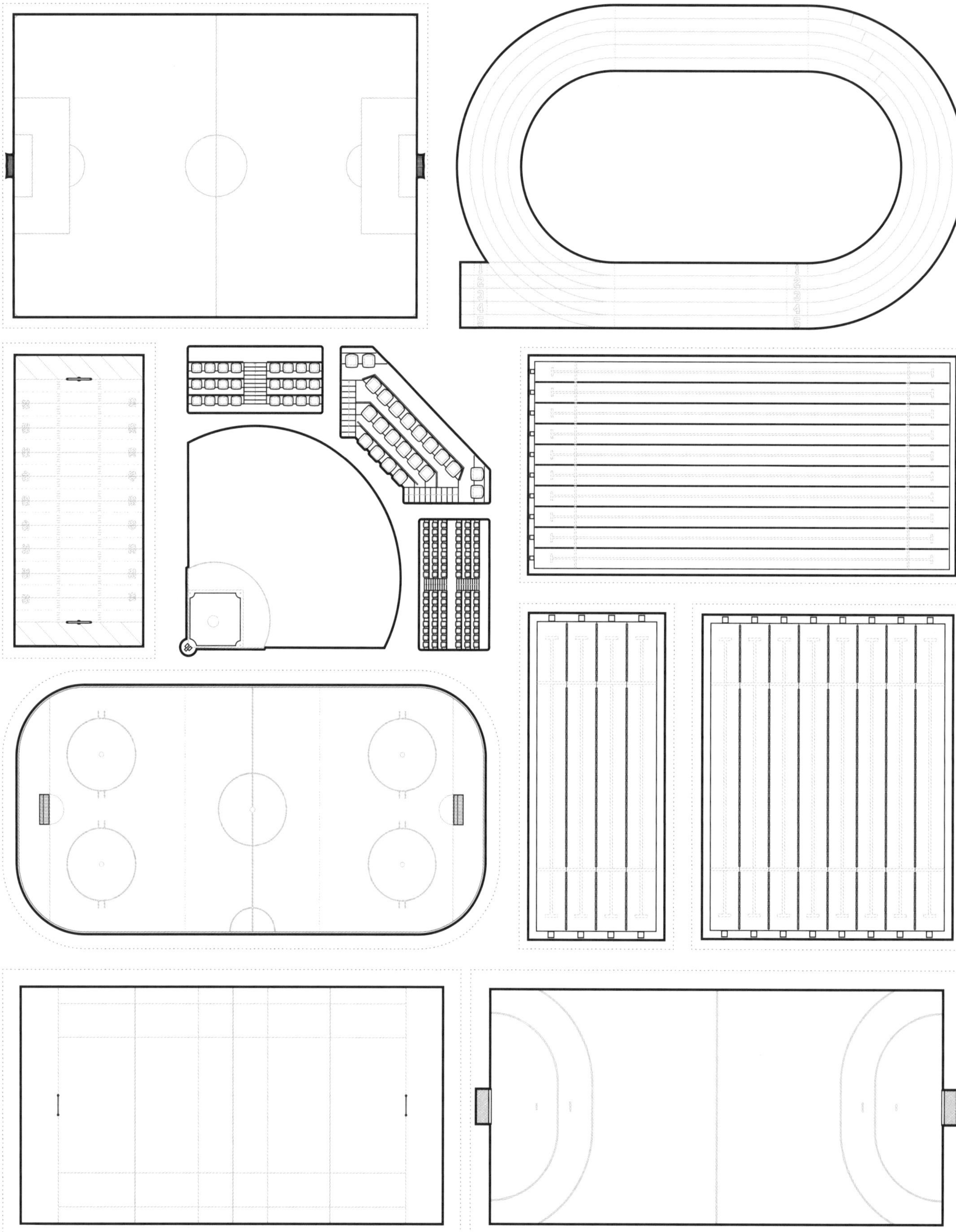

Kit for a
Stadium

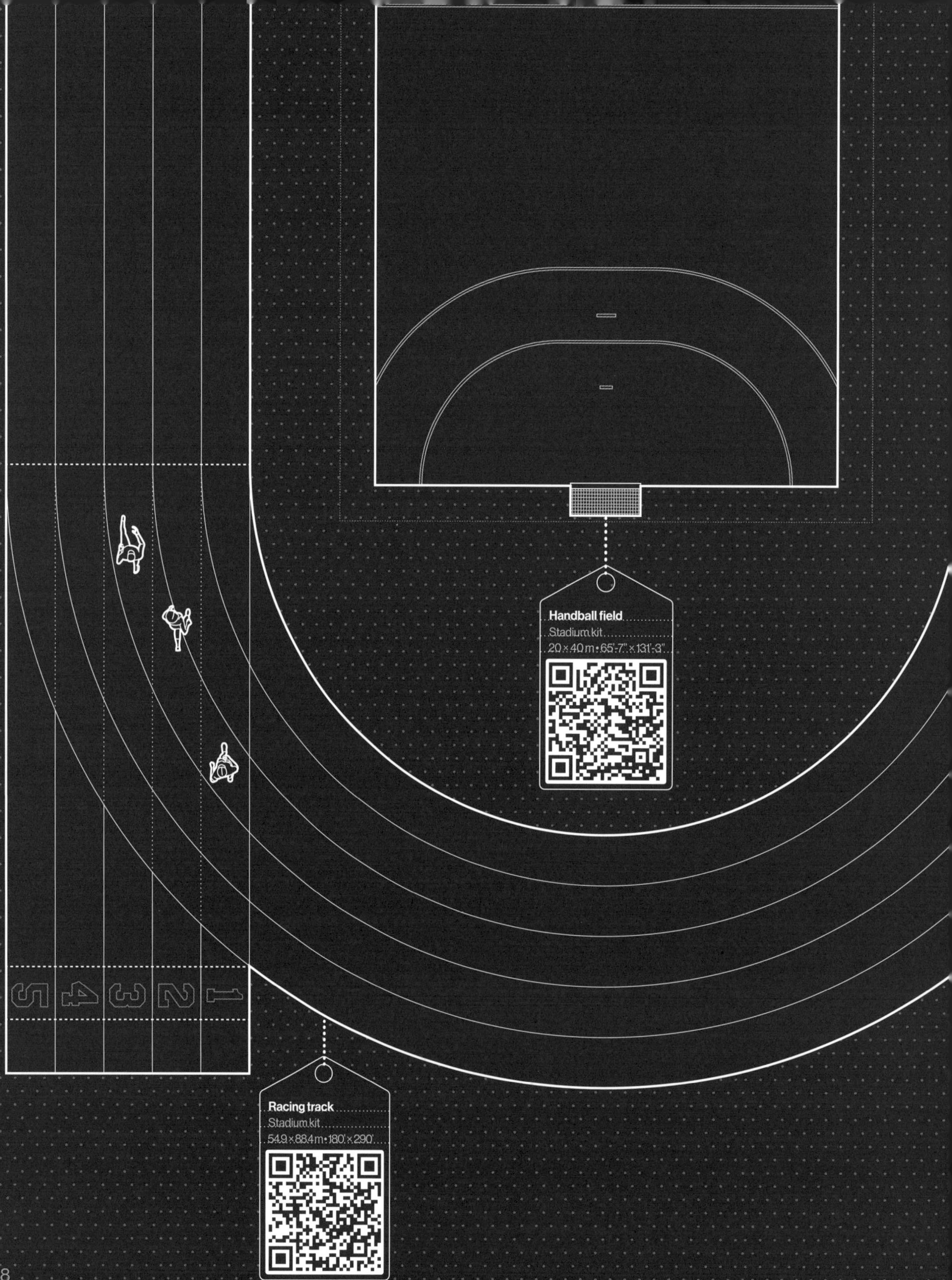
5
4
3
2
1
Handball field
Stadium kit
20 × 40 m • 65′-7″ × 131′-3″
Racing track
Stadium kit
54.9 × 88.4 m • 180′ × 290′

Tribune L
Stadium kit
6.2 × 11.4 m • 20'-3" × 37'-5"
Olympic pool
Stadium kit
26.2 × 51 m • 85'-11" × 167'-4"

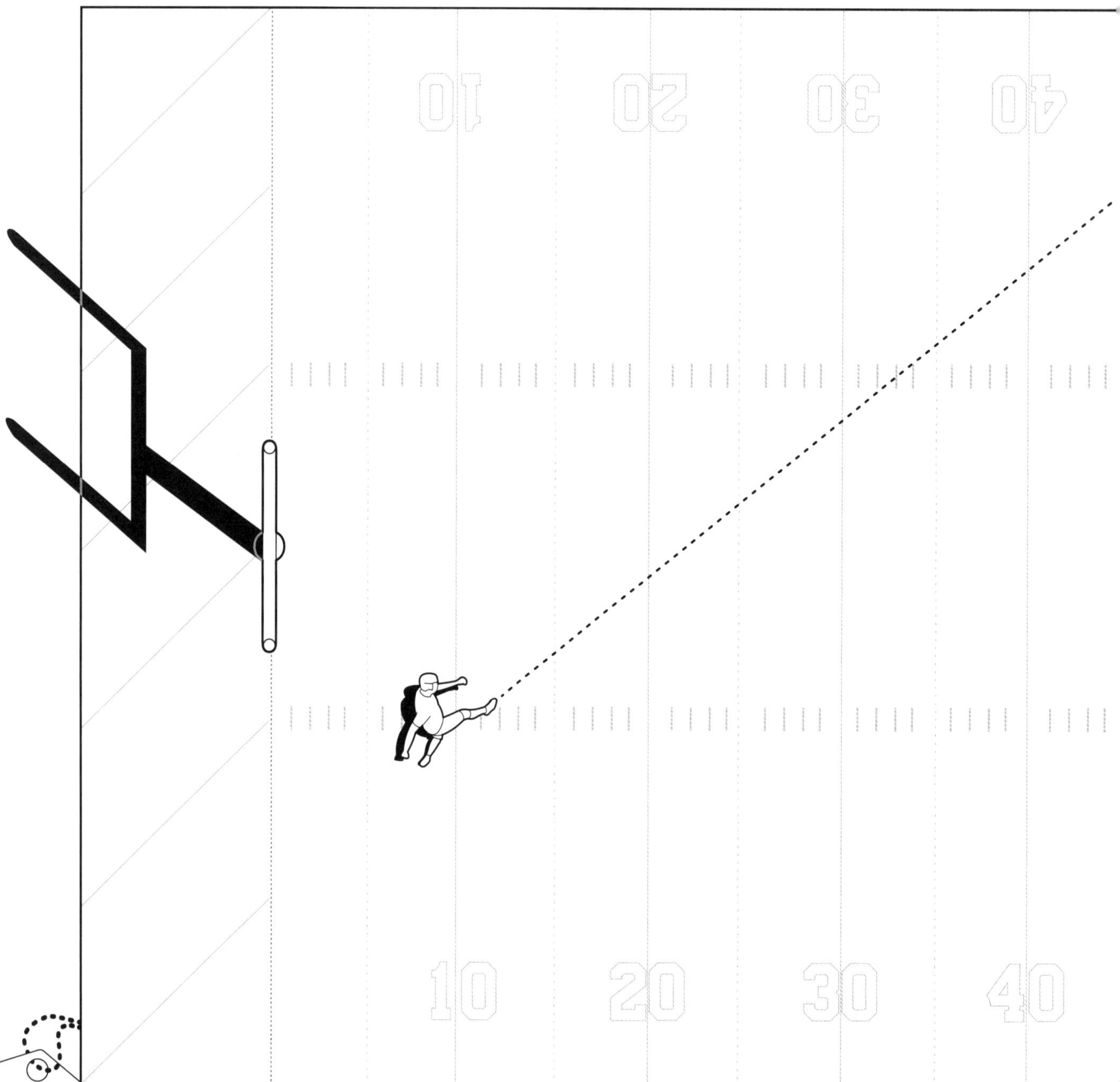

American football field • Stadium kit
49 × 110 m • 160′ × 360′

Hockey rink
Stadium kit
61 × 30 m : 200' × 98'-5"

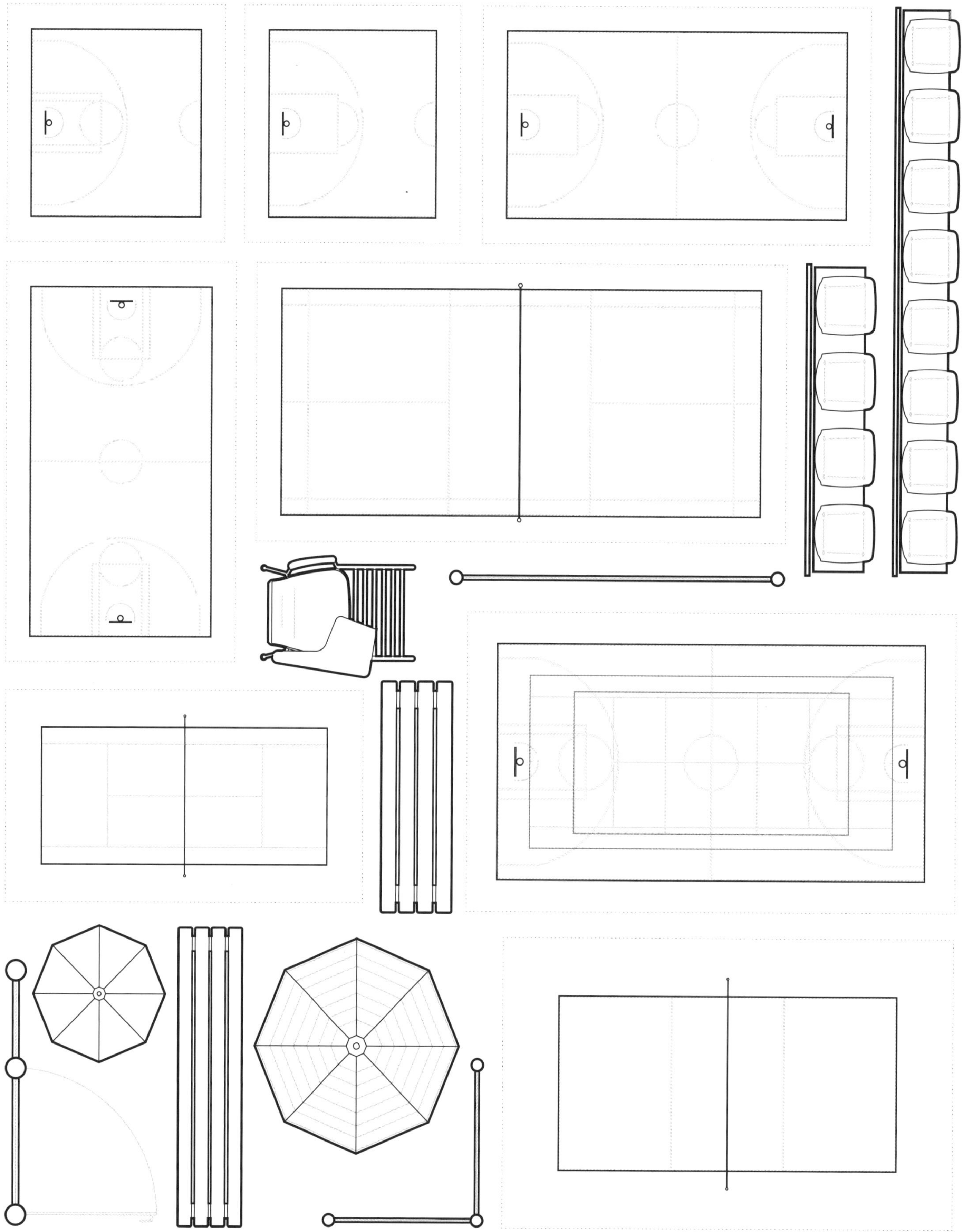

Kit for a
Sports Court

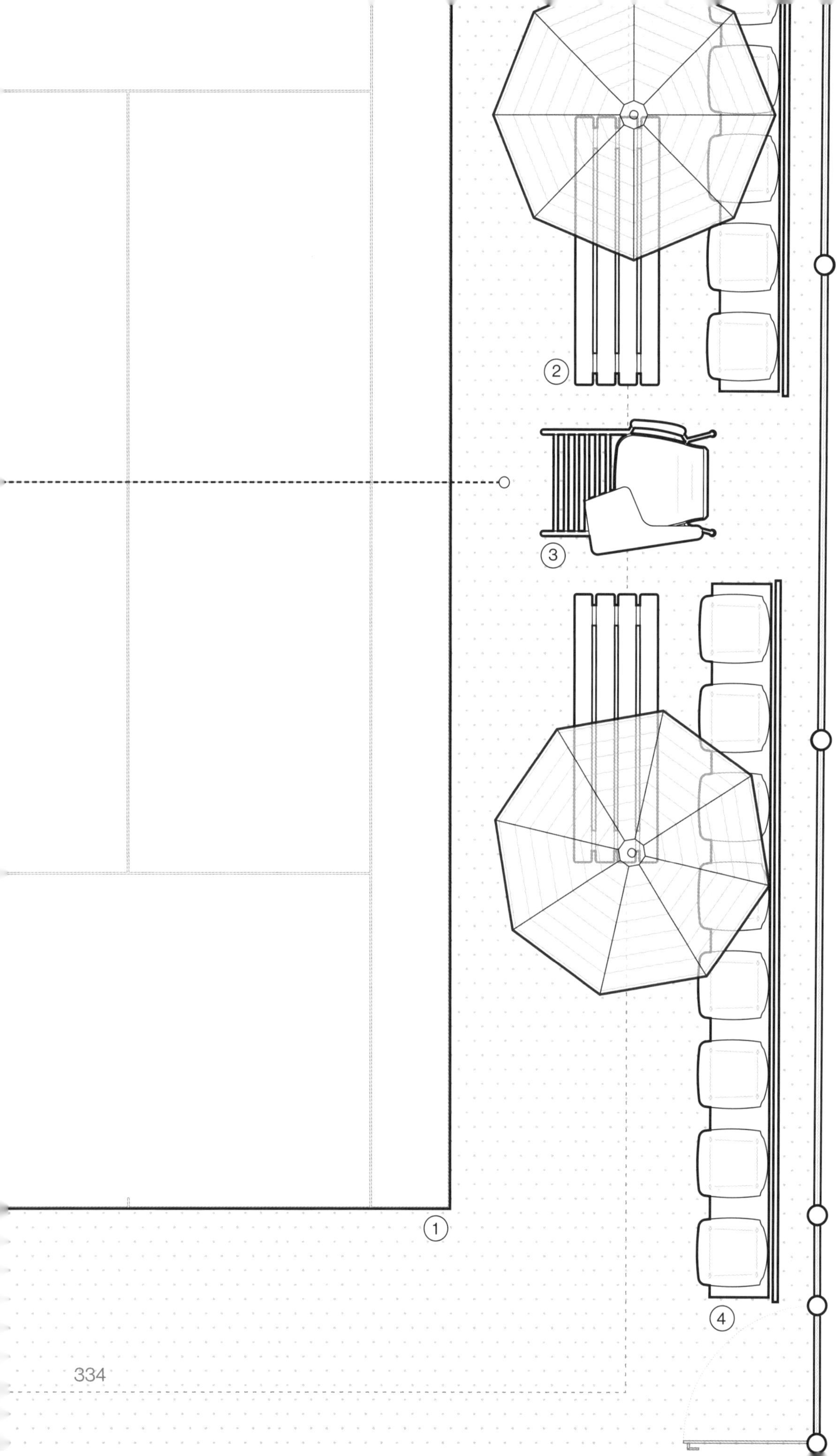

1

Tennis court
Sport court kit
11 × 23.7m • 36' × 78'

2

Tennis bench S
Sport court kit
0.46 × 1.4 m • 1'-6" × 4'-7"

3

Referee chair
Sport court kit
0.84 × 0.65 m • 2'-9" × 2'-2"

4

Public bench L
Sport court kit
0.55 × 4.82 m • 1'-10" × 15'-10"

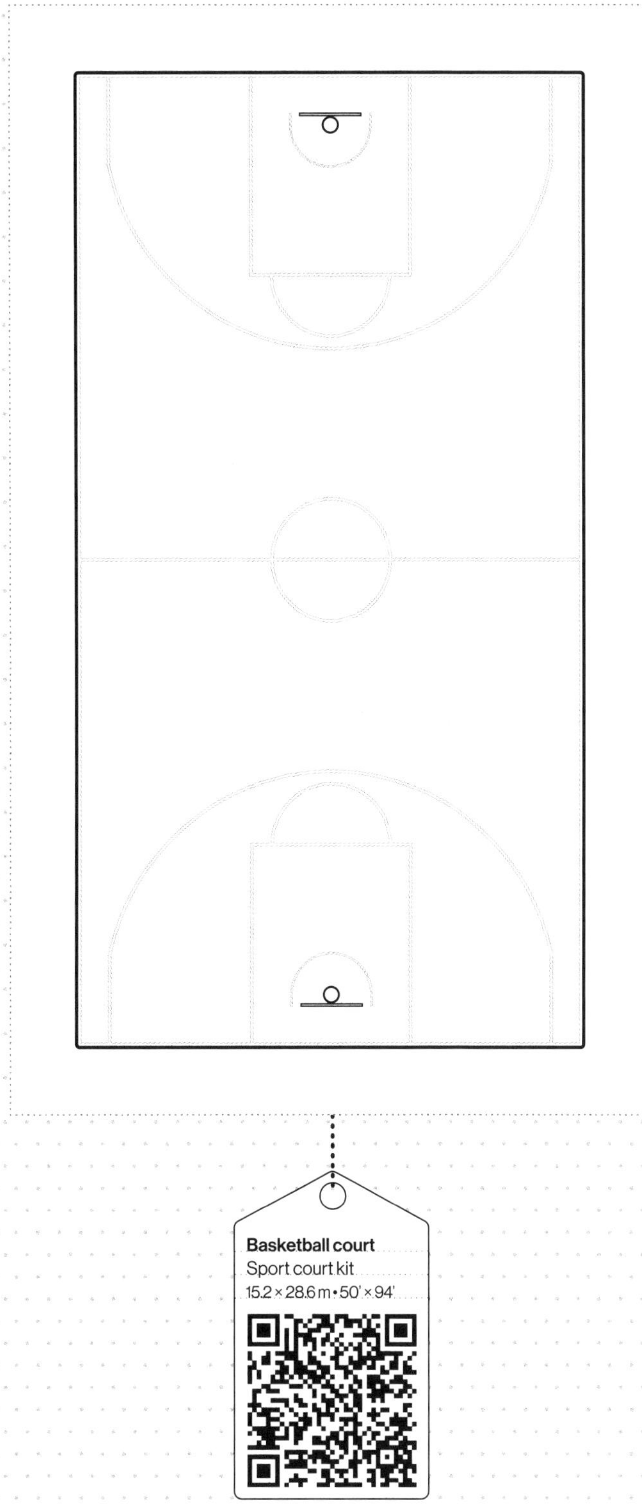
Basketball court
Sport court kit
15.2 × 28.6 m • 50′ × 94′

Volleyball court
Sport court kit
9 × 18 m • 29'-6" × 59'

Half basketball court
Sport court kit
15 × 14 m • 49'-3" × 45'-11"

Kit for a
Golf Course

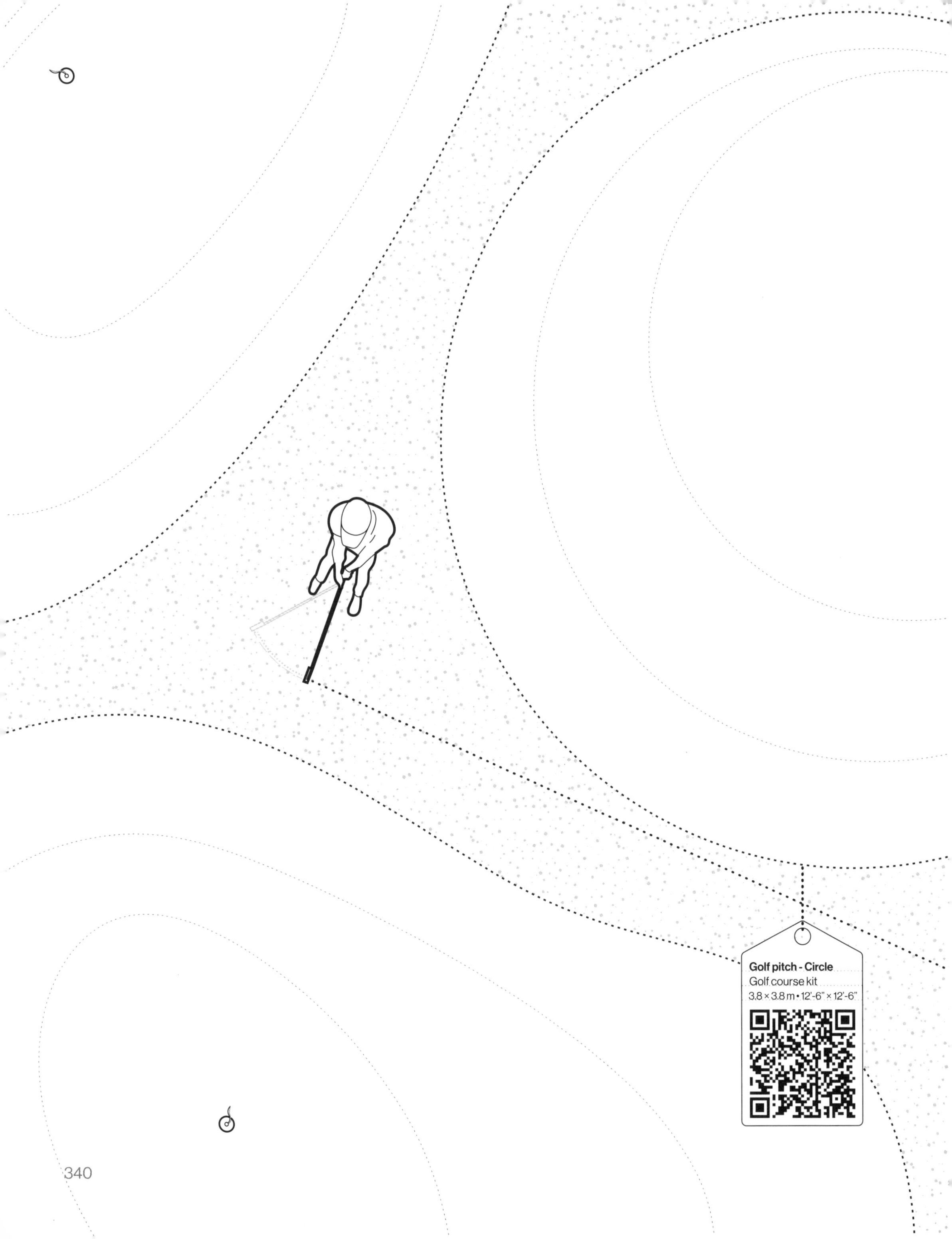
Golf pitch - Circle
Golf course kit
3.8 × 3.8 m • 12'-6" × 12'-6"

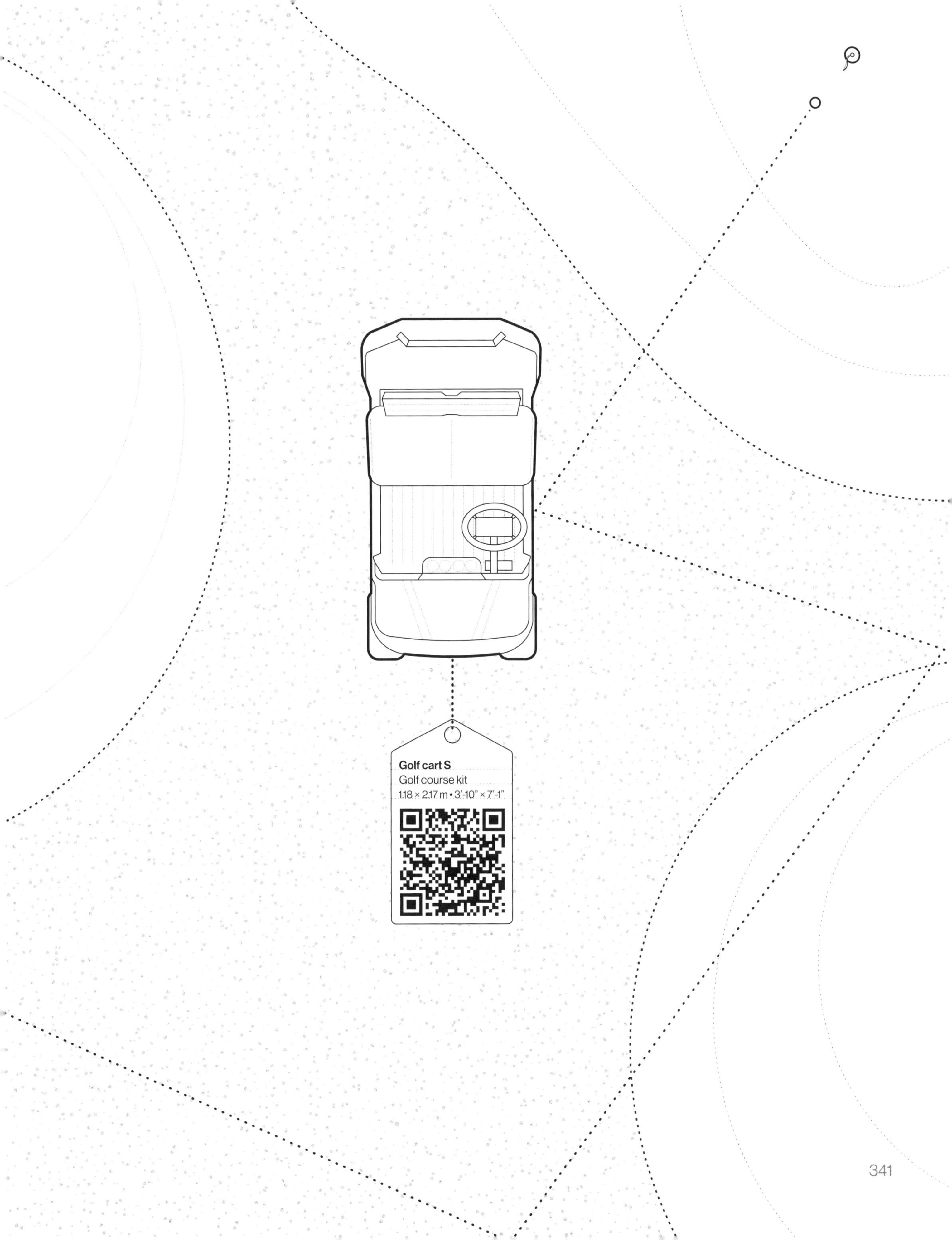
Golf cart S
Golf course kit
1.18 × 2.17 m • 3’-10” × 7’-1”

Mini golf - Zigzag
Golf course kit
1.44 × 4.7 m • 4'-9" × 15'-5"
Mini golf - Loop
Golf course kit
2.6 × 2.93 m • 8'-6" × 9'-7"
Mini golf - L-shaped
Golf course kit
2.38 × 2.6 m • 7'-10" × 8'-6"

Mini golf - Square
Golf course kit
1.33 × 3.6 m • 4'-4" × 11'-10"
Mini golf - Jagged
Golf course kit
1.65 × 4.57 m • 5'-5" × 15'

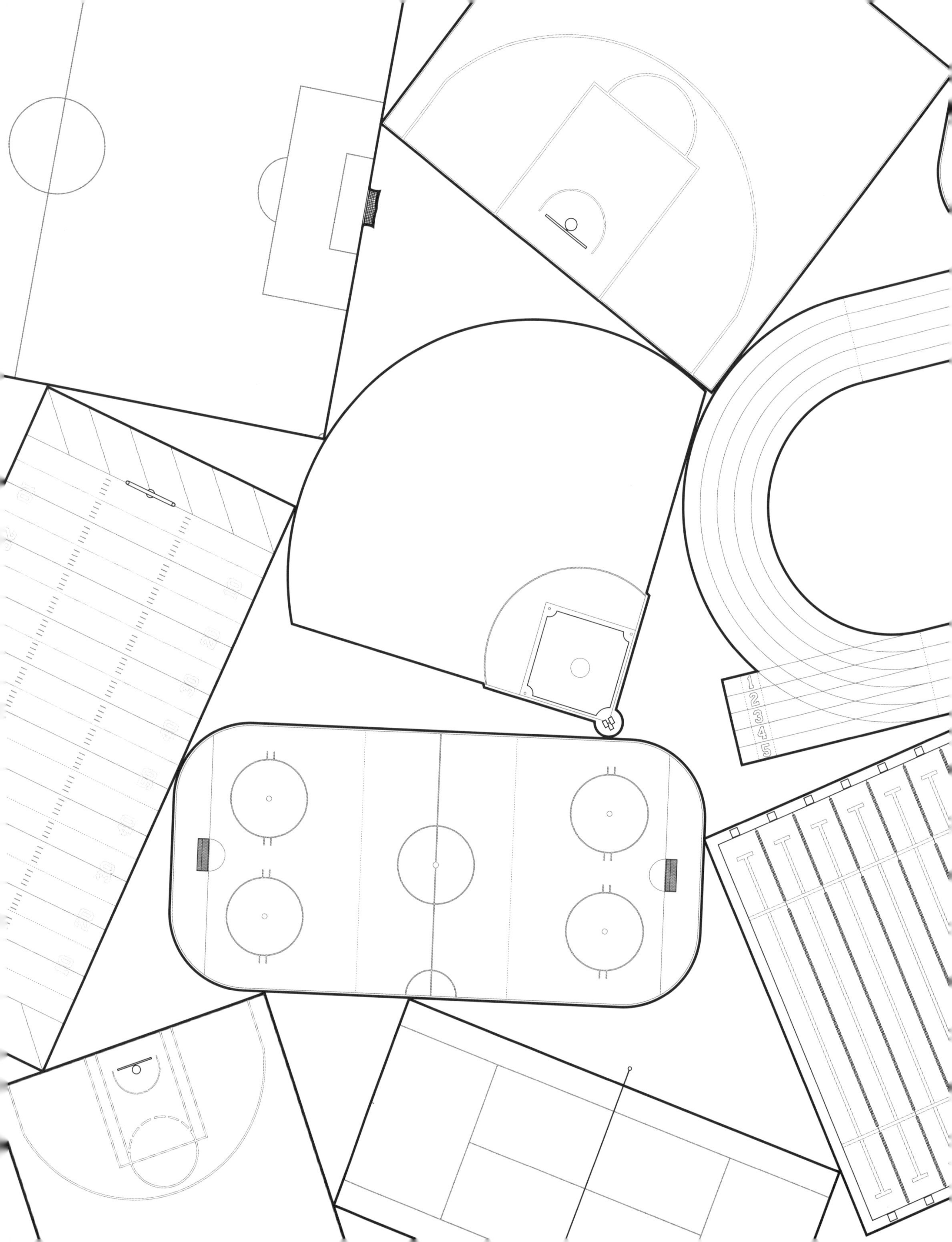
1
2
3
4
5

A Catalog of Sports Fields

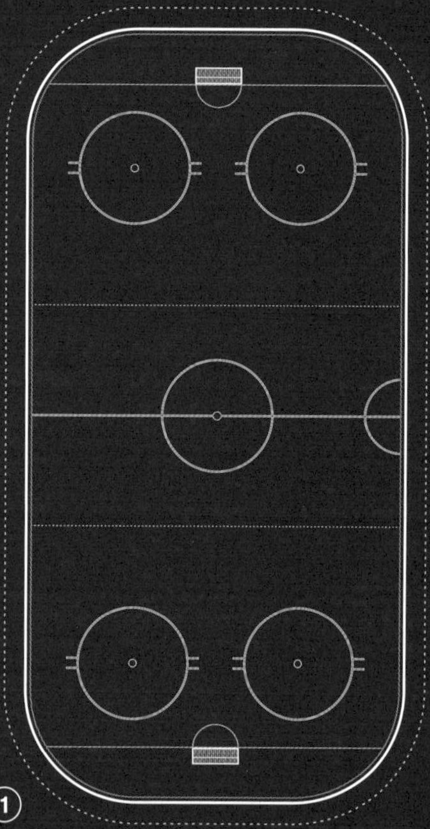

1

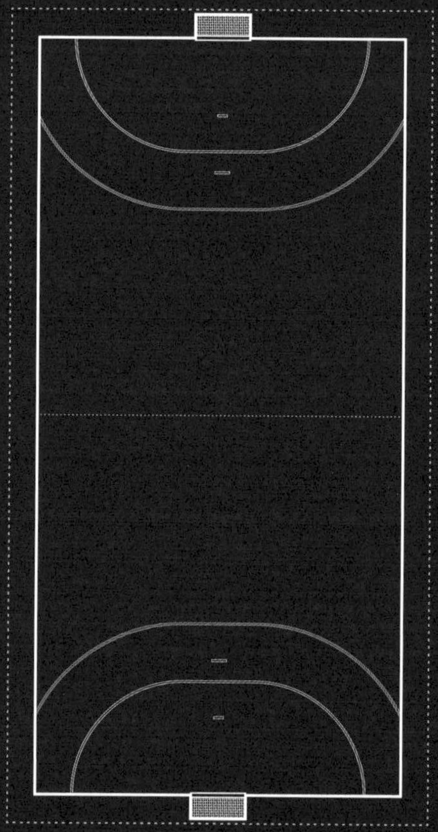

2

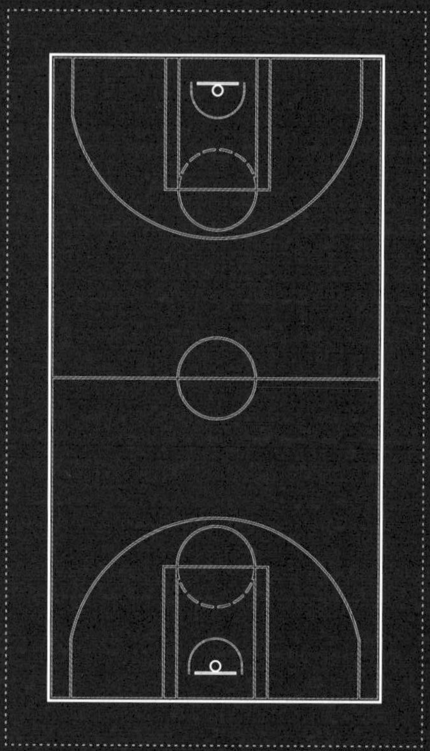

3

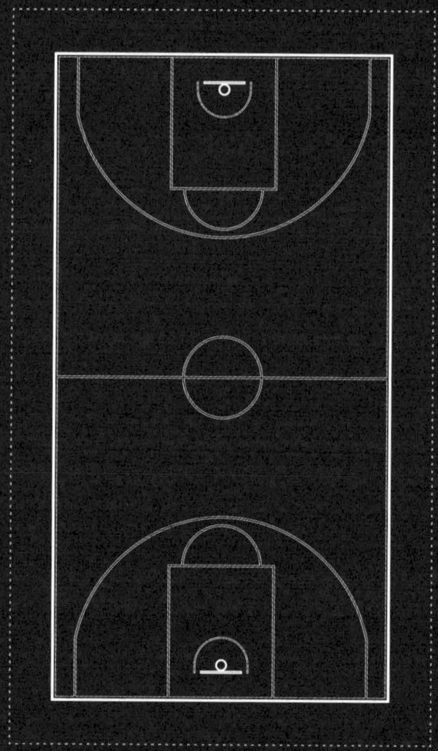

4

5

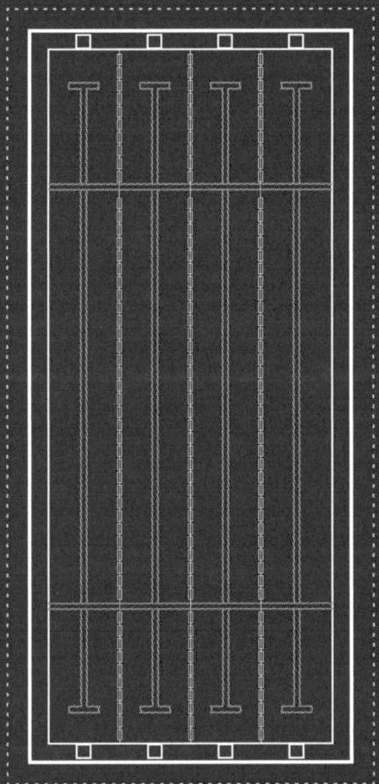

6

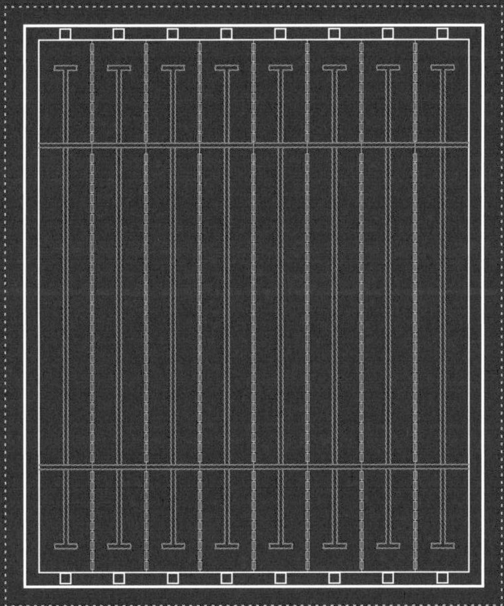

7

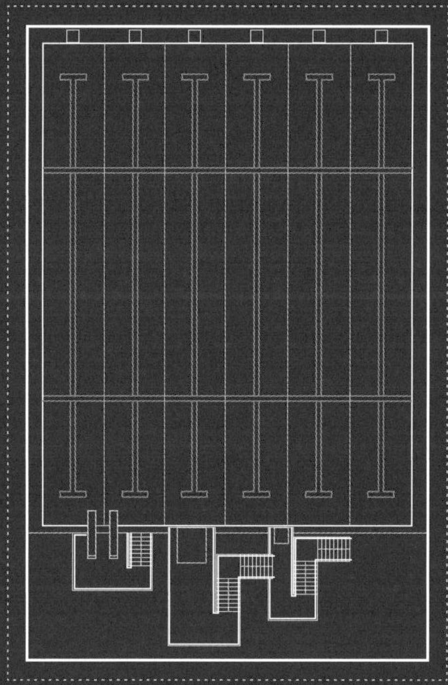

8

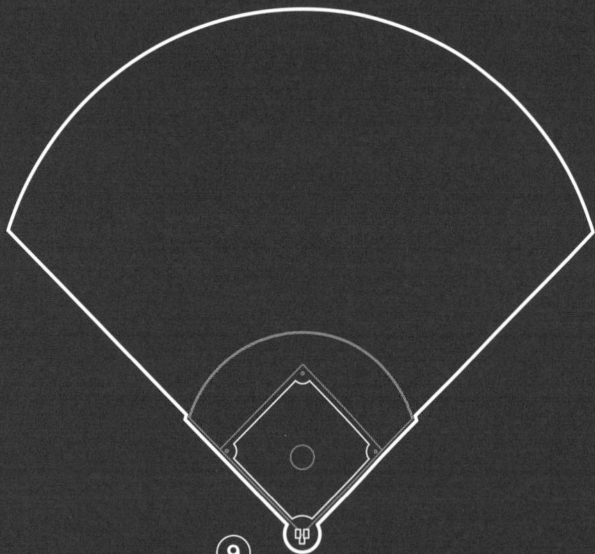

9

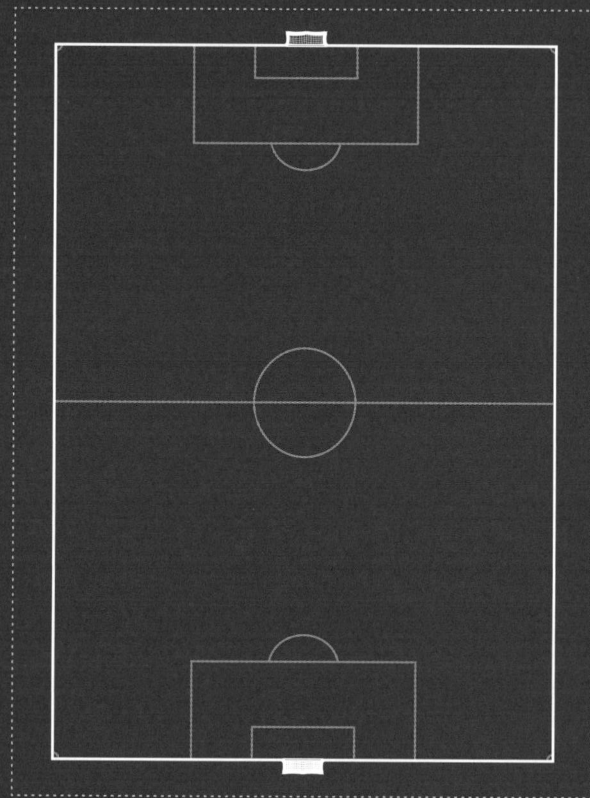

10

11

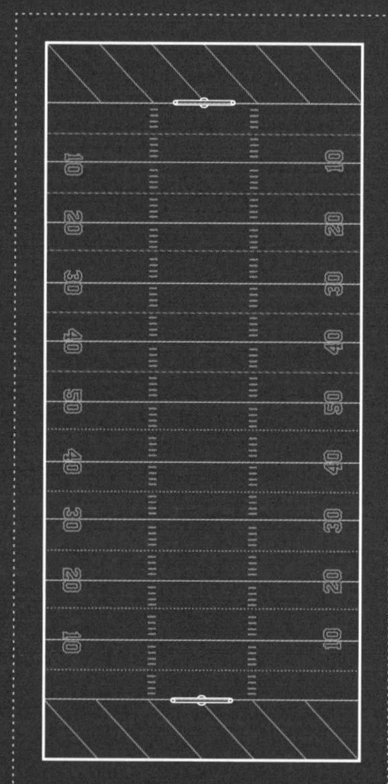

12

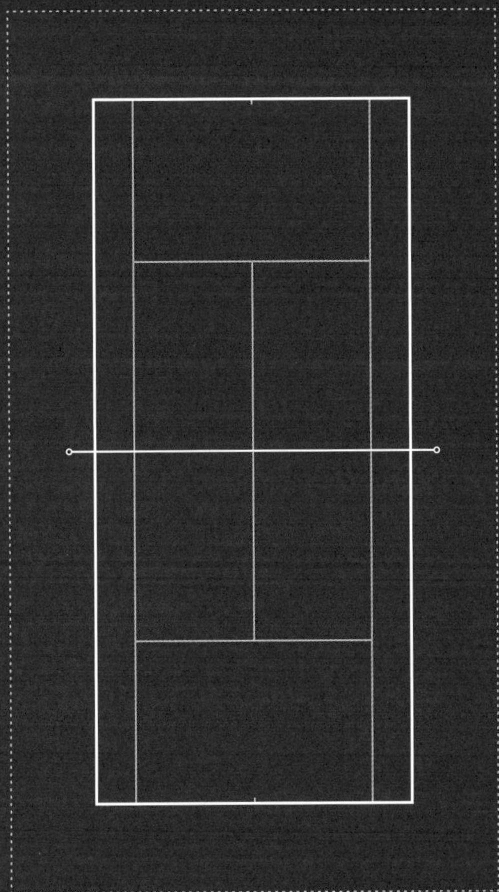

13

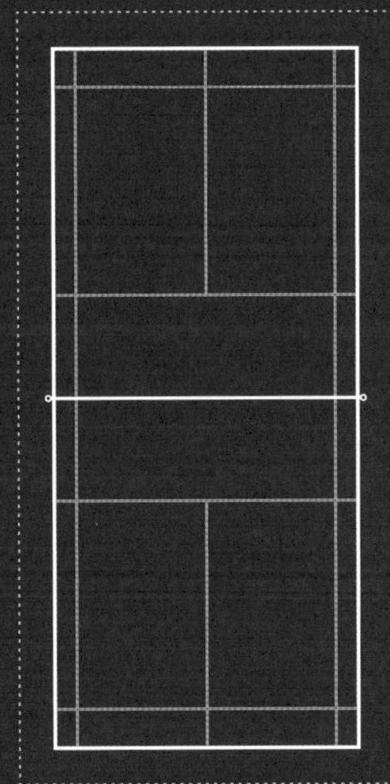

14

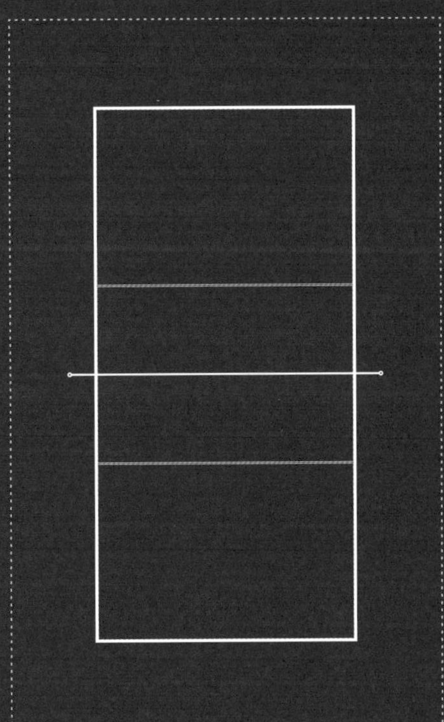

15

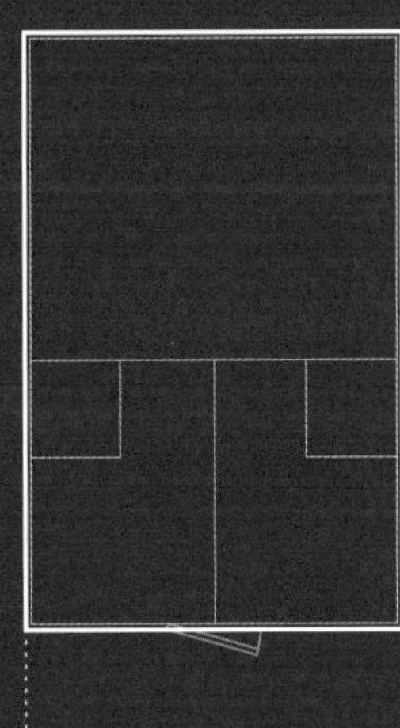

16

1. **Hockey rink**
Sport fields
61 × 30 m • 200' × 98'-5"

2. **Handball court**
Sport fields
20 × 40 m • 65'-7" × 131'-3"

3. **Basketball court (NBA)** • Sport fields
15.2 × 28.6 m • 50' × 94'

4. **Basketball court (FIBA)** • Sport fields
15.2 × 28.6 m • 50' × 94'

5. **Olympic pool**
Sport fields
51 × 26.2 m • 167' × 86'

6. **3-lane pool**
Sport fields
26.2 × 11.2 m • 86' × 37'

7. **8-lane pool**
Sport fields
26.2 × 21.2 m • 86' × 70'

8. **Diving pool**
Sport fields
26.2 × 17.8 m • 86' × 58'

9

Baseball field
Sport fields
125 × 140 m • 410' × 460'

10

Football field
Sport fields
90 × 120 m • 295' × 394'

11

Rugby field
Sport fields
70 × 122 m • 230' × 400'

12

American football field • Sport fields
49 × 110 m • 160' × 360'

13

Tennis court
Sport fields
11 × 23.7 m • 36' × 78'

14

Badminton court
Sport fields
6.1 × 13.4 m • 20' × 44'

15

Volleyball court
Sport fields
9 × 18 m • 29'-6" × 59'

16

Squash court
Sport fields
6.4 × 9.75 m • 21' × 32'

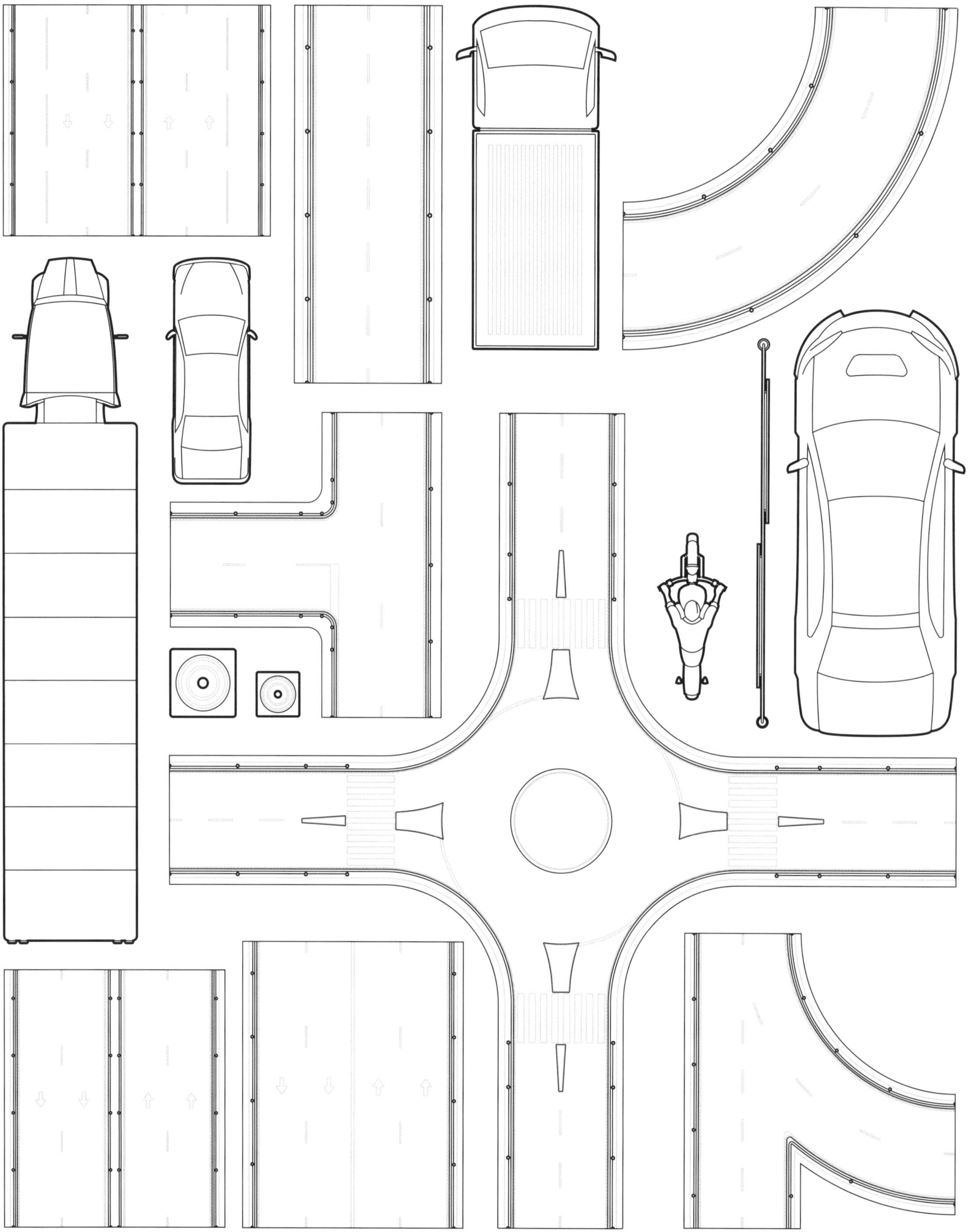

Kit for a
Road

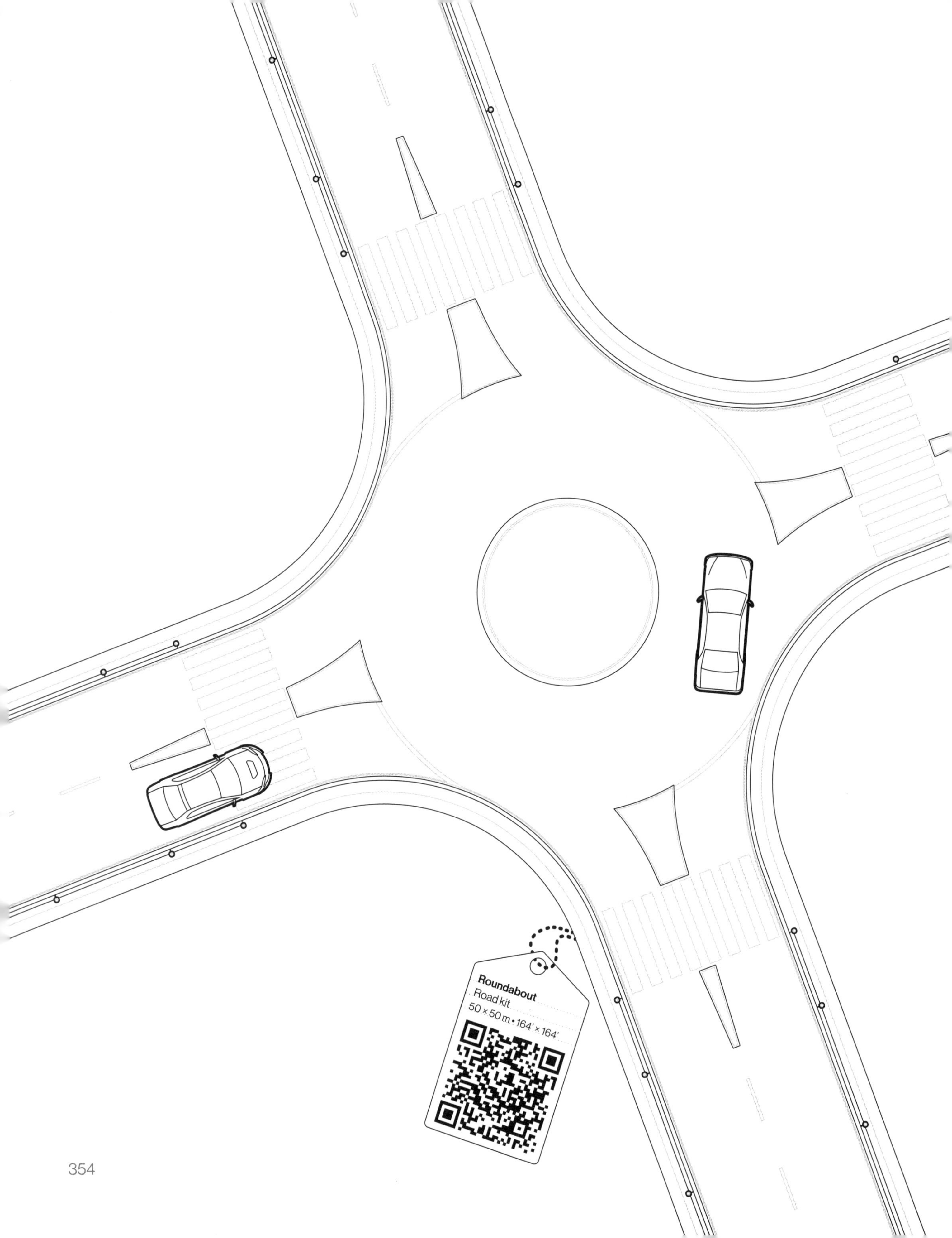
Roundabout
Road kit
50 × 50 m • 164′ × 164′

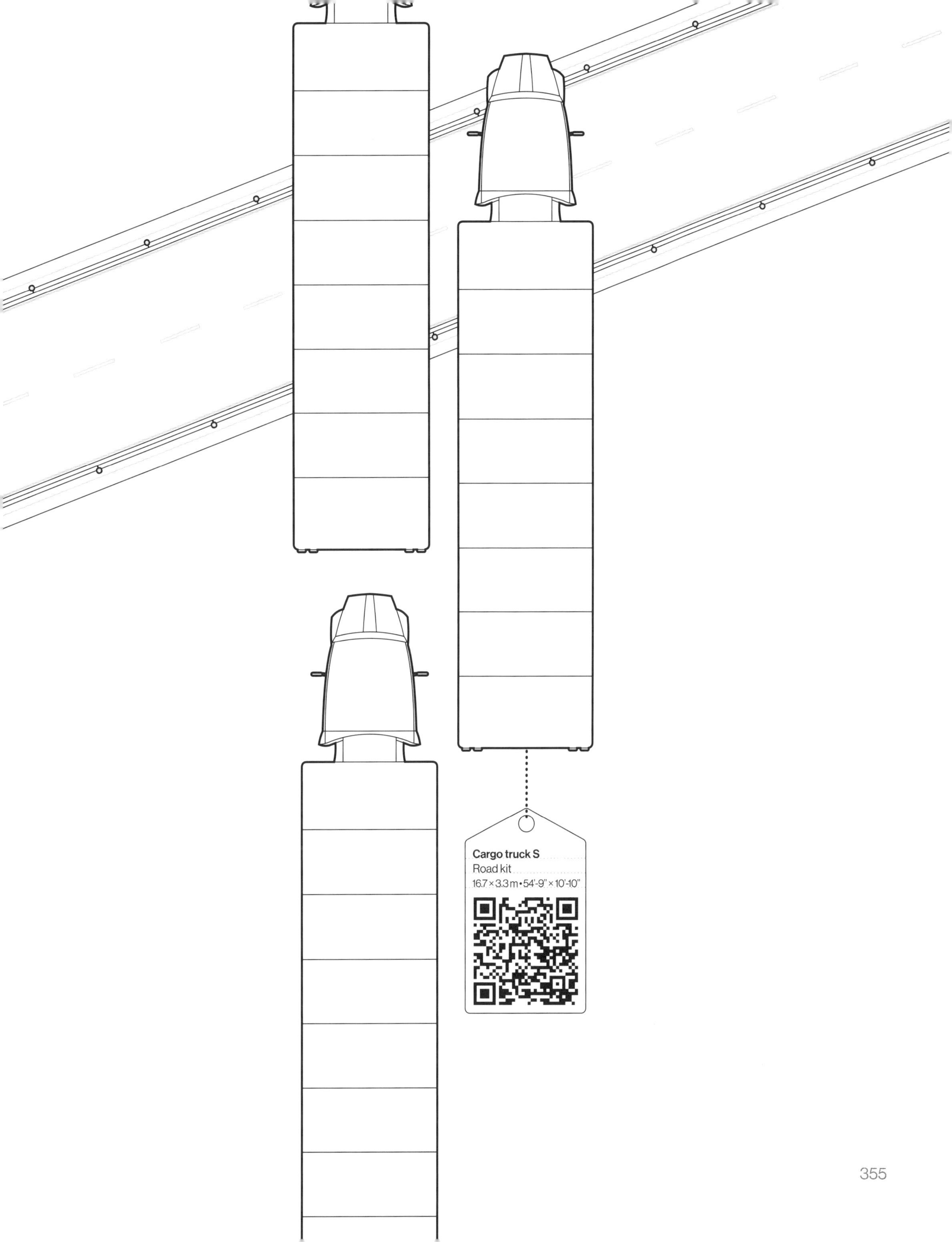
Cargo truck S
Road kit
16.7 × 3.3 m • 54'-9" × 10'-10"

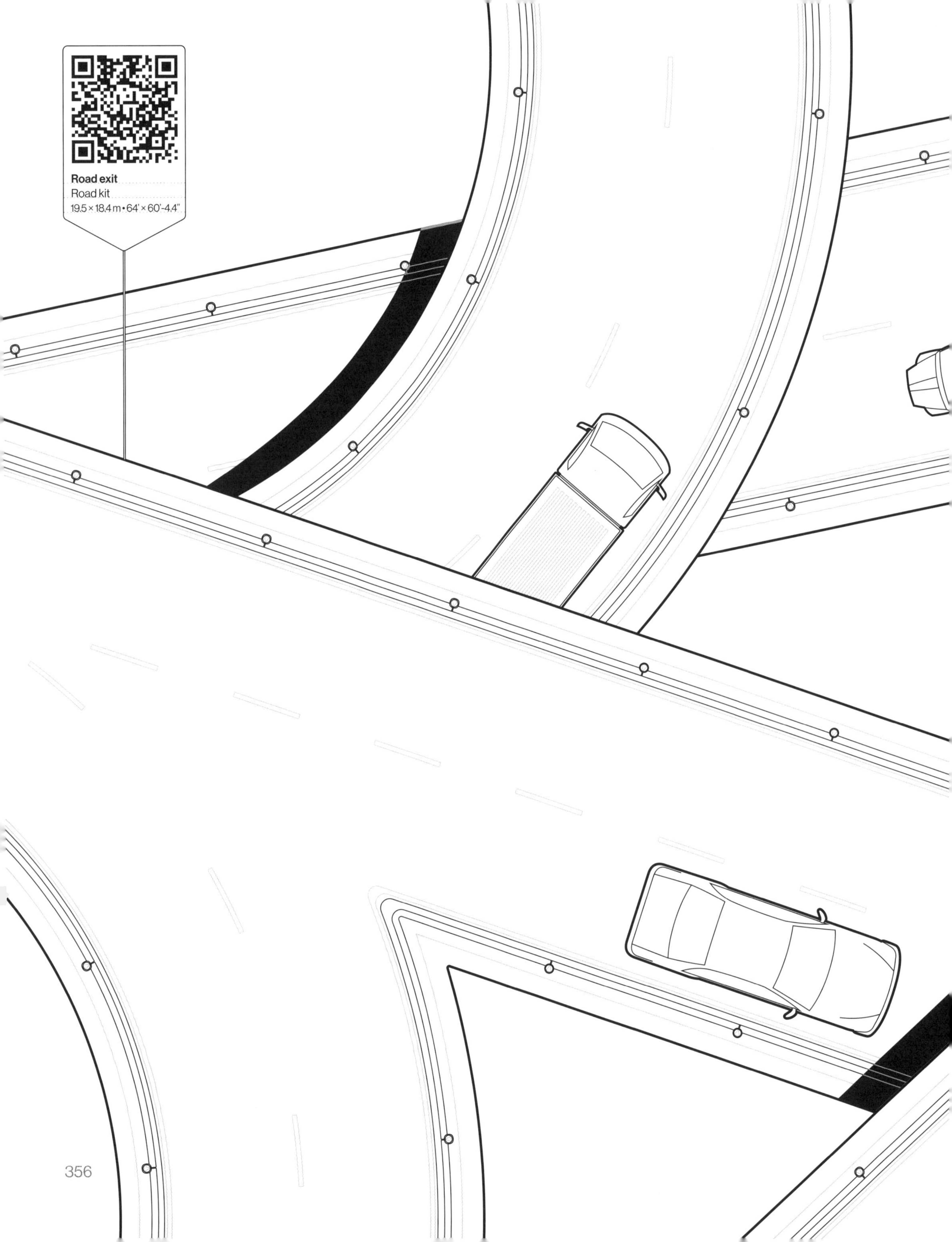
Road exit
Road kit
19.5 × 18.4 m • 64' × 60'-4.4"

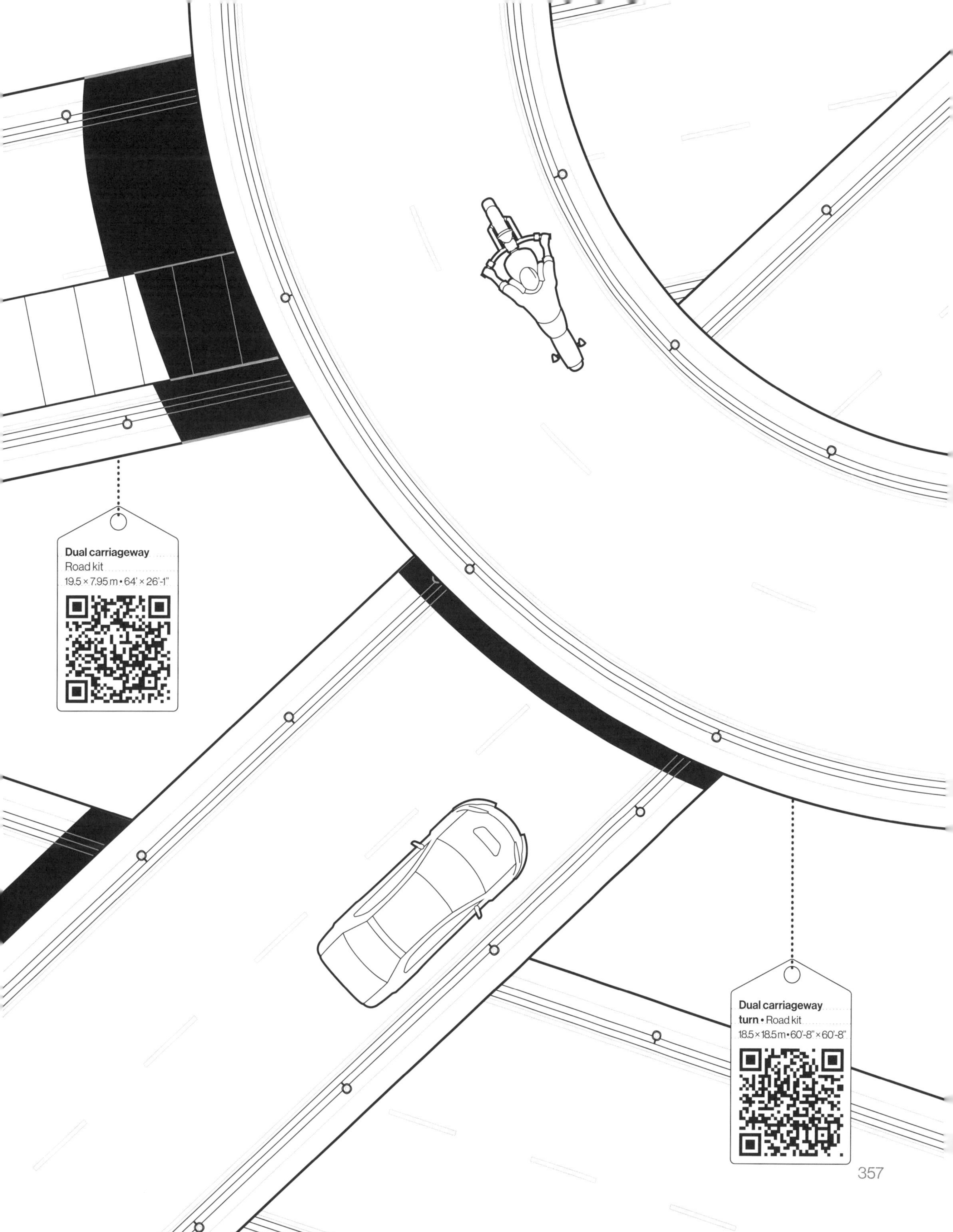
Dual carriageway
Road kit
19.5 × 7.95 m • 64' × 26'-1"
Dual carriageway
turn • Road kit
18.5 × 18.5 m • 60'-8" × 60'-8"

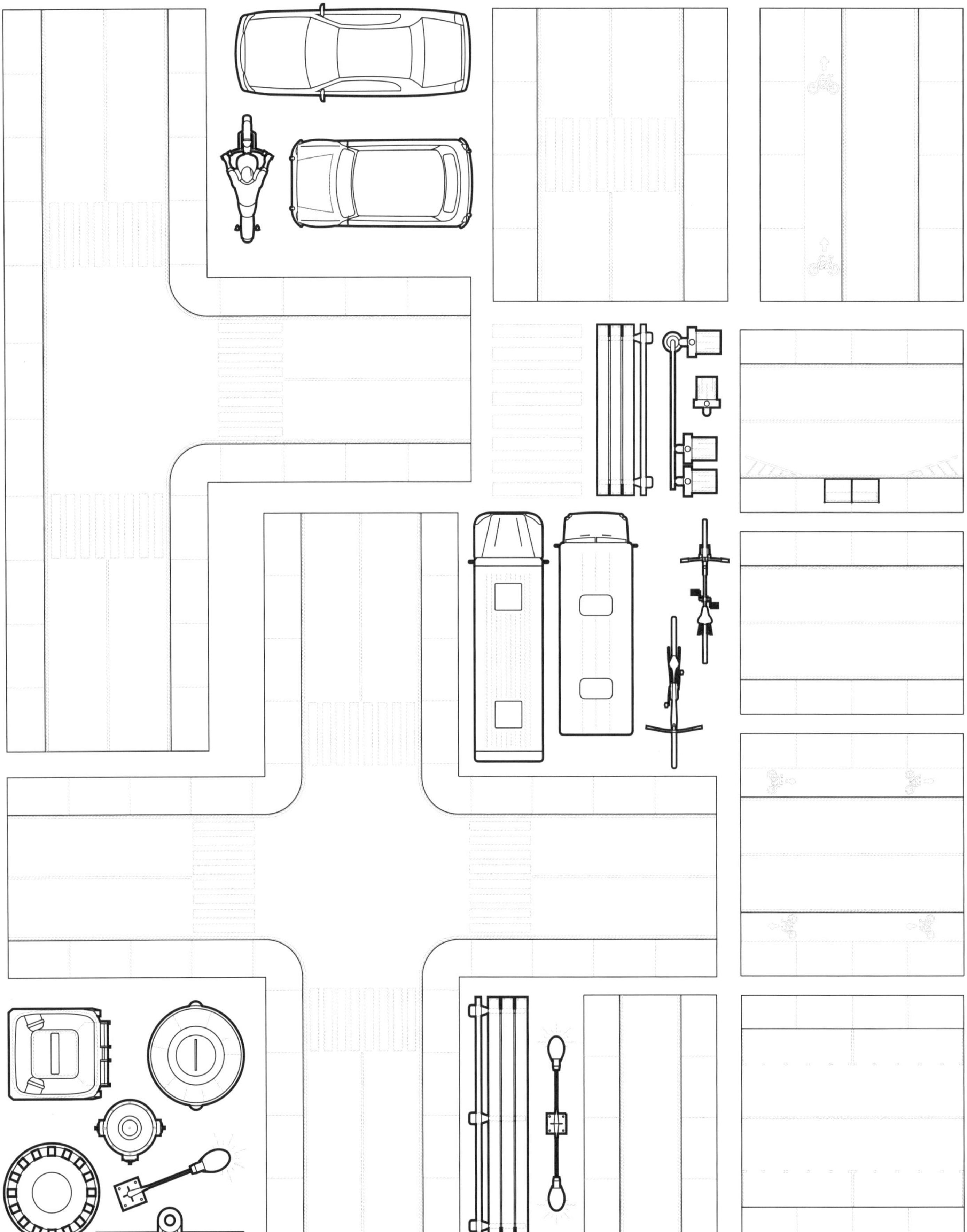

Kit for a
Street

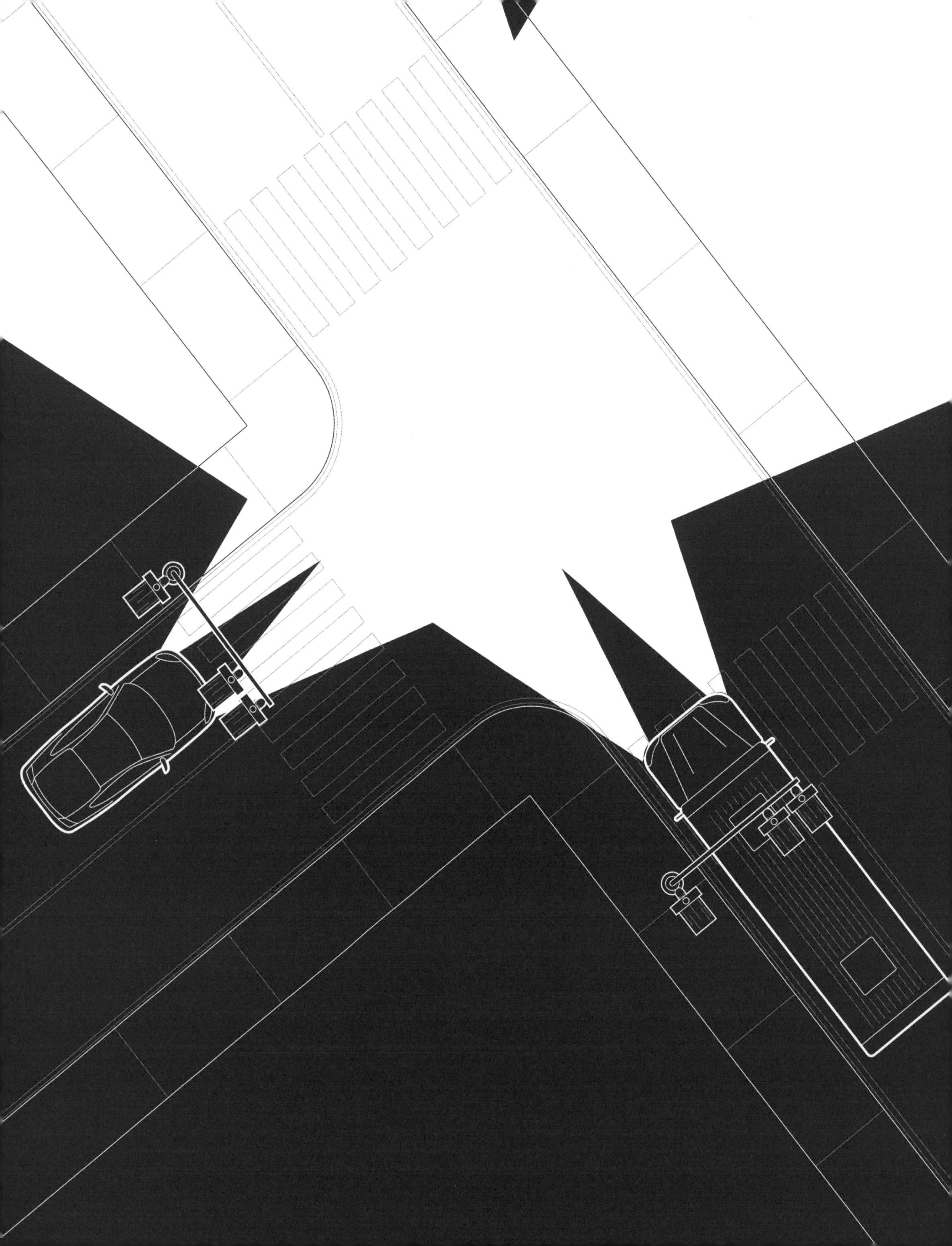

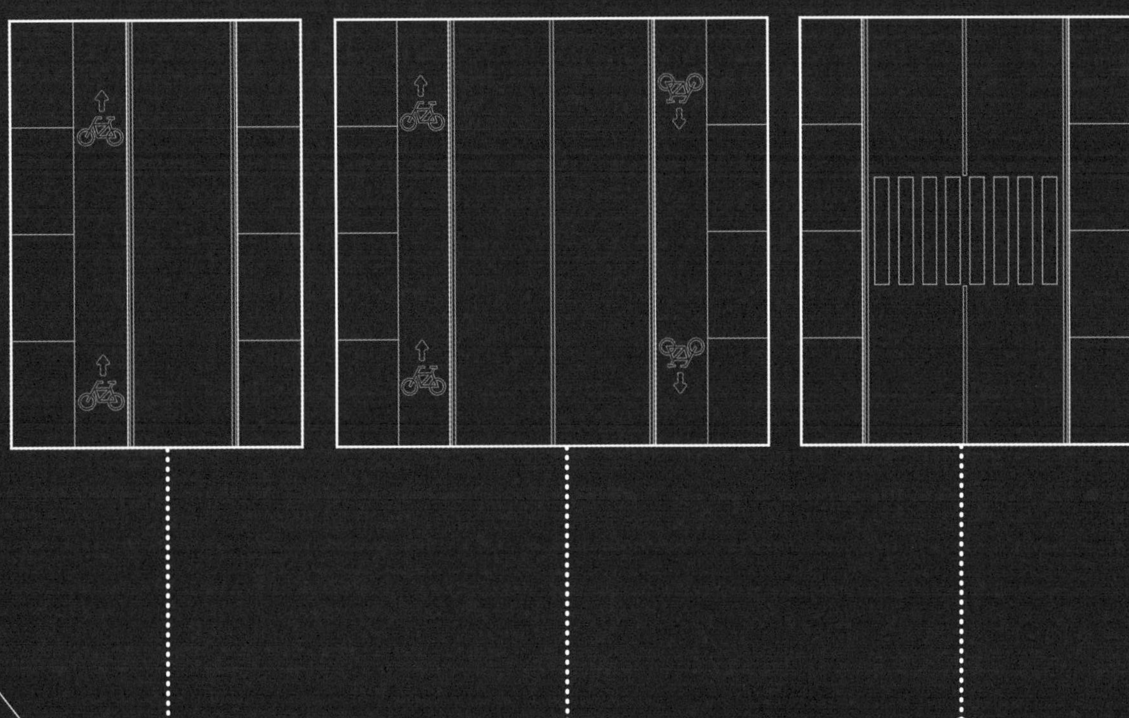

One-way street with bike lane • Street kit
12 × 8.2 m • 39′-4″ × 26′-11″

Two-way street with lane • Street kit
12 × 12.6 m • 39′-4″ × 41′-4″

Two-way street with crossing • Street kit
12 × 9.6 m • 39′-4″ × 31′-6″

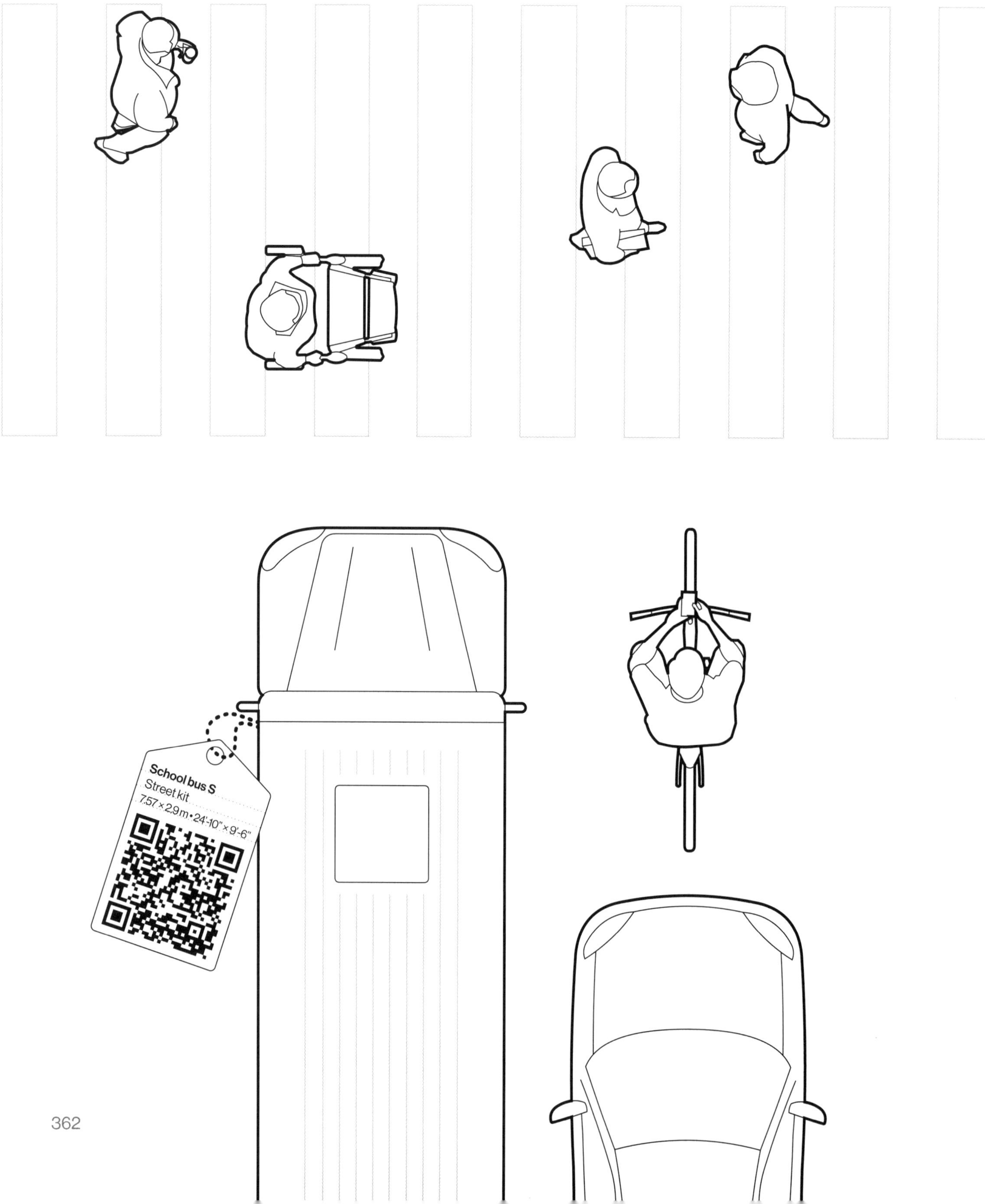
School bus S
Street kit
7.57 × 2.9 m • 24'-10" × 9'-6"

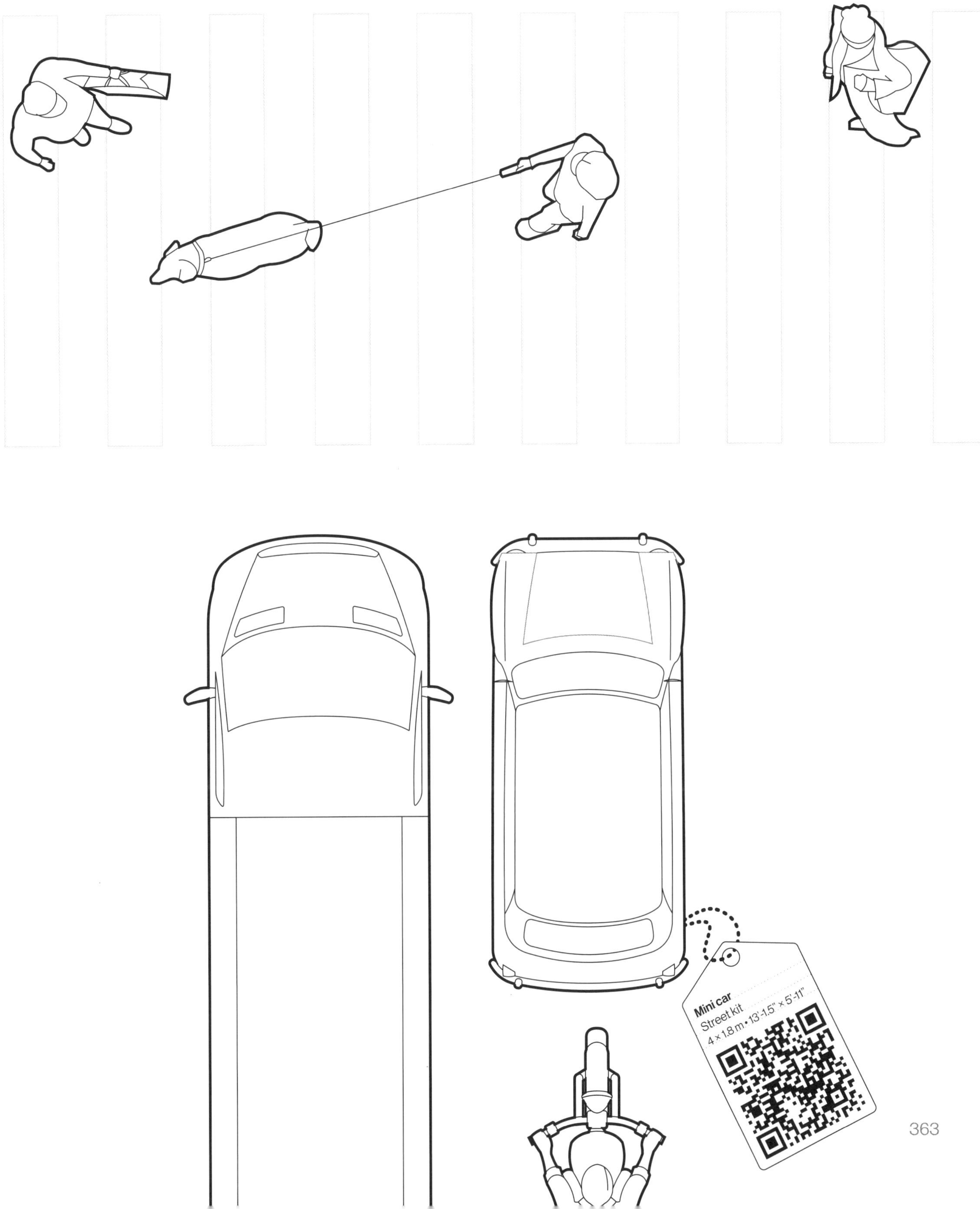
Mini car
Street kit
4 × 1.8 m • 13'-1.5" × 5'-11"

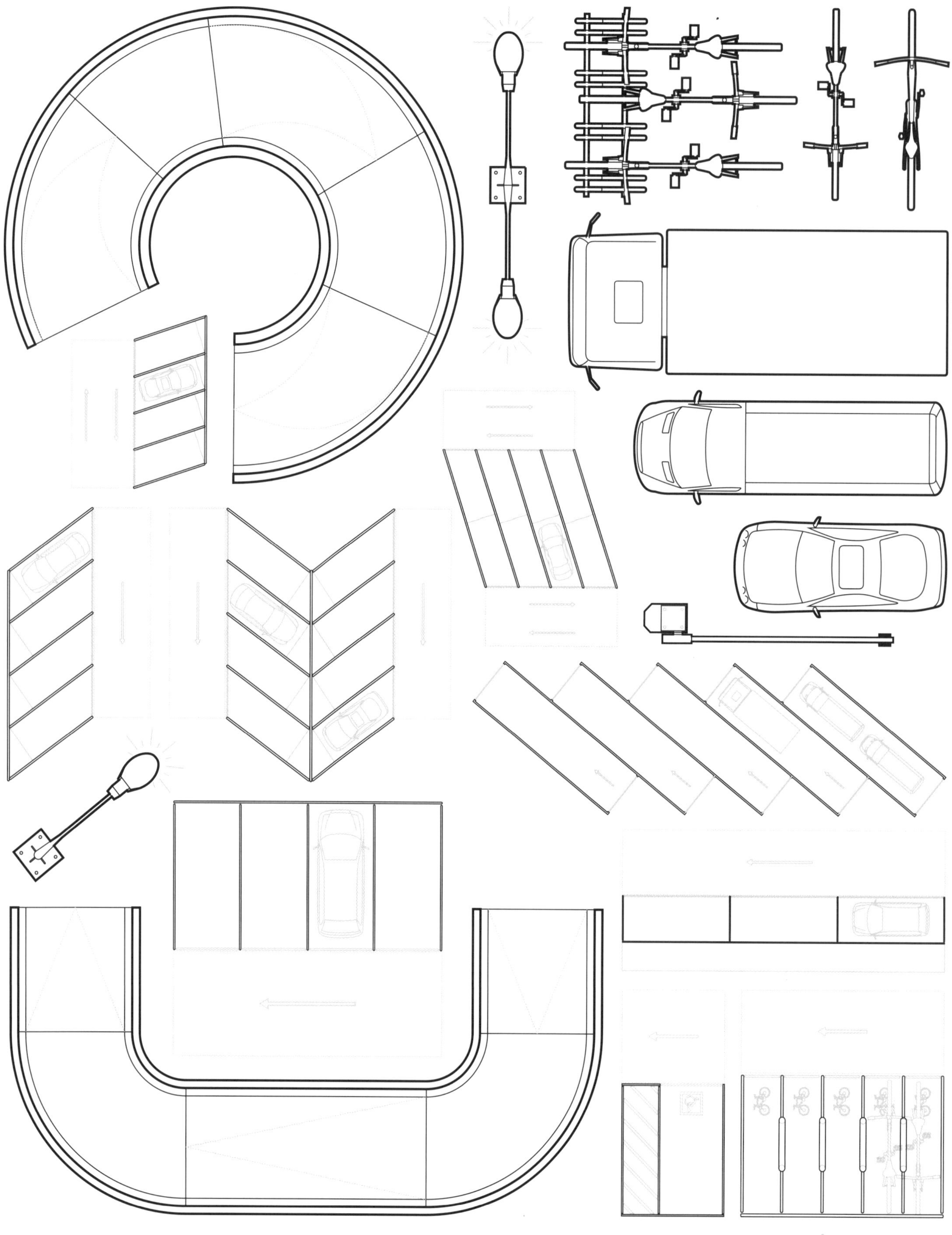

Kit for a
Parking Lot

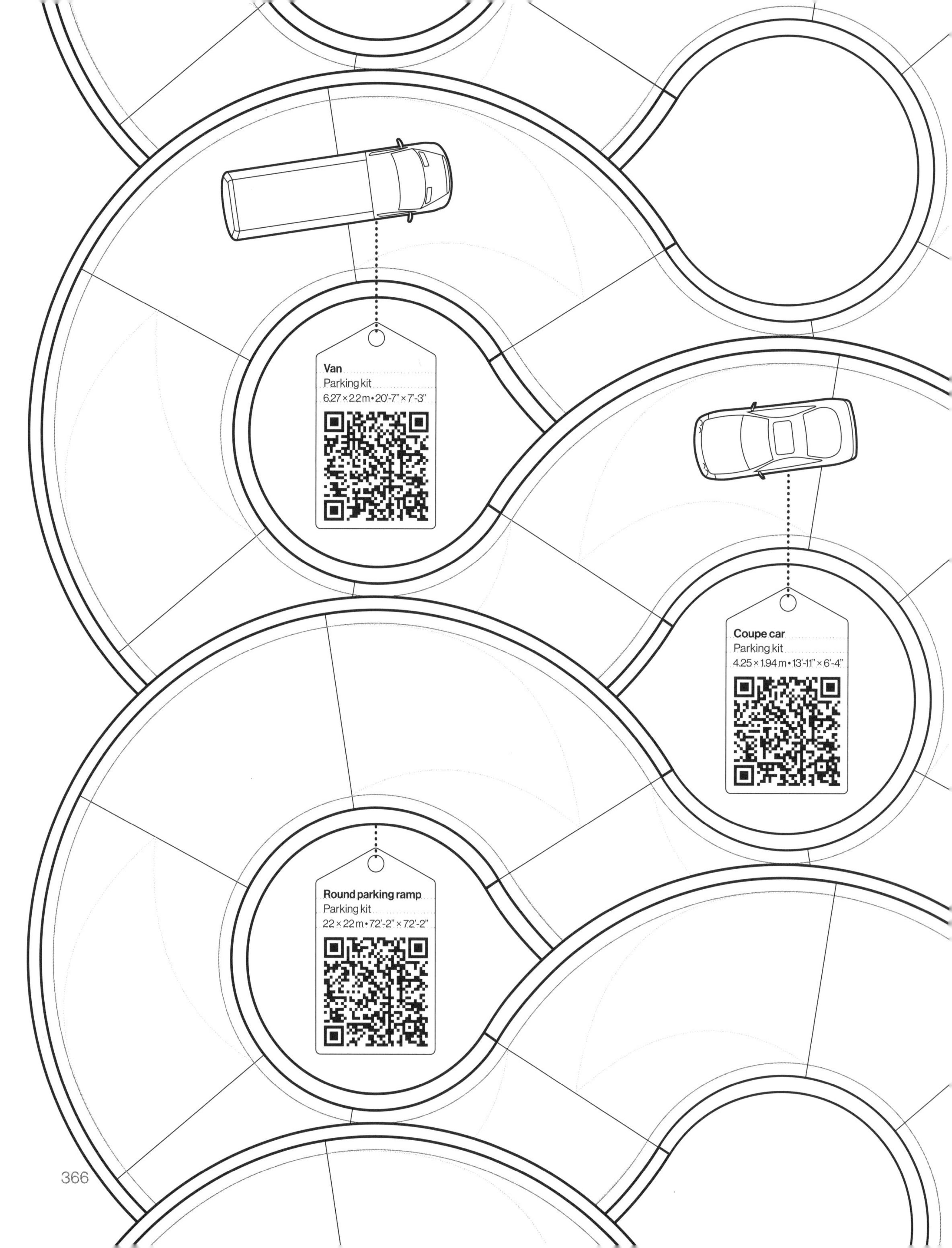
Van
Parking kit
6.27 × 2.2 m • 20'-7" × 7'-3"
Coupe car
Parking kit
4.25 × 1.94 m • 13'-11" × 6'-4"
Round parking ramp
Parking kit
22 × 22 m • 72'-2" × 72'-2"

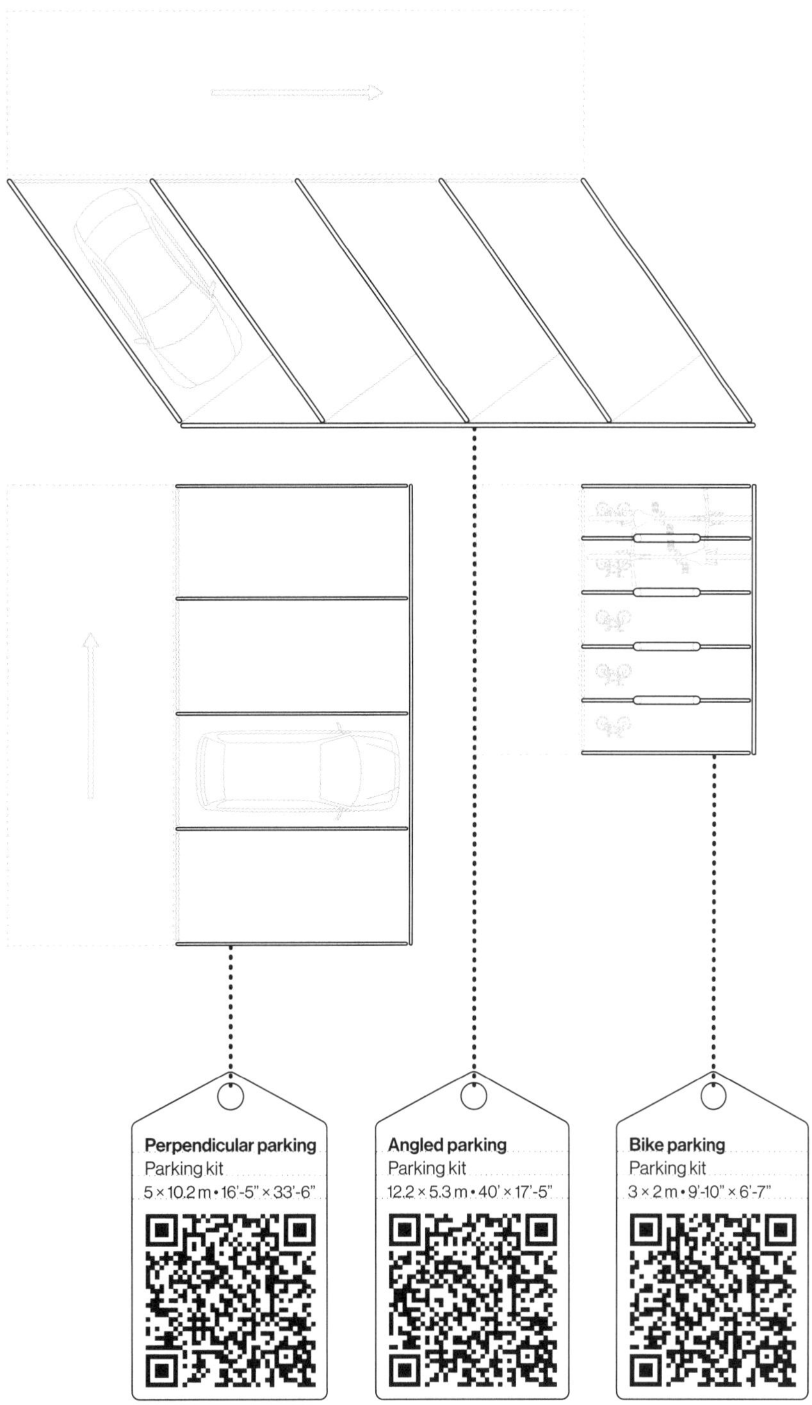

Perpendicular parking
Parking kit
5 × 10.2 m • 16'-5" × 33'-6"
Angled parking
Parking kit
12.2 × 5.3 m • 40' × 17'-5"
Bike parking
Parking kit
3 × 2 m • 9'-10" × 6'-7"

U-parking ramp
Parking kit
31.3 × 15.5 m • 102'-8" × 50'-10"

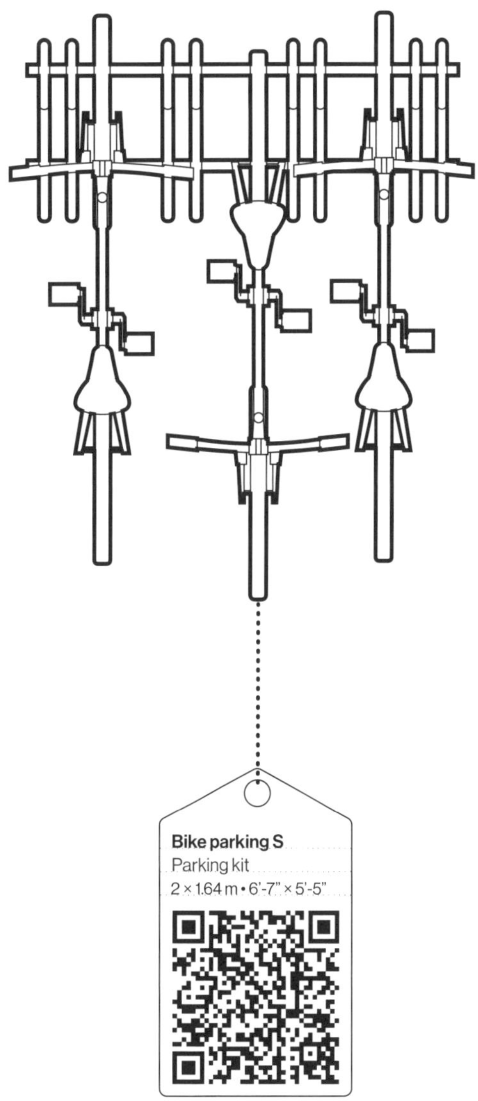
Bike parking S
Parking kit
2 × 1.64 m • 6'-7" × 5'-5"

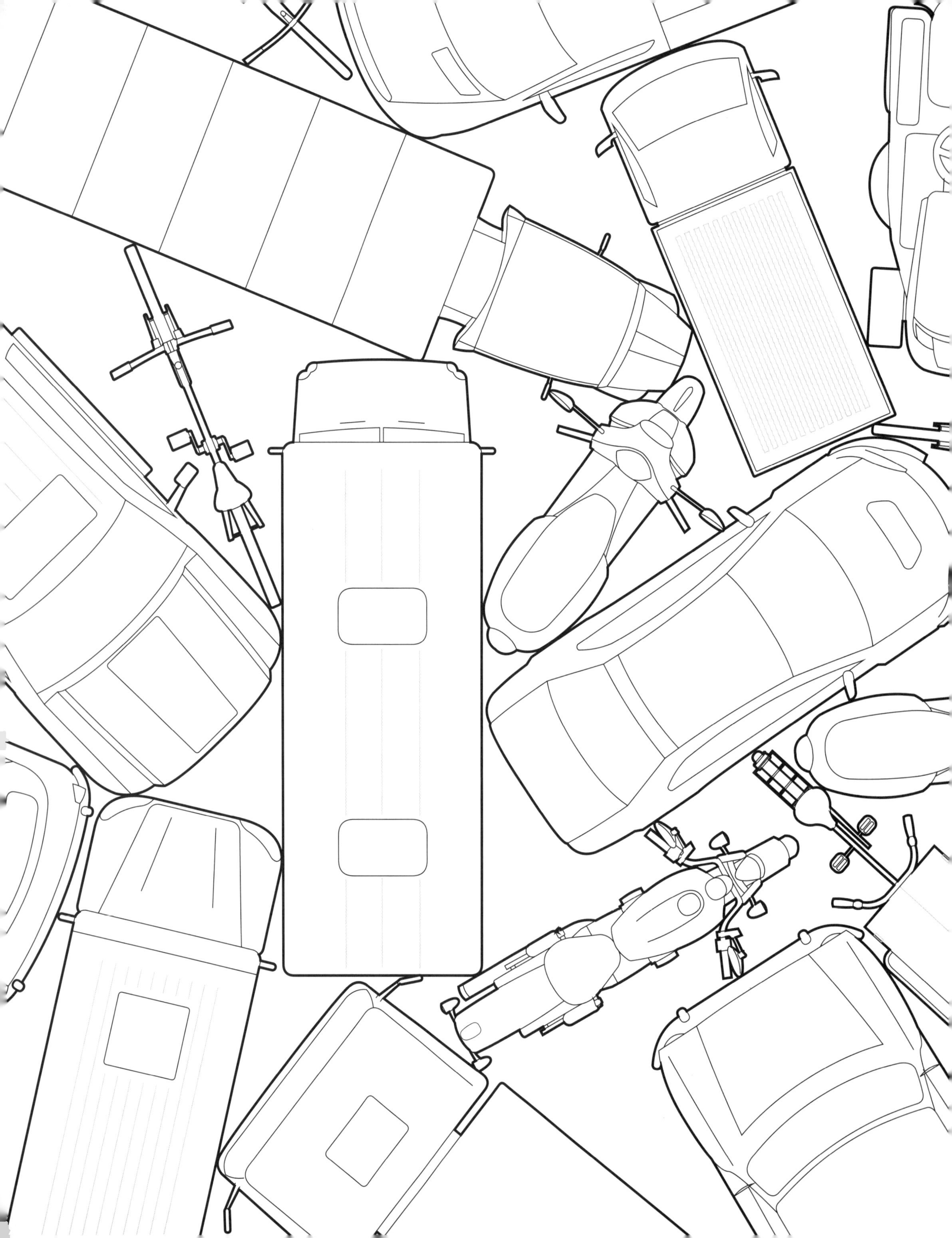

A Catalog of

Transportation

1

2

3

4

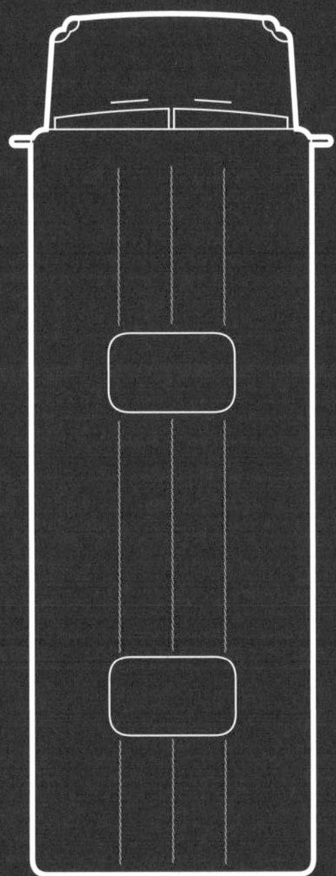

5

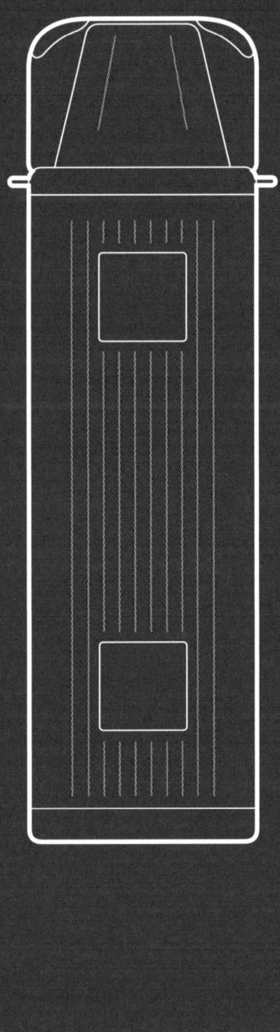

6

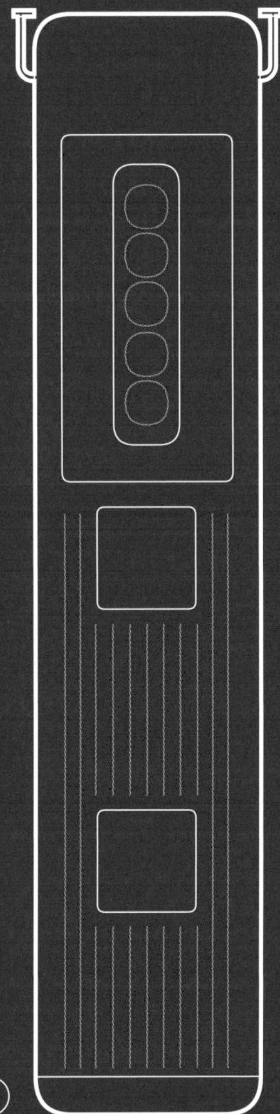

7

8

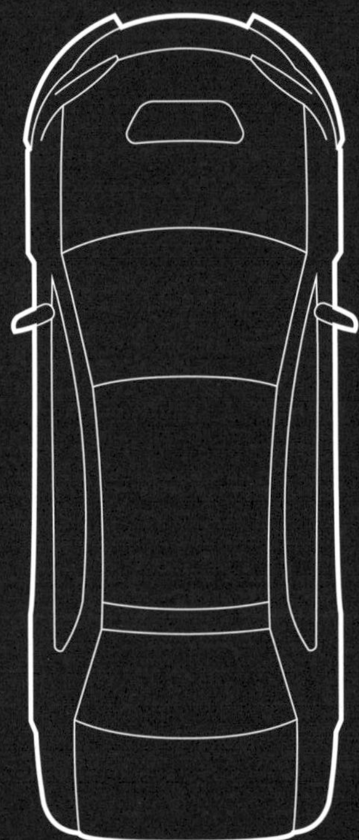

9

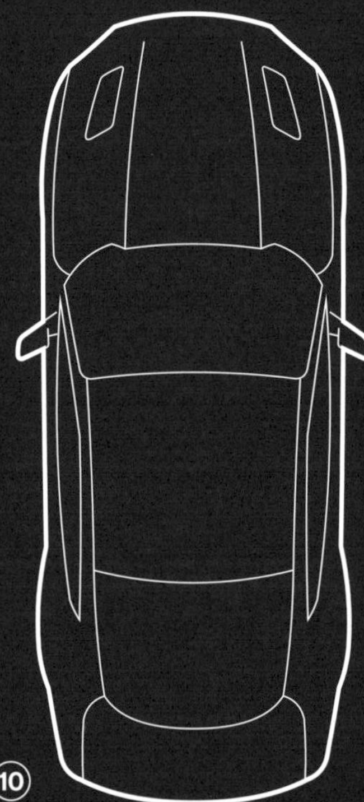

10

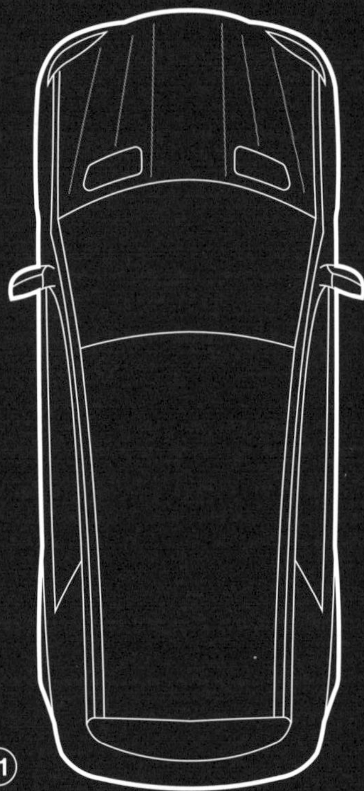

11

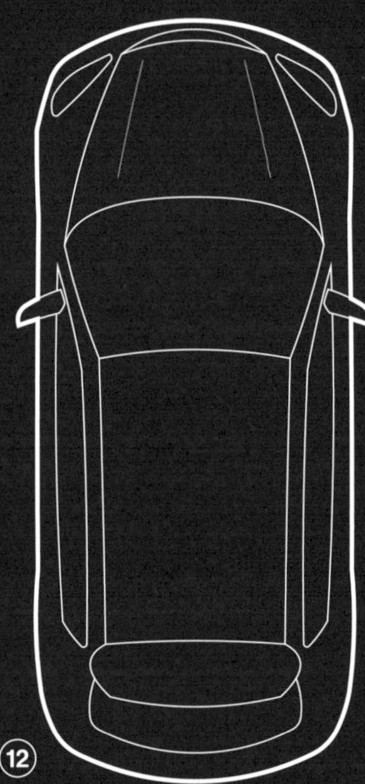

12

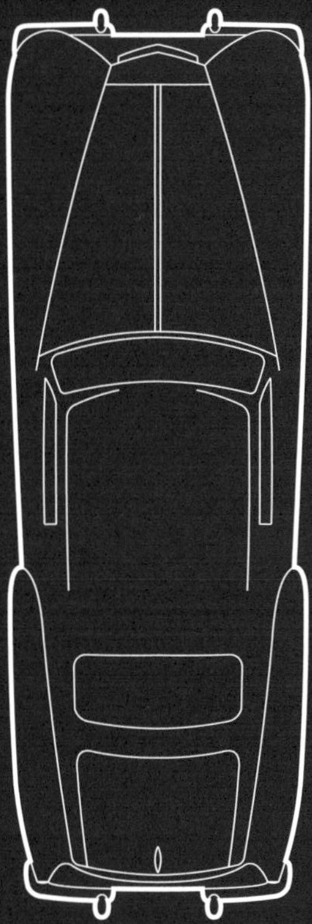

13

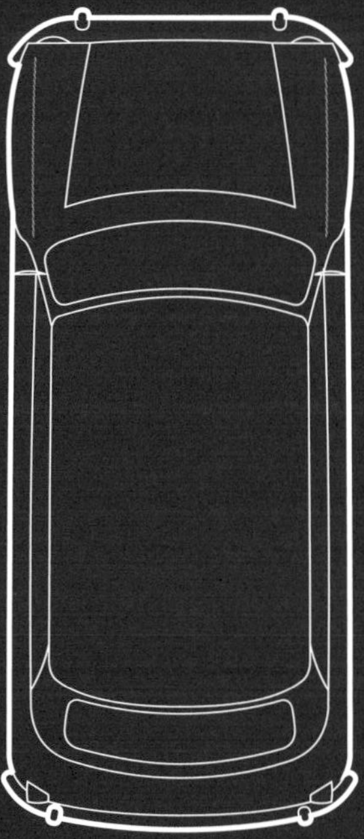

14

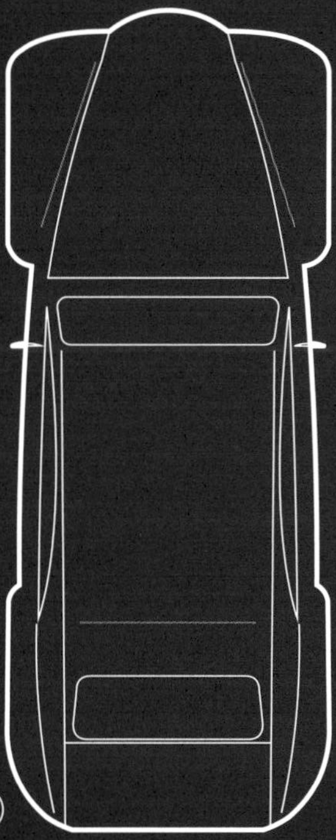

15

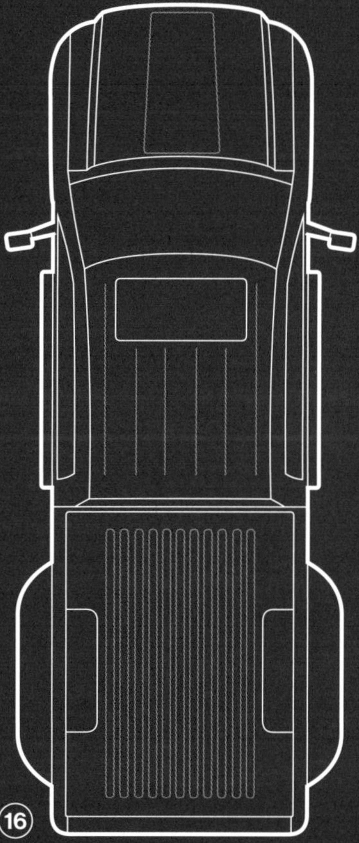

16

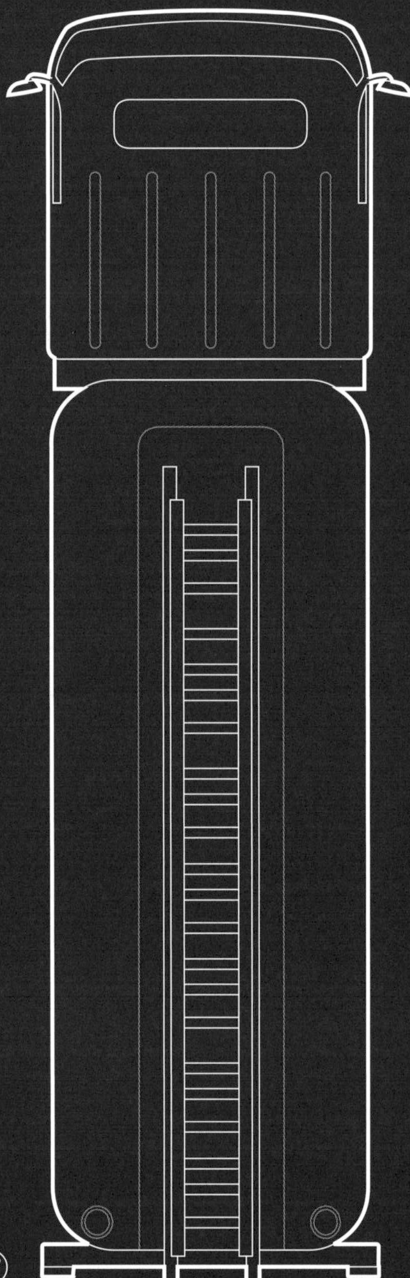

17

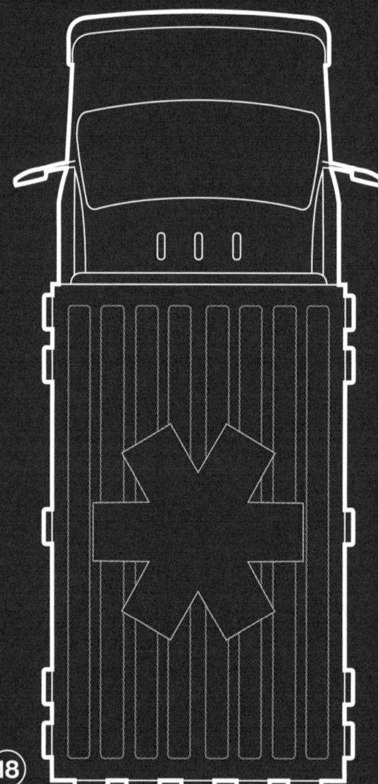

18

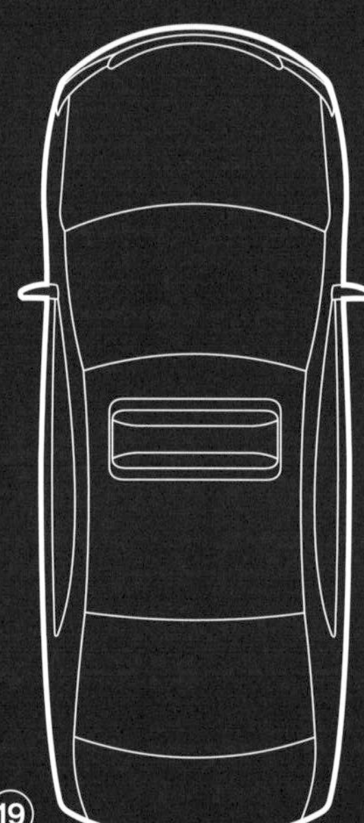

19

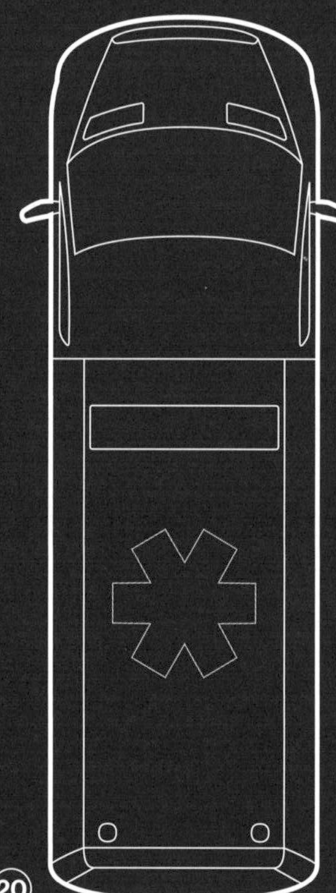

20

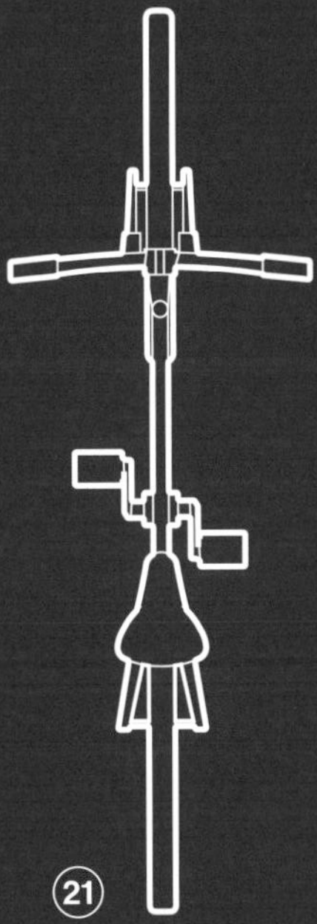

21

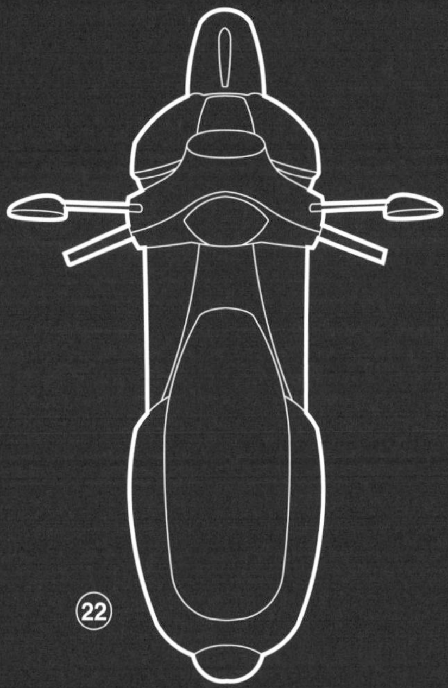

22

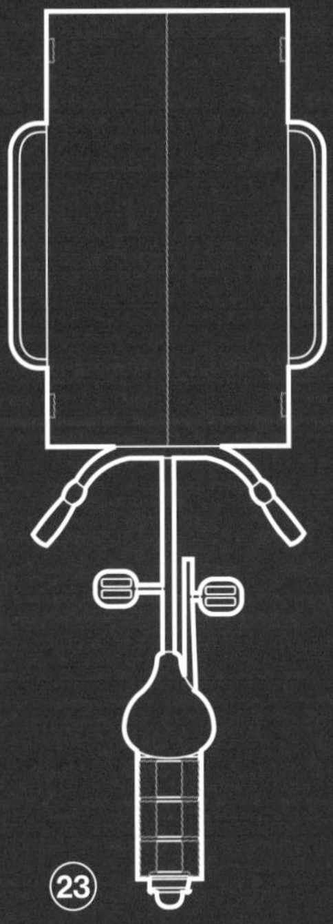

23

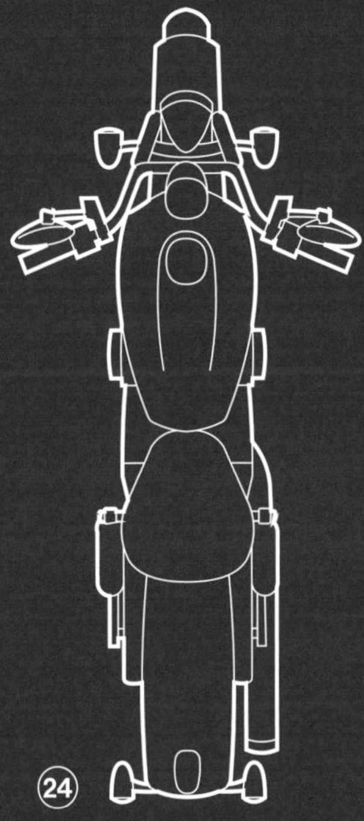

24

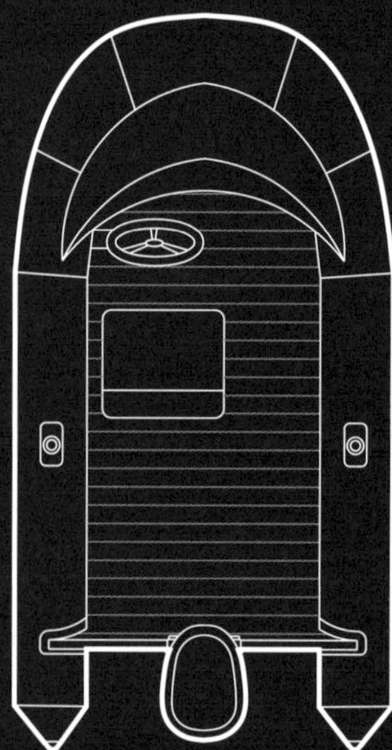

25

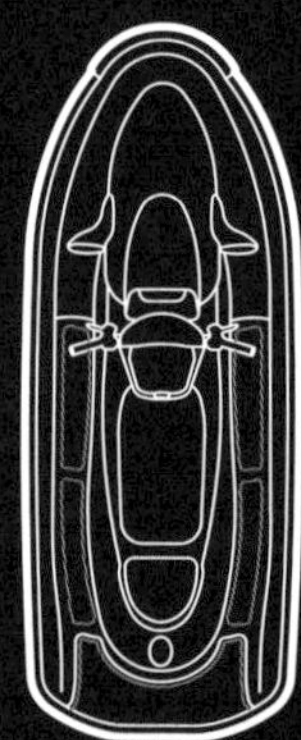

26

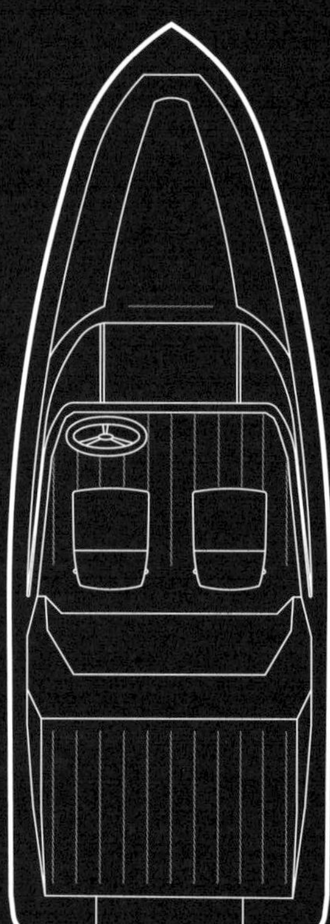

27

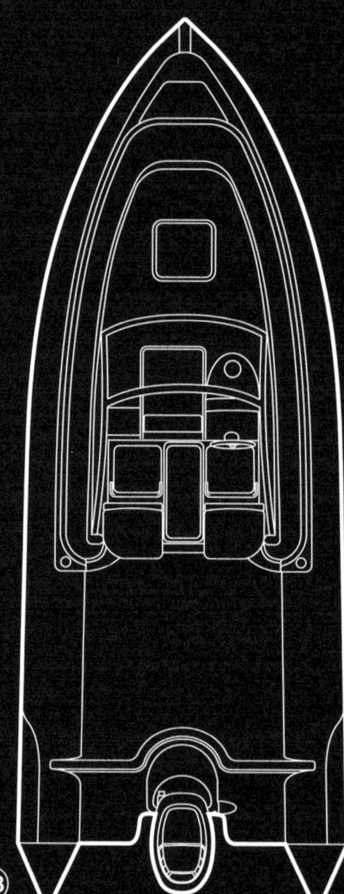

28

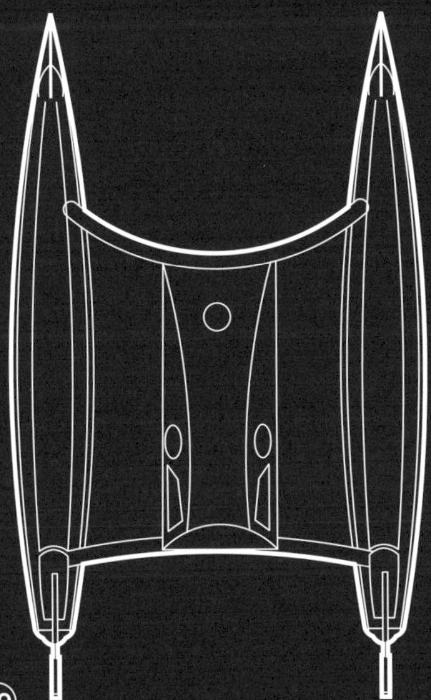

29

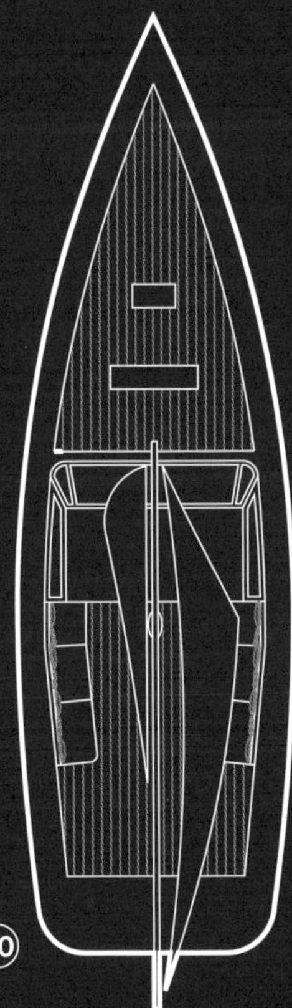

30

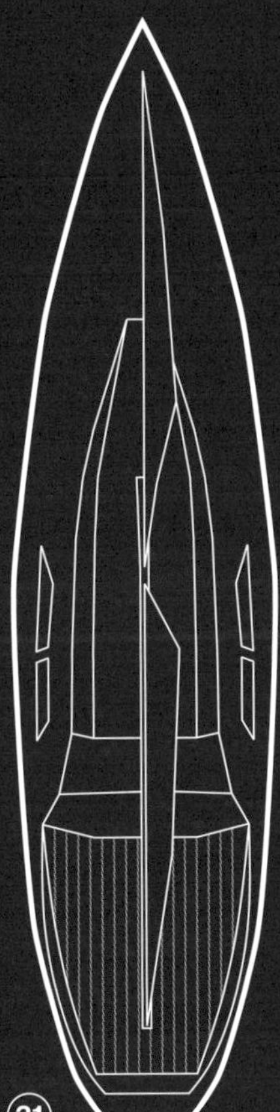

31

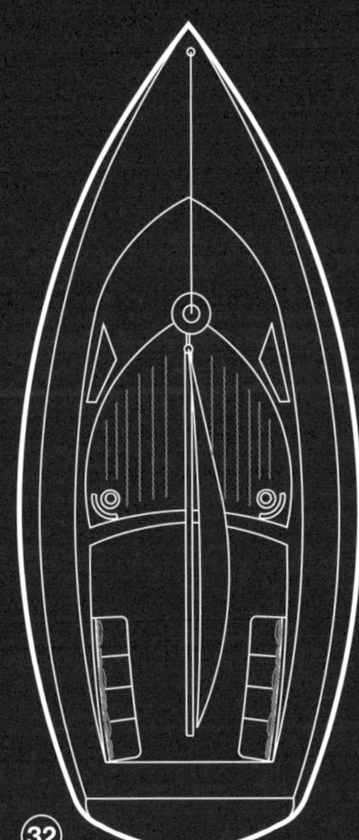

32

1
Box truck L
Transportation
8 × 2.5 m • 26'-3" × 8'-2"
2
Box truck S
Transportation
7.1 × 3.2 m • 23'-3.5" × 10'-6"
3
Cargo truck S
Transportation
16.7 × 3.3 m • 54'-9.5" × 10'-10"
4
Cargo truck L
Transportation
18 × 3.3 m • 59'-1" × 10'-10"
5
School bus S
Transportation
7.5 × 2.9 m • 24'-7" × 9'-6"
6
School bus L
Transportation
8.7 × 2.9 m • 28'-6.5" × 9'-6"
7
Bus B
Transportation
12.1 × 3 m • 39'-8.4" × 9'-10"
8
Articulated bus
Transportation
16.9 × 3 m • 55'-5.4" × 9'-10"

9

Liftback car L
Transportation
4.4 × 1.9 m • 14'-5" × 6'-3"

10

Sports car M
Transportation
4.4 × 2 m • 14'-5" × 6'-6.7"

11

Hatchback car L
Transportation
4.5 × 2.1 m • 14'-9" × 6'-11"

12

Liftback car M
Transportation
4.4 × 2.1 m • 14'-5" × 6'-11"

13

Luxury car
Transportation
4.8 × 1.6 m • 15'-9" × 5'-3"

14

Mini car
Transportation
4 × 1.8 m • 13'-1.5" × 5'-11"

15

2CV car
Transportation
4.3 × 1.7 m • 14'-1.3" × 5'-7"

16

Pickup car
Transportation
5.2 × 2.3 m • 17'-1" × 7'-6.6"

17

Fire truck
Transportation
9.8 × 3.2 m • 32'-2" × 10'-6"

18

Ambulance hospital truck • Transportation
5.5 × 2.6 m • 18'-1/2" × 8'-6"

19

Taxi car L
Transportation
4.5 × 2 m • 14'-9" × 6'-7"

20

Hospital truck
Transportation
5.7 × 2.1 m • 18'-8" × 6'-11"

21

Bicycle L
Transportation
1.8 × 0.6 m • 5'-11" × 2'

22

Scooter S
Transportation
1.9 × 1.2 m • 6'-3" × 3'-11"

23

Cargo bike
Transportation
2 × 0.7 m • 6'-7" × 2'-3.6"

24

Motorbike
Transportation
2 × 0.9 m • 6'-7" × 2'-11.4"

25

Motor boat S
Transportation
3.1 × 5.8 m • 10'-2" × 19'

26

Jet-ski
Transportation
1.2 × 3 m • 3'-11" × 9'-10"

27

Sports yatch
Transportation
2.7 × 7.3 m • 8'-10" × 23'-11.4"

28

Motor boat M
Transportation
3.3 × 8.7 m • 10'-10" × 28'-6.5"

29

Catamaran
Transportation
5.1 × 8.3 m • 16'-9" × 27'-3"

30

Sailing boat M
Transportation
3 × 10.6 m • 9'-10" × 34'-9"

31

Sailing boat S
Transportation
2.2 × 9 m • 7'-2.6" × 29'-6"

32

Sailing boat L
Transportation
3.8 × 9 m • 12'-5.6" × 29'-6"

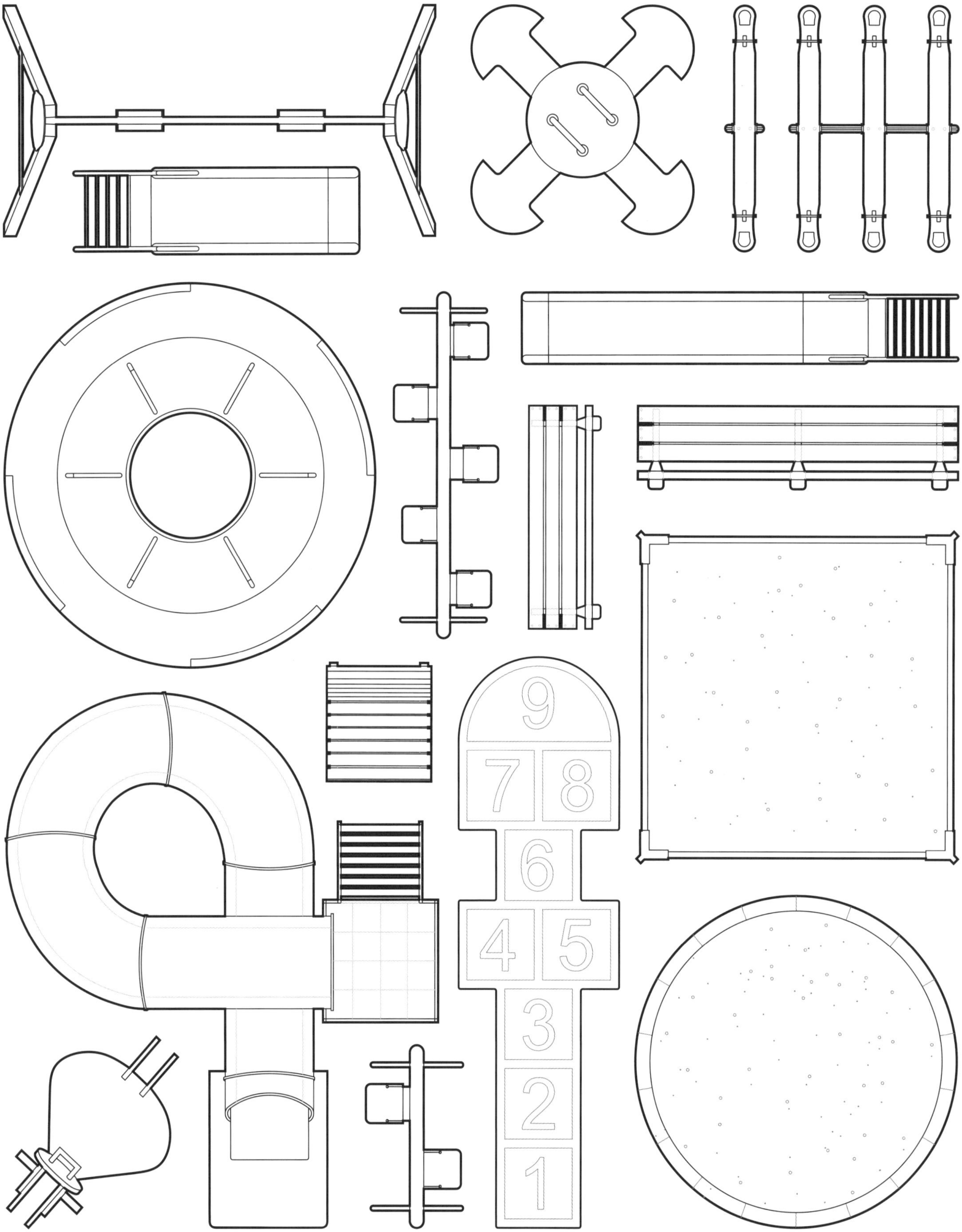
9
7
8
6
4
5
3
2
1

Kit for a
Playground

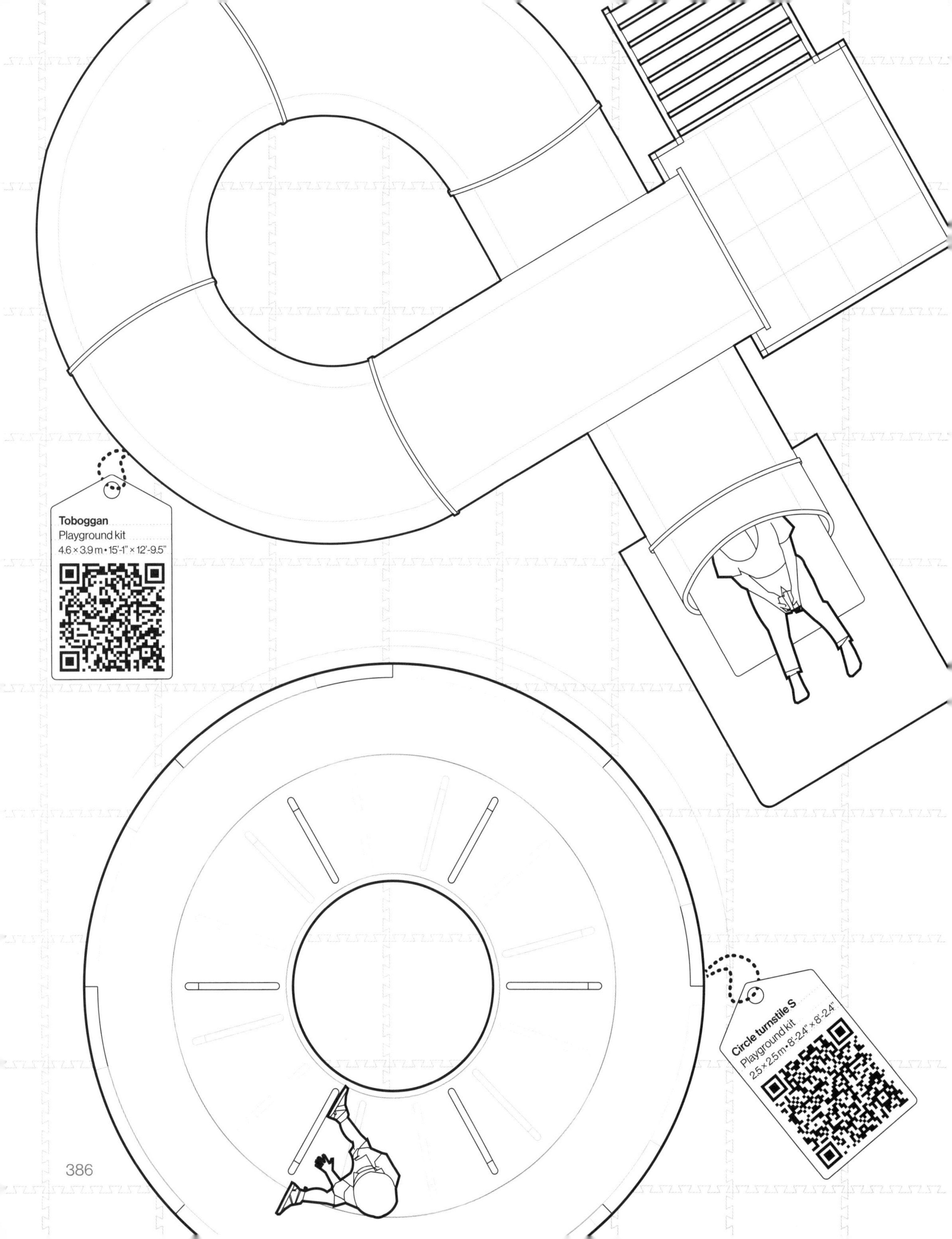
Toboggan
Playground kit
4.6 × 3.9 m • 15'-1" × 12'-9.5"
Circle turnstile S
Playground kit
2.5 × 2.5 m • 8'-2.4" × 8'-2.4"

Hopscotch
Playground kit
2.4 × 0.7 m • 7'-10" × 2'-3.6"

Sandpit square
Playground kit
2.1 × 2.1 m • 6'-10.7" × 6'-10.7"

Swing M
Playground kit
1.9 × 3.7 m • 6'-3" × 12'-2"

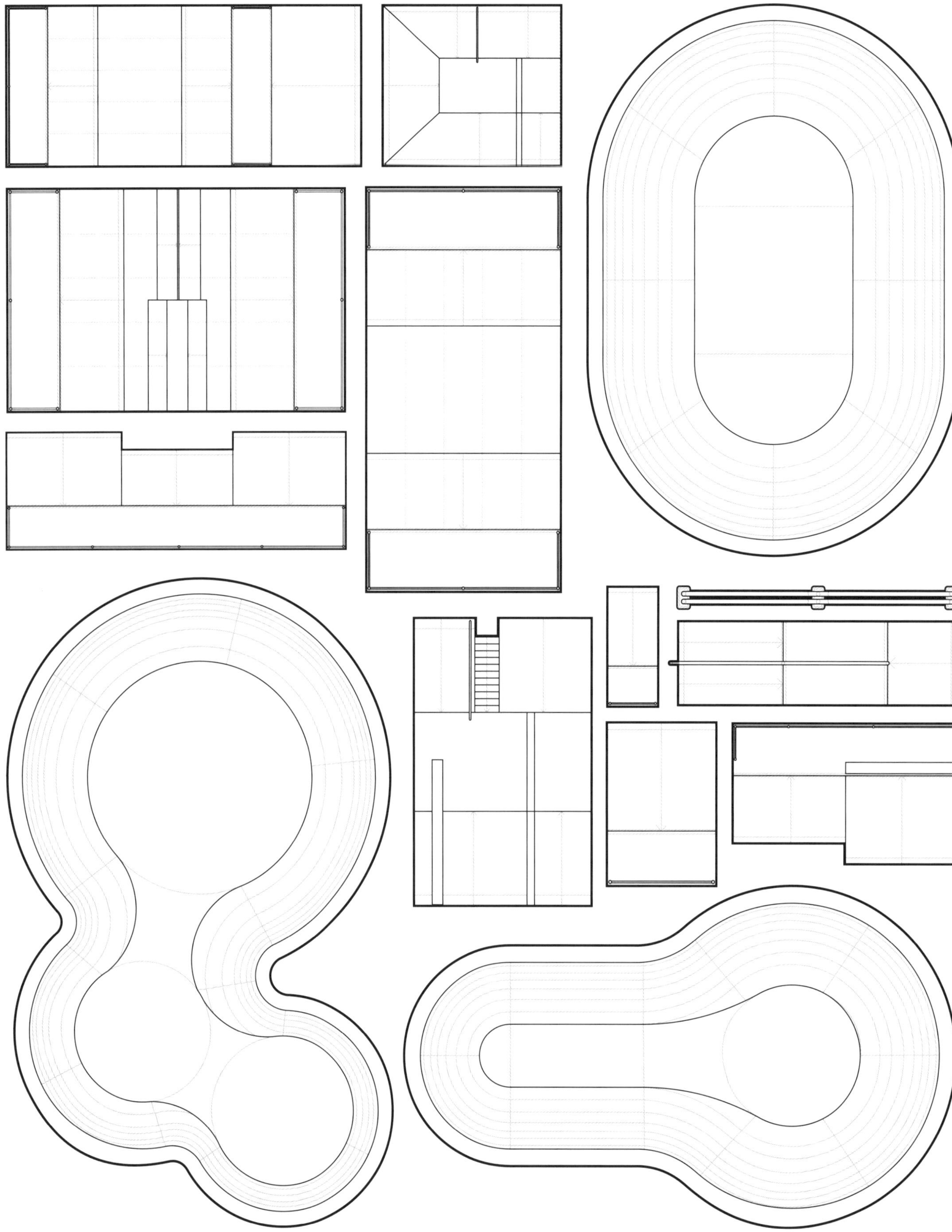

Kit for a
Skate Park

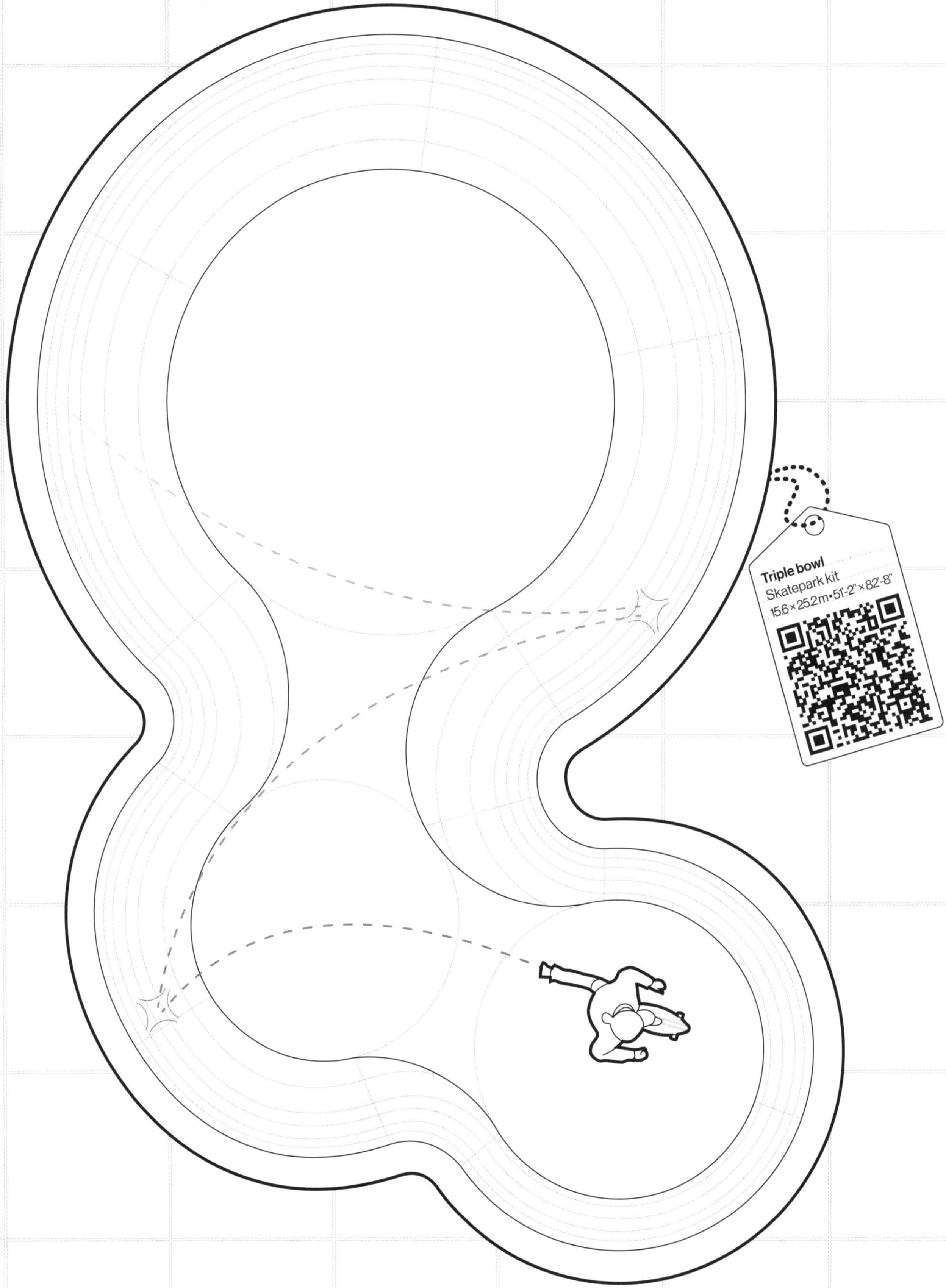
Triple bowl
Skatepark kit
15.6×25.2m•51'-2"×82'-8"

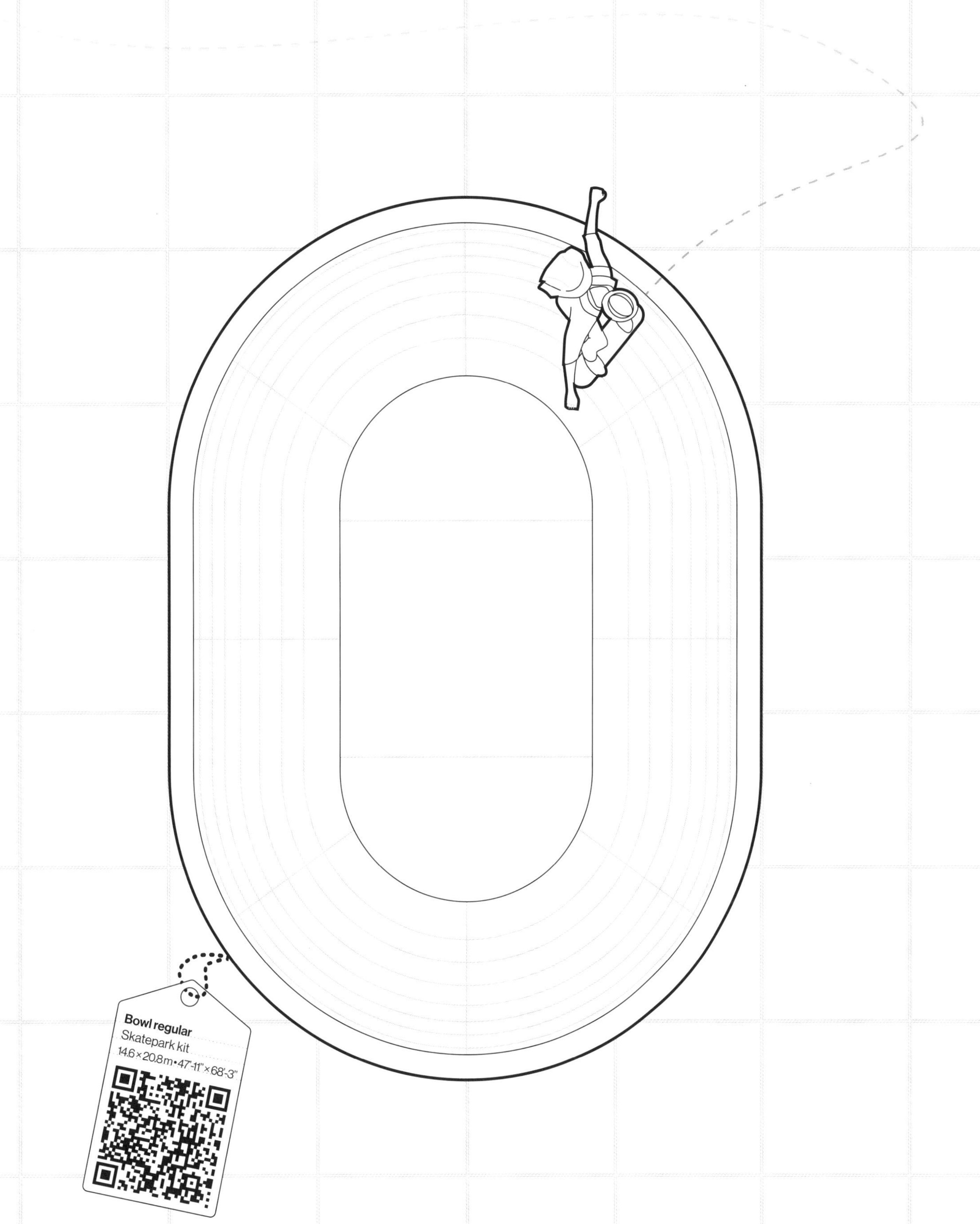
Bowl regular
Skatepark kit
14.6 × 20.8 m • 47'-11" × 68'-3"

Skate box
Skatepark kit
5.8 x 7.5 m • 19' x 24'-7"

Bowl S
Skatepark kit
12 × 20.1 m • 39'-4" × 65'-11"

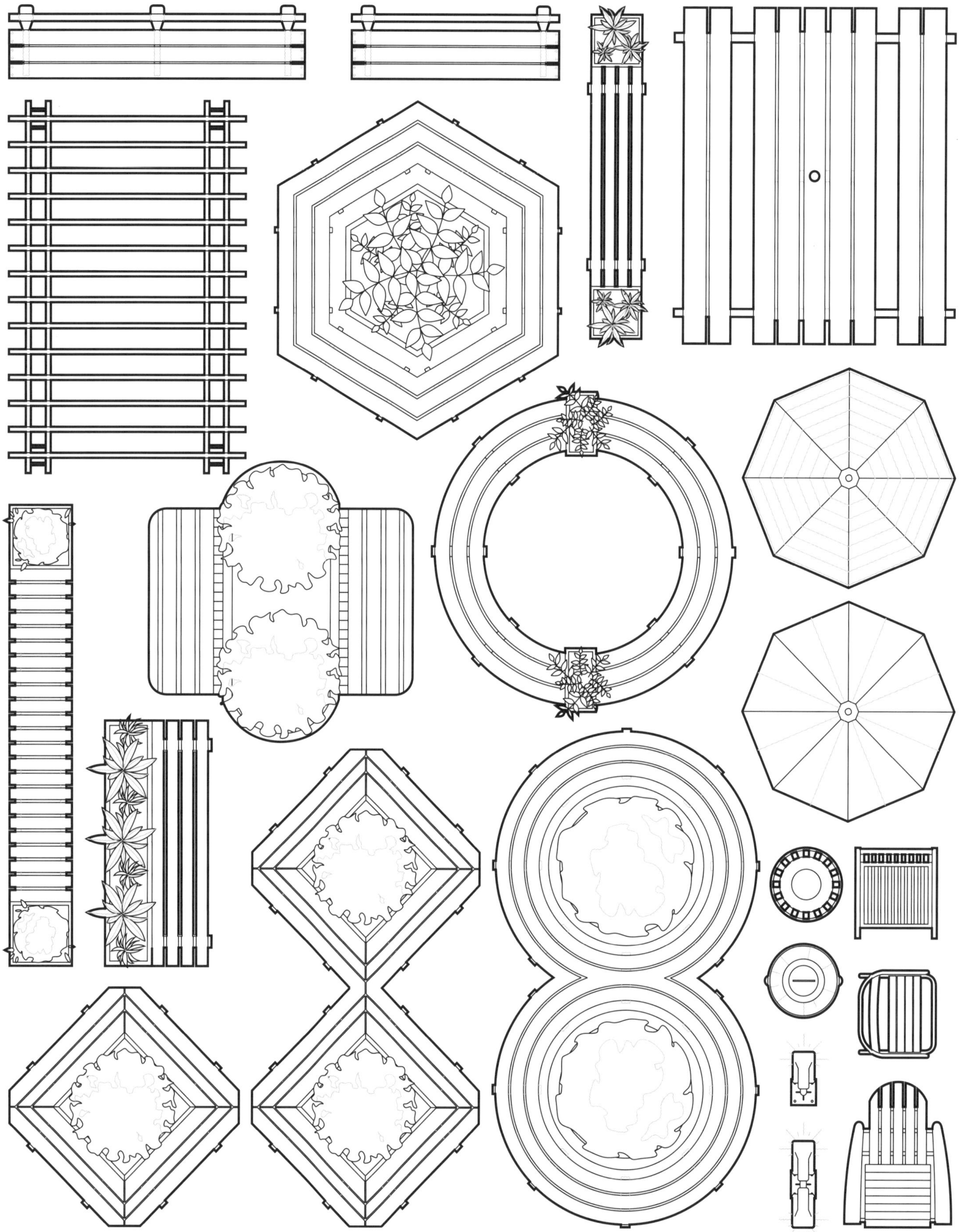

Kit for a
Public Park

Hexagonal bench
Public park kit
2.8 × 3.15 m • 9'-2" × 10'-4"
Picnic table
Public park kit
2.1 × 2.5 m • 6'-11" × 8'-2.4"

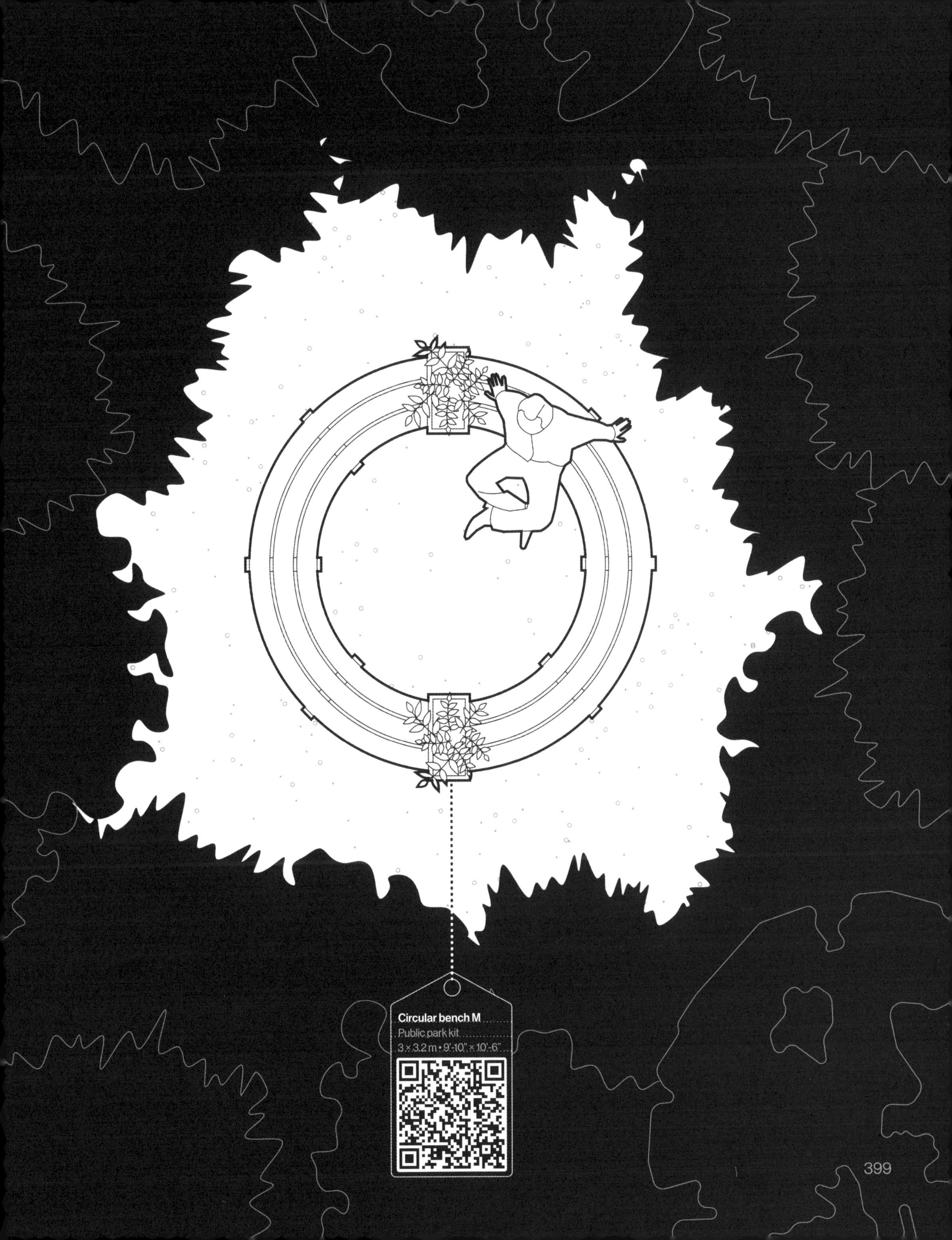
Circular bench M
Public park kit
3 × 3.2 m • 9'-10" × 10'-6"

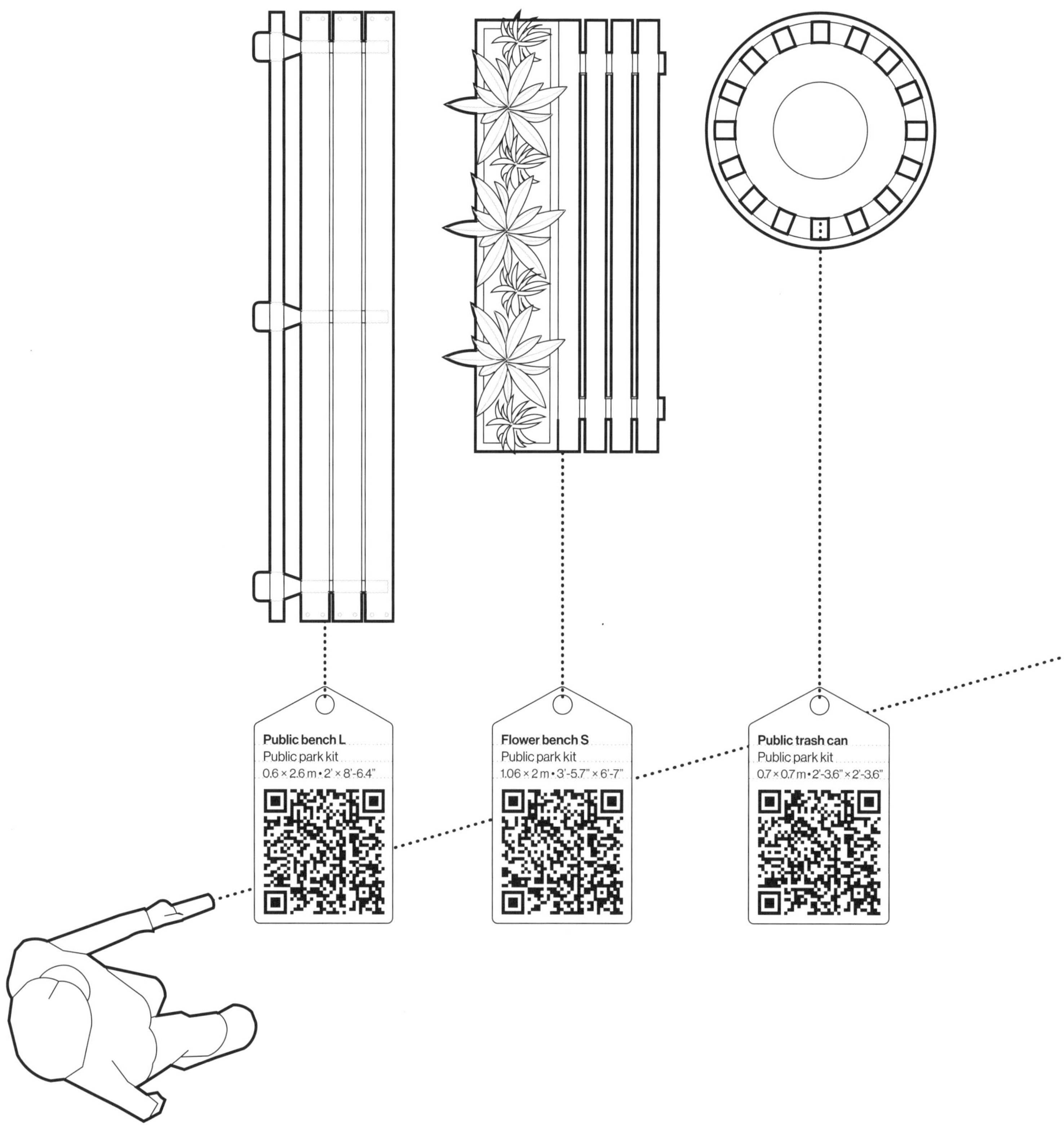
Public bench L
Public park kit
0.6 × 2.6 m • 2' × 8'-6.4"
Flower bench S
Public park kit
1.06 × 2 m • 3'-5.7" × 6'-7"
Public trash can
Public park kit
0.7 × 0.7 m • 2'-3.6" × 2'-3.6"

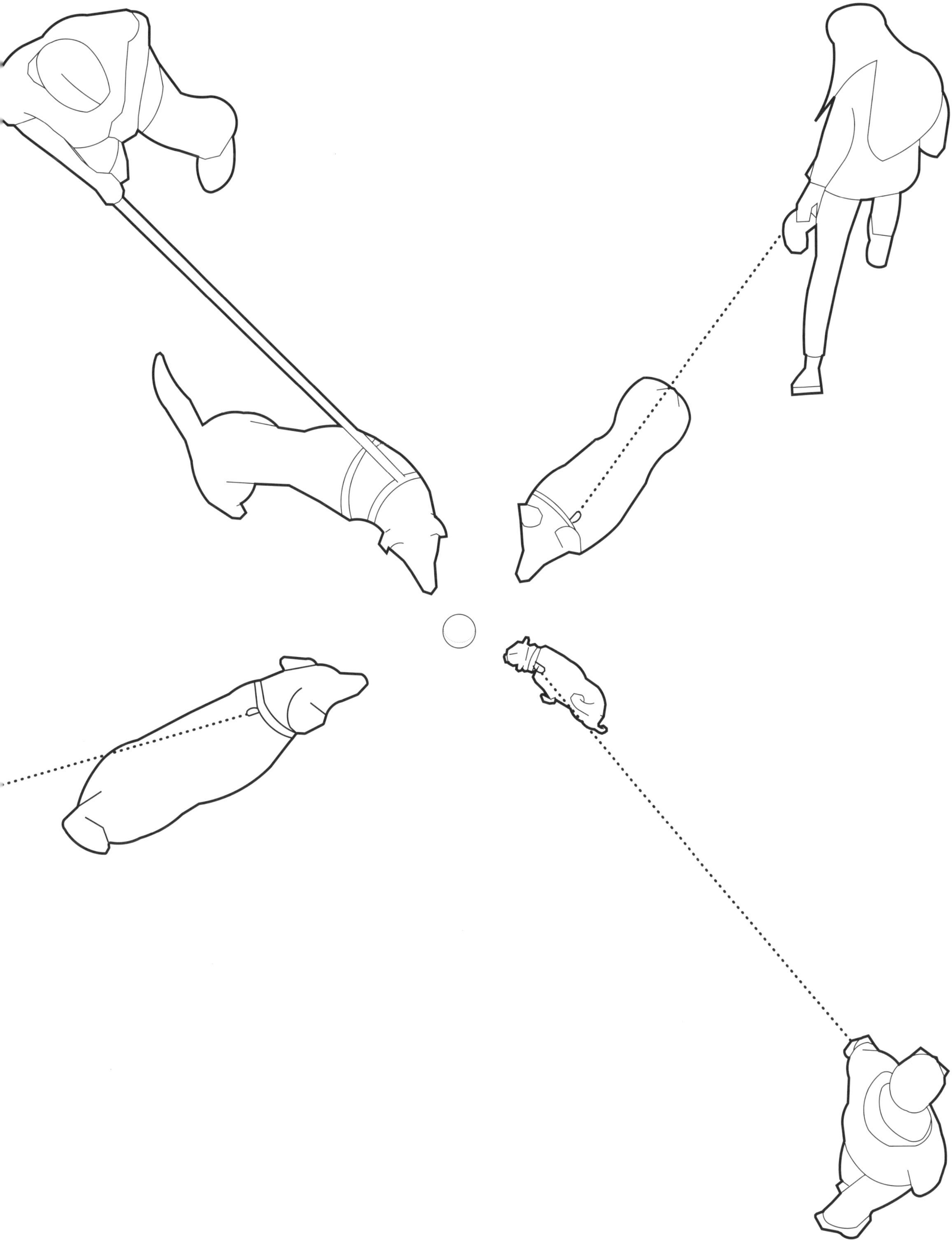

A Catalog of

Urban Furniture

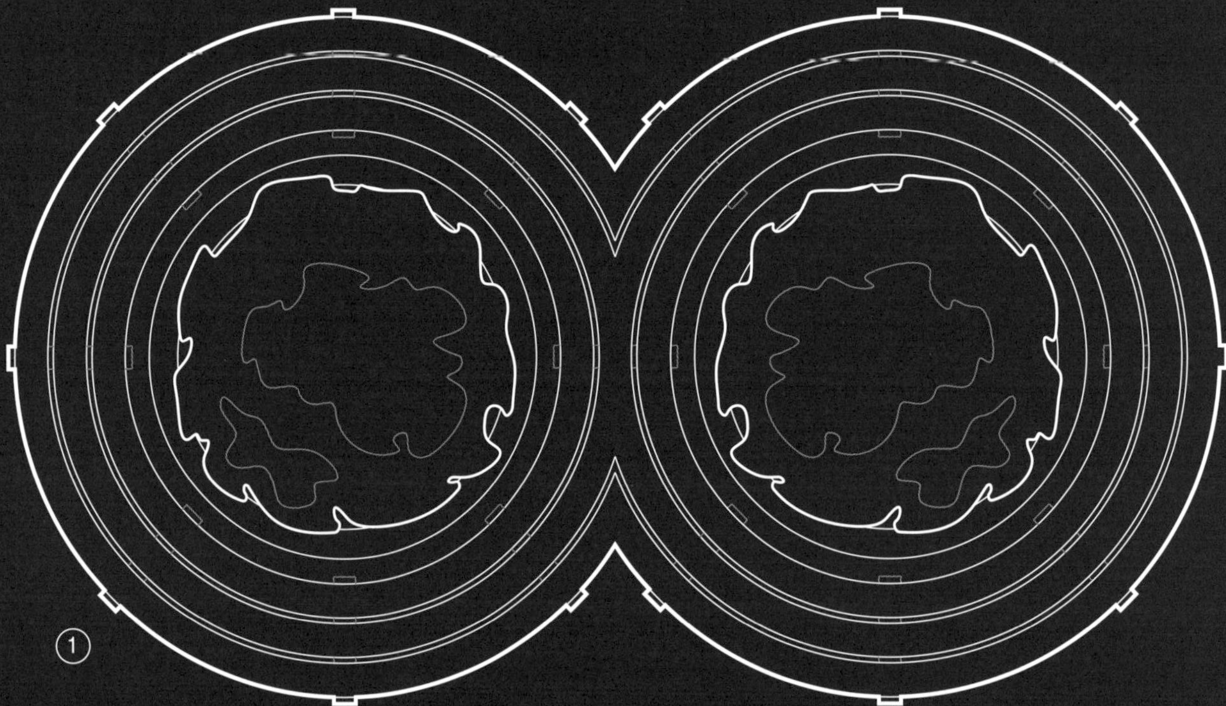

1

2

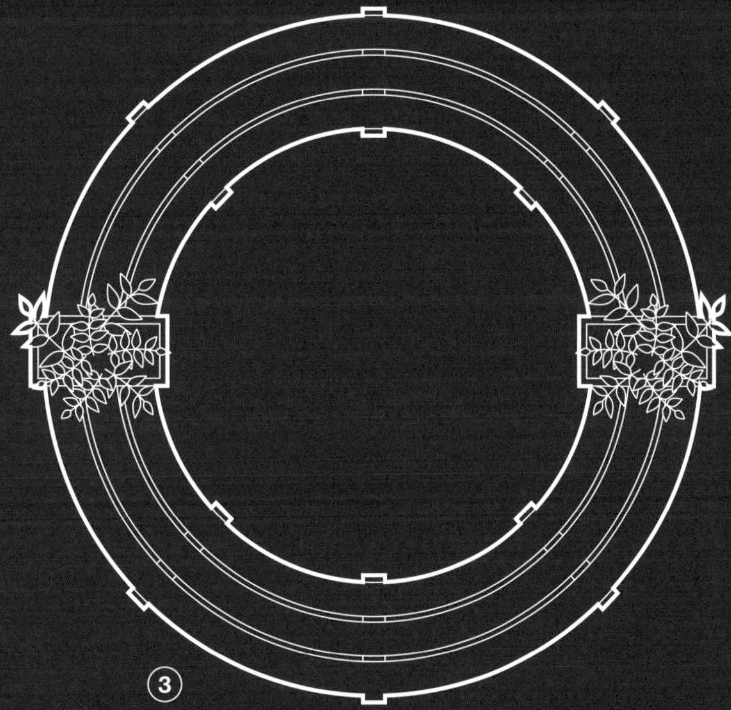

3

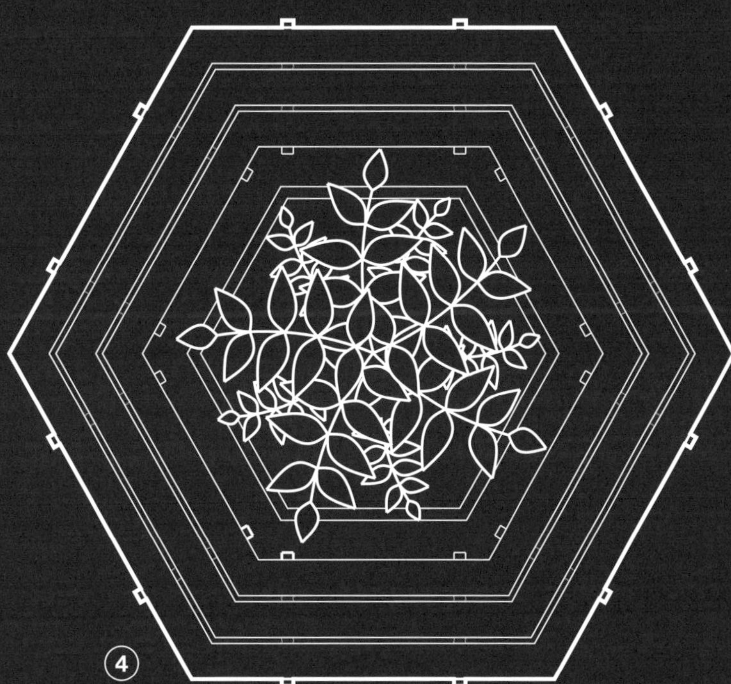

4

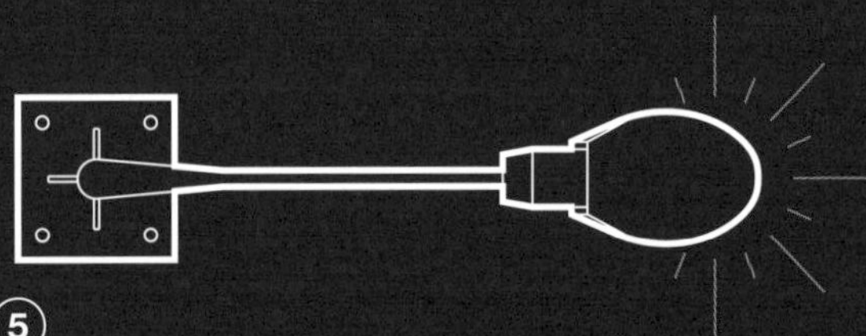

5

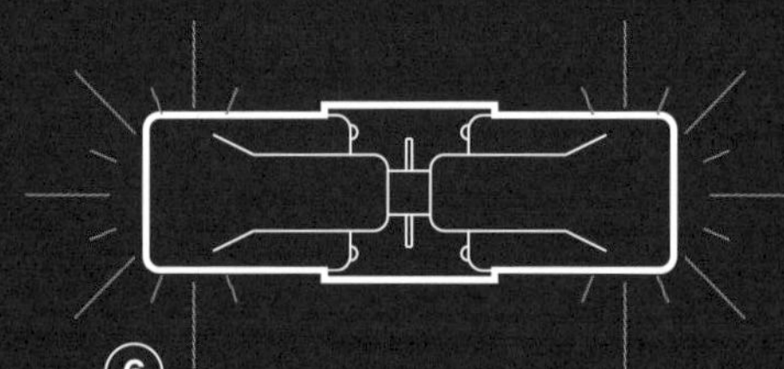

6

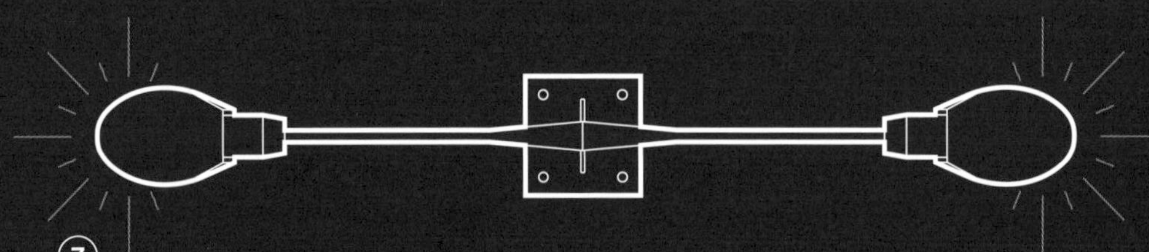

7

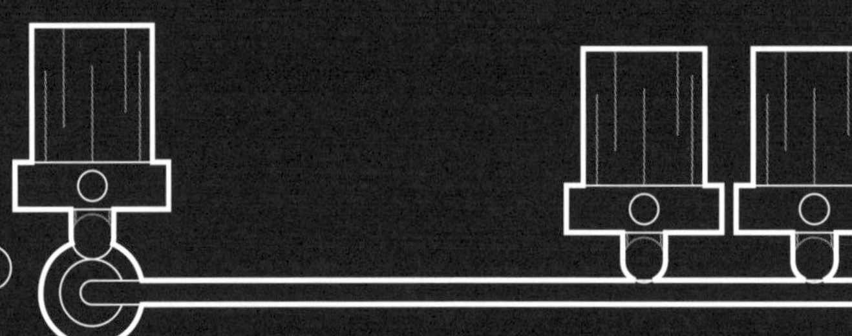

8

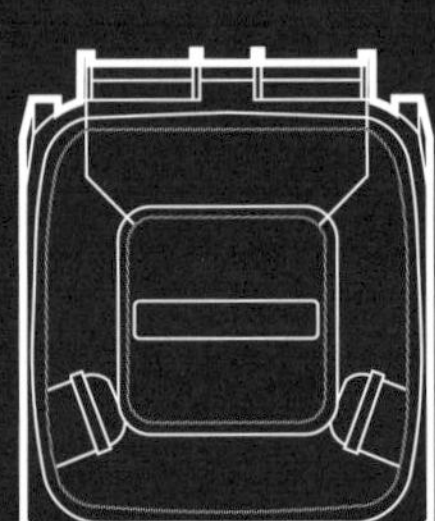

9

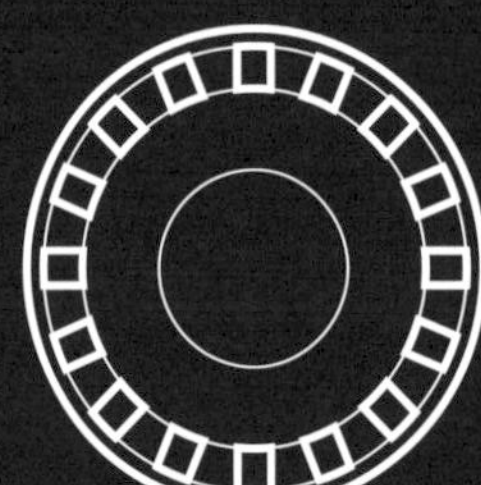

10

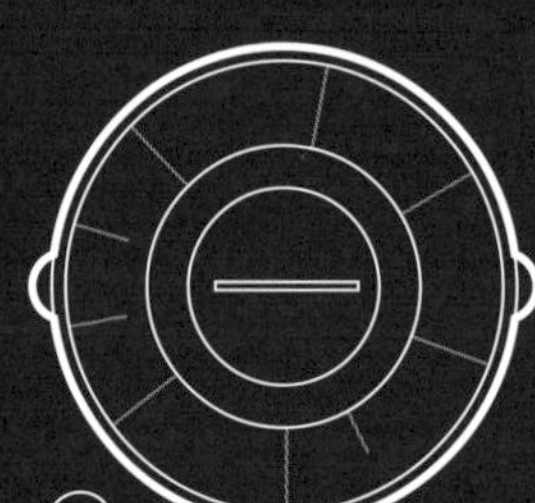

11

12

13

14

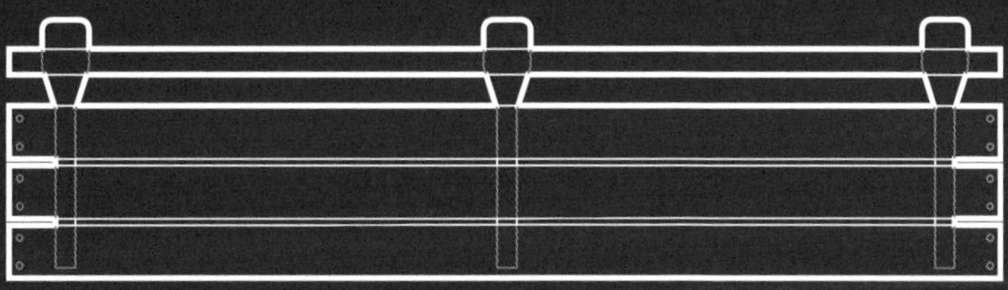

15

16

1
Circular bench L
Urban furniture
5.5 × 3 m • 18'-1/2" × 9'-10"
2
Square bench M
Urban furniture
2.2 × 4.5 m • 7'-2.6" × 14'-9"
3
Circular bench M
Urban furniture
3 × 3.2 m • 9'-10" × 10'-6"
4
Hexagonal bench
Urban furniture
2.7 × 3.1 m • 8'-10" × 10'-2"
5
Street lamp S
Urban furniture
0.5 × 1.5 m • 1'-7.7" × 4'-11"
6
Modern lamp M
Urban furniture
0.5 × 1.3 m • 1'-7.7" × 4'-3"
7
Street lamp M
Urban furniture
0.5 × 2.8 m • 1'-7.7" × 9'-2"
8
Traffic light L
Urban furniture
2.5 × 0.9 m • 8'-2.4" × 2'-11.4"

9

Trash can
Urban furniture
0.7 × 0.6 m • 2'-3.6" × 2'

10

Public trash can
Urban furniture
0.7 × 0.7 m • 2'-3.6" × 2'-3.6"

11

Public trash can with cover • Urban furniture
0.7 × 0.74 m • 2'-3.6" × 2'-5"

12

Fire hydrant
Urban furniture
0.5 × 0.44 m • 1'-7.7" × 1'-5"

13

Flower bench S
Urban furniture
1 × 2 m • 3'-3.4" × 6'-7"

14

Bench with flowers
Urban furniture
0.55 × 3.1 m • 1'-10" × 10'-2"

15

Public bench L
Urban furniture
0.7 × 2.7 m • 2'-3.6" × 8'-10"

16

Public bench S
Urban furniture
0.6 × 2 m • 2' × 6'-7"

Kit for a
Private Garden

Lawn mower S
Private garden kit
1.57 × 0.6 m • 5'-2" × 2'
Lawn mower L
Private garden kit
2.8 × 1 m • 9'-2" × 3'-3.4"

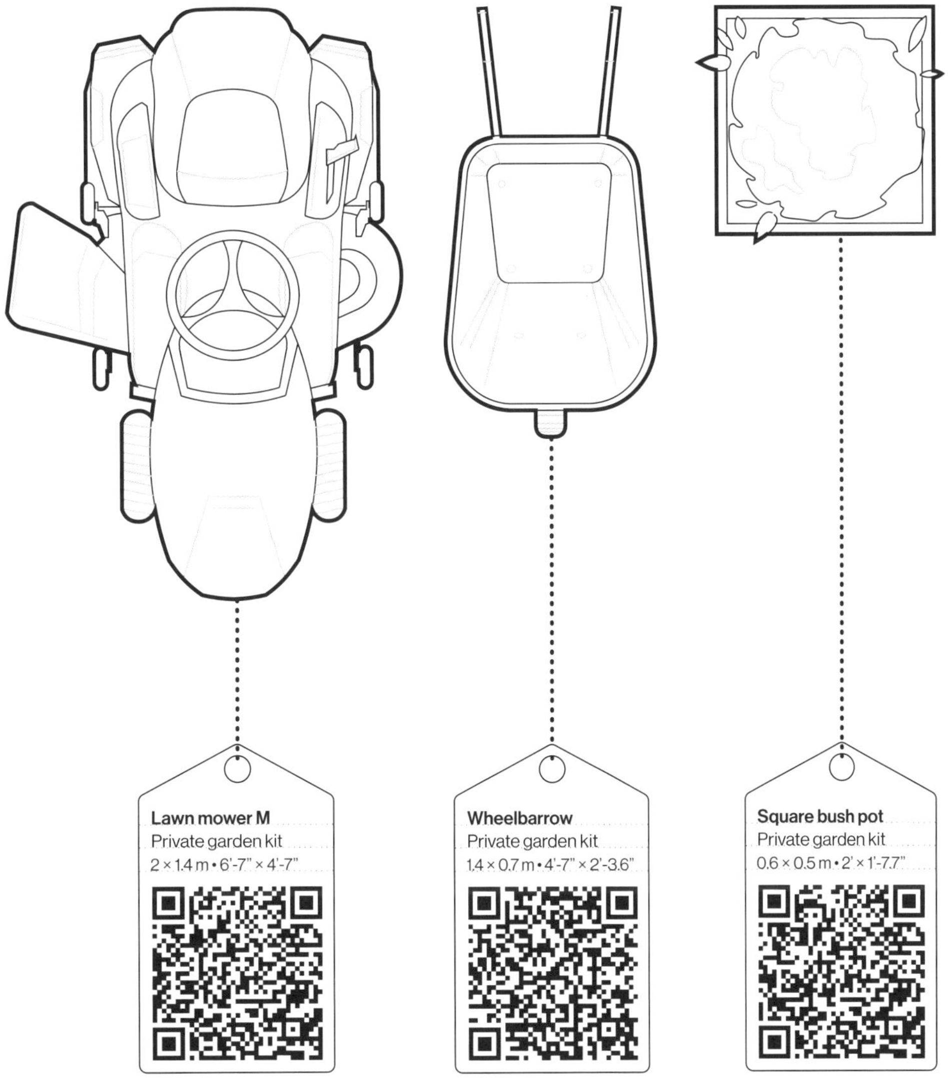
Lawn mower M
Private garden kit
2 × 1.4 m • 6'-7" × 4'-7"
Wheelbarrow
Private garden kit
1.4 × 0.7 m • 4'-7" × 2'-3.6"
Square bush pot
Private garden kit
0.6 × 0.5 m • 2' × 1'-7.7"

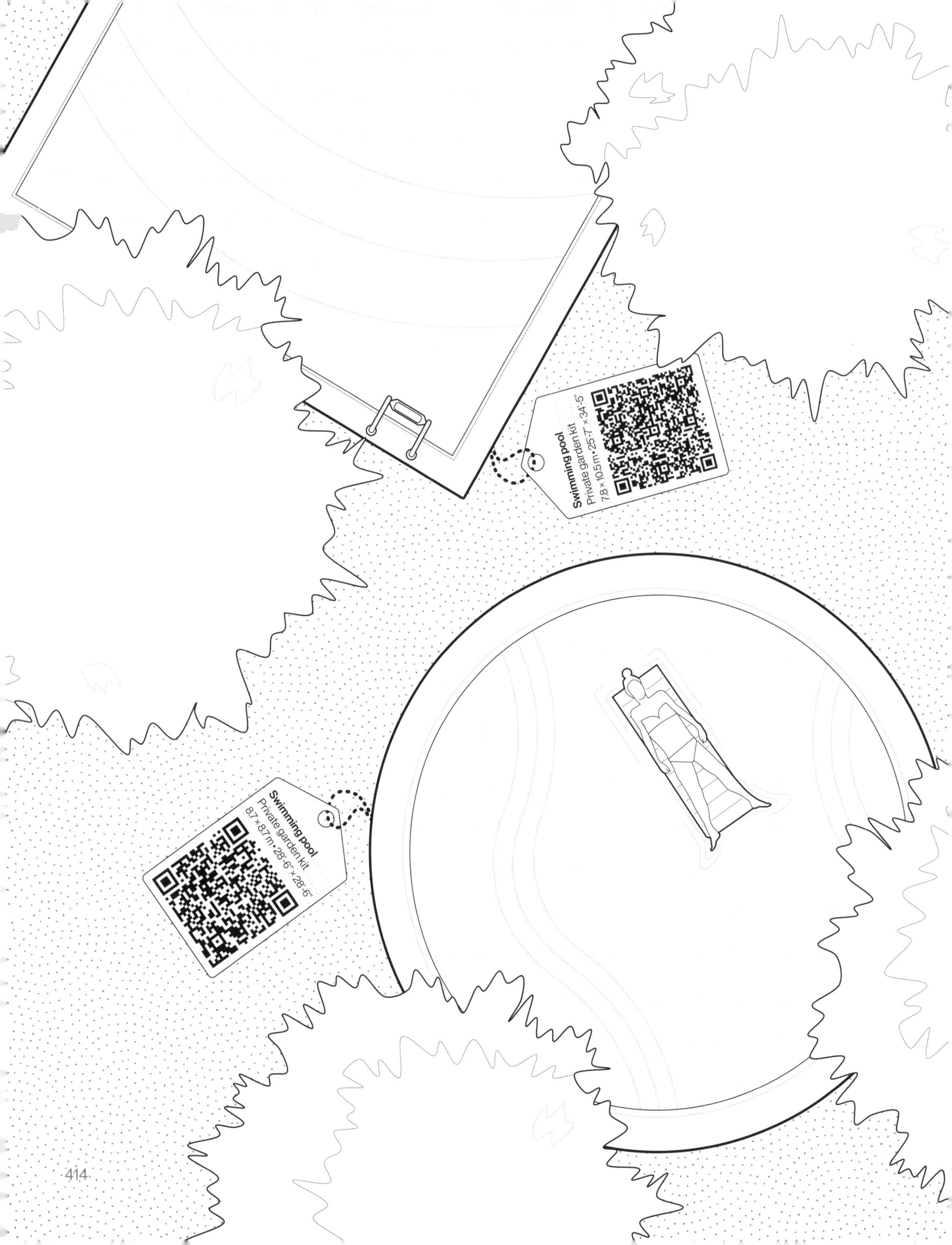
Swimming pool
Private garden kit
7,8 × 10,5 m • 25'-7" × 34'-5"
Swimming pool
Private garden kit
8,7 × 8,7 m • 28'-6" × 28'-6"

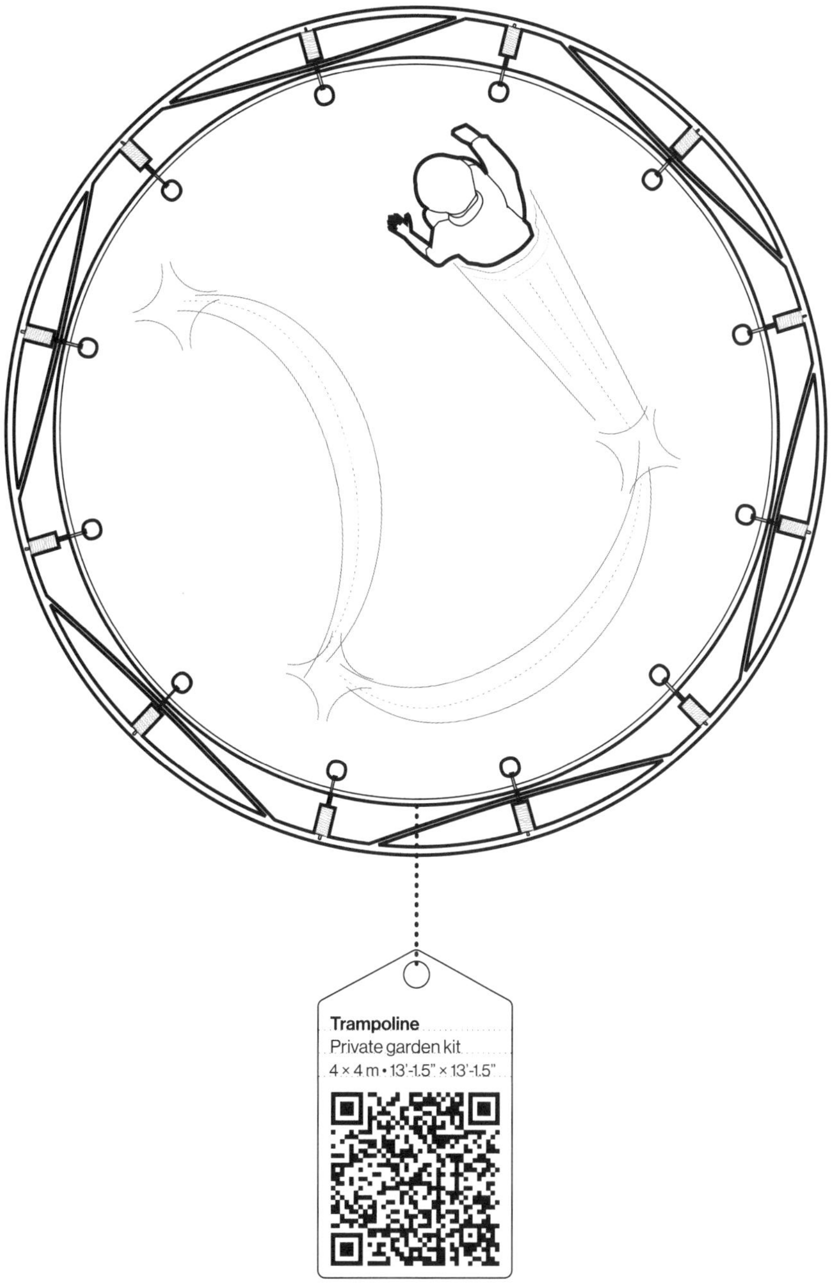
Trampoline
Private garden kit
4 × 4 m • 13'-1.5" × 13'-1.5"

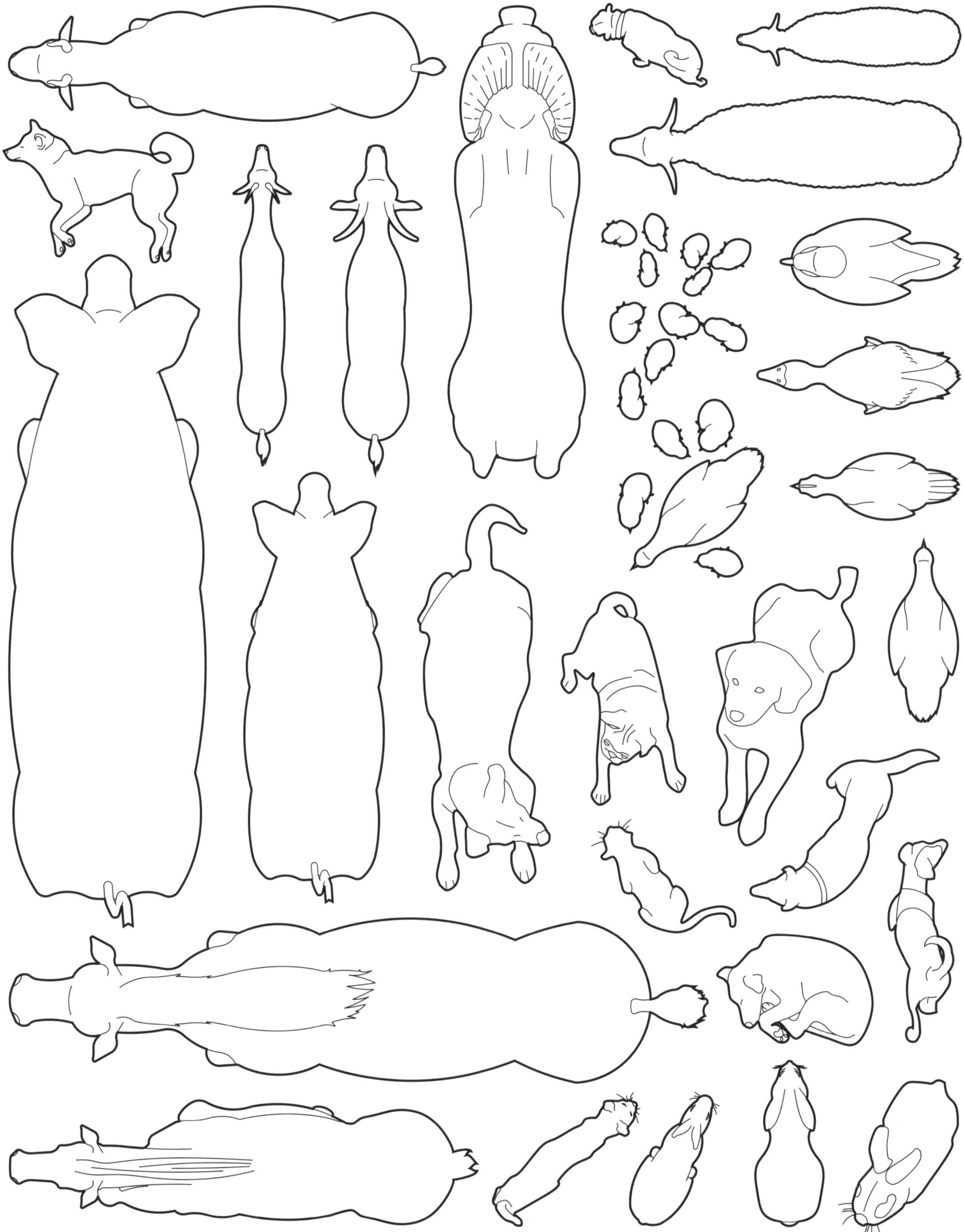

Kit of
Animals

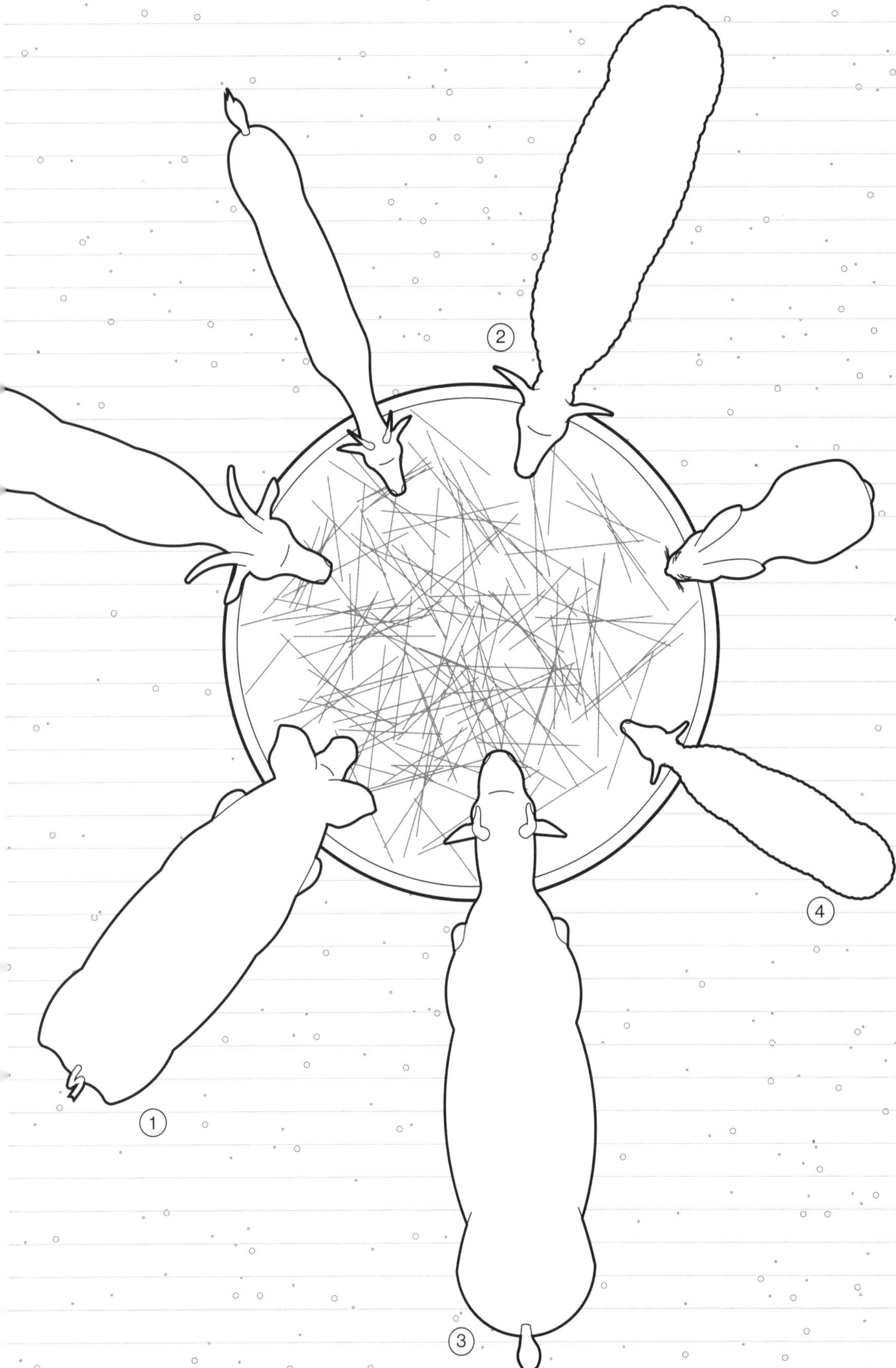

1

Pig
Animals kit
0.47 × 1.5 m • 1'-6.5" × 4'-11"

2

Sheep
Animals kit
0.33 × 1.2 m • 1'-1" × 3'-11"

3

Bull
Animals kit
0.59 × 2.34 m • 1'-11" × 7'-8"

4

Lamb
Animals kit
0.2 × 0.77 m • 8" × 2'-6.3"

Shiba inu
Animals kit
0.9 × 1.06 m • 2'-11.4" × 3'-6"

Group of chickens
Animals kit
0.4 × 0.52 m • 1'-4" × 1'-8.5"
Pug
Animals kit
0.2 × 0.5 m • 8" × 1'-8"

Cat
Animals kit
0.11 × 0.42 m • 4" × 1'-4.5"

A Catalog of

Trees

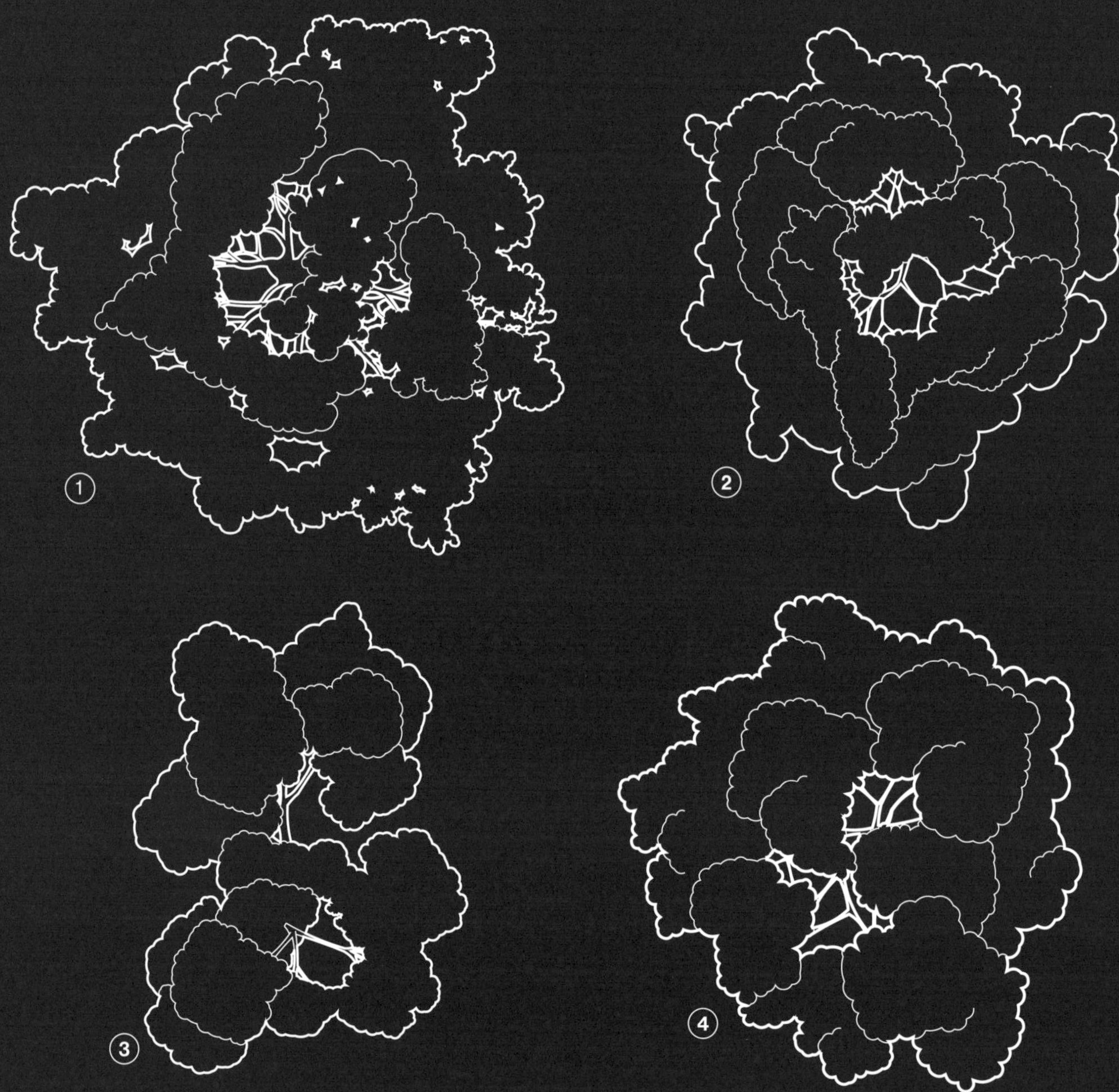
1
2
3
4

⑤

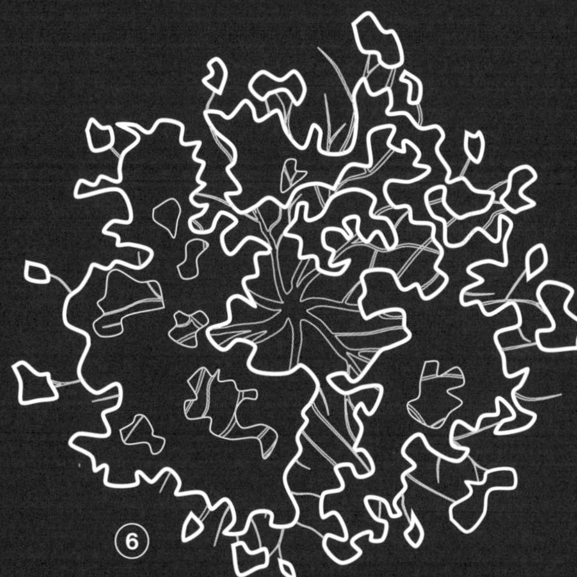

⑥

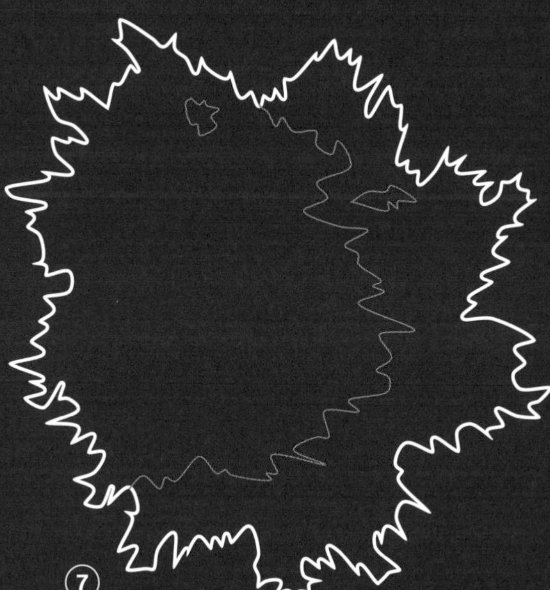

⑦

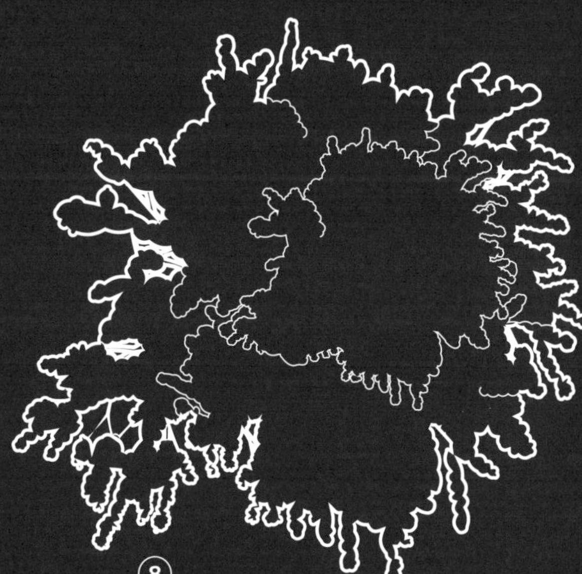

⑧

⑨

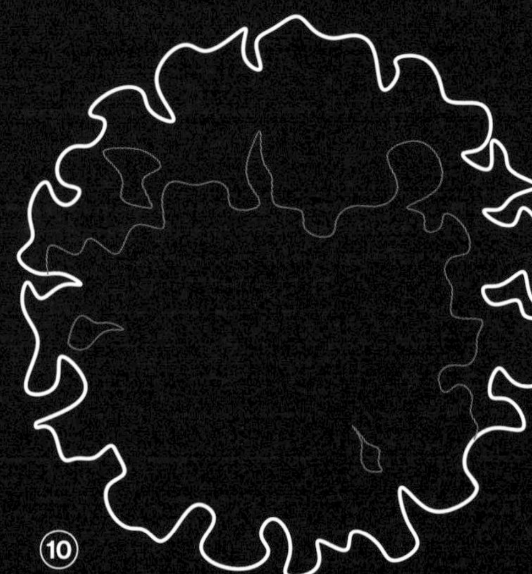

⑩

⑪

⑫

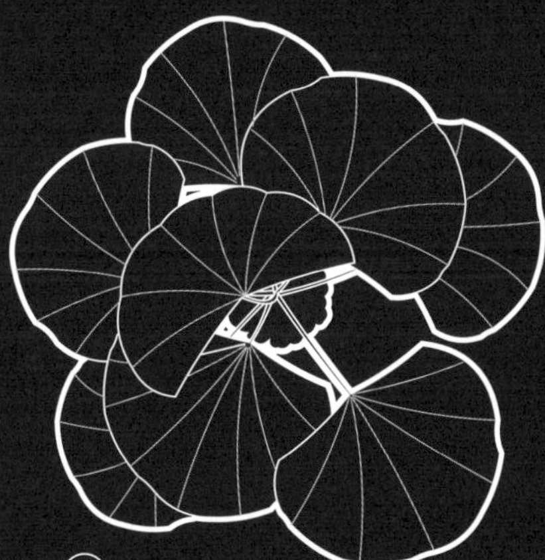

⑬

⑭

⑮

⑯

1
Elm tree
Trees
5.73 × 6.1 m • 18'-10" × 20'
2
Bleech tree M
Trees
4.55 × 4.45 m • 14'-11" × 14'-7"
3
Bleech tree S
Trees
4.7 × 3.5 m • 15'-5" × 11'-6"
4
Birch tree L
Trees
5 × 4.85 m • 16'-5" × 15'-11"
5
Acacia tree
Trees
4.46 × 4.85 m • 14'-8" × 15'-11"
6
Oak tree
Trees
4.6 × 4.9 m • 15'-1" × 16'-1"
7
Linden tree
Trees
4.8 × 4.7 m • 15'-9" × 15'-5"
8
Fir tree
Trees
4.1 × 4.4 m • 13'-5.4" × 14'-5"

9

Spruce tree
Trees
4.4 × 4.4 m • 14'-5" × 14'-5"

10

Maple tree
Trees
3.9 × 3.8 m • 12'-9.5" × 12'-6"

11

Pine tree S
Trees
2.6 × 2.97 m • 8'-6.4" × 9'-9"

12

Pine tree L
Trees
3.6 × 3.4 m • 11'-10" × 11'-2"

13

Ruffled fan palm L
Trees
1.98 × 1.98 m • 6'-6" × 6'-6"

14

Banana palm
Trees
2.86 × 2.97 m • 9'-5" × 9'-9"

15

Palm tree L
Trees
6 × 5.3 m • 19'-8" × 17'-5"

16

Palm tree S
Trees
3.1 × 3 m • 10'-2" × 9'-10"

Do It Yourself

Paper Cutouts, Just For Fun!

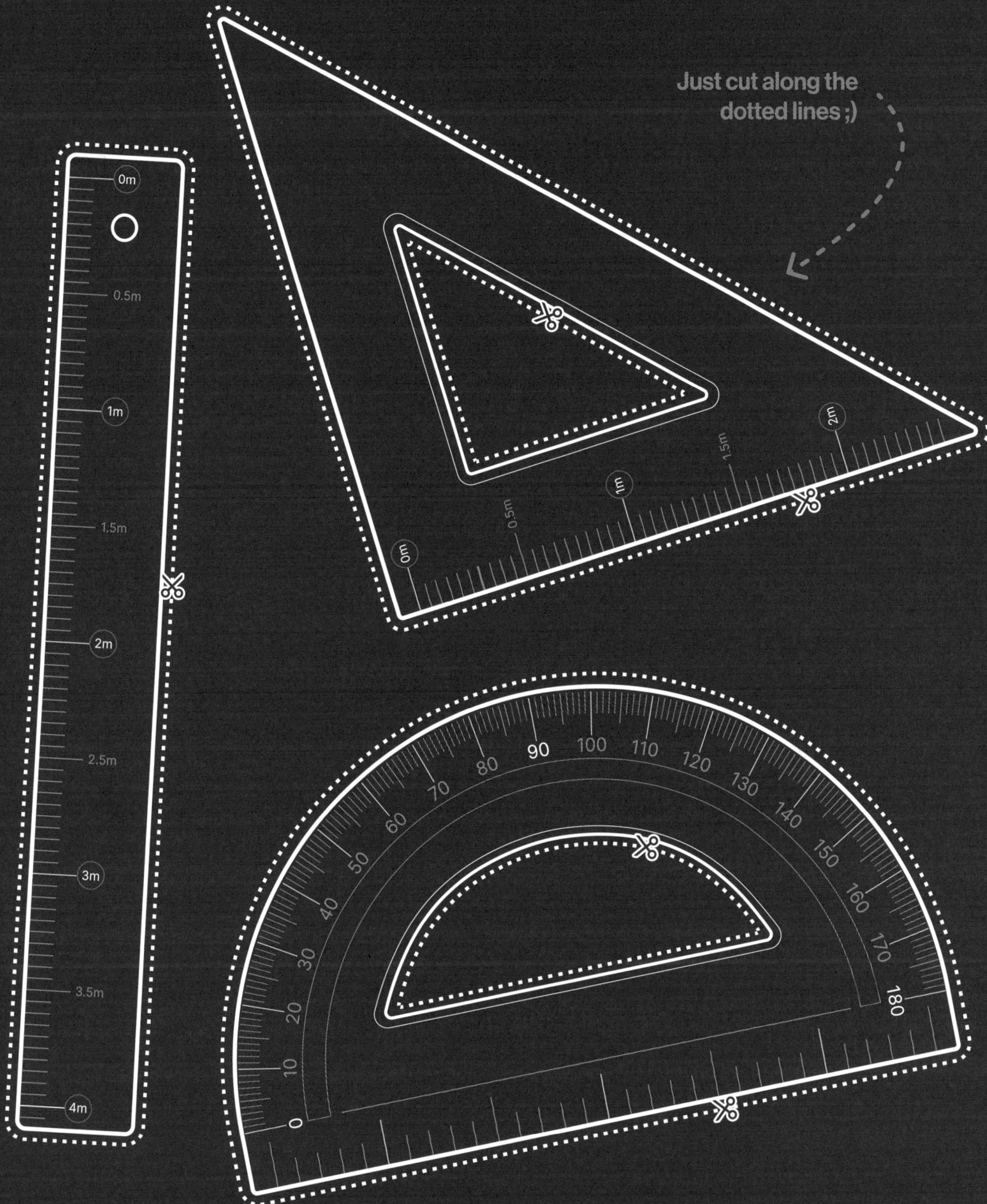

Let's get your tools ready!

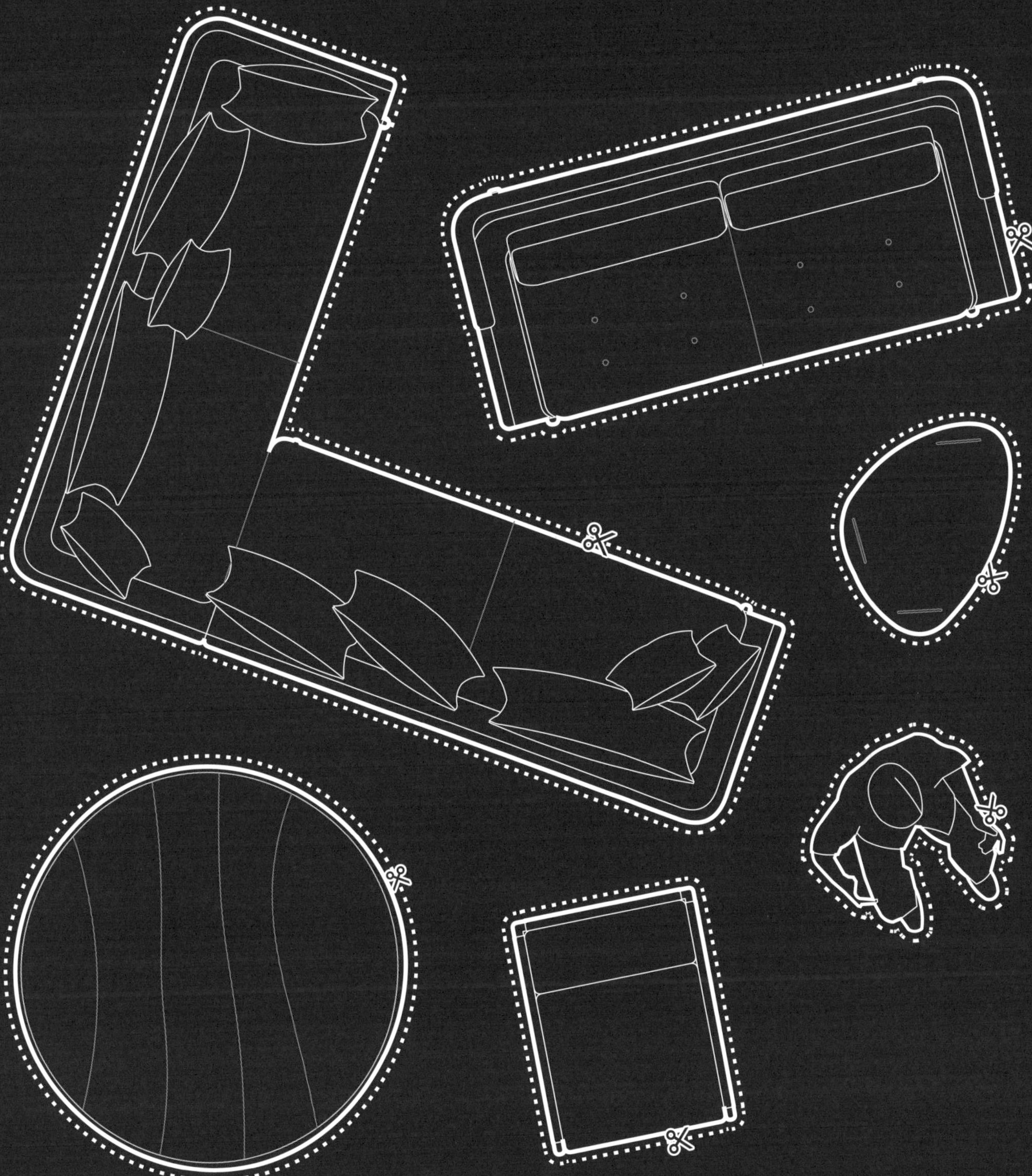

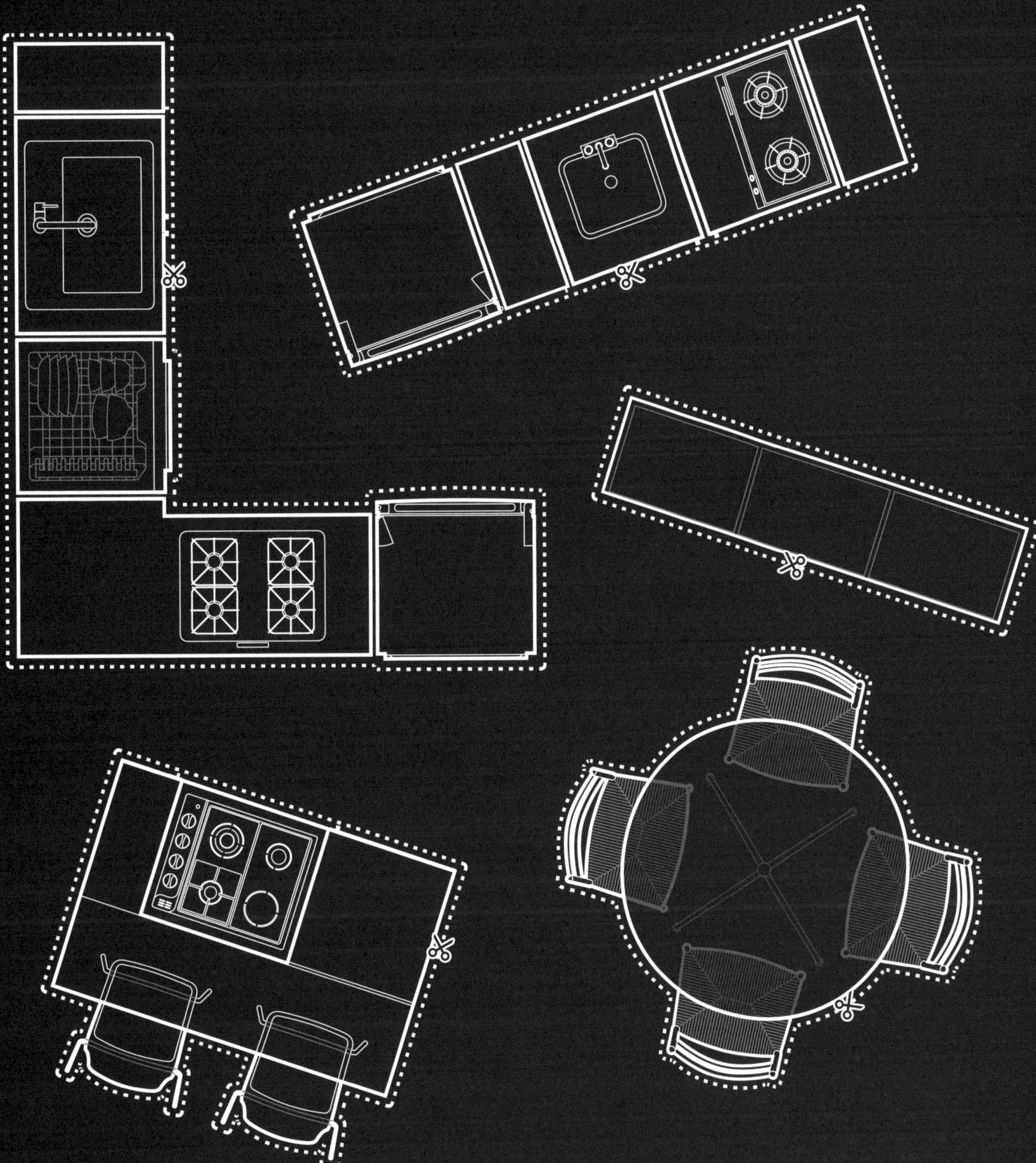

Plan your Kitchen

Some furniture
Some category
Some size

References

All Kits, Catalogs, and Footnotes

Private Office Kit
For the Office
17 items

Meeting Room Kit
For the Office
15 items

Archive Room Kit
For the Office
19 items

Office Chairs Catalog
For the Office
16 items

Open Space Kit
For the Office
23 items

Quiet Open Space Kit
For the Office
26 items

Hot Desking Space Kit
For the Office
18 items

Office Desks Catalog
For the Office
16 items

Conference Room Kit
For the Office
17 items

Lecture Room Kit
For the Office
19 items

Communal Kitchen Kit
For the Office
21 items

Plants Catalog
For the Office
16 items

Lounge Area Kit
For the Office
17 items

Lobby Area Kit
For the Office
20 items

Waiting Room Kit
For the Office
16 items

Lounge Items Catalog
For the Office
16 items

Office Bathroom Kit
For the Office
13 items

Gym Room Kit
For the Office
20 items

Recreation Room Kit
For the Office
15 items

Office Fixtures Catalog
For the Office
16 items

Master Bedroom Kit
For the House
20 items

Single Bedroom Kit
For the House
19 items

Dressing Room Kit
For the House
17 items

Beds Catalog
For the House
16 items

Living Room Kit
For the House
21 items

Dining Room Kit
For the House
15 items

Study Room Kit
For the House
20 items

Seatings Catalog
For the House
16 items

Kitchen Kit
For the House
23 items

Bathroom Kit
For the House
22 items

Washing Room Kit
For the House
16 items

Appliances Catalog
For the House
16 items

Kid's Bedroom kit
For the House
18 items

Game Room Kit
For the House
15 items

Library Room
For the House
19 items

House Fixtures Catalog
For the House
16 items

Patio Kit
For the House
17 items

Garage Kit
For the House
16 items

Storages Catalog
For the House
16 items

Stadium Kit
For the Outdoor
13 items

Sports Court Kit
For the Outdoor
18 items

Golf Course Kit
For the Outdoor
21 items

Sports Fields Catalog
For the Outdoor
16 items

Road Kit
For the Outdoor
16 items

Street Kit
For the Outdoor
27 items

Parking Lot Kit
For the Outdoor
20 items

Transportation Catalog
For the Outdoor
32 items

Playground Kit
For the Outdoor
17 items

Skate Park Kit
For the Outdoor
14 items

Public Park Kit
For the Outdoor
25 items

Urban Furniture Catalog
For the Outdoor
16 items

Private Garden Kit
For the Outdoor
24 items

Animals Kit
For the Outdoor
29 items

Vegetation Catalog
For the Outdoor
16 items

Intro

1. The Architect's Data, Fourth Edition, Ernst Neufert, Wiley Blackwell, 2012
2. Bauentwurfslehre, Ernst Neufert, Ullstein Verlag, 1936
3. Architectural Graphic Standards, Charles George Ramsey, Wiley and Sons, 2016
4. Architectural Graphics, Frank Ching, Wiley, 2015
5. Constructing Architecture, Andrea Deplazes, Birkhauser, 2018
6. See "Paradigms of Architectural Knowledge", Zachary Tate Porter, SITE magazine, https://www.thesitemagazine.com/read/paradigms-of-architectural-knowledge
7. An Icon Retires, Ikea Museum's website, https://ikeamuseum.com/en/explore/the-story-of-ikea/an-icon-is-retired/
8. After 70 successful years, Ikea is turning the page, article on Ikea's website, https://www.ikea.com/global/en/newsroom/retail/after-70-successful-years-ikea-is-turning-the-page-201207/
9. Typical examples of such portals can be found on Herman Miller's website or Knoll's.
10. See Wikipedia's "Architecture" page and revision history dating back to 2001.
11. See ArchDaily (https://www.archdaily.com), Dezeen (https://www.dezeen.com), AD (https://www.architecturaldigest.com), Architect's Newspaper (https://www.archpaper.com).
12. See Architectural Graphics Standards' website, https://www.graphicstandards.com/
13. Building Types Online, Birkhauser, 2013
14. Five years of Figma, Dylan Fields, 2020, https://www.figma.com/blog/meet-us-in-the-browser/
15. "Autodesk has ruled architecture for decades. These startups are trying to unseat it", Sam Lubell, Fast Company, 2023
16. See preface of Architects' Data, p.13, Ernst Neufert, Wiley Blackwell, 2012
17. See Kits, https://www.rayon.design/kits
18. "Shearing Layers" diagram, in "How Buildings Learn: What Hap-pens After They're Built", Steward Brand, Penguin Books, 1995
19. Find "Office" chapter on p.32, Housing chapter on p.172, Outdoor chapter on p.304
20. Links to all blocks in Reference chapter.
21. We highly recommend Gary Larson's "Far Side Gallery" (Sphere, 1989).

For the Office

For the House

For the Outdoor

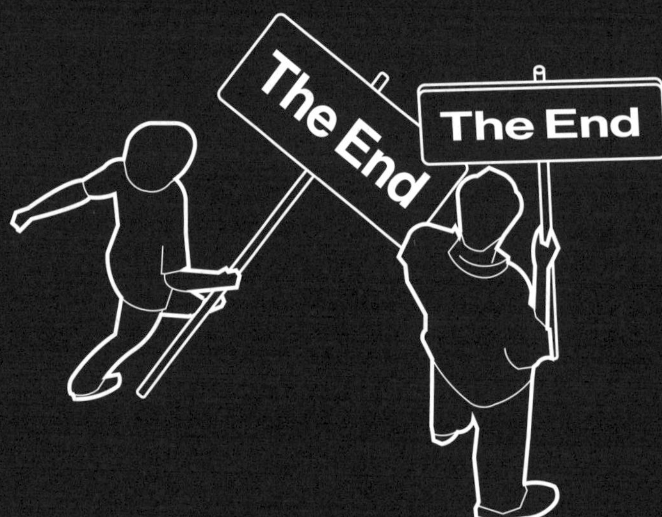
The End
The End